William Harrison Clarke

The face of Jesus

Thoughts for the mature concerning the nature of the Word of God

William Harrison Clarke

The face of Jesus
Thoughts for the mature concerning the nature of the Word of God

ISBN/EAN: 9783744646727

Printed in Europe, USA, Canada, Australia, Japan

Cover: Foto ©Lupo / pixelio.de

More available books at **www.hansebooks.com**

"ye was so marred more than any man."—*Is. lii.: 14.*
" And His Face did shine as the sun."—*Matt. xvii: 2.*

THE
FACE OF JESUS;

OR,

THOUGHTS FOR THE MATURE

CONCERNING THE

NATURE OF THE WORD OF GOD.

BY

A BELIEVER IN THE INTERNAL EVIDENCE OF
DIVINE REVELATION.

" And it was written in Hebrew, Greek and Latin."—*John xix: 20.*
" This is my body which is given for you."—*Luke xxii: 19.*
" This is my blood of the new testament which is shed for many."
—*Mark xiv: 24.*

London:
F. PITMAN, 20 PATERNOSTER ROW., E. C.

Toronto, Ont.:
HUNTER, ROSE & CO., 25 WELLINGTON ST.
1883.

ENTERED AT STATIONERS' HALL.] [ALL RIGHTS RESERVED.

"Seek the Lord and His strength ; seek His Face evermore."—Ps. cv. 4.

Entered according to the Act of the Parliament of Canada, in the year one thousand eight hundred and eighty-three, by HUNTER, ROSE & Co., in the office of the Minister of Agriculture.

THE ORDER OF CONTENTS.

	PAR.
Introduction	1
The Face of Jesus	14
The Preparation for Regeneration	28
The Retrospect	53
The Religious Teacher	68
The Miraculous Conception	80
Serious Questions	85
The Literal Sense of the Word	93
Flesh and Blood	99
The Son of Man	117
The Crucifixion	125
The Son of God	139
The Human Form	142
The Trinity in One	155
Abstract Spiritual Principles	163
The Internal Sense	174
Degrees of Order	178
Triune Principles of the Word	185
The Love of Self the Origin of Evil	190
The Love of the World	196
The Form of the Literal Sense of the Word	207
The Brazen Age, or Natural Degree	214
The Silver Age, or Spiritual Degree	216
The Golden Age, or Celestial Degree	219
The Style of the Literal Sense	221
The First Chapter of Genesis	225
States	227
The First Day of Creation	236
The Proprium of Man	255
The Second Day of Creation	278
The Rational Faculty	280
The Opening of the Rational Faculty	288
The Formation of the Rational Faculty	292
The Material Degree of the Mind	296
The Maternity of the Virgin Mary	311
Prayer	327
The Lord's Prayer	333
The Third Day of Creation	351

THE ORDER OF CONTENTS.

The Two Affections	361
Correspondences	369
Trees	373
Numbers	390
The Birth of the Holy Child	395
Miracles	442
Divine Worship	457
Idolatry	484
Music and the Sound of the Voice	489
The Influences of Angels and Spirits	502
The Order of Spiritual Descent	518
The Corporeal Principle of the Mind	538
The Material Body of the Lord	551
A Miracle of the Third Day	563
The Fourth Day of Creation	613
Interior Motives	623
Spiritual Quarters	653
The Consecration of the Holy Child	658
Baptism and Circumcision	660
The Book of Life	669
Offering Sacrifice	677
The Fifth Day of Creation	689
The Infancy of Jesus	706
Interpretation of Scripture	712
The Light of Nature	722
The True Source of Intellectual Culture	728
Dreams and Visions	734
The Parts of Galilee	756
The Sixth Day of Creation	767
Pleasures	776
The Form of Heaven	792
Marriage	808
Adultery	824
The Holy Supper	833
The Transfiguration	845
The Last Temptation	858
The Sabbath	868
The Life of Regeneration	873
The Pulpit and the Press	879
Conclusion	889
Summary	905

INTRODUCTION.

§1. The thoughts expressed in these pages are not self-intelligent opinions derived from fanciful or speculative metaphor, but they are founded upon the coherent internal understanding of that Word of Eternal Life which the Lord has given to men. <!-- John 3:27; Ps. 127:1; 2 Cor. 3:6; John 6:63; John 6:68 -->

2. A thoughtful comparison of the different portions of the Word of God, with the mind divested of preconceived or traditional ideas, may reveal to the rational intelligence glimpses of the Divine Truth which may be found within, and illustrated by the Word from its own pages. <!-- John 5:39; Mark 7:9; Matt 24:27; Ps. 119:18; Ps. 119:80 -->

3. In order to perceive Divine Truth, the first requisite on the part of the reader is a life in the constant effort to shun all evil, both in will and thought, because it is wrong, and thus is in opposition to the Divine Laws which have been given for the elevation of man's spiritual nature; with an inward acknowledgment, that all life and spiritual thought are from the Lord; that man in himself alone is helpless, and that all the power to overcome evil is from Him alone. <!-- John 14:23; John 14:15; John 15:5; Ps. 37:27; Ps. 119:142; Ps. 119:130; John 14:6; John 15:4; Ps. 84:11 -->

4. Those only who possess this first requisite will perceive truth in the thoughts here written concerning the nature of the Divine Word ; for in order that interior truth may enter the mind, there must be an innocent state of life, in which one feels that he knows nothing, and that he is simply a receptacle of life and thought. *"Blessed are the pure in heart : for they shall see God."* <!-- Luke 24:45; Ps. 51:6; Matt. 18:1,2; John 14:10; Ps. 40:17; Matt. 5:8 -->

6 THE FACE OF JESUS:

| Requisites for comprehension. | Prove by comparison. |

References.

1 Thess. 5:21
Deut 13 : 3
Mark 12 : 29
Mark 12 : 30
Matt. 22 : 37
Deut. 6 : 5
Mark 12 : 31
Lev. 19 ; 18
Rom. 13 : 9
James 2 : 8
John 5 : 43
Matt. 15 : 9
Matt. 12 : 36
1 Tim. 4 : 16
Mark 12 : 33
Matt. 22 : 40

5. The second requisite is, that these thoughts shall be tested by their harmony with the simple truth of the Word, which is, "*The Lord our God is one Lord: And thou shalt love the Lord thy God with all thy heart, and with all thy soul, and with all thy mind, and with all thy strength. This is the first commandment. And the second is like, namely this, Thou shalt love thy neighbour as thyself. There is none other commandment greater than these*," and not by their agreement with some cherished doctrine ; for there are popular religious theories and systems in existence even at the present time, which tend to obscure this fundamental law of spiritual life, on which rests " *all the law and the prophets.*"

Matt 16 : 12
John 7 : 16
Matt. 24 : 11
Matt 24 : 23
John 5 : 31
2 John 1 : 9
John 5 : 32
Jer. 33 : 3
Matt. 12 : 37
2 Tim. 3 : 16
Is. 43 : 6
Matt. 6 : 20
Matt. 11 : 28
Acts 18 : 28
Is. 8 : 20

6. If the tendency of these thoughts is to lead us more into the love of self and the world, and thus away from the Lord, or the Word, then are they false and should meet with condemnation, for they would be dangerous to spiritual life. But if they lead the mind to perceive in the Divine Revelation a satisfactory internal evidence that it is inspired Truth, thus placing it upon a higher plane of thought, so that we shall not only delight in searching for its hidden treasures, but obey the written Precepts, and thus be led to the Living Word, the Lord Himself, then, when the book is finished, the judgment of the candid reader will readily determine whether these principles are good and true, or are the invention of man, and are thus evil and false.

Matt. 6 : 33
Hos. 6 : 3
Ps. 19 : 7
Rev. 2 : 17

7. To those only who possess a thorough knowledge of the literal contents of the Sacred Scriptures, and whose minds are capable of mature reflection from

Order of study. Salvation from sin.   The Advent of the Lord.

many years of living experience, will the summary of these thoughts find a sympathetic response. Not only should the marginal references be examined, but as far as possible each statement should be verified by means of a Concordance, and the following paragraphs and pages should be read and studied consecutively.

8. In this progressive order the mind may perceive from internal spiritual evidences, that the principles of Divine Love and Wisdom contained within the Word, applied to the life by obedience to them, will save a man from his sins, or from the love of self, which is the origin of all sin;—that this Divine Love and Wisdom is embodied in the Word in the name and by the representation of the life of the Lord Jesus Christ as the Son of God and Son of Man;—that the Lord Jesus Christ and the Word are identical, and that the Word is the body of the Lord, or His "*flesh and blood*" within the life of a regenerate man.

9. This Word, or the Divine Love and Wisdom, was "*in the beginning*," and "*was God*," and is the "*Life which is the light of men, the true Light which lighteth every man which cometh into the world.*" This Word is the "*bread which cometh down from heaven.*" The man who feeds upon its Divine truths by learning and obeying them, will be nourished and grow up into spiritual life, or in the image and likeness of God, which is salvation from sin.

10. The Lord comes into the world, or what is the same thing, the Word is given both to the material and spiritual mind, for this purpose, for it treats only concerning spiritual principles, and has no connection with physical-material science or things in the natural

References.
Ps. 37:31
Mark 1:27
Ps. 50:23
Job 33:5
Ps. 119:133

Deut. 8:3
Luke 17:33
Matt. 4:4
Deut. 8:6
Jer. 7:23
Ex. 15:26
Ex. 19:5
Is. 9:6
Is. 43:11
Heb. 5:9
John 1:4
Ps. 136:5
Mark 14:22
Luke 22:19

Jer. 10:12
John 1:1

John 1:9

John 6:33
John 6:51

Ps. 17:15
Matt. 1:21
John 10:10

1 Cor. 15:46
Matt. 13:34

8   THE FACE OF JESUS:

A Book of Spiritual Science.   Personification of the Word.

References.	
John 1 : 14	world excepting by comparison or analogy for the sake of illustration. This Word "*was made flesh*," or a living principle of spiritual life, "*and dwelt among us.*"
John 6 : 51	"*I am the living bread which came down from heaven; if any man eat of this bread, he shall live forever, and the bread that I will give, is my flesh, which I will give for the life of the world. For my flesh is meat indeed, and my blood is drink indeed.*"
John 6 : 55	
John 8 : 51	11. The Word contains a living Human Principle, by obedience to which a man's spirit will be re-created, and in the work of regeneration, the enlightenment of the rational faculty by the revelation of the Internal Sense of the Word is represented by the birth, life and passion of the Lord Jesus Christ as the Son of Man, and the Son of God, or the Divine Human Principle of the Word in the man who is being regenerated.
John 3 : 3	
Is. 60 : 19	
Ps. 119 : 105	
1 John 1 : 1	
1 John 1 : 2	
Luke 8 : 17	
Col. 3 : 3	
Rev. 22 : 4	12. The Divine Truth, or the Lord is thus personified with a Living Face and made sentient to the material mind, so that the interior spiritual faculty enclosed within, may extract and feed upon the interior truth thus embodied within the literal sense or covering, which is upon the Face of the Word.
Ps. 80 : 14	
Is. 40 : 11	
Rev. 7 : 17	
Ps. 80 : 3	
Heb. 1 : 3	13. In order to see the "*brightness of His glory*" as it shines from within the Word, we "*must become as little children,*" conscious of our ignorance in ourselves, and depending rationally upon the Lord for enlightenment. To the mature "little ones" who may be aided in finding coherence and unity in the Internal Sense of the Word of God, by which alone its Divinity can be proved, these pages are thoughtfully inscribed.
Matt. 18 : 2	
Ps. 51 : 17	
Ps. 64 : 10	
Ps. 119 : 104	
Ps. 119 : 90	
Eph. 4 : 13	
1 Pet. 1 : 8	
Numb. 6 : 25	"THE LORD MAKE HIS FACE TO SHINE UPON THEE, AND BE GRACIOUS UNTO THEE."

THE FACE OF JESUS.

14. It is not pleasant to gaze upon the face of the dead, for there is neither life nor expression within the pale countenance by which thought may be communicated to others; and often, when the covering is tenderly and hesitatingly turned down, we are filled with grief and sorrow, and wish that we had not looked upon those rigid features which were once flushed with animation; for the person whom we loved is not there, and the cold form must be carried away out of sight.

15. There is one Face which loving hearts and eyes do not shrink from beholding, and the more it is gazed upon, the more its beauty and glory will appear, for it communicates life and light to those who reverently uncover, and devoutly look.

16. During the centuries of the past, many hands of artistic genius have endeavored with skilful crayon and brush to portray the countenance of the "*King of kings, and Lord of lords.*" They could not reproduce what they had not seen, and the results of their talented efforts have simply been representations of the visage of a suffering man, whose pitiful expression touches our hearts with emotion.

Ps. 89:48
Ps. 39:11
Is. 33:17
Jer. 22:10
Heb. 2:15
Is. 25:8
Luke 24:5
1 Cor. 15:42

Ps. 27:8
Ps. 105:4
Matt. 17:2
Matt. 10:26
Is. 38:19

1 John 4:12
Exod. 33:20
John 1:18
Is. 53:3

17. We turn from these pictures of Jesus with a dissatisfied and pained feeling, and wish that those faces had been called by some other name, for they are but likenesses of the mental conceptions of the painters, fitted to some earthly model whom they have seen or imagined. Such delineations of the Son of Man, in themselves, are dead, for apart from the canvas, they are only representations of grief, tender love, and the yearning for that sympathy which we would gladly give to those patient expressive faces, were we able to extend it by our personal presence.

18. These faces of Jesus are produced from the minds of the artists, by the contemplation of the story of the Evangelists as related in the Gospels, but no earthly painter will ever live who can design either the features or form of the Lord Jesus Christ as a physical man in time or space, for no man has ever thus seen Him, nor will He ever thus appear, and every attempt to personify Him in this form, will destroy all perception of His Omnipresence, without which He would not be Divine.

19. When we look into a living human face, there is imparted to us an intuition of the quality of the life of the man whom we behold, although we may at first be somewhat hasty in our judgment; but if men were constantly

THE NATURE OF THE WORD OF GOD. 11

Beautiful Faces. — **Inward quality.**

living according to the laws of spiritual order, the interior qualities of their minds would be manifested by the shape and expression of their countenances. *John 7:24; Is. 26:3; Ezek. 28:15*

20. Those who would then possess affection for, and intelligence in the spiritual truths of the Word, would have beautiful faces in which there would be no trace of pride or vanity. The eyes would beam with love and wisdom, and with the gentleness of the dove. The brow would have no frowning wrinkles; the cheeks would not be wreathed in hypocritical smiles, and the mouth would not indicate sensuality and selfishness. *Zech. 9:17; Ps. 149:4; Ps. 19:17; Ps. 45:11; Cant. 5:12; Cant. 5:13; Cant. 5:16; Ps. 37:30*

21. But since mankind from the early ages have disobeyed the laws of Divine Order, the face does not truly represent the real man within, and we must be charitable in our opinion of others, especially until we can know something of the quality of the interior motives of their lives. *Gen. 6:5; Matt. 7:15; Matt. 7:20*

22. We are charmed with a beautiful face, but often learn that it is but a covering for a hypocritical and false life, whereas in the plain and homely countenance we learn to appreciate the life of the man within, and we are led to love him for his inward qualities instead of the exterior face. Our love for others must be deeper than the external face, for when the *Ezek. 28:17; Ps. 147:11; Is. 33:17; Eccl. 12:1-7*

The marred visage.	Where the Divine Face may be seen.

Is. 46 : 4
Ps. 71 : 9

years of infirmity arrive, the brightness of the eye will be dimmed, and decay will mark its inevitable progress with pallor and furrows.

Ps. 51 : 5

23. Although the visage may be marred by the evil lives of ancestors, or by sickness or

Ps. 51 : 6
Ps. 37 : 23

injuries, yet the love which animates the good man warms his countenance with affection, and his eyes are filled with the lustre of intelligence,

Matt. 13 : 43

so that his whole face shines with light to those who know and love him, because they have similar qualities of life. The evil man does not

Is. 32 : 6

recognize this warmth and brightness, but attributes all the intentions and actions of the good man to the same motives by which his

Mal. 3 : 18

own life is governed, until he is convinced to the contrary.

John 14 : 9
John 1 : 18

24. The Face of the Lord is seen only in the Word which He has given and preserved

Is. 64 : 4

among mankind. To those who here see Him, and whose lives are warmed and guided by the

John 1 : 41

truth here painted, "*His Face doth shine as the Sun*," for they perceive within this Face, those

John 1 : 45
Matt. 1 : 16

interior qualities of Love and Wisdom from which the names Jesus and Christ are derived, which prove from this interior or spiritual

Ps. 104 : 24
Rev. 22 : 14
Is. 60 : 1

source, that through all the ages of the past spiritual history of man, "*the Word was God*," and the only evidence which reveals to the per-

Ps. 19 : 8, 9

plexed mind that it is from a supernatural

THE NATURE OF THE WORD OF GOD.

The painted face.	The Living Face.

origin is to be found from that interior light which causes "*His Face to shine.*"

25. To those whose lives are not principled in the simple commandments of life which may be read upon this very Face of the Lord, there is no true light shining from within, and His Face appears to them painted like the countenance of a common man like themselves, an outgrowth of their own imagination.

26. In order to behold the Face of Jesus, let us thoughtfully follow the progress of a serious and earnest man who has come to Him by night, and who cannot yet see His Face, keeping our minds fixed upon this one person, who will in the succeeding pages, be called a regenerating man, and as far as possible bring him close to our own hearts, so that we may observe his various states of mind and internal experiences, as he is led by the Lord by means of instruction from the Word, to be prepared for the first and succeeding states of regeneration, until the Face of Jesus becomes illuminated and shines as the sun.

27. Many devout readers may perceive that this serious man is representative of their own inward life and desires, and through his spiritual journey of trials and blessings, be also led to see the Living Face of the Lord Jesus Christ.

Side references: Matt. 11:29; Luke 9:29; John 1:11; John 1:5; Ps. 50:21; Ps. 107:43; Ps. 95:6; Ps. 112:4; Ps. 37:37; Ps. 37:39; Ps. 37:31; Ps. 37:3; Is. 45:22; Ps. 37:5

THE
PREPARATION FOR REGENERATION.

<small>John 18 : 38</small>

28. After many years of mental conflict, as the appearances of truth which were implanted in the mind during the period of early educa-<small>Ps. 90 : 12</small> tion begin to be dissipated, and the thoughtful <small>Ps. 39 : 13</small> moods of maturity cast their serious rays over <small>Ps. 60 : 11</small> the future, there often flows into the mind an <small>Ps. 39 : 4</small> intense yearning to know what is really true, in <small>Exod. 33 : 20</small> which the spiritual nature shall rest as upon a <small>Ps. 18 : 2</small> solid Rock, in the utmost security of a rational <small>John 6 : 68 9</small> faith, both in relation to this world and the im-<small>Heb. 11 : 1</small> mortal life beyond.

<small>P . 31 : 1</small>

29. While in this state of mind, there is no <small>2 Tim. 1 : 12</small> doubt in regard to the existence of an Infinite God, nor in His Divine Providence, neither is <small>Amos 5 : 14</small> there any doubt but that a good life tends to <small>Ps. 63 : 3</small> elevate man to happiness, and that an evil life <small>Amos 5 : 15</small> will kill the development of his spiritual nature, <small>Rom. 6 : 23</small> and fill his life with misery. The mind thus <small>Rom. 7 : 15</small> recognizes that good and evil, truth and falsity, <small>Deut. 30 : 15</small> are both received by the nature of man, and <small>Rom. 12 : 21</small> that the one condition is to be sought, and the other is to be avoided.

<small>Ps. 18 : 21</small>

30. In fact, a man may have had the belief <small>Ps. 34 : 22</small> that he has trusted in God many years, and <small>Nahum 1 : 7</small> constantly have sought illumination from above,

| Religious motives. | Realization of ideals. |

and endeavored to love his neighbor as himself, in all his earthly affairs, acknowledging God in all his ways, and in humility utterly disclaiming self-merit; or, with religious motives, he may have been of such a sensitive disposition that prevailing doctrines have been to him a source of irritation and irrationality, and he has become retired and isolated from the popular opinions of his fellow-men in regard to serious thought.

<small>Matt. 7:7
Prov. 3:5, 6
Matt. 23:12
Ps. 34:13
Matt. 15:8,9
Mark 7:7
Deut. 8:2
Is. 32:16, 17</small>

31. When the years of maturity dawn, the past has been characterized by affliction and suffering in various forms. With some, loved ones have been summoned above, leaving the sad heart to mourn in grief; business ventures have not succeeded; property has vanished, and apparent friends have proved false. With others, a devastation fully as hard to bear, has been the crushing of cherished ideals when the motives seemed to be pure; but rest assured, O wounded spirit, that not a single ideal has been entertained, but which, if the inward motives have been unselfish, will yet bloom in beautiful fruition, in that world of elevated thought, where all things or principles are substantial and real to clearer perceptions than we can possess in our material degree of thought.

<small>Ps. 89:48
Ps. 38:6
2 Sam. 12:23
Matt. 6:19
Prov. 23:5
Ps. 35:15
Ps. 25:16,17
Ps. 42:5
James 1:3
Is. 54:11
Is. 54:14
Is. 3:10
Is. 55:12
Is. 55:13
Is. 35:5, 6
2 Cor. 4:18</small>

32. In the spiritual world, men are real men in the human form, tangible angels and spirits

<small>Rev. 22:8, 9
Luke 20:38</small>

Luke 20:36	without wings, with all their superior faculties
Jer. 17:10	in acute exercise, living in the use of, and sur-
Rev. 22:14	rounded by the very ideals which their inmost
John 4:36	ruling affections have created by their daily course of life.
Ex. 24:7	33. If the effort of the life, in the inward
Rom. 5:19	motives, has sought the Divine Guidance in
Gen. 27:8	love and obedience during this life, the sur-
Deut. 11:27	roundings there will typify the actual state of
Ps. 65:4	one's life. With those whose lives have
Is. 65:17	been principled in the truths of the Word, the
Is. 65:10	affections will be represented by such objects
Is. 65:25	as innocent lambs; the thoughts will be repre-
Ezek. 34:31	sented by beautiful birds, which principles are
Ps. 84:3	also represented in the Word where beasts and
Is. 35:9	birds are mentioned in a good connection.
Jer. 31:13	Loving friends will commingle their joys, and
Rev. 19:7	aid each other in imparting the knowledges
Acts 20:35	given them. With their minds illuminated by
Rev. 21:23	the Sun of the Heavens, they will constantly
Is. 58:11	seek to love others better than themselves.
Jer. 31:12	Even the residences, gardens, trees and flowers,
Ps. 37:11	will in their beauty and usefulness represent
Ps. 119:165	the nature of the man who has yielded himself to be led by the Lord.
Deut. 8:20	34. On the other hand, the surroundings of
Jer. 7:24	the man whose continual life has been evil, will
Jer. 18:12	partake of the nature which he himself, and not
John 5:40	the Lord, has created; for he has been led by

| Nature of evil men. | Self-Love. |

the love of self and the world, resisting every gentle invitation of Him who says, "*Behold, I stand at the door and knock,*" that He may enter and lead to heavenly joys. He will be attended and infested by crawling and creeping things, venomous serpents, carrion birds who feed on putrefying flesh, and wild beasts of prey, and the ground on which he walks will be filled with sulphurous pits, and his fields will be over-run with weeds, thorns, and covered with the desolation of the wilderness. The world which the poor sufferer in delirium tremens sees about him, with its coiling snakes, and frightful, loathsome animals which he deliriously fears, is for the time real to him in the insanity he has brought upon himself by his own free choice and act.

Is. 30 : 1
Rev. 3 : 20
Is. 56 : 11
Is. 34 : 15
Is. 30 : 6
Is. 65 : 4
Is. 34 : 14
Ps. 38 : 5
Deut. 29 : 23
Hab. 2 : 15
Ezek. 8 : 10
Hab. 2 : 7
1 Cor. 6 : 10

35. It is not gratifying to the pride of man to contemplate the nature of self-love, and yet it is necessary to consider it in its true aspect, so that in due time in the progress of these pages, the Divinity of the Word shall clearly be perceived as the "power of God unto salvation" from sin. Self-love constitutes that state of life which is described in the Word as hell, for from this evil love all sin originates as from a corrupt fountain. A man in this state regards nothing but what is in the interest of himself, with which he is so absorbed that the

Is. 55 : 8
Is. 1 : 6
Is. 1 : 2
2 Peter 1 : 4
Rom. 1 : 16
Jer. 49 : 16
Matt. 23 : 33
Jer. 2 : 13
Is. 47 : 10,11

light from heaven cannot penetrate, for he believes only in himself, and inwardly denies the truths of the Word, which from the beginning to the end have reference to the principles of love to the Lord and the neighbor, although outwardly he may profess reverence for sacred things, and even class himself among the chosen people of God. The presence of the Lord with man first exists when he inwardly loves his neighbor, for the Lord is within this love, which is opposed to the love of self.

36. Man, in his hereditary nature is filled with the love of self, in which he does not regard the Lord, nor his neighbor, and if this evil principle were not restrained by that mercy of the Lord which constantly surrounds every person, all men would be precipitated by this ruling love into that life of sin and misery which the word hell fitly expresses, for he who hates his brother-man, would, if not restrained by the fear of discovery and the loss of reputation, take his life, or rejoice at his death.

37. The nature of every man is such that if he should be left to himself and his own government, unless he were prevented by external restraints, he would plunge into all kinds of wickedness, and not rest until he had subdued all persons in the universe, and not only obtained possession of their wealth, but made

them slaves to his will. If he were permitted, he would rush headlong into the perpetration of every evil to the utmost of his power, thus bringing his nature lower than the wild beasts, for they kill and devour other animals to appease the cravings of hunger, but the evil man seeks to destroy the souls of the innocent, to gratify the desires of his infernal lusts. Thus man, being utterly evil, can never have dominion over himself without Divine help, for evil cannot govern evil and bring it into order, but the Lord, by His Omnipotent mercy, restrains man from evil by every possible influence, without violating his freedom.

Jer. 22 : 13
Is. 57 : 20
Is. 24 : 5
Is. 14 : 9
Jer. 22 : 19
Jer. 22 : 17
Ps. 10 : 8
Is. 26 : 13
Jer. 10 : 23
Ps. 139 : 8
Lev. 1 : 3

38. In this depraved condition of the nature of man, the Lord pities those who suffer on account of sin, and is never angry with anyone. He never leads into temptation, nor punishes any person, neither does He curse any sinner, but to the man who sins, it seems as if God is angry, and that He punishes and destroys, because in his perverted state of life, the man himself is angry with the Divine Laws which he has violated. For this reason, the Word in many places is written as God appears to the thoughts of evil men, so that by the appearance of truth it may reach sinners in their lowest condition. Thus through their own fears they may be led to believe that there is a God who

Is. 63 : 9
Ps. 103 : 13
Ps. 103 : 8
Rev. 3 : 10
Ps. 7 : 11
Hos. 4 : 9
§28
John 7 : 23
Lev. 26 : 24
Ezek. 13 : 17
Ezek. 13 : 3
Ezek. 13 : 2
Ps. 90 : 11
Deut. 28 : 67

Ps. 93:1	
Mal. 3:2	
Ps. 107:28	

governs all things in the universe, and in their selfish dread of punishment, hoping in some way to appease the wrath of their angry God, they are led to acknowledge their need of Divine assistance.

Ezek. 18:20	
Is. 59:12	
John 8:34	
Rom. 5:12	
Ezek. 18:4	
Rev. 22:12	
Ezek. 17:18	
Ezek. 17:19	
Ezek. 11:21	
Ps. 4:4	
Heb. 12:1	
Ezek. 18:21	
Ezek. 11:19, 20	

39. Every man must bear the punishment of his own sins as long as he persists in a sinful course of life. By sin, a man closes the door of Eternal Life, without which a man is spiritually dead, for "*the soul that sinneth, it shall die.*" It is not the retribution of sin which man is to fear and be saved from, for there is no escape from the penalty of any violated law, either physical or spiritual, but the very root of sin itself, the love of self, is to be dug out, and a Divine principle from the Word of God is to be implanted in its place by a regenerate life, which is salvation from sin.

Ps. 86:5	
John 6:37	
Matt. 24:35	
Ezek. 18:22	
Ezek. 13:14	
Ezek. 13:15	
Ezek. 13:16	
Jer. 50:39	
Is. 34:13	
Luke 13:24	

40. The Lord always forgives, and never casts anyone away from Him. He has come into the world by means of the Word, and plainly declares, "*Let the wicked forsake his way, and the unrighteous man his thoughts: and let him return unto the Lord, and He will have mercy upon him, and to our God, for He will abundantly pardon.*" The man who is ruled by the love of self is like a desert filled with stagnant pools, poisonous brambles, and deadly vines. As rapidly as the man digs these out

Heavenly implanting. — Need of Divine Revelation.

by striving against his evils, and fills the stagnant pools with living water from the Word with the strength given him from above, in the same proportion the Lord implants the fruitful vines and fragrant flowers, "*and the desert shall rejoice and blossom as the rose. It shall blossom abundantly, and rejoice even with joy and singing.*"

Ps. 15:2
Is. 41:18
Hab. 3:19
Jer. 17:7, 8
Is. 35:1, 2
Hos. 14:6

41. As the Kingdom of Heaven is within the good man, so the dominion of hell is within the evil man, "*for out of the heart proceed evil thoughts, murders, adulteries, fornications, thefts, false witness, blasphemies,*" and when this inward evil principle is comprehended, a satisfactory explanation will be perceived concerning the great conflicts so frequently mentioned in the Psalms and Prophecies between man's foes and enemies, as well as in the historical relations, for this warfare consists of the spiritual combats and temptations which arise from his own evils during the progress of regeneration, and are not the external enemies which appear to be described in the literal sense of the Word, for, "*a man's foes shall be they of his own household.*"

Luke 17:21
§30
Matt. 15:18, 19
Mark 7:21, 22
Ps 64:1
Je· 6:25
Ps. 27:2
Ps. 56:2
Ps. 5:8
Ps. 25:2
Matt. 10:36

42. Hence the need of a coherent Divine Revelation which shall meet the spiritual wants of man's nature to the utmost, from the man who can only be led through fear and external

John 17:21
1 Kings 8:56
Is. 45:23
Ezek. 12·18

§28

Ps. 139 : 6
John 5 : 46, 47
Deut. 27 : 3
Rev. 21 : 5
John 17 : 17

1 Pet. 1 : 25
Eph. 2 : 21

John 8 : 47
John 16 : 25
Ps. 69 : 11
Deut. 18 : 21, 22
Ps. 78 : 2
Mark 4 : 34
Deut. 18 : 20

Ps. 97 : 9
Is. 55 : 8

Is. 34 : 14
Is. 55 : 2
John 16 : 29
Jer. 30 : 9
Rev. 11 : 8
Is. 7 : 18
John 16 : 30

representations of the appearances of truth, to him whose cultivated perceptions are led by love and interior thought. For this reason, the art of writing and printing was provided by the Lord so that there might be a communication of Divine Truth from Him to the mind of man, in such form as would reach every condition of depraved life, and the Word has thus been given in its literal sense of historical narrative and prophetic utterance, for the sake of the true spiritual meaning within, which is so coherent in its form that there is not a single contradiction. The literal sense from beginning to end is written, according to appearances, by a wonderful analogy or correspondence between earthly things and spiritual principles, which will be briefly illustrated in succeeding pages.

43. In studying the Word, the mind at first is incapable of being instantaneously removed from the historical narration to the Internal Sense, until by searching its pages diligently, with the knowledge that all the statements contain within them eternal spiritual realities, and that the names of all persons, places and things are representative of principles within the mind of the regenerate man, the reader may be led to perceive the spiritual correspondence. The historical relation always adheres to and fills the mind at first, and it was given to man in

| Parables. | Value of the literal sense. |

this form in order that it may be read with delight by children, and those who are in the simple and innocent state of life which children represent, and who receive instruction in Divine Truth by means of parables.

44. The whole Word of God treats only of spiritual principles, and has nothing to do with physical science or earthly things excepting by correspondence, and in no other form or place in the universe is the Lord revealed in spiritual truths; for all books which contain illustrations of the true doctrine of life, which is to love the Lord and the neighbor, are derived from the knowledge of the truth within the Word, without which no one would know of God, neither that there is an immortal life after the death of the physical body, or corporeal frame, nor could we know of His character which is naturally represented in the personification of the Lord Jesus Christ.

45. Without this literal sense of the Word, there would be no form, or body, to hold the spiritual contents, as the spiritual body of man could not exist in this world without a corporeal frame of flesh and bones. If the literal sense of the Word should be taken away from men, and all knowledge of its simple truths should be obliterated, there could be no redemption from sin.

Hab. 2:2
Ps. 34:11
Mark 10:15
Ezek. 20:49
Matt. 13:3
Is. 43:9, 10
John 18:36
89
Is. 34:16
Deut. 17:18, 19
Jer. 30:2
Mal. 3:16
Jer. 36:4
Rev. 1:3
Luke 24:44
Prov. 8:34
Is. 9:8
Ezek. 33:30
Ps. 147:19
1 Thess. 2:13
Jer. 23:7
Prov. 22:23
Eph. 5:26
Eph. 6:17

46. This Word which is called the Holy Bible, is the Lord Himself, who has descended into this world into the lowest forms of created substances, the dead material matter of paper and ink, used to inscribe the words and thoughts which contain Divine Truths. These Divine Truths taken by the understanding from this paper and incorporated into the life of man, will save him from his sins, and raise him into Eternal life and happiness.

47. This Word is the *"flesh and blood"* of the Lord, which we are to eat and drink; this is His Body which is given for us; the *"bread and wine"* upon which our spiritual bodies are to be nourished, that we may grow into the images of His Form, and likenesses of His Face, redeemed by Him from the love of self, through the Living Human Principles of the Word.

48. When the internal principles which exist within this Word are revealed to the man who is living in obedience to its truths, the literal sense in itself alone becomes dead to him, especially the appearance of earthly history, just as the corporeal frame dies when the spiritual body is withdrawn,—because he sees the reality of the picture which has been represented in a dead form which has life only from the spirit which is within it.

| A startling statement. | The Divine Humanity. |

49. This statement may at first startling to those who have always imagined an historical man called Jesus, outside of the Word, and have thus far thought of Him as a terrestial being, in corporeal flesh and blood, walking upon the earth in the land of Palestine, and surrounded by a few apostles and disciples, when the Internal evidence reveals that only in the Word, or in the lives of those who have obeyed its truths, has the Lord ever been seen by finite eyes, either by angels or men.

John 7 : 17
Acts 13 : 12
John 8 : 58
Is. 44 : 6
§ 43
Hos. 11 : 9
1 Tim 6 : 16
Is. 28 : 9
John 8 : 32

50. But when it is perceived that the Lord Jehovah from Eternity is the same Lord Jesus Christ, the Alpha and Omega of whom the Word in its spiritual sense treats from Genesis to Revelation, and that He is the One only Infinite Personal God, then the devout mind can rest in Him without distraction.

Is. 41 : 4
Is. 43 : 12
Heb. 13 : 8
Rev. 1 : 8
Rev. 22 : 13
Hos. 13 : 4
Is. 60 : 20

51. When it is further discovered that He is the unchangeable, loving Father, who, in the narrative of the Sacred Scriptures, came into the world in Divine Truth in the representation of the Son of God and the Son of man, and that the Humanity which He assumes is the living principle of the Word within the lives of men who are being regenerated, then the rational believer, in reading the literal sense by its correspondence with spiritual principles, may discover its true Divinity and exclaim in

Is. 9 : 7
John 10 : 27
John 17 : 6
John 17 : 14
John 17 : 22
John 17 : 25
John 17 : 26
John 20 : 27

its own literal language "*My Lord and my God!*" for the Lord is not denied, but is then seen in glimpses of His true glory. By means of the spiritual meaning of the Word, separated from the "traditions of men," the mind is led to Him alone, and He is then elevated above all earthly science, and is perceived to be the "*King of kings, and Lord of lords,*" over the heavens and the earths, over angels and men.

52. Only those earnest and sincere minds who love to obey the truths of the Word are capable of bearing the interior light which shines from the Word, and, if they desire, may see a faint outline of its intellectual glory illustrated in the succeeding pages.

THE RETROSPECT.

53. As we stand at the threshold of the Eternal World and look back upon our past lives, we can with gratitude see that all our griefs and trials have proved to be blessings in the guidance of the Divine Providence. The object of their permission has been to impress upon our minds the unstability of all external material things, and to lead us to reflect upon subjects pertaining to our eternal welfare.

54. All our mental conflicts and sufferings occur in the natural mind, and not in the spiritual mind, for the mind has an external and

| The material mind. | The real resurrection. |

internal nature. The natural, or material mind, has its faculties occupied through the senses which act in this physical world by means of the corporeal frame. Within this frame of flesh and bones, the real or spiritual body exists which gives life and form to these earthly substances.

55. This corporeal frame, or external covering, is composed of the animal, vegetable and mineral substances of the earth upon which we live, and with which it must be daily supplied in the form of food which contains these same substances. When this corporeal frame dies, and the spiritual body cannot live within it, the man then will exist in the Spiritual World, which is not far away distant in some other material planet, or realm of space and time. Then the dead corporeal frame must be buried out of sight and its substances be decomposed into their earthly elements.

56. No other bodily resurrection will take place, than the entrance of the spiritual body into the spiritual world. The death of the physical frame and the resurrection of the spiritual body will occur alike to all persons, both the good and the evil, without any freedom of choice; but the real resurrection is the advent of the Lord by the Word into the nature of man, kindling his natural mind with regen-

§8
Rom. 8:7
§33
Heb. 10:5
Job 10:11
1 Cor. 15:44

Gen. 3:19
Gen. 1:29
2 Kings 3:17
1 Tim. 6:8

James 2:26
§45
Ps. 118:17
Matt. 3:2
Luke 21:31
§30
Job 34:15
Eccl. 12:7

1 Cor. 15:50
Hos. 6:2

John 5:28
John 5:29

John 5:24
John 5:25
Col. 3:1

John 6:40	erate life, by his own desire and through his
John 6:44	own efforts in conjunction with the strength
John 6:45	which the Lord gives, for all spiritual life is from the Lord alone.
John 11:23	57. The literal sense of the Word appears to
Acts 24:15	teach that the earthly body will rise again at a general resurrection of the dead, and men have
§ 48	been permitted to believe in this appearance of
Acts 17:22	truth, for the reason that if this opinion had not
Matt. 22:32	been prevalent, mankind would have denied
Matt. 22:23	that there is an immortal life beyond the grave, and it is better to believe such a doctrine, if it
Col. 1:5, 6	implies that the man within the corporeal frame
1 John 5:13	is to live to eternity, for if men should deny
1 John 5:11	that life is eternal, and actually be persuaded
1 John 5:12	that they would utterly perish with the death
1 John 2:28	of the corporeal frame, there would be no in-
Ps. 49:20	centive to live a holy life, and only natural and animal life would then exist on the earth.
1 Cor. 15:40	58. The natural mind exists within the
§ 38	spiritual body, and the corporeal frame is only
Eph. 4:4	a means given by which we may first have our
Ps. 36:9	being and existence. Although all life and
Amos 4:13	thought exist from the spiritual world, yet
Gen. 2:7	when we are children, we receive our first in-
1 Cor. 13:11	struction through the senses which operate externally by means of the organism of the corporeal frame, from things in the material uni-
Is. 32:3	verse which surround us. We therefore see,

THE NATURE OF THE WORD OF GOD.

Perception.   **Death of natural ideas.**

hear, feel, taste and smell, or have perception of the qualities of objects outside of the corporeal frame, by means of the senses which are within.

Acts 17 : 21
Ps. 34 : 8
1 Cor. 12 : 17
1 Cor. 12 : 18

59. These senses belong to the natural or external mind of the spiritual body, and by means of instruction in the wisdom of this world in all branches of science known to the natural mind, a man may be so highly educated in earthly knowledge, as to stand upon the pinnacle of fame, on account of his attainments in learning, and yet his spiritual and internal mind may not be opened in the least degree.

§39
Prov. 1 : 7
Prov. 23 : 15
Is. 5 : 21
1 Cor. 3 : 18
Jer. 9 : 23
Matt. 11 : 25

60. Thus a man is in a natural state or condition of thought, and he does not turn his mind toward spiritual principles until he has been brought down so low in his own estimation, that he feels utterly devastated of everything which he called and believed to be his own,—until he cries out in the anguish of his spirit for the Divine Light to illumine his path. It is not unusual for the preparation for a regenerate life to be extended over a period of many years, even after a man has publicly professed his belief in the prevailing religious doctrines of the people among whom his lot has been cast.

Is. 29 : 14
Heb. 12 : 11
Ps. 119 : 67
Is. 2 : 11
Is. 2 : 17
Ps. 143 : 4
Ps. 13 : 6
Ps. 34 : 6
Ps. 34 : 5
Ps. 10 : 17
Ps. 61 : 7
Amos 4 : 12
1 Tim. 6 : 12
Ps 146 : 8

61. When natural ideas and appearances of truth begin to perish, then arise conflicts and

Matt. 8 : 24
Matt. 8 : 25

| The Divine guidance. | Helplessness of man. |

Matt. 8:26
2 Pet. 2:9
Prov. 3:7
Prov. 16:9
Prov. 1:31
Ps. 1:6
Is. 42:16
Ps. 61:2
1 Cor. 10:13
Prov. 14:12
1 Cor. 8:2
Job 23:10

temptations, and the consequent mental suffering. In our natural self-hood or individuality, we desire all events in our lives to succeed as we have planned, and we also desire that other people shall do our bidding; but there is an Omniscient Loving Man who gently seeks to lead our thoughts higher than natural things, as rapidly as we are able to bear the discipline, although we often imagine that we know best what is for our good, for we call those things good which favor our natural desires, and it is characteristic for us to recognize more readily the hand of Providence when we appear to be favored, than when events seem adverse.

Ps. 55:4
Ps. 66:10
1 Pet. 4:10
Rom. 8:18
2 Cor. 4:17
Ezek. 33:13
1 Tim. 6:7

John 1:3
Deut. 28:66

62. In our disappointments we experience depression, and ultimately are filled with discouragement. We do not perceive the great object of the Divine Purpose, although we must suffer in order that it shall be attained; but when the talents which we thought our own seem to fail us, then we are sometimes led to realize that we cannot even think, by our own volition, any more than we can cause our own life-blood to flow through our veins and arteries.

Ps. 116:3
43
Ps. 115:17
Deut. 4:22

63. In this helpless condition a man feels as though he were dead, and in reality he is dead, for he has no life which originates from himself, and into this experience of the death of natural

The Day of Judgment.

things, a man must enter who is about to be regenerated, for it is truly the Day of his Last Judgment, the consummation of the reign of natural principles.

Rom. 8 : 13
Matt. 24 : 29
1 Thess. 5 : 2

64. Before the resurrection of spiritual life can take the place of the natural, or before the advent of the Lord can enter the world of man's internal mind, all external things in themselves alone must die to the man, and in this state of preparation it seems as though he were left by himself alone in the desolation of darkness, with no avenue of help, and in his despair he calls upon his God to lead him to the True Light, which shall guide his uncertain steps.

Ps. 22 : 15
2 Cor. 1 : 9
Jer. 17 : 5
Ps. 107 : 8
Ps. 107 : 39
Lam. 3 : 47
Luke 21 : 26
Ps. 107 : 19
Ps. 55 : 22
Ps. 73 : 24

Is there no light?

65. Through all these years, from early childhood, his memory may have been stored with the words of the Holy Scriptures, but after many years, in the order of his education in the sciences of the natural world, he meets with statements in the Word which seem to conflict with his acquired knowledge, and he begins to doubt concerning the Divine origin of the Word, and then the darkness becomes thicker; for to what other volume can he look for guidance toward a heavenly life? What other book can lead him to see the "*Light which lightens every man who cometh into the world?*"

2 Tim. 3 : 15
Is. 30 : 2
Is. 30 : 3
Jer. 47 : 2
1 Cor. 14 : 33
Is. 5 : 24
Ps. 82 : 5
Is. 10 : 3
Ps. 49 : 14
Ps. 73 : 25
John 1 : 9

The true world.	A mental sepulchre.

Ps. 9:8
1 John 5:4
1 John 2:15
1 John 2:16
1 John 2:17

66. What world is this desolate man about to enter? It is not the natural world in which he has been groping, which has gradually been perishing to him and is now dead, for no light for the immortal spirit can come from that world which has no spiritual life.

Heb. 4:1
Heb. 3:12
§30
Heb. 4:2
Ps. 88:11
Ps. 88:3
Is. 28:16
John 11:25, 26

67. In this state of doubt, even the letter of the Word which is illustrated by earthly comparisons, has become dead to him, because he perceives no life within it. But in the lowest vale of this mental cemetery, is a solid pillar of polished marble, bearing in plain, raised letters, the familiar words, "*I am the resurrection and the Life: he that believeth in Me, though he were dead, yet shall he live, and whosoever liveth and believeth in Me, shall never die.*"

THE RELIGIOUS TEACHER.

Is. 24:1
Is. 24:2
Jer. 14:18
Lam. 2:20
Jer. 8:1
1 Tim. 4:16
Titus 1:11
Eph. 4:14
James 1:12
Col. 4:17
Matt. 23:5

68. Down within this mental sepulchre, many a professional religious teacher has stood and gazed upon the remains of his natural education, even after many years of proclaiming doctrines from the Word. Perhaps he has turned from his vocation, or wandered for a while in some new doctrine for relief, only to be brought into greater despair. Or perhaps in his hour of temptation, the love of fame or honor has overcome him, and he has redoubled his efforts in the old routine of labor and doctrine, and

Adulation.	Conflicting statements

become even more interested in external things than before, so that his worshippers have increased in numbers, and he has become a recipient of that homage from men and women, which is so flattering to vanity in every profession. . — Matt. 20:28; Matt. 23:6; Matt. 23:7; Matt. 23:8

69. Or perhaps he may feel unfitted for any other profession, and for the sake of a living, continue to preach traditional doctrines without entering into farther investigation, or else seek to gratify his natural delight of ruling over the minds of other men, which is a love of dominion arising from the love of self. — Micah 3:11; Matt. 23:16; Jer. 5:31; Matt. 23:15

70. It is the privilege of a religious teacher to possess more knowledge of the literal sense of the Word than others, and in his studies to confirm the doctrines of his particular ecclesiastical system, he has met with many conflictions in comparing one portion of the literal sense with another, and it is with much effort and evasion that he has endeavored to make one passage harmonize with another. — 1 Tim. 4:6; Jer. 18:18; Luke 7:30; Ezek. 7:26; Matt. 24:21; Micah 3:6

71. He finds in one place the statement, "*Thou canst not see my face: for there shall no man see me and live;*" and yet in the same chapter he reads that "*The Lord spake unto Moses face to face, as a man speaketh unto his friend;*" also, "*thou Lord art seen face to* — Ex. 33:20; Is. 6:5; Judg. 13:22; Ex. 33:11; Gen. 32:30; Numb. 14:1

John 5:37	*face;"* when also it is declared in the New Testament, "*Ye have neither heard his voice at any time, nor seen his shape.* "*No man hath seen God at any time.*"
John 1:18	
Is. 45:7	72. He reads that God creates evil, and that He brings evil upon men; that He casts down into hell; that He hardens the heart; that He sends curses; that He commands His people to kill the man who serves other gods; that He will hide His eyes from those who spread out their hands; that He will not hear when many prayers are made; that He repents; that He cometh with fierce anger; that He destroys sinners; that in the prophecies He utters words of wrath and vengeance toward His own chosen people; and he finds many other sayings which he cannot reconcile as consistent with the attributes of Divine Love and Wisdom which shine forth in the Gospels, and therefore he does not say much concerning the Old Testament record. Thus he feels that He is at the mercy of scoffers, and begins to doubt the Divine authority of the Word; but he does not outwardly express his thoughts, and continues his routine of religious teaching as before.
Jer. 19:15	
Ezek. 31:16	
Ex. 4:21	
Mal. 2:2	
Deut. 13:9	
Is. 1:15	
Ex. 32:14	
Is. 13:9	
Jer. 15:7	
Jer. 50:15	
Jer. 50:28	
Nahum 1:2	
John 15:13	
Eph. 4:32	
Matt. 5:44	
2 Pet. 3:3	
Micah 3:7	
Ps. 146:4	
Mal. 2:1	73. But should he inwardly ask for more Divine Light to enter his mind, with willingness to be led, with a desire to lead others as the letter of the Word should become more illumi-
Jer. 17:16	
Mal. 2:7	
Dan. 12:3	

God has no perverse attributes. | Belief in the Word.

nated, he would in due time be permitted to see clearly that all these perverse expressions are intended to convey to the depraved natural mind, the appearance of truth, as the Lord seems to the man who is deeply engulfed in the love of self; but from the Spiritual Sense, the Word teaches that the Lord Himself is pure, unchangeable Love from Eternity to Eternity, whose desire is that every man shall turn from his evil ways and permit Him to lead all His creatures into angelic life. Those who obey the truths of the Word in loving the Lord and their neighbor, readily perceive that He has none of the perverse attributes which belong only to evil men. Evil men, in their freedom will not go to the Lord, or the Word, because they love evil rather than good.

Jer. 23 : 36
James 1 : 14
§33
Ps. 18 : 26
Ps. 18 : 25
James 1 : 13
Ps. 18 ; 30
Mal. 3 : 6
Ezek. 18 : 32
Ezek. 33 : 11
1 Pet. 1 : 22
2 Sam. 22 : 26, 27
Jer. 8 : 3

74. Any person who reads the Word for the purpose of confirming false principles by the appearances of truth according to which the Word is written, may do so in many places; but it is one thing to confirm false principles by passages from the Word, and another thing to believe simply what is spoken in its pages. The man who in an innocent state of mind, thinks that it is truth because he is instructed that the Lord spoke it by the mouth of His holy prophets, when he is led to understand its true meaning by what is said in the spiritual

Rev. 5 : 4
Ps. 56 : 5
1 Cor. 2 : 14
John 3 : 12
2 Pet. 3 : 16
John 14 : 11
Ps. 26 : 6
Ps. 32 : 8
Luke 1 : 70
Ps. 71 : 17
Micah 4 : 2

Is. 61:10	interpretation of the Word, readily perceives the Divine Truth and is filled with joy. Thus
Is. 50:10	the Lord permits a man in simplicity at first to believe that He is angry, punishes and repents,
Is. 48:17	so that he may be restrained from evil and led to do good.

'75. The question at once reasonably arises, that if the internal meaning of the Word is the

Ps. 104:31 real interpretation, why is it permitted that
Rev. 1:7 holy spiritual principles which are divine and
Dan. 7:13 true, should be obscured by such gross mis-
Ps. 97:2 representations? Is it consistent with the
Ps. 4:2 character of a just God to say one thing and
Is. 45:21 mean another? Why not declare the pure
Is. 45:19 simple truth at once, and avoid all the conflic-
Is. 53:8 tion and misinterpretation which has always
1 Sam. 9:27 existed concerning the Word of God?

Is. 40:28 76. These are honest inquiries, and are not
Is. 40:31 to be set aside, although the answer to them
2 Thess. 2:0 cannot at once be made clear to the apprehen-
Ps. 25:14 sion. If men were in their true order of spiri-
Gen. 1:31 tual life as they were in the most ancient times
James 1:15 before the "serpent," or the love of self, had
Gen. 2:17 drawn the whole race of man from spiritual into natural life, there would have been no need that the Word should have been written
Lev. 16:2 according to the appearance of truth as it seems to the natural mind.

77. It was thus written on account of the nature and condition of man's life, which through continuous ages has become so immersed in the corporeal and sensual ideas belonging to a life, or succession of lives, filled with the love of self, that he can only be led upward to spiritual life by such means as his mind can grasp, which must meet him in whatever condition of life and thought he may be existing.

Rom. 3 : 23
Jer. 40 : 3
Job 15 : 16
Jer. 31 : 30
Ps. 31 : 3
Job 33 : 27
Job 13 : 28

78. By nature, "*men love darkness rather than light*," and must blindly feel their way upward from the dark subterranean caverns, by forms which to them are real and tangible to the external sense of touch, which enable them to be guided into more acute senses of the perception of truth. These forms have within them, and even upon the face, qualities which will reveal their beauty and symmetry to the sense of sight in all their proportions as they approach the illuminating influence of the Internal Sense of the Word, and all will be led to the Light, who in their state of darkest obscurity, in humble obedience live in love to others from a child-like trust in Him who is the Sun of Heaven.

John 3 : 19
John 8 : 12
Job 33 : 29
Job 33 : 30
Is. 59 : 10
Is. 29 : 18
Ps. 96 : 6
Is. 42 : 18
Ps. 102 : 16
Ezek. 10 : 4
John 14 : 21
Mal. 4 : 2

79. The Lord will not leave the man who is willing and obedient, to grope in darkness, if

John 14 : 18
Ps. 16 : 10

The experienced physician.   Danger of fatalism.

Ps. 119 : 18
Rev. 22 : 7

he desires to open his eyes to the Light that shines from the obscure forms within the Word.

THE MIRACULOUS CONCEPTION.

Ps. 139 : 14
Ps. 145 : 9
Ps. 19 : 1
Job 32 : 8

Jer. 30 : 17
Matt. 8 : 7
Ex. 23 : 25

80. The physician who studies the intricate anatomy of the corporeal frame, observes how orderly every part does its own sphere of work, independent of the volition of the man who lives within it. He spends his life and thought in his arduous profession in the endeavor to bring into order those disarrangements of the physical system which originate from evil influences for which he cannot account.

3 John 11
1 Pet. 3 : 15
1 Cor. 10 : 12
§61
Luke 1 : 1
Is. 44 : 7
Ps. 24 : 1
Ps. 119 : 89
Is. 37 : 16
Zech. 12 : 1
Dan. 2 : 28
Ezek. 43 : 2
Ezek. 12 : 25
Ezek. 12 : 13

81. He hears religious doctrines proclaimed which he is told that he must believe without questioning. They seem to be confirmed from the Word, but to his clear perception they do not appear to be in harmony with the laws of order, which he recognizes must prevail in everything that is natural and divine, without which order, even the heavens and the material universe would not cohere; but he is unconscious that the Word treats of higher principles than disorderly natural births, and ignominious earthly history, and he is tempted to confirm himself in fatalistic principles, and think no farther.

82. It is right for him to affirm that God never violates the laws of order, although man in his fallen nature constantly disobeys them. In the temptation to discard the Word of God, the physician is not yet aware that the Internal Sense teaches that all births which are there recorded have only reference to spiritual births, and that the statement embodied in the prevailing doctrine of the MIRACULOUS CONCEPTION does not refer to the order of the birth of a physical or material child, excepting for spiritual illustration, for no natural birth ever occurred upon this earth excepting through the orderly means of a natural father and mother. This account of apparent earthly history is true spiritually, but it refers entirely to the spiritual birth of the Lord within the interior mind of the man who is to be regenerated.

Col. 4 : 6
Is. 44 : 8
Matt. 22 : 16
Rom. 8 : 5
1 Pet. 4 : 12
Luke 20 : 21
Hag. 2 : 7
1 Tim. 1 : 4
Luke 1 : 31
1 John 5 : 1
2 Pet. 3 : 2
Luke 17 : 25
Matt. 23 : 36
John 5 : 17
John 3 : 5
1 John 4 : 7
1 John 4 : 16
1 John 2 : 29

83. Farther along in these pages it will be illustrated from the Word that the state of life which precedes the advent of the Lord is typified by the mother Mary, who represents that virgin state of innocence at which the man has arrived in his reformation from evil and falsity, in which he is actuated by affection or desire for truth from the Word, for a man must be reformed or walk in the way which leads to holiness, before the work of regeneration can proceed. The knowledges of the simple living

James 1 : 5
Prov. 8 : 17
Mal. 3 : 1
Luke 1 : 43
John 14 : 23
Matt. 4 : 17
Gal. 5 : 6
Prov. 10 : 24
Rom. 7 : 6
1 Thess. 3 : 13

| Simple truths. | The appearance and the reality. |

<table>
<tr><td>Heb. 1:10
Gen. 1:2
Rom. 8:14

Luke 1:35
Eph. 2:1

Matt. 1:23
§48
Amos 5:4
Job 22:28
Ps. 15:1
John 20:25
Luke 2:34
§56
Is. 43:15
Heb. 6:13
Is. 43:18
Luke 21:27
§61</td><td>truths of the Word precede the "*beginning*" which God creates, and the "*Spirit of God moving upon the face of the waters*" or upon these truths in the external memory is signified by "*the power of the Highest shall overshadow thee*," or the Father quickening them with life. Thus the "*holy thing which is born of thee*," is named "*Emmanuel*," "*God with us.*"
  84. Yet if a man obeys the simple truths of the Word as they shine from the literal sense, and everywhere teach him to love the Lord and his neighbor, it will not be injurious for him to believe in the appearance of this spiritual fact which relates to the advent of the Lord into the regenerate life of men, because he may thus perceive a Divine Authority for the truths given by the Lord, as from a physical Person, and he will be clearly enlightened in the world to come, if not in this world, unless he is self-persuaded from pre-conceived opinions which are fostered by the love of self.</td></tr>
</table>

SERIOUS QUESTIONS.

2 Tim. 3:1

Ps. 46:1
Ps. 46:2
Ps. 46:3
Ps. 46:7

  85. In the minds of candid readers a very important question arises, viz. : If the religious doctrines of the Christian world which are founded upon the appearance in the Word of the physical Incarnation of the Son of God in the corporeal flesh, as a visible Person,—should

| A Vital consideration. | Mental food. |

be utterly swept away as an event of earthly history, would not the tendency be for thinking minds to discard the entire Word of God, and look upon it as a book of "*cunningly devised fables?*"

86. This is a serious inquiry, and will lead us to consider whether the Divinity of the Word depends upon external proof, or whether it contains within its thoughts and utterances, an Internal Evidence which cannot be dissipated by sophistry, or arguments from self-intelligent reasonings.

87. If the external or literal sense of the Holy Scriptures should be taken away, will mankind have any Revelation in which the soul can rest as the Word of God, or in any other way be saved from sin? "*If the foundations be destroyed, what can the righteous do?*"

88. This is certainly a momentous question; for if the literal form of the words of the Sacred Scriptures should perish, man could not be regenerated and saved from his sins; neither could heaven, or the principles of heavenly life, enter the world of his mind, for these principles as recorded in the Word must fill his inner life and be externally manifested in love to the neighbor.

89. The "*flesh and blood*" of the mind, or the spiritual body, must be fed with spiritual

Marginal references:
§51
Titus 1:13
Ps. 45:6
Titus 1:14
1 Peter 1:16
Titus 2:11
Titus 2:12
Titus 2:13
Titus 2:14
Ps. 93:5
Titus 2:1
Ps. 94:11
Ps. 99:5
Ps. 99:7
Ps. 102:12
Ps. 104:5
Ps. 11:3
1 Cor. 3:11
Hab. 1:12
Acts 4:12
1 John 2:27
1 John 3:24
John 3:3
§47

Earthly food.   The new birth.

Ps. 78:25	substances, and this spiritual food is found
Deut. 8:16	only in the Word of God. The food which the
Micah 5:4	corporeal frame derives from the three king-
Gen. 9:3	doms of the natural world, the animal, vege-
Ps. 65:9	table and mineral substances which must daily
John 6:27	be eaten to supply its life, will not nourish the
Matt. 6:25	spiritual body. And yet the soul of man could
Prov. 30:8	not exist on earth if the corporeal frame were
Lev. 25:19	not nourished with physical substances of its
	kindred nature.
Is. 55:1	90. The actual life of the physical frame is
Ps. 22:26	derived from the spirit, nevertheless the earthly
Luke 12:22	body must be fed and sustained from earthly
1 Cor. 9:4	substances in order that man may live within
Dan. 1:5	it, for Heaven depends upon earth as a basis.
Is. 66:1	"*Thus saith the Lord, The heaven is my throne, and the earth is my footstool.*"
	91. If there were no earths in the universe,
Ps. 89:11	the life of man could have no beginning, for
Ps. 83:18	there would be no place for his corporeal frame
	to be created and continue in existence. The
	soul is created within and gives form to this
1 Thess. 5:23	corporeal frame, and as the physical structure
Col. 1:10	is developed in strength and size, the man
	within increases in knowledge preparatory to
Josh. 24:15	receiving spiritual life, if he will so choose to
Is. 66:9	accept and attain it. This spiritual life is typi-
John 3:7	fied in the Word, at its beginning under the
1 John 5:18	figure of a new birth, or the advent of the

THE NATURE OF THE WORD OF GOD. 43

| The Holy Child. | The dead Literal Sense. |

Lord, which is analogous in its order to the physical birth of man, the Lord Jehovah being the Father of the Holy Child.

92. The analogies or correspondences of the Word in the literal sense, are taken from earthly things, and at first the mind only perceives the sign or representation which is used in the historical form of the Sacred Writings. The whole Word, not only the books of the Old Testament, but the four Gospels and the book of Revelation, is thus written according to natural appearances, and the names of persons, places and things, are not to be considered in themselves, for they represent spiritual principles in man, a statement which, with many others of a similar purport, will often be reiterated in the succeeding pages.

Margin references: 1 John 3:9; § 82; Matt. 16:27; § 42; Is. 7:11; Matt. 16:3; 1 Cor. 14:10; 1 Sam. 24:13; Mark 16:20; Luke 21:25; Acts 7:36; § 43; Judg. 14:14; Is. 28:10

THE LITERAL SENSE OF THE WORD.

93. Earthly things in themselves are dead. The food which we eat is dead. The meat contains flesh and blood which are dead, and the bread contains dead vegetable and mineral matter; but the life within the corporeal frame feeds upon these dead physical substances and is sustained, while without the life within, even the corporeal frame itself is dead.

94. The Literal Sense of the Word in itself is dead, for it is made from the dead material

Margin references: Col. 3:2; Is. 40:6; Is. 40:7; Lev. 11:27; Deut. 14:21; John 3:31; Jer. 31:40

| Bread and water. | Corporeal frame of man. |

<small>1 Cor. 15:37
Gal. 5:24
John 4:13
John 2:21
Matt. 5:6
Micah 7:14
Job 23:12
Ps. 146:7</small>

representatives of earthly things, which in themselves are dead. But when they are taken into the mind, or spiritual body, to appease the "*hunger for righteousness*," they sustain it with nourishment, for they form that flesh and blood, or that bread and water which is to be vivified with Life from the Lord.

<small>1 John 2:23
Rev. 22:19
John 3:36
John 1:32
Ps. 78:20
489
Matt. 16:11
John 6:31
Ps. 78:72

John 6:35
Mark 12:13</small>

95. The Literal Sense of the Word must not be denied, rejected, or crucified, for it is the Lord Himself in the world, who has thus descended from Heaven into substances which are to serve for spiritual food. This food is dead in itself, because it is an appearance of truth, containing no living principle for man until it is brought forth into life. If this spiritual food of the literal sense should be taken away, man would spiritually die, and the Advent of the Lord in man could not take place, neither could the Infant Jesus be sustained in the beginning of man's spiritual life.

<small>Ps. 8:4
Job 33:12
454
Job 14:10
Is. 38:11
Acts 23:8
Gal. 2:20
John 14:19</small>

96. Man, in his corporeal frame, appears to be a living creature in himself, and this is all that we see of him with our external eyes. When the spiritual body is withdrawn, we see him here no more, and there has not been a created man or angel in existence without first living within a corporeal frame, which is not the man himself, but is simply the covering or

| A disfigured form. | Divinity within this form. |

garment in which he first appears upon the stage of life.

97. This corporeal frame may appear disfigured and without symmetry, on account of the hereditary tendency to evil which has descended from depraved ancestors. It may be "despised and rejected of men; a man of sorrows and acquainted with grief: and we hid as it were our faces from him: he was despised, and we esteemed him not," and yet within this visage and form so marred, there may be a beautiful, tender and loving man, who has struggled against his inevitable natural surroundings, into whose inner life the Lord has entered to create him an angel of Heaven. Job 16:16
1 John 1:10
Ps. 106:6
Is. 53:3

Is. 52:14
Is. 29:19
Rom. 7:22
Jer. 31:33

98. The Word has been given to men as meat and drink to nourish the flesh and blood of the spiritual body. In its external appearance without any interior sense it is dead, but when it is applied to the life, and man imbibes and obeys its literal utterances, recognizing an internal divine principle clothed by disfigured words which often do not seem to cohere in unity, there is revealed to the spiritual perception that within these dead forms of expression there is Eternal Truth in which alone is to be found its Inspiration and Divinity. "*For that which had not been told them shall they see; and* Job 36:31
Ps. 111:5
2 Cor. 10:7
Ezek. 40:20
Is. 62:9

Is. 42:7
Luke 4:18
Ps. 24:10
Is. 52:15

Spiritual flesh.   Eating flesh.

Rom. 15 : 21 — *that which they had not heard shall they consider.*"

FLESH AND BLOOD.

Is. 40 : 26
John 1 : 14
Rom. 1 : 3
Heb. 2 : 16
Rom. 7 : 25
Rom. 3 : 20
John 3 : 6
Ps. 16 : 9
Eph. 6 : 12
Eph. 6 : 17

99. When it is understood what the spiritual meaning of FLESH conveys to the mind, then it may be perceived how the "*Word was made flesh and dwelt among us.*" It may therefore be useful to consider briefly the general meaning of this word as it is found in the Literal Sense of the Word, bearing in mind that every expression which there describes anything which is in the natural world, represents some spiritual principle of the mind, which is a corresponding receptacle of the principles of the Word. All spiritual principles begin with the Lord, or the Word, and descend through different degrees until they form and govern the mind of the man who obeys them.

Matt. 16 : 17
Ezek. 36 : 26
Gal. 6 : 8
2 Cor. 3 : 3
John 6 : 53
John 6 : 41
John 6 : 52

100. The words "*flesh and blood,*" are often used in the Word, and every thoughtful person knows without argument that they do not mean to convey the literal expression. When the Word represents the Lord Jesus as saying that we must "*eat His flesh, and drink His blood,*" even the most external and material mind might reasonably ask, "*How can this man give us his flesh to eat?*"

John 6 : 57
John 6 : 65

101. In its highest meaning, " flesh " signifies the Divine Love of the Lord which proceeds

| Living flesh. | The Word made flesh. |

from Him through the Heavens to the world of the mind of man. This Divine Proceeding is the "*Spirit that quickeneth,*" which is within "*the words that I speak unto you,*" for "*they are spirit and they are life.*" All persons who apply the truths of the Word to their interior motives, find within them an inward principle of life which is above the nature of the earthly life. The Divine Love is thus proclaimed by the Word, "*For God so loved the world, that He gave His only begotten Son, that whosoever believeth in Him should not perish, but have everlasting life.*" This SON OF GOD is the Divine Life of the Word within the man who believes and obeys its precepts. "*I am the living bread which cometh down from heaven: if any man eat this bread, he shall live for ever. The bread which I will give is my flesh, which I will give for the life of the world.*"

John 6 : 50
John 6 : 63

Eph. 5 : 8
Is. 61 : 8
Ps. 118 : 27
1 John 3 : 19
John 3 : 16

Rom. 5 : 8

Matt. 14 : 33
1 John 5 : 20
John 6 : 51

102. In order to sustain spiritual life, the Word must be partaken of as food, and this food is the flesh which is given "for the life of the world." The Life which is within this flesh is Eternal Life, or the Life of the Lord in the inmost principle of the mind of a regenerating man, which Life is derived from the Word, the "bread which cometh down from heaven."

Ezek. 2 : 8
Jer. 15 : 16
Matt. 25 : 46
1 John 2 : 25
John 10 : 28
Eph. 3 : 16
John 6 : 32
John 3 : 34

103. The word "flesh" as applied to man, has two meanings, one in reference to good,

Gen. 6 : 12
Jer. 32 : 27

The heart of flesh.	The renewed heart.

Rom. 7:5
Rom. 8:8
Gen. 6:5
Rom. 8:6
Ps. 36:1
Ps. 36:4
Rom. 7:9

Jer. 17:5

1 John 3:12

Jer. 17:9
Ps. 7:9
John 6:63

Ps. 65:2
Ps. 145:21
Luke 3:6
Ps. 84:2
Ezek. 37:5,6
Ps. 104:30

Joel 3:17

and the other to evil. Before the beginning of regenerate life, it refers to the self-hood of man's nature, to his ruling motive, or the "heart," which is hereditarily perverse and opposed to the living truths of the Word, and is that state of life in which he thinks only of himself and those who belong to him. The good or evil principle is indicated in the Word by the subject which the scriptural passage is treating of, as for example, "*Cursed be the man that trusteth in man, and maketh flesh his arm, and whose heart departeth from the Lord,*" where it is plainly indicated that the man curses himself, or closes the entrance to spiritual life, who trusts in his own natural evil principle, for "*The heart is deceitful above all things, and desperately wicked : who can know it?*" and also "*The flesh profiteth nothing,*" and in many other places.

104. The good principle represented by flesh in relation to man, when he has permitted the Lord to assume control of his nature, by active conjunction with the truths of the Word, is thus illustrated, "*Behold, I will cause breath to enter you, and ye shall live : and I will lay sinews upon you, and will bring up flesh upon you, and cover you with skin, and put breath in you, and ye shall live : and ye shall know that I am the Lord.*"

Interior principles.   Shedding blood.

105. If the Word is believed to be of Divine authority, the thoughtful reader will perceive that the word "flesh" must have reference to inward spiritual principles, especially in such passages as the following, "*Come and gather yourselves together unto the supper of the great God: that ye may eat the flesh of kings, and the flesh of captains, and the flesh of mighty men, and the flesh of horses, and of those that sit on them, and the flesh of all men, both free and bond, both small and great.*" Acts 4:4
1 Pet. 2:6
Rom. 1:8
Gal. 1:16
2 Cor. 4:6
Rev. 19:17, 18

Is. 31:3
James 5:3
Is. 17:4

106. The word BLOOD in its highest sense when found in the Word signifies the Divine Wisdom of the Lord as it proceeds from Him to the intellectual faculty of the man who receives it as it is clothed and given expression in the truths of the Word. The correspondence of the word "blood" is derived from the red fluid which circulates through the arteries and veins of the corporeal frame in which physical life resides, "*for the life of the flesh is in the blood.*" Matt. 26:28
Ex. 24:8
Dan. 2:20
Dan. 2:21
Matt. 13:54
Rev. 19:13
Heb. 9:22
Heb. 9:23
Deut. 12:23
Lev. 17:11

107. The Divine Life of the Lord courses through the arteries and veins of the historical narratives and prophetic utterances of the Word, and enters the affections and thoughts of the man who drinks this blood by learning and obeying its Divine Truths. "*This is my blood of the new testament, which is shed for*" John 10:15
2 Cor. 4:10
Phil. 2:16
Rev. 11:11
Matt. 26:27
Deut. 4:10
Mark 14:24

1 John 1 : 7	*many*," which redeems and cleanses from sin,
1 John 1 : 9	for it is the heavenly principle from the Divine
Heb. 9 : 20	Love and Wisdom, working within the blood
Rev. 5 : 9	of the spiritual body of the regenerating man,
Phil. 2 : 13	who drinks it from that cup which runneth
Ps. 23 : 5	over with Divine Truth. He who drinks this
John 7 : 37	blood by learning and obeying the simple
1 Cor. 10 : 4	truths of the Word, will bear good-will to all
John 7 : 38	people from an inward desire for their spiri-
2 Tim. 2 : 10	tual happiness.
Deut. 30 : 19	108. All things in the Word relate to good or evil and truth or falsity, because man
Ezek. 38 : 7	during his earthly life is in an intermediate state between good and evil influences. Thus
Luke 13 : 1	"blood," before regenerate life begins, signifies
Lam. 4 : 14	the intellectual principle of the natural mind
Zeph. 1 : 17	which perverts and falsifies the Divine Truth
Ex. 7 : 17	in the Word, and turns it so that it agrees with
Jer. 46 : 10	the love of self, or with doctrines which favor
Micah 7 : 2	selfish principles. These are they of whom it
Is. 34 : 3, 7	is said, "*The mountains shall be melted with their blood: and their land shall be soaked with
Rev. 16 : 6	blood.*" But concerning those whose spiritual
Heb. 13 : 20	blood is quickened by obedience to the truths
Ps. 72 : 14	of the Word, it is said, "*He shall redeem their soul from deceit and violence: and precious shall their blood be in His sight.*"
Ex. 16 : 4	109. Thus it may be understood that "flesh
Judg. 19 : 19	and blood," or "bread and wine," represent the

| Washing in blood. | The death on the cross. |

spiritual meat and drink which is to be eaten and drunken from the Word. 1 Cor. 10 : 3
Joel 2 : 26

110. In the Spiritual Sense of the Word, "blood" does not refer to the physical shedding of blood, nor the sacrificing of the life of a corporeal Person to propitiate the wrath of another Person, for the mind should rest in One Person only, in whom are the Three Principles represented in the Word, in man, and in nature. A true circle can have but one center. Deut. 19 : 20
Luke 22 : 20
1 John 5 : 3
Deut. 6 : 4
1 John 5 : 7
1 John 5 : 8

111. There are many persons of tender and trusting natures, who through the fear that they shall "crucify the Son of God afresh, and put him to an open shame," feel constrained to abide in doctrines derived from a literal interpretation of many passages of the Word. If their lives are inwardly pure, the Lord will reveal how He washes us *"from our sins in His Own Blood."* 1 John 4 : 18
Heb. 6 : 6
1 John 2 : 24
Is. 29 : 23
Is. 29 : 24
Rev. 1 : 5

112. The death of the Son of Man upon the cross signifies the violence done to the simple living truths of the Word, on which hang "*all the law and the prophets,*" when traditional teachings from the literal sense are confirmed in such a manner as to obscure those plain truths of life, on which rest the civil, moral and spiritual laws of the universe, and which in some form have been known among all nations. Matt. 26 : 2
Is. 53 : 9
2 Tim. 4 : 4
Matt. 7 : 12
1 Tim. 1 : 5
1 Tim. 1 : 6
1 Tim. 1 : 7
1 Tim. 1 : 8
Rom. 2 : 14

Why flesh and blood are used. | Anti-christ.

Matt. 22:1	113. The reason why it was written "flesh
Mark 3:23	and blood," instead of saying the Divine Love
Mark 4:2	and Wisdom of the Lord, or the spiritual prin-
Mark 4:13	ciples of good and truth derived from Him, is
Mark 4:33	because the Literal Sense of the Word was
Ezek. 17:2	named from things on earth which correspond
Acts 10:11 Acts 10:12	to spiritual principles in heaven, so that there
Jer. 32:14	may be a conjunction of the angel principles
Ps. 148:13	which constitute the Spiritual Sense, with men
Ps. 18:9	who read the Word in its Literal Sense. Those
Deut. 32:1	on earth who apply its truth to their lives,
Deut. 32:2	gather true spiritual food from the interior or
Deut. 32:3	angelic sense, for they are those blessed ones
Deut. 32:4	of whom it is said, "*Hereafter ye shall see*
John 1:51	*heaven open, and the angels of God ascending*
1 Sam. 28:13	*and descending upon the Son of man.*" The
Gen. 28:12	"Son of Man" is the Living Truth of the Literal
Matt. 25:31	Sense of the Word.
John 17:5	114. The Spiritual Sense of the Word reveals
Ps. 93:2	that the true doctrine which asserts that "God
1 Tim. 3:16	was manifest in the flesh" may be rationally
Is. 1:18	received by the enlightened mind, and that
1 John 4:3	"*every spirit that confesseth not that Jesus Christ is come in the flesh is not of God: and this is that spirit of anti-christ, whereof ye have heard that it should come; and even now already*
2 John:7	*is it in the world. For many deceivers are*
Rom. 10:9	*entered into the world, who confess not that Jesus*
Luke 21:8	*Christ is come in the flesh. This is a deceiver*

Salvation by the Commandments. · The Will of God.

and an antichrist. He that biddeth him God speed is partaker of his evil deeds." 2 John : 11
1 Tim. 5 : 22

115. In its effect upon the life of the man who is in the effort to obey the precepts of the Word, and who perceives an interior Divine Principle within the external expression, it is not essential that he should believe in a corporeal Incarnation of the Lord Jesus Christ, outside of the regenerate man in whom He lives. He saves a man from his sins by his life according to his obedience to the Commandments of the Word, and not by means of an irrational faith in mysteries which when literally interpreted are not according to the laws of Divine Order.

Deut. 4 : 1-5
John 1 : 12
John 4 : 23
1 John 2 : 5
Is. 43 : 10
1 John 2 : 3
John 9 : 37
Ezek. 18 : 31
Ezek. 18 : 27
Ezek. 13 : 23
1 John 2 : 18
Mark 4 : 11
Rom. 11 : 25

116. We should think spiritually concerning the "flesh and blood" of the Lord, or the Word, which is the Body he assumes in the world, and not reason materially upon this theme. In order to love the Lord even as we would love a fellow-being, we are not to adore a physical image of His Person, but we should strive to do those things which He reveals in the Word, which is the only visible expression of His Face and Form. The Internal Sense of the Word cannot be discovered by the natural mind, and is only revealed by the Lord to those who love to do His Will as it is revealed in the Word. All who desire a knowledge of the in-

Eph. 5 : 30
Eph. 5 : 32
John 20 : 11
John 20 : 12
1 Cor. 10 : 16
John 15 : 10
John 15 : 12
Mark 12 : 32
John 15 : 14
John 15 : 26
Ezek. 1 : 28
Ezek. 2 : 19
Ezek. 3 : 1
Ezek. 3 : 10
Ezek. 3 : 12
1 Cor. 8 : 3

The Lord Jehovah.	The suffering Son of Man.
Ezek. 3 : 17 Ezek. '3 : 22 Ezek. 3 : 23	ternal proof of Divine Inspiration, may find it within the Revelation God has given.
	## THE SON OF MAN.
John 14 : 7 John 14 : 29 John 14 : 26 John 14 : 20 Matt. 16 : 13 John 3 : 28 John 8 : 29 John 8 : 46 John 13 : 21	117. In the revealing of the Internal Sense of the Word, the Divine Man of the Gospels is not taken away and denied, for it is shown unto the true believer that He is the Lord Jehovah. The "Son of Man" of the Literal Sense is lifted up from the historical record of an humble Jewish peasant, and it is perceived that He is the Living Divine Truth which shines from the Literal Sense. Upon carefully searching the Four Gospels it will be found that the expression "*Son of Man*" represents one spiritual principle, while the "*Son of God*" is used to express another.
Luke 9 : 22 Mark 9 : 31 Mark 10 : 33 Mark 10 : 34 Luke 24 : 7 Matt. 17 : 22 Matt. 17 : 23 Luke 18 : 32 Matt. 20 : 18 Matt. 20 : 19	118. It is the "SON OF MAN" who is "delivered to the chief priests"; who is "condemned," "mocked," "scourged," and "crucified." It is the "Son of Man" who is "tempted;" who is delivered into the hands of sinful men;" who wears the "crown of thorns;" who is "spitefully entreated and spitted on;" who is "killed, and is raised again on the third day," and not the "Son of God."
Luke 22 : 22 Mark 14 : 21	119. It is the Divine Truth of the Literal Sense of the Word which has thus suffered and

been obscured by dead rites and ceremonies of external worship without internal spiritual life; with traditional teachings filled with condemnatory dogmas; with preachings which abrogate the simple Commandments, and supplant them with doctrines which prevent men from seeing the plain truth of loving the Lord and the neighbor, and which hold inquiring minds under the yoke of the fear of wrath, or the condemnation of the elders. *"Well hath Esaias prophesied of you as it is written. This people honoreth me with their lips, but their heart is far from me. Howbeit in vain do they worship me, teaching for doctrines the commandments of men; for, laying aside the commandment of God, ye hold the tradition of men." "And he said unto them, Full well ye reject the commandment of God, that ye may keep your own tradition."*

Matt. 26:24
Matt. 26:67
Luke 11:39
2 Tim. 3:5
Titus 1:15
Ps. 119:136
Ps. 62:4
Ps. 119:134
Gal. 5:1
Mark 7:6, 7
Is. 29:13
Col. 2:22
Titus 1:16
Ezek. 33:31
Mark 7:9
Ezek. 33:32

120. The contrast between the burdensome commandments of men and the simple truth of the Word, is thus plainly illustrated, *"He hath showed thee, O man, what is good; and what doth the Lord require of thee, but to do justly, and to love mercy, and to walk humbly with thy God?"* From the face of the plain truths of the Word, such as the Commandments of Life, there shines an Interior Light for the mind who obeys them. The Divine Law of Love to

Ezek. 33:33
Micah 6:8
Micah 7:18
Micah 7:19
Ps. 119:135
Hab. 3:4
Prov. 6:23
Is 9:2

| The fundamental precept. | The personification of Divine Truth. |

Matt. 4:16
Is. 52:10
Lev. 19:18
Matt. 5:43
Ps 15:3
Ps. 15:4

the Neighbor is clearly revealed in the Word of the Old Testament, "*Thou shalt not avenge, nor bear any grudge against the children of thy people; but thou shalt love thy neighbor as thyself: I am the Lord.*"

Jer. 44:22
Matt. 24:15
Dan. 9:26
Dan. 9:27
Ezek. 22:26
Ezek. 20:36
Luke 6:26
John 15:7
John 16:15
Deut. 6:25
Ps. 111:10
John 14:22
Titus 1:3
Jer. 8:9
Ps. 143:5
Ps. 27:13
Luke 12:8
Phil. 2:11
John 14:17
Prov. 19:23
Prov. 8:1
1 Cor. 1:24
Col. 2:3

121. In the spiritual history of mankind, these plain Living Truths had become so obscured by the quality of external worship represented by the Jewish rites and ceremonials, and which illustrate the same principles existing in the nature of man at the present day, that when the spiritual principles of the Commandments are more clearly revealed by becoming personified to the external mind in the life of, and utterances from the appearance of the Lord as a man,—in the Literal Sense of the Evangelists,—they are rejected and set aside for more elaborate and irrational doctrines. But when the mind is abstracted from physical appearances, and the Lord is acknowledged within these truths, it will be perceived that the Lord, or the Divine Truth dwells within regenerating men, as recipients of His Life from the Word. The personification of Divine Wisdom is very clearly presented to the external mind in the eighth chapter of the Book of Proverbs.

Is. 18:3
Ps. 24:9

122. The "Son of Man" is to be "lifted up from the earth" as the mind recedes inwardly,

or is elevated from the earthly appearance of the Literal Sense of the Word, and He will thus "draw all unto him" who look for Him within the Word. "*How sayest thou, The Son of man must be lifted up? Who is this Son of man? Then Jesus said unto them, Yet a little while is the light with you.*" "*I am come a light into the world, that whosoever believeth on me should not abide in darkness.*" Farther along in these pages it will be illustrated that light is a correspondent of spiritual truth, and that the Divine Truth, or the Word, is the Light proceeding from the Sun of Heaven.

Col. 3 : 4
1 Thess. 1 : 5
John 12 : 32
John 12 : 34
Ps. 24 : 8

John 12 : 46
Rom. 10 : 4
Rom. 10 : 11
Ps. 27 : 1
Ps. 74 : 16
Hos. 6 : 5
Eph. 5 : 14

123. The "*Son of Man shall come in His glory*" to the mind of man when the Word shall shine with light from its Spiritual Sense. This light will illuminate the mind of every believer when he perceives the Eternal principles of Divine Love and Wisdom within the earthly clothing of the Literal Sense. In entering this Portal of Glory the external mind must experience sufferings akin to the death of the corporeal frame, for all earthly thoughts of spiritual principles must perish before the Light from Heaven can be borne.

Acts 1 : 11
2 Thess. 1 : 7
Mark 13 : 26
Is. 60 : 3
Is. 62 : 2
Ps. 104 : 1
Rev. 10 : 1
Gen. 28 : 17
Ps. 118 : 18
Ps. 118 : 19
Ps. 118 : 20
Matt. 7 : 13
Matt. 7 : 14

124. So shall the Sacred Story of the Gospels be made the Life of Jesus within the man who receives the Word into his life, and in the trials and temptations which he will spiritually

Joel 1 : 3
Joel 2 : 27
Ps. 26 : 7
John 13 : 37

| The spiritual crucificixion. | Familiar comparisons. |

James 4 : 1	undergo, will he perceive within himself the
Rom. 6 : 5	crucifixion, as the appearances of truth in the
Rom. 6 : 6	literal sense are dissipated, and at the end of
Matt. 28 : 6	the third day, or full state of preparation, the
Mark 8 : 31	Lord will raise him from dead earthly repre-
Mark 16 : 6	sentatives, to perceive that the Living Principle
Mark 16 : 19	of the Internal Sense is the SON OF GOD. Then
Matt. 27 : 54	will he realize the true meaning of that Divine
Luke 1 : 46 Luke 1 : 47	History, which in its Literal Sense has been
Luke 2 : 29	the guide and comfort of millions, and for
1 Peter 5 :10	which thousands have suffered martyrdom.

THE CRUCIFIXION.

Deut. 4 : 39	125. In meditating upon the forms of expres-
Jer. 17 : 15	sion contained in the Word which contain the
Ezek. 13 : 14	Divine Truth, the imagination should not revert
2 Cor. 6 : 2	to the centuries of past earthly history outside
Is. 49 : 7	of one's own spiritual world or experience. It
Is. 49 : 8	is true that in the apparent history of the men
Is. 49 : 9	of old, in the narrative of the journeyings of
Is. 49 : 10	the Children of Israel, and other incidents,
Is. 40 : 11	there may be comparisons made with our own
Is. 40 : 12	struggles through the journey of life. Such
Ps 78 : 3	comparisons are only external, and are familiar
Ps. 78 : 1	to all religious people, and the Internal Sense
Ps. 78 : 4	does not consist of such similitudes, but is
Ps. 78 : 5	founded upon the unchangeable law of the cor-
Ps. 78 : 6	respondence between natural ideas or things,
Ps. 78 : 7	and spiritual principles.

126. The passion of the "Son of Man," ending with the death upon the cross, represents the violence which is done to the Divine Truth, or THE WORD, when it is externally honored, but is not received into the inner life. It signifies the death of the spiritual faculties of man, which results from perverting the vital truth of the Word, the law of love, by covering it over with the traditions of men. This effect is not to be seen outside of man's spiritual nature, but its tendency is to close the gate of true perception of the character of the Word.

Is. 53 : 12
Is. 59 : 6
Matt. 23 : 27
John 5 : 44
Matt. 23 : 23
Matt. 23 : 33
Matt. 23 : 27
Matt. 23 : 26
Eph. 4 : 17
Eph. 4 : 30

127. When this gate is closed, it is promulgated from the Literal Sense that the Lord is a God of wrath and retaliation, like a perverse man who is filled with jealousy and revenge, whose wounded honor and sense of justice, according to the teachings of men, can only be satisfied by certain conditions, which an unselfish man would shrink from proclaiming to his fellow-men. To those who thus think of the Lord, while in this state, it cannot be revealed that He is the Word which in the life of a regenerating man is the Humanity being made Divine.

Is. 3 : 26
Lam. 1 : 4
Ps 2 : 5
Hos. 5 : 10
Ex. 32 : 10
Deut. 32 : 42
Luke 6 : 37
Is. 50 : 9
Matt. 13 : 13
Is. 42 : 20
Is. 41 : 28
Is. 42 : 9

128. The Internal Sense reveals that the Lord Jehovah is Pure, Infinite and Unchanging Love, flowing without respect to persons to all His creatures whether they are governed by

Zech. 2 : 10
Is. 32 : 1
Acts 10 : 34

| Laws of Divine Order. | False doctrines. |

<table>
<tr><td>2 Sam. 22 : 33
Acts 26 : 18
Job 36 : 22
Is. 55 : 9
Rom. 11 : 33
1 Chron. 16 : 30
Is. 60 : 21

Job 37 : 23

Rev. 22 : 17

Ps. 25 : 10
Prov. 11 : 5
Ps. 55 : 5
Ezek. 3 : 21
Dan. 4 : 27

Matt. 14 : 36
Ps. 23 : 3
Jer. 10 : 13
Ps. 139 : 10

Matt. 26 : 55
Is. 47 : 14
Is. 40 : 24

Lev. 19 : 14
Is. 57 : 14</td><td>good or evil principles, doing all in His Omnipotence to elevate men into spiritual life without violating His Divine Laws of Order, or the freedom of the will of man. It is impossible for Him to violate His laws of order. He cannot turn the world backward from its course in the firmament, for it would cause destruction to the whole physical universe, and the Heavens which depend upon it. He cannot cause a good man to become an evil spirit, neither can He drive a man through the Heavenly Portal who will not freely walk in the paths which lead to Heaven. The re-action of a man's own evils upon himself often bring him into such a state of anguish and despair, that they force him to seek those avenues which are lighted with heavenly truths from the Word.

129. The only tangible way in which the Lord guides us, is by means of these heavenly truths. We hear no other audible voice, we touch no other guiding hand, nor do we see Him in any other Form. When His plain teachings of simple spiritual and moral duty are covered over with the stubble of the commandments of men, so that the mind, from these traditions, is filled with false ideas of the nature of the Lord or the Word, which causes the simple truth of spiritual life to be cast aside for doctrines which tend to foster the love of</td></tr>
</table>

THE NATURE OF THE WORD OF GOD. 61

| Death of spiritual perception. | Imprisoned thought. |

self in the most insidious form, such doctrines kill the spiritual perceptions of the man who reads the Word. Mal. 2 : 8
Is. 8 : 15

130. Thus the Son of Man "is rejected and despised of men," and it should be constantly borne in mind that the Word is addressed only to the persons who possess and read it. Those principles in the nature of man which confirm and proclaim doctrines from the Literal Sense of the Word which are irrational and are inconsistent with the Divine Loving Nature, tend to despise the simple commands of obedience which the Word utters, and these false principles are the Jews who crucify the "Son of Man." John 12 : 48
Hos. 4 : 6
Jer. 11 : 6
Rom. 16 : 18
Jer. 44 : 29
Ps. 36 : 3
Ezek. 2 : 6
Amos 2 : 4
Jer. 38 : 19

131. These Jews are externally religious, and attend jealously to all the requirements of public worship, and loudly vindicate the honor of God, but inwardly they condemn all who do not favor their traditions. They are tempted to execrate those persons who are in the simple interior life of keeping the Commandments, whose Living Faith teaches that the obedient are devoid of self-righteousness, and whose strength is wholly in the Lord. John 5 : 16
Matt. 15 : 2
John 5 : 18
Luke 6 : 7
John 10 : 31
John 7 : 13
Matt. 5 : 5
Is. 49 : 5
Ps. 68 : 34

132. The "traditions of men" thus obstruct the avenues to the perception of the Internal Sense of the Word, with the man who is bound in thought by their influence. But he who by Matt. 15 : 3
Numb. 16:33
Dan. 12 : 9

Living Principles. | Substitution.

Jer. 42 : 6
Gen. 22 : 18
Gen. 26 : 24
Is. 24 : 19
Col. 1 : 18
Rom. 8 : 2
Phil. 1 : 20

obedience to the Commandments of the Word sees the Living Principles of the Internal Sense when it is revealed to him, "fears not," for although they reveal that the body of the literal sense is dead in itself alone, yet within that Dead Body he sees and feels the Life of the Son of God from which his own spiritual body is nourished.

133. Before the Internal Sense is confirmed

Ps. 19 : 11
Luke 12 : 5
Heb. 12 : 25
Heb. 12 : 27
Heb. 12 : 28
John 8 : 43
Heb. 13 : 9

in his life, he is warned by the Word to fear those false principles which darken the perceptions, for in their interpretation of the Word the "traditions" destroy not only the entrance to, but the Spiritual Life within, by the perversion of the Literal Sense to sustain errors which shut out the light from Heaven. "*Fear not them which kill the body, but are not able to*

Matt. 10 : 28
Heb. 13 : 6

kill the soul: but rather fear him which is able to destroy both soul and body in hell."

134. From a remote period in the history of

Deut. 4 : 23
Deut. 4 : 19
Lev. 16 : 22
Lev. 16 : 10
Gen. 3 : 1
Ps. 140 : 3
Micah 7 : 17
Ps. 58 : 4

man, there has been in his perverted nature, a fallacy of substituting for the simple truth in religious duties, such principles which most agree with and favor the Love of Self. This enticing principle is represented under the form of a "serpent," because as serpents live and move with their bodies close to the earth, so sensual principles are closely connected with the external body. Sensual principles are

THE NATURE OF THE WORD OF GOD. 63

| The earthly serpent. | The heavenly serpent. |

those by which the mind is affected by means of the senses, from such external things as are represented in the Literal Sense of the Word from things in the natural world. By the external body is not meant the corporeal frame, but the external principles of the mind or spiritual body, which come in contact with external things by means of the senses. All sensation in the corporeal frame is actuated by an inflowing of perception from the senses of the spiritual body which is within.

Gen. 2:9
Ps. 45:8
Ezek. 33:10
Ezek. 33:11
Ezek. 33:12
Rom. 8:9
1 Cor. 6:17
1 Cor. 6:20
Col. 1:9
Eph. 2:22

135. When a man is becoming regenerated from the wilderness of the love of self, the sensual or corporeal principles of his mind are governed by internal principles, and are lifted up above earthly motives in proportion as Internal Principles are perceived within the Literal Sense of the Word. The Internal Principle is signified by "Moses," who represents the Lord, or the Word, and who reveals to the mind its interior truths, which, when obeyed with a living faith will revive a man from a state of spiritual death, and quicken him with Eternal Life. *"And as Moses lifted up the serpent in the wilderness, even so must the Son of man be lifted up; that whosoever believeth in him shall not perish, but have eternal life."*

Is. 11:8
Is. 51:3
Is. 11:9
Eph. 3:20
Ezek. 10:3
Ex. 24:18
Ex. 14:31
Ex. 34:35
Is. 63:12
Heb. 9:19
John 3:14
Matt. 10:16
Num. 21:9

136. The Literal Sense of the Word is written by spiritual correspondences with ter-

1 Cor. 10:11

| Exterior representatives. | Fear of punishment. |

<table>
<tr><td>Col. 1 : 16</td><td></td></tr>
<tr><td>Mark 6 : 31</td><td></td></tr>
<tr><td>Lam. 4 : 2</td><td></td></tr>
<tr><td>2 Peter 1 : 9</td><td></td></tr>
<tr><td>Lam. 4 : 1</td><td></td></tr>
<tr><td>Deut. 23 : 29</td><td></td></tr>
<tr><td>John 12 : 35</td><td></td></tr>
</table>

restrial, physical and natural objects and ideas, thus from sensual and visible things. When the mind rests only in these outward representatives, and does not perceive the spiritual principle within, a spiritual blindness is occasioned, in which the light of simple truth is turned into darkness, so that the mind can only see that which is physical and natural.

137. When this is the case with a man who reads the Word, he cherishes such doctrines from the Literal Sense which most agree with his ruling love or fear, and he naturally delights in those principles which favor the evasion of the responsibility of that obedience by which the love of self must be overcome, without which, heavenly truth cannot gain admission.

<table>
<tr><td>Is. 28 : 19</td></tr>
<tr><td>Jer. 10 : 8</td></tr>
<tr><td>Ps 73 : 18</td></tr>
<tr><td>Mark 4 : 10</td></tr>
<tr><td>2 Tim. 4 : 3</td></tr>
<tr><td>1 Sam. 15 : 22</td></tr>
<tr><td>James 3 : 15</td></tr>
</table>

138. The fear of the punishment for sin actuates such a man to seek in some way to propitiate what he supposes to be the wrath of an avenging Deity, not being aware that every sin will bring its own punishment, and that whoever is in a life of sin is immersed in its punishment. The idolater, or the man who is governed by the love of self, thus brings offerings to his deformed god, which is a reflection of his own life, and pacifies his mind with the thought that he has purchased favor, and thus has averted punishment. With greater anxiety to escape the punishment of his sins than to

<table>
<tr><td>Ezek. 14 : 10</td></tr>
<tr><td>Jer. 37 : 9</td></tr>
<tr><td>1 John 3 : 7</td></tr>
<tr><td>2 Thess. 2 : 3</td></tr>
<tr><td>Jer. 5 : 25</td></tr>
<tr><td>1 Cor. 10 : 14</td></tr>
<tr><td>Col. 3 : 5</td></tr>
<tr><td>Ezek. 33 : 25</td></tr>
<tr><td>Ezek. 6 : 13</td></tr>
<tr><td>Ezek. 23 : 49</td></tr>
<tr><td>1 Cor. 8 : 4</td></tr>
<tr><td>Ezek. 36 : 25</td></tr>
</table>

Atonement.   Peace on earth.

combat his hereditary evils, and overcome | Ezek. 36 : 25
them, he hails with joy the offer of a substitute, | James 4 : 7
for the penalty which he fears, and which | Rom. 10 : 27
he finds provided in doctrines which only
in appearance seem to be confirmed from | Deut. 28 : 58
the Literal Sense of the Word. The only
atonement which the Internal Sense of the | Acts 22 : 6
Word reveals, is the conjunction of a man's | Hag. 1 : 12
life in his interior motives, with the Living | Ps. 18 : 44
Truths of the Word. | Rom. 13 : 12

THE SON OF GOD.

139. LIVING TRUTHS are those which a man | Is. 35 : 16
manifests in his life by loving to do them, but | Mal. 2 : 5
before regeneration begins, the natural prin- | Rom. 7 : 21
ciple of his life is opposed to candid obedience, | Rom. 7 : 14
and he seeks to "climb up some other way." | John 10 : 1
Jesus, the Son of God, is the Interior Truth of | Mal. 2 : 6
the Word which the regenerating man delights | Is. 38 : 20
in obeying. He is "*the Way, the Truth, and* | John 14 : 6
the Life." The Word is "*the door,*" by obedi- | John 10 : 9
ence to which, from affection for its truths, "*if* | Matt. 25 : 21
any man enter in, he shall be saved." The Good | Heb. 4 : 11
Shepherd leads by the truths of the Word to a | John 10 : 11
life of "*peace on earth and good-will to men;*" | Heb. 4 : 9
"peace on earth" signifying a state of blessed- | Lev. 26 : 6
ness resulting from the cessation of conflict | Mark 4 : 39
between the spiritual and natural principles | Ps. 55 : 18
within, as the love of self is overcome through | Rev. 21 : 7

E

| The Good Shepherd. | The Divinity manifested. |

a life of obedience to the Word. "*The Good Shepherd giveth his Life for the sheep.*" By "sheep" in the Word are meant those persons whose ruling motive is to obey the Divine Truth, because they love the life to which it leads. A "shepherd" signifies the Lord. The Lord is the Word, and thus the Word is the Good Shepherd.

John 10:14
John 10:27
John 10:16
John 10:4
John 10:7
Ps. 23:1

140. Those false principles which are confirmed from the literal sense, which fill the mind only with natural ideas concerning the Word, and which obscure the perception of the plain living truths, are the "*thieves and robbers*" which "*climbeth up some other way,*" and which "*cometh not but for to steal, and to kill, and to destroy.*"

John 10:8
John 10:12
Jer. 22:29
Is. 59:9
Is. 56:10
Joel 2:6
Jer. 4:23

141. The interior Living Principle of the Word is the actual Life of the Lord from whom all life exists. It is the Infinite Love and Wisdom existing in successive degrees of heavenly order until it descends into the dead forms of natural language, based upon the dead forms of natural objects, so that the Lord may manifest Himself to the natural mind of man in a Human Form, and lead him to perceive the Divinity within this Human Principle. "*And I saw, and bare record that this is the Son of God.*" Thus does He come "*that they might*

2 Sam. 22:47
Jer. 4:2
1 John 4:8
Ps. 73:23
2 Cor. 4:7
Gen. 20:19
Is. 66:18
Ps. 69:32
Ps. 107:42
John 1:34
Ps. 145:7

have life, and that they might have it more abundantly," who *"open the door"* of the Word. *" Behold, I stand at the door and knock : if any man hear my voice, and open the door, I will come in to him, and will sup with him, and he with me."*

Man is to open the door.	The form of the Human Principle.

Is. 55 : 7
Ex. 34 : 6
Rev. 19 : 9
Luke 12 : 36
Luke 12 : 37

THE HUMAN FORM.

142. By Form, is meant the mode or order of operation. A spiritual principle takes its form according to its intended use, or object of its creation. The corporeal frame of man takes its form from the spiritual body within it, and this form is created in such shape that the attainment of his earthly and spiritual life may be fulfilled, the culmination of which is, that he may be of use to his fellow-beings both here and in the other world, according to the faculties with which he is endowed by the Lord.

Is. 45 : 18
Is. 43 : 7
Ex. 4 : 11
1 Cor. 15 : 49
Col. 2 : 17
Col. 3 : 10
Luke 4 : 4
Eph. 4 : 24
Eph. 4 : 16
Eph. 4 : 12
Is. 43 : 21

143. In order to attain this sphere of usefulness on earth, he has all the physical organs given which depend on each other. His legs and feet support and carry him from place to place in the journey of life. The organs within the trunk above, are used for the nourishment of the whole system and the sustaining of life. By his arms and hands he performs the duties of life, earns his living, and manifests the life within, so that his ultimate power resides

Eph. 1 : 22
Eph. 1 : 23
Is. 33 : 15,16
1 Cor. 12 : 12
1 Cor. 12 : 20
Is. 59 : 16
Ps. 24 : 3
Ps. 24 : 4

| The Earthly Form. | The Divine Form. |

1 Cor. 4:12
1 Cor. 12:25
Is. 51:11
Col. 2:19
2 Cor. 3:18

in his hands and fingers. Each finger is made to serve the other, while the thumb, as chief minister serves them all. The head contains the brain in which resides the intelligence which directs all thought, speech and actions, and which shines through the expression of the face.

Rom. 12:4

144. The science of anatomy explains the use of each exterior and interior principle of the corporeal frame, every minute organ of

1 Cor. 2:13
1 Cor. 2:10
1 Cor. 3:16
Gal. 5:14
1 Cor. 2:12
1 Cor. 6:19
1 Cor. 3:17
2 Cor. 6:16

which has its corresponding spiritual principle within the mind or spiritual body of man. The form of man is given him in its actual shape, in order that he may love the Lord and the neighbor with the utmost facility. To inhabit this temple of the spirit with any other motive, is to desecrate and pervert it, by profaning it with idolatry, or the worship of self.

Eph. 1:17
Eph. 1:18
Eph. 2:10
Gal 5:25
Is. 11:2
1 John 4:2
1 Peter 4:6

145. In order to comprehend what is meant by the Human Form, or Human Principle, of the Word, it will be essential to perceive what principles constitute the spiritual nature of man; and in order to understand the nature of man, there must exist some finite idea of the nature of God, from whom man has his being and existence.

Is. 46:9
Is. 40:26
Is. 40:20

146. There is One Lord Jehovah from whom all life originates, and who perpetually keeps all things in existence by constant creation.

The Creator.	The Spiritual Sun.

He is the Substance and Form from which angels, spirits and men receive their substance and form, and when their lives are formed by the Living Principles of the Word, they become images and likenesses of Him. All things are created by the Lord from Himself, and the Word in no place communicates the thought that He created all things out of nothing, for nothing can produce nothing.	Heb. 10 : 34 Ps. 139 : 15 Ps. 139 : 16 Is. 66 : 22 Heb. 11 : 3 Rev. 4 : 11 Is. 45 : 12 Col. 1 : 17
147. The Lord is Infinite Love and Infinite Wisdom, from whom all affection and thought exists in man. This Infinite Love and Wisdom constitute One Essential Life in One Person, and the mind may be aided in perceiving these two principles by means of the correspondence of the sun of the natural world with these spiritual principles.	Jer. 31 : 3 Prov. 3 : 19 John 15 : 9 Deut. 10 : 1? Jer. 31 : 35 Judges 5 : 3
148. The sun sends forth heat and light, which respectively represent the Divine Love and Wisdom. The sun itself represents the Lord in Essence and Person. The heat represents His Love; the light represents His Wisdom, and the going forth of the heat and light united in the rays of the sun as they proceed to vivify with life all the living things of the earth, represents the Divine Proceeding, or the operation of the Holy Spirit. Thus, as there is heat, light, and operation or effect, and but one sun from which they exist, so in the	Ps. 19 : 6 Rev. 22 : 5 Job 31 : 26 Rev. 1 : 16 Is. 6 : 16 Luke 17 : 2. Ps. 80 : 1 Jer. 20 : 9

| The Father, Son and Holy Spirit. | The natural man. |

Matt. 28 : 19	Lord, as One Person there is Divine Love, Divine Wisdom, and the Divine Proceeding, called in the Word, the Father, Son, and Holy Spirit.
1 John 5 : 7 1 John 5 : 8 John 20 : 22	149. From this Infinite Trinity in One Person, a triune principle exists in all finite things in heaven, man, and earth, each created thing being receptive of Love, Wisdom, and Power, according to its nature and capacity.
Job 33 : 4 Job 12 : 10 Ps. 31 : 24 Luke 24 : 45 Jer. 5 : 24 Jer. 13 : 10 Is. 47 : 8 Obad. 3 Ps. 10 : 3 Ps. 10 : 4 Gal. 5 : 16 Gal. 6 : 3 Gal. 6 : 7 Luke 6 : 31 Luke 19 : 14	150. Man has no life in himself, and even in his spirit is only a dead receptacle of Life from the Lord. Man's spiritual nature consists of two faculties : the WILL, which is the receptacle of Love from the Lord, and the UNDERSTANDING, which is the receptacle of Wisdom from the Lord. In his natural state, he does not recognize this principle of life, but attributes all that he thinks, says, and does, to what he supposes to be his own knowledge, which is only so in appearance. His will, instead of regarding the Love of the Lord, from which its life is derived, burns only to gratify the love of self, and does not inwardly seek the welfare of others, but puts himself first in thought, if he does not outwardly do so. He does not make the rule of his life, "*As ye would that others should do to you, so do ye also unto them,*" and does not inwardly desire the Lord, or the Word, to be his guide.

THE NATURE OF THE WORD OF GOD. 71

| A dead man. | A living man. |

151. In this state of life he is dead, for he has no spiritual life, and is actuated by no higher motives than the animals which perform earthly uses, although his natural understanding may be filled with sagacity and learning. He differs from the beasts in this respect: his understanding is enlightened with truths which he does not obey, although he has the faculty for obedience, while a beast has no understanding of truth, but an instinct which flows into his brain, which he obeys according to the laws of the order of his nature. The animal attains the full end of his being in this physical world, while man possesses faculties by which he may attain angelic life.

Ps. 49 : 12

Prov. 26 : 12

1 Cor. 3 : 19
1 Cor. 3 : 20

Is. 43 : 20

Dan. 12 : 10

152. The faculties which constitute man are, the perception of goodness, which is made acute by the desire for spiritual life, and the faculty of understanding truth when it is presented to the mind. In order that spiritual life may enter the will of man, he must obey the truth which he knows. He must bring it forth into life. This truth is found only in the Word, or in books derived from the Word.

Hos. 14 : 9
Ps. 107 : 9
Is. 40 : 18
Rom. 13 : 10
Deut. 30 : 20
Rom. 13 : 10
Ps. 40 : 6
Luke 4 : 20

153. This truth brought forth into the life of the man who reads it from the Word, will change his will from being ruled by the love of self, to an acknowledgment of the Lord, for he then gives up his own life of hereditary evil,

Ps. 119 : 116
Jer. 36 : 15
Heb. 10 : 7
Jer. 36 : 8
1 Peter 4 : 2

| The Body of the Lord. | The Trinity in Unity. |

Rom. 6:10
Rom. 14:8
Ps. 136:25
Matt. 26:26
Prov. 30:5
1 Cor. 11:26
Lam. 3:58
Is. 26:12
Matt. 13:23

John 14:3
Col. 3:24

Col. 3:15
1 Tim. 3:15
Is. 1:17
Is. 56:1
Ps. 119:23
Ps. 62:11
Luke 11:13
Is. 6:3
Is. 52:7
Is. 52:13

Is. 52:6

Ps. 111:9

and the Lord, or the Word, enters, and he begins to grow into the form of a true man. The truths therein which he feeds upon, constitute the Body of the Lord, which is given to him in the natural or literal form of the Word. The nourishment derived from this Body will regenerate his life, and bring the two faculties of the will and understanding into harmonious operation, so that they will become receptive of the Divine Love and Wisdom, and he will be converted into a true rational man according to the laws of heavenly order.

154. The Word in its operation within the regenerating man is in the Human Form, for it contains within its literal form a Divine Principle, which, when applied to the life, will change his thoughts from natural to spiritual conceptions, from animal to human life, and this Power from the Word in man is the Divine Proceeding, or the Holy Spirit, and thus the Word is the Divine Humanity which the Lord assumes in the will and understanding of the spiritual man, and hence is the explanation of what is meant by the Human Principle of the Word.

THE TRINITY IN ONE PERSON.

155. As the Divine Love and Wisdom operate in the spiritual nature of man by means of

THE NATURE OF THE WORD OF GOD. 73

| The Divine Trinity reflected. | Clouds and smoke. |

the Word, and thus its Triune Principle may be seen, so the effect of the will and the understanding, going forth into his words and actions, reflects this Divine Trinity in a regenerating man. Here the distracted mind may rest in the One Living God who is Incarnated in the Word, the Word made flesh and dwelling in the will and understanding of the man who is to live forever as an angel in heaven. Here is the Lord Jesus Christ, Jehovah God, the Divine Love and Wisdom of the Word, Incarnated and made manifest in the "flesh," or regenerated will of the man to whom he speaks by the Word, "*If ye love me, keep my commandments.*"

<small>Mark 9 : 5
1 John 1 : 3
Jas. 2 : 24

1 Cor. 8 : 6
John 14 : 10
Ps. 91 : 1
Ps. 91 : 16
Rom. 9 : 33
John 1 : 10

John 1 : 36

John 14 : 15</small>

156. The perplexed mind may behold in the Word, this One Personal God from Eternity, and think of Him as always the same and unchangeable in His Divine Love and Wisdom, and in the Eternal Past, Present and Future, abide in Him alone. Thus may we think of Him as within the Sun of the Spiritual Heaven, THE WORD, with His Heat and Light steadily shining without diminution, although its rays are often obscured by the evils and falsities of the men who misinterpret His Love, and make Him appear as a God after their own hearts, just as the earth is surrounded by clouds and smoke, and inclines its poles away from the illuminating centre of its orbit, so that the in-

<small>Is. 44 : 24
Heb. 13 : 8

Rev. 4 : 8
2 Peter 1 : 19
Deut. 4 : 36

Is. 4 : 5
Is. 5 : 30
Rom. 1 : 25
Ezek. 18 : 20
Hos. 13 : 2
Hos. 13 : 3
Is. 14 : 31</small>

fluences of the perpetual sun appear to vary according to the declinations and exhalations from the earth's surface, and its rays do not enter in their fulness of power.

Eph. 3 : 19

157. The Triune Principles of the Word are personified in the names of the Father, Son, and Holy Ghost, so that thoughts concerning God should take the Human Form in the mind. All men are sons from fathers, and yet there is but One Father of all to whom the mind reverts as the Creator. Without such a mode of presentation, men would have had no idea of One Personal Being, for the mind must behold sentient forms in order to abstract spiritual principles therefrom, otherwise the mental eyes could not have seen any higher attributes in the Deity than they would perceive in the clouds and murky atmospheres which surround the earth, and thus behold no Infinite Being in the Human Form.

Matt. 28 : 19
John 5 : 26
Heb. 12 : 9
Eph. 4 : 6
Rom. 1 : 19
1 Cor. 8 : 5
Rom. 1 : 20
Rom. 1 : 21
Micah 4 : 12
Rom. 1 : 23
Jer. 5 : 21
Jer. 16 : 20

158. Enlightened reason has been given man to recognize that God could consist of but One Person, although there have been doctrines prevalent which taught that there is more than One Person, derived from material thoughts concerning the Literal Sense of the Word. The apparent separation of the Father and the Son is based upon the physical appearance of the Incarnation as an event outside of the ex-

Is. 33 : 6
Is 46 : 9
Is. 43 : 10
2 Pet. 1 : 20
Gal. 4 : 8
Jer. 10 : 11
Luke 22 : 42
John 8 : 16
Ps. 22 : 1

perience of the man who reads or hears the
Word. If the Word contained no Internal
Sense within the external forms of expression
which clothe it, it could not be Divine, although
it treats of sacred things in the Literal Sense,
because without the soul within the literal
expression, many utterances based upon the
appearances of truth could not be reconciled
with that rationality which is enlightened from
above.

159. This is why the Lord has permitted it
to be revealed that the Word contains an Internal Sense, which communicates to the mind
of a man who is seeking spiritual life, that the
Lord Jesus Christ is the Divine Love and
Wisdom within the life of him who receives it
in his will and understanding, and thus to him
the Word is God.

160. It would not be truly rational to say
with the mouth that the Lord is One Person,
and inwardly think of a Father in Heaven and
a human Son upon the earth, for then the mind
inwardly would be in confliction on account of
the separation of the two principles represented
by the Father and the Son, which in the Lord
must be united and unchangeable, without
states, or seasons of being greater or less in
power, according to the appearance of more or
less love in the changeable nature of man. If

John 8 : 14
John 7 : 16
John 7 : 28
John 7 : 26
John 7 : 33
John 7 : 34
John 8 : 15
John 7 : 36

Is. 30 : 18
John 9 : 32
John 10 : 37
John 10 : 38
John 9 : 5
Hag. 2 : 9
Is. 33 : 10

Ps. 2 : 10
John 10 : 30
Rom. 15 : 6
2 Tim. 1 : 7
Is. 65 : 16

John 17 : 23
James 1 : 17
Numb. 23:19
Ps. 102 : 27

| The Son not a physical man. | The Rational faculty closed. |

by the Son it should be understood in the least that it conveys to the mind that it is a physical corporeal frame of the Lord upon this terrestrial globe, then the idea of the Father and the Son becomes that of Two Persons, and the thought is then distracted from the true Spiritual Sense of the Word. Thus the Lord Jesus Christ is not to be thought of as a physical man or Person on the earth, but His Commandments in the Word are to be obeyed and loved, which is the only way in which He can be loved, for the Word is His Person, and these Commandments loved and brought forth in the life of a regenerated man, constitute the ultimate degree or External Form of the Divine Humanity.

§ 19
§ 24
§ 44
§ 46
§ 49
§ 50
§ 51
Matt. 23 : 5
Matt. 28 : 7, 8
Numb. 15:40
John 14 : 21
John 1 : 1
Is. 48 : 18
Matt. 28 : 9
Matt. 28 : 10
Matt. 28 : 17

161. When the mind, in its abstraction from earthly things and their appearances in the Word, meditates upon the Divine Principles of this One Person, or the Commandments of the Word, spiritual perception flows in from Heaven, for Heaven is from the Lord, and there the angels know of but One Person. Where the idea of more than One Person exists in the mind, the door of the rational faculty, through which spiritual light enters, will be closed by the fallacies which result from the thoughts of more than One, because the effect in the mind is to create as many Gods as there are Persons, for the man then desires to worship each Per-

1 Cor. 12 : 1
§ 48
John 12 : 26
Is. 6 : 1
John 12 : 23
Rev. 4 : 1
Rev. 4 : 2
§ 74
§ 60
§ 64
§ 70
Jer. 16 : 11
Jer. 16 : 12
Jer. 16 : 13

THE NATURE OF THE WORD OF GOD. 77

| One Human Form. | Causes of anxiety. |

son, and is not fixed upon the vital Center of Life, and spiritual life can recognize but One Person in One Being or Human Form in which is the Infinite Human Principle.

2 Kings 17:29
Deut. 8:19
Ex. 34:14
Zech. 14:16

162. The external form of the face and body does not constitute the human principle of man, but the Understanding of Truth and the Love of Good, which actuate his life, and the operation of these two principles by which he manifests them to others, form the Triune Human Principle which exists in man because it is derived from the Infinite Human Principle which is within the Word of God.

¶ 19
¶ 23
Acts 17:23
Acts 17:24
Acts 17:25
Acts 17:26
Acts 17:28
Acts 17:29

SPIRITUAL PRINCIPLES ABSTRACTED FROM LITERAL EXPRESSIONS.

163, Spiritual principles cannot be apprehended, unless a person, by intelligent rational discipline has obtained power to abstract the mind from all things of time and space which belong to this physical world. Time and space belong only to the things of this world, and we shall soon exist beyond their influence, where spiritual principles are real and palpable to the senses. This reality exists even now while we are imprisoned in the corporeal frame, but we are so absorbed with the things of sense, from which arise all our cares and anxieties, that it is difficult to realize that we are spiritual beings,

§ 161
Jer. 35:13
1 Cor. 6:14
2 Pet. 3:11
Ps. 75:3
2 Cor. 5:1
2 Cor 5:2
2 Cor 5:3
2 Cor 5:4
2 Cor 5:5
2 Cor 5:6
2 Cor. 5:7
2 Cor. 4:8
Eph. 3:9

| The Spiritual World a reality. | Thoughts within words. |

<small>Eph. 3 : 10
Col. 1 : 16
Heb. 6 : 18
Heb. 6 : 19</small>

and that we are surrounded with a spiritual universe more real than the objects which we see in the physical world about us.

<small>2 Cor. 7 : 1
2 Cor. 5 : 10
2 Cor. 5 : 8
2 Cor. 5 : 9
2 Cor. 5 : 17
Rom. 8 : 35
Gal 5 : 22
Rom. 5 : 5
Rom. 16: 16
Jude. 19
Is. 44 : 18</small>

If we were solicitous about those principles which will exist after the death of the corporeal frame, and which constitute Eternal Life in Heaven, our perception of spiritual things would be quickened, for when we love these truths we drink them in with delight and perceive their reality, because that which a man loves constitutes his life, and if he does not love a life founded upon true spiritual principles, he cannot comprehend them when they are presented to his mind.

<small>John 3 : 12
Jer. 51 : 15
Jer. 51 : 16
Ezek. 3 : 27
1 Cor. 4 : 19
Titus 2 : 8
Eccles.10: 12
1 Cor.14 : 25
1Cor. 14 : 19
§ 58
§ 60</small>

164. All spiritual ideas must first be presented to the mind in natural language, or by natural forms. If a person is communicating thought to our minds by means of speech, we hear the sound of his voice, and the words which he utters. The sound of the words is not what the mind retains, but the idea is extracted which the words convey. The result is the same when we read a book. We see the letters which form the words, and the words convey ideas which exist in the mind of the author, and these ideas are associated with things of this world, either in relation to science or history, or are connected with the natural imagination as found in works of fiction.

| Power of abstraction. | Measurement of progression. |

165. It is possible to apprehend spiritual principles abstracted from time and space while in this life, and to perceive that they constitute the reality from which all things are derived. If we think interiorly, we shall perceive that the Lord Jehovah in His Infinite Love and Wisdom, exists above or within all conceptions of time and space, and also that all affection and thought in man exist independent of time and space. Our thoughts can even now reach forward to higher development in spiritual intelligence, and our affections become warm with joy when we contemplate the attainment of greater love for the Lord and the neighbor, while the weak corporeal frame may be prostrated with infirmity, and be confined within the fixed limits of the walls of a room. When our minds are absorbed with subjects which we love, we do not regard the passing hours, but when we are in seasons of temptation and grief, the time passes slowly and the days and nights seem long.

1 Cor. 2 : 5
1 Cor. 2 : 6
1 Cor. 2 : 7
1 Cor. 2 : 8
1 Cor. 2 : 9
Ezek 10 : 19
John 8 : 23
Eph. 4 : 6
Col. 3 : 2
James 4 : 14
Heb. 11 : 10
1 John 1 : 4
1 Pet. 1 : 8
1 Pet. 3 : 9
Ps. 41 : 3
Ps. 77 : 10
Ps. 79 : 11
1 Pet. 3 : 10
Luke 12 : 34
Ps. 27 : 5
Matt 24 : 22

166. The order of a man's regenerate life is measured by successive states or degrees of advancement from evil to good, and thus progression in Divine principles is made. These progressions are not measured by days, months, or years, but by obedience to the truths of the Word. Regeneration is only attained through

John 8 : 12
Ps. 92 : 12
Mark 4 : 28
2 Pet. 3 : 18
Is. 58 : 2
Eph. 4 : 15
Ps. 3 : 1

successive struggles in which the conflict between good and evil within the man results in the victory of the Lord over every evil and false principle, and then dawns the Sabbath of peace which is sanctified by the Lord. Thus the regeneration of a man's spiritual life may be thought of, abstracted from earthly time and space, and therefore all the principles of good and evil may be thought of independent of material things in themselves.

167. All books of earthly sciences, history, and fiction, have relation to natural things and ideas, but the Word of God treats only of principles concerning the regeneration of man, or of his spiritual life, and the mind must be abstracted from the natural form of things narrated therein, and the spiritual principles represented by them will be perceived in the place of the literal appearance.

168. The apparent history of events in the Word thus becomes true history of the spiritual states of man in the order of his regeneration, which occur historically as they are related. All the narratives become historical facts, for in their order they are representative of the progress of the regenerating man toward the Life of Heaven. All the wars and combats, with their apparent historical surroundings and circumstances, are representative of principles

| Typical characteristics. | A spiritual panorama. |

which the characteristics of the men typify, either good or evil, true or false. These historical narratives being representative of true spiritual history which must occur in the order of the regeneration of man, the rational mind will clearly perceive that it is not essential for salvation from sin, to believe that they were occurrences of actual physical history in successive earthly events.

	Joel 3:10
	Joel 3:11
	Rev. 15:3
	John 16:33
	Matt. 5:17
	Matt. 5:18
	Matt. 24:34
	Mark 1:15
	Rom. 13:8

169. A portrait hanging upon the wall, or found in an album, is representative of a person. The picture is not the person, but serves to bring the original form before the mind, and as the copy of the face appears before the sight, so the qualities of the man as we have known him, or have read of him, appear before our thoughts.

	§ 18
	John 1:7
	John 17:24
	John 17:8

170. So the Word of God is a panorama of true spiritual events in the history of each regenerate man, for spiritual principles alone are true and eternal. In the Letter of the Word nothing is apparent but mere history which in many instances seems remote from Divine principles. Within the form of the Literal Sense are concealed heavenly truths which cannot be seen as long as the mind and eyes are confined to the historical narratives, and they cannot be revealed to the mind until the thoughts are abstracted from the Literal

	Ps. 102:18
	Ps. 102:19
	Rom. 15:4
	Ps. 102:25
	Ps. 102:26
	Is. 60:2
	1 John 5:21
	1 Cor. 4:5
	Luke 10:21
	1 Cor. 4:20
	Is. 2:2

F

Sense, which is derived from the Internal Sense. It is contrary to the laws of order to think of the Internal Sense being derived from the Literal Sense, just as it would be to accept the husk in place of the ear of corn within.

171. In the abstraction or removal of the mind from the earthly things mentioned in the Literal Sense, when the coherent spiritual sense appears, and during its perception, the Literal Sense in itself alone then dies to the illuminated mind, for it has no life in itself independent from the Internal Sense, as the corporeal frame does not live from itself when the man enters the spiritual world.

172. The Literal Sense of the Word is the corporeal frame which holds its Spiritual Body, and while the mind is occupied with the external appearances, the internal contents cannot appear, for they are the truths which exist in the Spiritual World from which all the truths in this world are derived, and which govern the lives of angels and spirits, for man increases in knowledge after he enters the other world, by means of instruction from the Word. The Sense of the Letter, being corporeal, does not enter the other world, but the spiritual principles which are historically related, are Eternal Truths, a proof of which can only be demonstrated to the man who lives according

Self-intelligent wisdom.   A " hard saying."

to the Light which shines from the Face of the Word.

173. A man who is filled with self-intelligence, and deems himself wiser than others, cannot perceive the light from the Internal Sense, and spends his efforts in seeking confirmations of literal physical events to prove his position, utterly rejecting the affirmation that the Word of God treats of spiritual principles alone, teaching heavenly truths by means of natural forms and ideas. The time is rapidly approaching in the history of intelligent men, when self-intelligent science and human erudition, in darkness will make war upon the outer court of the Temple of God. Then will its gate of pearl open, and the Light from the Altar will shine through and disperse the enemies of Divine Truth.

| Lev. 26 : 12 |
| Jer. 8 : 8 |
| Jer. 50 : 31 |
| Jer. 50 : 32 |
| Is. 55 : 2 |
| Matt 23 : 12 |
| Matt. 28 : 13 |
| Matt. 28 : 15 |
| Mark 1 : 22 |
| Luke 13 : 35 |
| Rev. 22 : 10 |
| Zech. 10 : 11 |
| Is. 54 : 17 |
| John 2 : 19 |
| Ezek. 43 : 3 |
| Ezek. 43 : 4 |
| Ezek. 12 : 15 |

THE INTERNAL SENSE.

174. The reason that the Internal Sense of the Word has not been known among religious men in the past, and why it has not been understood clearly that the Lord has only " dwelt among us" by the Word, is, because the state of the affections and thoughts of men have not hitherto been able to bear it, and at first it will be a " hard saying" to many, for it will seem to them that these interior principles have

| Is. 40 : 21 |
| Ex. 6 : 3 |
| Ephes. 3 : 5 |
| John 8 : 26 |
| John 1 : 39 |
| 1 Cor. 3 : 2 |
| John 6 : 60 |
| John 20 : 22 |

| The Living Word. | Orderly laws of science. |

<small>John 20 : 13
Ezek. 43 : 5
Luke 4 : 32
John 20 : 14
John 20 : 26
John 20 : 29
Luke 24 : 32
Luke 24 : 36</small>

"taken away their Lord," but the light from the Internal Sense reveals Him as the Living Word, and all who desire may there see Jesus "standing" in the Human Form, and know that He is both the Lord and the Word, when they perceive Him guiding their footsteps by the Word into those paths which lead to perfect peace.

<small>Deut. 29 : 29
2 Thess. 2 : 1
2 Thess. 2 : 2
Phil. 3 : 14
Phil. 3 : 15
Is. 53 : 1
Phil. 3. : 20
1 Cor 2 : 11
Phil. 4 : 7
Amos 3 : 7
Luke 23 : 38
Ps. 118 : 26
1 Cor 1 : 7
Is. 62 : 11
Matt. 24 : 3
Is. 19 : 12
Luke 21 : 9
Luke 21 : 11
Matt. 24 : 4
Luke 21 : 36
Luke 21 : 28</small>

175. Many years ago, the Lord revealed the undistorted, coherent, and rational interpretation of the Internal Sense of the Word, in which He plainly declares Himself to be the Word, and that all the physical appearances which are there narrated are purely correspondences of spiritual principles from the Lord which exist in the mind of man by means of the Word. This Revelation of the Internal Sense is from the Lord alone. It was written in Latin, and was placed upon the shelves of the libraries of the principal Universities of Europe, to await the time when men should be prepared to receive it as Divine Truth : when earthly knowledge should begin to undermine the physical appearances in the Letter of the Word and prove them inconsistent with the orderly laws of natural science, so that thinking men who read the Word would be compelled to acknowledge an inward spiritual principle higher than metaphor, which is consistent and

coherent, and thus be led to higher intuitions of their own being and of the realities of the spiritual world. — Luke 21 : 32

176. The Word of God will neither be rejected nor despised by those who there perceive the Lord, for the knowledge of the Internal Sense will protect it from all the assaults of false principles, perverted reason, and atheism. — Luke 21 : 33 / Luke 21 : 22 / John 5 : 19 / John 5 : 20 / Ps. 91 : 4

177. The spiritual descendants of the historical Jews do not yet perceive that the MESSIAH has come, for He has not come in the external earthly glory for which they have been looking. The Son of Man has come "*in the clouds of heaven with power and great glory,*" by the Internal Sense of the Word, which reveals that Jesus is the Divine Love, and that Christ is the Divine Wisdom embodied in the Word, from the reception and union of which in the regenerated will and understanding of man, spiritual life in unity is produced, and is externally manifested in Love to the Neighbor. — Matt 23 : 31 / Matt. 25 :13 / John 4 : 25 / Matt. 23 : 39 / John 18 : 20 / Matt. 24 : 30 / John 4 : 26 / 1 Cor. 1 : 30 / 1 Cor. 2 : 16 / 1 Cor. 2 : 15 / 1 Cor. 3 : 9 / Eph. 4 : 13 / Eph. 5 : 1

DEGREES OF ORDER.

178. There are Three Distinct Degrees of Order in all things of the spiritual and material universe, each depending on the other, and these three degrees are contained within each sub-division or particle derived from any object. As the full illustration of this subject would — Gen. 18 : 2 / Lev. 24 : 8 / Ps. 104 : 27

occupy the entire pages of a book, a brief outline simply can be given.

179. The earth contains an Animal, Vegetable, and Mineral kingdom. The Animal Kingdom is the highest in respect to the inflowing of life, the Vegetable Kingdom is next in order, and the Mineral Kingdom is the lowest. All objects contain Length, Breadth, and Thickness, and they have Substance, Form and Use. A Circle contains a Centre, Diameter, and a Circumference, and it is formed from the Centre. It is a common rule in universal nature that whatever is purest and most noble, is Innermost, and occupies the Centre.

180. If a circular pillar should have three equal divisions, the lowest of brass, the intermediate division of silver, and the highest of gold, and be melted upon a heated plane surface, the brass would first subside and spread itself out so as to form the circumference, the silver would form a concentric circle within, while the gold, which was the highest, would form the inmost or centre of the substances of this circle. In Degrees of Comparison, the Superlative is the highest or inmost, the Comparative is the intermediate, and the Positive is the lowest or outermost. The Mind of Man contains the Will, or inmost principle, the Understanding, or intermediate, and the Life,

| Three Heavenly degrees. | Three Heavens. |

or union thence proceeding, which is the external manifestation. [2 Cor 4:11]

181. There are three degrees of heavenly life, the Celestial, or inmost, the Spiritual, or intermediate, and the Natural, or external. The word *natural*, when applied to the mind or principles of the Word, signifies the lowest or ultimate principle, but it has nothing in common with terrestrial or physical things, excepting by correspondence. The Natural Principle constitutes the external mind. In the Internal Sense of the Word, the names *Abraham, Isaac,* and *Jacob,* represent these three principles of the Word, and all other names are representative of sub-divisions of these principles, or their opposites, according to the subject which is being treated of. The words *Canaan, Assyria,* and *Egypt,* as well as *Judea, Samaria,* and *Galilee,* are also significative of the same principles, also *Zion, Jerusalem,* and *Nazareth,* and the names of the rivers *Euphrates, Jordan,* and the *Nile.*

[1 Cor. 15:40]
[1 Cor.15:44]
[1Cor. 15:46]
[1 Cor. 15:54]
[1 Cor 15:43]
[Hos. 2:22]
[Ex. 3:6]
[Matt. 8:11]
[Josh. 5:12]
[Is. 19:23]
[John 4:3]
[John 4:4]
[Ps. 147:12]
[Luke 1:26]
[Rev. 9:14]
[Ps. 114:5]
[Gen 15:18]

182. There are Three Heavens, which, like the pillar of gold, silver, and brass, are perfectly distinct from each other, viz., the Inmost or Third Heaven, the Middle, or Second Heaven, and the Ultimate, or First Heaven, and the principles of these Three Heavens lie within the plane surface of the Literal Sense of the

[§ 180]
[2 Cor 12:2]
[§ 180]
[Rev. 1:10]

Three interior receptacles.   Four senses within the Word.

<small>John 8 : 31</small>
<small>Luke 13 : 21</small>
<small>Matt. 13 : 33</small>
<small>Acts 10 : 36</small>
<small>Luke 9 : 33</small>
<small>Luke 9 : 34</small>
<small>Acts 10 : 37</small>
<small>Luke 9 : 35</small>
<small>Luke 24 : 15</small>
<small>Luke 24 : 8</small>
<small>Luke 24 : 9</small>

<small>Is. 42 : 5</small>

<small>Rev. 21 : 17</small>
<small>Matt. 6 : 20</small>

<small>Col. 1 : 16</small>
<small>Col. 1 : 26</small>
<small>Col. 1 : 27</small>
<small>Col. 1 : 28</small>

<small>Zech. 1 : 18</small>
<small>John 19 : 23</small>
<small>Eph. 2 : 20</small>

Word. The interiors of the mind of a regenerated man become receptacles of these Three Heavenly Principles, which give them form. In each Precept of the Word there are Three Interior Senses within, or in addition to the Literal Sense, descending in successive order from the Lord, through the Three Heavens until they rest upon the Literal Sense, which, when taken into the natural thoughts of a regenerating man, becomes the plane surface upon which they are spread in continuous order so that the understanding as it is enlightened may perceive the Inmost, Middle, and Ultimate meaning which the natural words enclose.

183. Wherefore the Word is in each Heaven, and all the knowledge of the Lord is there obtained from the Word in its respective Internal Sense, for all angels are regenerated men. Thus the Word was given that men may be prepared for Heaven, and there continue to derive their celestial and spiritual life from its truths. Descending through the Three Heavens, it is accommodated in its Internal Sense to the quality of the lives of the angels of each Heaven, and finally rests in its Literal Sense for the minds of men in this world. Thus the Word has a fourth sense on account of the Literal Sense being a foundation for the natural mind, as the earth must exist in order that a

Fulness of the Literal Sense. Concentration of Mind.

man may have his being commenced, and a place in which to begin the life of regeneration, which begins from the truths of the literal sense, in which the whole Word rests in its fulness.

Amos 9:6
Is. 51:16
Is. 34:1
Col. 2:9
Col. 2:2

184. In the endeavor to concentrate the mind upon the One Divine Man, the WORD, from whom all regenerated men are created, it may be of assistance to present an illustration of some of the Divine Attributes, with their derivatives in man, representing the Triune Principles of the Word in abstract form.

Col. 2:6
Col. 2:10
Col. 1:22
Col. 1:23
Col. 1:12
Col. 1:13
Col. 1:16

Make Thy Face to Shine upon thy servant; and teach me the way of Thy statutes. Ps. 119:135.

Abstract Principles.		Living Principles.

TRIUNE PRINCIPLES

OF

THE WORD,

OR

THE DIVINE HUMANITY

OF

THE LORD JESUS CHRIST.

END,	CAUSE,	EFFECT.
SUBSTANCE,	FORM,	USE.
CELESTIAL,	SPIRITUAL,	NATURAL.
INFINITE,	ETERNAL,	SELF-EXISTENT.
OMNIPOTENCE.	OMNISCIENCE,	OMNIPRESENCE,
LOVE,	WISDOM,	POWER.
CREATOR,	REDEEMER,	REGENERATOR.
JEHOVAH,	GOD,	ALMIGHTY.
FATHER,	SON,	HOLY SPIRIT.
DIVINE,	HUMANITY,	REVELATION.
GOODNESS,	TRUTH,	HOLINESS.

THE NATURE OF THE WORD OF GOD.

Personification of Divine Truth.		Eternal Life.
	ANOINTED.	Ps. 2 : 2
	COUNSELLOR.	Is. 9 : 6
	EMMANUEL.	Matt. 1 : 23
	GOOD SHEPHERD.	John 10 : 11
	GOVERNOR.	Ps. 22 : 28
	INTERCESSOR.	Is. 59 : 16
	JUDGE.	Micah 4 : 3
	KING OF GLORY.	Ps. 24 : 10
	KING OF KINGS.	Rev. 19 : 16
	LAMB OF GOD.	John 1 : 29
	LIGHT OF THE WORLD.	John 8 : 12
	LORD OF LORDS.	Rev. 17 : 14
	MEDIATOR.	I Tim. 2 : 5
JESUS	CHRIST. ETERNAL LIFE	1 John 5 : 20
	MESSIAH.	John 1 : 41
	MIGHTY GOD.	Is. 9 : 6
	PRINCE OF PEACE.	Is. 9 : 6
	SAVIOUR.	John 4 : 42
	SON OF DAVID.	Matt 21 : 9
	SON OF GOD.	Mark 1 : 1
	SON OF MAN.	Luke 19 : 10
	TEACHER.	John 3 : 2
	TRUTH.	John 14 : 6
	WAY.	John 14 : 6
	WONDERFUL.	Is. 9 : 6
	WORD.	John 1 : 1

THE FACE OF JESUS:

Regenerating principles.	Derivates from the Will.

TRIUNE PRINCIPLES

IN THE

REGENERATE MAN FROM THE WORD.

WILL,	UNDERSTANDING,	EXERCISE.
AFFECTION,	THOUGHT,	ACTION.
LOVE TO THE LORD,	LOVE TO THE NEIGHBOR,	SPIRITUAL LIFE
CHARITY,	FAITH,	GOOD WORKS.

185. From the Divine Love in the Will of the Regenerate Man there emanates

Adoration.	Desire.	Good-will.	Long-suffering.	Reconciliation.
Affection.	Devotion.	Gratitude.	Meekness.	Sacrifice.
Apprciation.	Emotion.	Holiness.	Mercy.	Temperance.
Benevolence.	Enthusiasm.	Humility.	Modesty.	Tenderness.
Charity.	Forbearance.	Innocence.	Patience.	Virtue.
Chastity.	Forgiveness.	Joy.	Peace.	Worship.
Compassion.	Gentleness.	Justice.	Pity.	Yearning.
Consolation.	Goodness.	Kindness.	Purity.	Zeal, etc., etc.

THE NATURE OF THE WORD OF GOD. 93

Qualities from the Understanding.   Evil principles.

186. From the Divine Wisdom in the Understanding of the Regenerate Man there emanates

Accomplishment.	Discernment.	Forethought. Invention.		Rationality.
Acknowledgment.	Discretion.	Honesty.	Judgment.	Representation
Communication.	Doctrine.	Illustration.	Knowledge.	Revelation.
Comprehension.	Education.	Inference.	Meditation.	Self-examination.
Confession.	Enlightenment.	Insight.	Memory.	Sincerity,
Conscience.	Explanation.	Integrity.	Perception.	Trust,
Contemplation.	Faith.	Intelligence.	Prudence.	Verity, etc., etc.

187. On account of the existence of the Love of Self and the World, from which all evil and falsity is derived, every good and true spiritual principle is perverted by the unregenerated man, and is changed into its opposite principle, and thus every natural idea which is in the Word has a good or evil meaning according to the subject which is being treated. The Divine Love and Wisdom flowing to the unregenerated man, cannot enter his life and cause him to be embued with spiritual principles, for it is perverted by his own nature, and instead of entering his will and understanding with vivifying influences, it becomes changed by the nature of man into the following Triune Principles :

LOVE OF SELF,	LOVE OF THE WORLD,	
EVIL,	FALSITY,	SPIRITUAL DEATH.
HATRED,	INSANITY,	
DEVIL,	SATAN,	

Evil qualities from the Will.	Evil qualities from the Understanding.

188. From the Love of Self in the Unregenerated man there emanates,

Adultery.	Debauchery.	Iniquity.	Love of rule.	Quarrelling.
Animosity.	Disapointment	Intrigue.	Malevolence.	Rancor.
Apathy.	Dislike.	Injustice.	Malice.	Retaliation.
Aversion.	Dissipation.	Intemperance.	Malignity.	Revenge.
Bitterness.	Destruction.	Indifference.	Meanness.	Ribaldry.
Brutality.	Harshness.	Jealousy.	Mercilessness.	Slavery.
Carnality.	Hatred.	Lasciviousness.	Murder.	Spite.
Complaining.	Immorality.	Lewdness.	Obscenity.	Suffering.
Concupisence.	Impurity.	Libertinism.	Oppression.	Tyranny.
Cruelty.	Ingratitude.	Lust.	Pride.	Violence, etc.,etc.

189. From the love of the World in the Unregenerated man there emanates

Atheism.	Distortion.	Hypocrisy.	Misguiding.	Profanity.
Betrayal.	Dulness.	Indiscretion.	Misrule.	Scepticism.
Blindness.	Deism.	Ignorance.	Negation.	Schism.
Concealment.	Envy.	Infidelity.	Obscurity.	Stupidity.
Covetousnesss.	Error.	Insanity.	Perfidy.	Theft.
Cupidity.	Falsity.	Irrationality.	Perjury.	Time serving.
Darkness.	Hallucination.	Knavery.	Policy.	Treachery.
Dishonesty.	Heresy.	Lying.	Perversion.	Unreliability, etc., etc.

| The nature of man. | The nature of the Devil. |

THE LOVE OF SELF THE ORIGIN OF EVIL.

190. In thinking of man as a spiritual being, the mind should be abstracted from the physical frame which we behold on earth, and we should consider those spiritual principles which constitute Man, so that he may be perceived as a being in the Spiritual World, and thus the principles of the Word apply to Angels and Spirits when obeyed, and to evil and false spirits, or Devils and Satans, when they are disobeyed and perverted.

	Lam. 3 : 40
	Lam. 3 : 41
	Joel 2 : 3
	Ps. 119 : 50
	Luke 2 : 35
	Heb. 2 : 1
	Heb. 2 : 2
	1 Cor. 11 : 19
	2 Thess. 2 : 8
	2 Thess. 2 : 9

191. Love and Wisdom, with all their derivates, emanate only from the Lord, or the Word. By a thoughtful reference to the preceding Dual and Triune classification of spiritual principles, it will be seen that no evil exists until Divine Principles reach the nature of man, and are perverted and violated by the freedom with which he is endowed. It may also be clearly seen that there is no Fallen God, who in the Literal Sense of the Word is called the Devil and Satan, and who in appearance seems to possess a power in his evil influence co-existent with the Infinite God.

	Heb. 1 : 1
	Heb. 1 : 2
	2 Cor 13 : 5
	Luke 6 : 45
	Jer. 11 : 8
	Rev. 12 : 9
	1 Pet. 5 : 8
	1 Pet. 5 : 9

192. The perversion of the Divine Love by man, in his own freedom turning it into evil, constitutes the Devilish Principle which actuates all evil spirits, who in their diabolical influences

	Is. 14 : 12
	Ps. 7 : 15
	Ps. 7 : 16
	Acts 19 : 16

Origin of the Devil.	The Selfhood of man.

Luke 7 : 21	upon the spirit of man, are Devils, and collec-
Deut. 32: 17	tively are called the Devil in the Word. The
Matt. 13 : 30	Love of Self is the opposite to the Love of the
Deut. 32 : 18	Lord, and from this evil love every species of
John 8: 44	wickedness originates, and he who loves him-
	self only, immerses all things of his will and
1 John 3 : 10	understanding in his Self-hood, so that his
Eph. 4 : 27	thoughts cannot be elevated from his selfish
John 8: 45	love to the Heavenly Principles of the Word.
Zeph. 1 : 15	He can see nothing from the Light of the
Prov. 4 : 8	Heavens which shines therein for the good
Amos 5 : 20	man, but his light is from the natural world
Joel 2 : 2 2 Cor. 3 : 14	alone, which is darkness in respect to spiritual light.
Matt. 16 : 24	193. The more a man loves himself, the more
Num. 15 : 31	he inwardly despises spiritual things, and de-
Matt. 10 : 33	nies them, and the door to the internal rational
Mal. 1 : 10	principle which is exercised by the light of
Matt 13 : 15	spiritual truth, becomes closed so that he can-
2 Cor 4 : 4	not be regenerated as long as he remains in the
Luke 3 : 3	Love of Self as his ruling motive. Thus he
	becomes merely Natural, and loves evils of
Num. 16 : 32	every kind : for the evil tendencies into which
Is. 53 : 6	every man is hereditarily born, reside in the
1 Cor. 2 : 14	Natural Mind, and are only removed from him
Prov. 4 : 27	in proportion as his interior mind which re-
Is. 45 : 8	ceives the Light of Heaven, is opened. The
Jer. 17 : 13	Self-hood of man resides in the Natural, or
Ezek. 8 : 9	External mind, and is nothing but evil. The

| The Great Adversary. | Divine influences never cease. |

Love of Self desires to rule over and destroy others, and thus becomes the Devil. This is the Ruling Spirit of the Dominion of Hell, the "Great Adversary" and Tempter which is to be conquered in man.

194. Since the evils of men are devils, all devils revealed within the Spiritual World of the Word, refer to the unregenerate principles of the hereditary nature which are inwardly filled with hatred, revenge, and adultery, notwithstanding they may be concealed by a devout exterior. Consequently all the devils revealed by the Word exist in the perverted nature of man, in opposition to the principles of Heavenly Order, and to a devout rational mind there is a satisfactory conclusion that the Devil, or personification in name of all evil principles collectively, is not co-existent with the Infinite God, and is not a Personal Evil One, and therefore God is not the Author of evil, nor the Creator of the Devil.

195. Although God creates the being of the evil man, and sustains his existence, He creates the faculty of attaining spiritual life with every individual, and sheds the heat and light of the Spiritual Sun as steadily upon evil men as upon those who open the door for its entrance, and He never will, even through Eternity, take away from man the power to open the door,

Ps. 106 : 41
Jas. 1 : 14
Nahum 1 : 11
1 Cor. 16 : 9
Eph. 6 : 11
Jas. 2 : 19
Rev. 16 : 14
Luke 4 : 33
Mark 7 : 21
Mark 7 : 23
Luke 4 : 36
Luke 4 : 41
Mark 9 : 25
Jude 6
2 Pet. 2 : 4
Ps. 25 : 10
Matt. 13 : 19
Matt. 13 : 38
Is. 45 : 5
Is. 45 : 6
Ps. 33 : 15
Luke 6 : 35
Heb. 4 : 13
Is. 45 : 24
Matt. 5 : 45
Ps. 121 : 6
Rev. 3 : 8
John 10 : 9
Jer. 42 : 12

and yet will never enter in opposition to his desire. Otherwise man would be a mere machine in the hands of an arbitrary and fatalistic Deity.

THE LOVE OF THE WORLD.

196. The Love of the World is opposite to the Love of the Neighbor, and is derived from the Love of Self. This false principle exists in those whose thoughts are entirely occupied with the affairs of this world in the effort to gain possession of its wealth and power, without being concerned whether others are injured by the means employed, using art and ingenuity in order to secure to themselves the property of others, which if they cannot succeed in accomplishing, they are filled with envy and covetousness.

197. It is not Love for the Neighbor for a person to love his wife, children, relatives and friends, because his own self-love and pride are wrapped up in these persons, but the Love of the Neighbor is represented by that principle in the Word, in which the light shines with brightness in this precept, "*Do unto others as ye would have them do unto you,*" which is the Divine Law of charity in feeling, judgment, speech and deed. To love the neighbor is to desire the regeneration of every man, even strangers, and those who have tried to injure

us, and it implies that our lives shall be in harmony with this Law of Love which will make us serve as living examples to others.

198. We are not to love a person as to his physical frame, but those principles which constitute his spiritual nature. We are to be useful to all, and faithful in the performance of the minutest duties which are presented for us to do, because the neglect of any duty, or the dishonest execution of work of any kind, causes others to suffer, so that this law enters into everything that we do, and thus it forms the Corner Stone or Fundamental Truth of the Word.

199. The neglect of this Divine Law of Love to the Neighbor, causes all the disorder and suffering in the universe, and this meek and humble Face which everywhere looks yearningly to man from the Word to arrest his attention as he reads, is that "*visage so marred more than any man.*"

200. The Love of the World nourishes every false doctrine which darkens the Light from the Word. Those men or spirits who are principled in this love are called Satan in the Word, which is the personification for all satans or false principles collectively. As satans are principled in falsity, instead of being wise they are insane in regard to spiritual truths, because

Rom. 12:14
Phil. 4:8
Col. 3:14
1 Tim. 4:12
2 John 5
2 John 6
1 John 4:13
Rom. 14:7
Luke 16:10
1 Cor. 7:31
Luke 16:12
Rom. 12:11
Rom. 12:10
1 Pet. 4:8
Mark 12:33
Ps. 81:13
Jer. 12:11
Rom. 8:22
Heb. 12:2
Ps. 69:20
Is. 53:2
Is. 52:14
Matt. 13:22
Mark 4:15
Job 1:6
Zech. 3:2
Matt. 4:10
Matt. 16:23
Jer. 5:4
Matt. 17:15

| Spiritual insanity. | God is no respecter of persons. |

1 John 1: 6 Matt. 16: 8 Jer. 9: 5 Jer. 9: 6 1 John 1: 5	not having them in their lives they cannot reason intelligently about them, although they possess the faculty of perceiving that Truth exists, they reject and despise it, loving "darkness rather than light."
Ps. 32: 2 Ps. 32: 7 Ps. 37: 28 1 John 5: 20 1 John 3: 2 1 John 5: 10 1 John 4: 20 John 3: 20 1 John 4: 5 1 John 3: 13 Ps. 1: 5 2 Pet. 2: 12 2 Pet. 2: 13 2 Pet. 2: 14	201. The regenerating man is principled in Love and Wisdom from the Word through the development of his Rational Faculty, and has Eternal Life and the True God, the Lord Jesus Christ, within him to make him a son of God, or a Divine man, while he who does not live according to the simple truths of the Word is principled in the Love of Self and the World, and his faculties are turned into hatred and insanity in regard to spiritual things, from which the result is Spiritual Death, and the destruction of every principle which can constitute him a man.
Rom. 10: 12 Rom. 10: 13 Joel 2: 32 John 5: 40 Matt. 10: 14 Gen. 6: 5 Deut. 27: 10 Deut. 2: 2 Rom. 2: 15 Rom. 2: 11 Rom. 2: 12	202. The Lord created every man with the faculty of attaining that true manhood which constitutes Eternal Life in Heaven, but He cannot force upon any man a gift which he will not freely receive and make use of. While all men are born with a natural tendency to evil, there is also implanted within them the faculty for obedience to those laws which will save them from sin. Those who obey the Light or Truth which is given them, will be led to the clearer Light of the Word as it is in the Internal

| Clear Light of the Word. | Application of the Word. |

Sense, and be saved from their sins by means of its Divine Truth working within them; but those who will not open the door by resisting their evils, so that Infinite Love may enter and raise them from that condition of misery and despair which they are continually bringing upon themselves, will not desire to abide with those who are warmed and enlightened by the Sun of the Heavenly World.

Rom. 2: 13
Ps. 36: 12
Luke 14: 33
Rom. 2: 8
Rom. 2: 9
Rom. 2: 1
Deut. 28: 15
Matt. 25: 40
Matt. 25: 41

203. The longer a man delays attending to those principles of life which are Eternal, the closer will he shut the door and fasten himself out from that unchangeable Infinite Love which will forever seek to enter, but which his confirmed spiritual insanity will oppose.

Ps. 119: 60
Prov 7: 24.
Luke 13: 25
Luke 13: 26
Luke 13: 27
Luke 13: 28

204. The Lord "knoweth our frame. He remembereth that we are dust." He knows the hereditary evils and temptations with which we have to contend. He never judges or condemns us, and in the Word He enjoins us not to judge others. Those who possess the Light which shines from the Word can apply it only to themselves, and see that it dwells richly in them, and then earnestly let their light so shine before men, that they may also see its spiritual life from its effect.

Ps. 103: 14
Ps. 103: 11
James 5: 11
Ps. 103: 12
Ps. 103: 6
Matt. 7: 1
Matt. 7: 2
Matt. 7: 3
Col. 3: 16
Matt. 5: 16
Phillip. 2: 15
Is. 60: 5

205. It is a serious and momentous thought, that if we have not yet opened the door to the Everlasting Love of Him who gave us being

Deut. 32: 20
Lam. 5: 21
1 John 4: 10

| Subjective application. | Eternal Punishment. |

1 John 4:15	that we might have Eternal joy in the true
1 Pet. 5:1	exercise of our yet undeveloped faculties,—
Heb. 3:3	there is danger that we may not desire to
2 Sam.14:14	overcome the Love of Self and the World.
2 Pet. 3:9	With His help, who is the Living Word, we
Ezek. 18:23	may attain that Eternal Life which is salvation
1 Pet.1:24	from sin, but the only time given to man to
Rom.13:11 2 Cor 6:2	"repent and believe" is the ever present Now.
Luke 11:28	206. All the spiritual principles contained
Ps. 119:11	within the form of the Literal Sense of the
Is. 51:7	Word are subjective, and are to be personally
Lev. 25:18	received by the regenerating man; they are not
Jas. 4:12	to be objectively applied, either to other persons
	or to apparent physical events. All the goods
Ps. 119:160	and truths which are held in the Literal Sense,
Col. 2:7	are to have their culmination in his regenera-
Matt. 13:49	tion, and all the evils and falses there portrayed,
Matt. 13:50	are representative of his own sinfulness, and
Jer. 7:15	are to be rejected and cast out, so that the
Is. 26:2	regenerating principles of the Word may enter
	and supplant them. As his evils are resisted,
Is. 55:7	overcome, and removed, he ascends from hell
Ps. 68:18	toward Heaven, for the state of heaven or hell
	exists in the Spiritual World of the mind of man,
	and neither state is a material place to which
John 6:54	mankind are destined. The appropriation of
	the Divine principles of the Word into the
John 17:3	thoughts and affections, thus governing the
	entire life, constitutes a state of Eternal Life or

THE NATURE OF THE WORD OF GOD.

Everlasting punishment.	Objective illustrations.

Heaven within the regenerating man, while all the evil and false principles which are being removed, and have been overcome in the order of his regeneration, which can never be separated from his individuality, are in a state of spiritual death, which is also eternal, for hell cannot exist with Heaven, and this constitutes the Everlasting Punishment of the wicked. By the "wicked" are meant subjectively all the evil and false principles which exist in the perverted hereditary nature of the regenerating man, which are opposed to the heavenly principles of the Word.	1 John 5: 12 Mark 9: 43 Mark 9: 45 Mark 9: 47 Mark 9: 43 2 Thess. 1: 9 Ps. 9: 17 Ps. 55: 15 Is. 14: 15 Ps. 37: 20 Matt. 25: 41
As all evil is death, and punishes itself, this is the Eternal Death of which the Word treats, and which can never enter Eternal Life. When a regenerating man sees the manifestation of wickedness in the lives of others, he at once recognizes an objective illustration of his own evil nature, and in humility he inwardly acknowledges his transgressions, and does not exalt himself above others, nor judge them, but in those wicked lives he beholds a representative state of his own evils, which is the hell from which he is being saved.	Rev. 20: 14 Ps. 92: 7 John 3: 36 Ps. 37: 35 Ps. 37: 1 Prov. 24: 17 Ps. 37: 9 Ps. 51: 3 Rom. 14: 10 Matt. 13: 51 Ps. 49: 15

THE FORM AND STYLE OF THE LITERAL SENSE OF THE WORD.

207. The order in which the spiritual principles of the Word descend into the plane of the Literal Sense is represented in historical form. Principles which precede, or which are prior, are first treated of in the order of discrete degrees, or degrees of altitude, for in the Internal Sense, all things which precede, signify higher, or interior principles, and those which succeed, signify lower, or more exterior principles. Thus the Adamic epoch, sometimes called the Golden Age, is not to be thought of as a period of the remote past, but it signifies a state vivified by the Celestial principles of the Word, as the order of spiritual descent is from the Celestial to the Spiritual degree, and from the Spiritual to the Natural degree, which three degrees are contained within the Literal Sense of the Word. These three degrees, consisting of interior principles, are sometimes termed the Three Heavens into which the mind of a regenerating man is elevated, who, in the order of his spiritual growth, begins with the most exterior principles which lie within the plane surface of the Literal Sense of the Word, as degrees of latitude.

208. In historical appearance, the Noatic or Silver Age seems to have been a successive epoch after the Golden Age, succeeded by the Israelitish or Brazen Age, but the regenerating man whose mind is open to perceive the Internal Sense of the Word, gives no thought to the appearance of physical events, but abstracts the coherent spiritual meaning from the historical connection of the words which contain these spiritual truths. The Golden Age is a present state of spiritual growth attained by a regenerating man whose will is actuated by a principle of love, as gold in the Word corresponds to Celestial principles; so the Silver Age is a present state of a regenerating man whose understanding

THE NATURE OF THE WORD OF GOD. 105

Column of degrees.	External evidence.

is enlightened by Spiritual Truth from the Word, and the Brazen Age is the state of a regenerating man who is living in the Truths of the Literal or Natural Sense of the Word, before his Rational Faculty has been opened to receive its Spiritual and Celestial principles. These spiritual principles descend from the Highest, or Inmost degree, through the Intermediate or Interior degree, to the Lowest or Exterior degree where they meet the mind of man in the Natural degree of thought as recorded in the Literal Sense. From obedience to the truths of this sense the order of his regeneration is upward from the Brazen, through the Silver, to the Golden Age, as illustrated by the column of degrees of gold, silver, and brass (§180), and the Golden Age is the Third Heaven to which the mind of the regenerating man is elevated, for the Three Heavens exist in the mind of one man who is vivified by the Celestial principles of the Word.

209. The WORD, in some form, has existed in all past time. When the Old Testament Record was given to man, and through what persons, there is no external history to give authentic proof outside of the Word itself. Added to this is the Word of the New Testament in the Books called Matthew, Mark, Luke, and John, ending with the prophecy of the Revelation.

It is not known who wrote the Gospels, and the subject of the authorship of all the Books of the Word will always be a matter of conjecture. The custom of using the date Anno Domini was not established until six centuries after the supposed Advent of the Gospel History, which may be ascertained by investigating the subject of Chronology in any reliable encyclopædia, without further comment.

Unsatisfactory as will be the result of this investigation, the external evidence of the superiority of the Word compared with other books, is in its having been so reverently guarded through successive generations, and by the general impression of its sacred character, resulting from a Divine inflowing into the External mind that it is a Book of Supernatural Origin. The strongest

Essence and Life of the Word.	Jehovah God.

external proof that it is from a Spiritual Source, is to be found in the witness of the lives of those who love and obey its Truths.

210. The Divine Truth is the Word which was "in the beginning," and which "was God"; not regarded as to the words and letters of the languages in which it was written, but as seen in its Essence and Life which is from within, in the meanings of its words and letters. From this Life within, the Word vivifies the Affections of the Will of the man who reads it devoutly; and from the Light of its Interior Meaning, it enlightens the Thoughts of his Understanding.

This constitutes the Word, because it is from the Lord, and speaks concerning the Lord, and is the Lord alone, as the rays of heat and light from the physical sun are called the sun, in common speech. No one, however, feels and perceives the Divine Life of the Word, the LORD JESUS, but the man who is in the spiritual affection for truth when he reads it, for he is then in conjunction with the Lord through the Word; there being something intimately affecting the heart and spirit, or the affection and thought, which flows with light into the Understanding, and bears witness of the Divine Truth.

211. In the Word of the Old Testament, the words JEHOVAH GOD frequently occur together, and also separately, as JEHOVAH, and sometimes GOD. Jehovah, or JESUS, signifies the Lord as to Divine Love or Goodness, and God, or CHRIST, signifies the Lord as to Divine Wisdom or Truth. Both terms, JEHOVAH GOD, or JESUS CHRIST, are used for the sake of the Heavenly Marriage, or harmonious conjunction of the Will and Understanding, which is to be effected by the regenerating principles of the Word which in all its particulars has reference to the marriage of Love and Wisdom in the mind and life of man.

The words JEHOVAH GOD are not used in the Literal Sense of the New Testament, but He is called the LORD JESUS CHRIST, through which name he is seen as the Divine Man from whom the two principles of Love and Wisdom exist, which form the Word,

Descent of Divine Truth.	The First Advent.

212. The Lord has descended as Divine Truth in the Word, and thus reaches the mind of man, by being adapted to his natural thoughts in its Literal Sense. No other principle than the Divine Truth, or the Word, is meant by the " Messiah," or " Christ," or the " Son of Man," or the " Son of God."

The Divine Humanity of the Lord, is the Word within the life of a regenerating man. The Humanity is the Literal Sense of the Word which is made Divine when a man is created spiritual by its Truths, for the Lord first introduces man into the truths of the Literal Sense of the Word, which is His Human Principle, and as these truths are united to good, or made alive by obedience, the Internal Sense of the Word is revealed, and becomes the Divine Humanity in the life of the regenerating man. By the union of the Literal and Internal Sense, or of the External mind with the Internal, by love and obedience to the Word, the mind is led from Natural to Spiritual and Celestial principles, and this is the Glorification of the Divine Humanity, the Word made Divine in the life of the man who obeys and loves its Precepts.

213. Thus by means of the Literal Sense of the Word in which He assumes the Human Principle, the Lord is born on the earth, or within the External mind of regenerating men, in order that they may be saved from their sins, by teaching them the principles of Heavenly Life, how they should live and believe, and thus attain Eternal Happiness.

As the First Advent of the Lord into the spiritual history of mankind during successive epochs, is the giving of the Literal Sense of the Word to the world, so the Second Coming, prophesied in the Literal Sense, is the unfolding of the Internal Sense to the minds of all who perceive its Interior Truths by living according to its Precepts.

THE NATURAL DEGREE.

214. The first thoughts of man concerning the Word rest in the Appearance of Truth according to which it is written, and the prevailing opinions of the religious world are based upon natural

Era of darkness.	Communication between Heaven and "earth."

thought concerning the Word as it is in the Literal Sense. When no internal principle is acknowledged within the Word, dogmas are formed and confirmed from the Literal Sense, derived from the Love of Dominion over the minds of men, which obscure the simple Doctrines of Life, and enshroud the Rational Faculty with darkness.

This cloud prevents the mind from perceiving that the Word contains an Internal Sense which alone constitutes its Divinity; for in the place of the simple Commandments of Life which are to be obeyed, doctrines have been earnestly promulgated that a man is to be saved by a mental act of faith without the effort to keep the Commandments, and thus the Living Precepts have been set aside and "darkness" has covered the "earth."

This era of darkness undergoes its consummation, or Last Judgment, when the Lord again comes into the world by opening the mind to perceive the Internal Sense of the Word from which the Literal Sense receives its origin and life, and the knowledge of the Eternal existence of this Divine Principle will gradually spread over and enter within the "earth" or External mind of those who are prepared to see the morning rays dawn from the mountains of the East.

215. The Word, which has been reverently preserved for our use for many thousands of years, is entirely written by representatives and significatives, so that it may hold the Internal Sense which is understood in Heaven, or the Internal mind of a regenerating man, when abstracted from the Literal Sense, and thus a communication may be effected with the natural mind, and the Lord's Kingdom in the Heavens may be united with the Lord's Kingdom on the earth; and unless these representatives or expressions by which the Word is written, contained principles concerning the Incarnation of the Lord in the regenerating man, the Literal Sense of the Word would not be from a Divine origin.

In order to contain this coherent spiritual principle within the Literal Sense, the Word could have been written in no other style, for it would not have been possible for the ideas and expressions of its external form to correspond with Celestial and Spiritual principles, and without this Internal Living Principle, the Word would be a dead letter, but it is vivified in the reader by the Lord, according to the nature and capacity of each individual, and thus the Lord lives in the regenerating man according to the state of his Love and Faith derived from the Word.

THE SILVER AGE, OR THE SPIRITUAL DEGREE.

216. The minds of those who are in the Spiritual Degree of regeneration are formed by doctrinal instruction in the Understanding, and not by immediate perception. The nature of this intellectual principle is, that Truths must be learned from the Word and retained in the memory by believing them to be true, and it is of such a quality, that should the doctrines be simply truths in appearance and not spiritually true, the mind is first impressed as though they were the truth, and the discrimination between Truth and its Appearance must be discerned by means of the Rational Faculty in order to discover what is True.

Thus Conscience is given to those who are living in this degree, which will be succeeded by the Perception which is possessed by those who have attained the Celestial Degree.

In the Celestial man, the Perception of Good in the Will is the ruling principle, which includes the co-operation of the Understanding, but in the Spiritual man, the Understanding of Truth is the governing principle, and the Rational mind examines the nature of doctrinal instruction from the Word to see if it be True, and then from obedience is led to love the Truth, and from this to love the Lord and the Neighbour.

217. The importance of studying the Word of God must continually be more apparent to the mature mind who has begun to walk in the paths of the regenerate life. The Internal Sense of the Word will not flow into the Understanding without effort on the part of man, and the Truths which are concealed within the Literal Sense, must be sought out from the " earth " of the Word,

just as the hidden treasure of gold and silver must be dug from the soil and rocks of the physical earth. These Truths are the riches which do not take to themselves wings and fly away, but they make the possessor rich with a wealth which he will carry with him and use in his spiritual growth. This wealth does not come to any man by the laws of earthly inheritance without his own effort, neither can he part with it by bestowing it upon others who are not prepared to receive it, but its nature is such that the more he seeks to communicate the secret of its production, by manifesting its quality in his external life so that others may see and be led to find the source of his riches, the more the Lord will fill him with the true and enduring wealth.

218. These spiritual riches do not come to any man who prays from morning until night for a Revelation from Heaven, and who hangs down his hands and his understanding, awaiting a blessing to be abundantly poured out more than he can think or ask, but he must go to work and search diligently with the means placed in his hands, which will always be provided for those who are willing and industrious, for "*the willing and obedient shall inherit the land.*" They shall possess the Good and Truth of the Word, which in their lives will be Love to the Lord and Neighbor.

The Lord gives to every intelligent man the faculty of perceiving the nature of the Word, and yet no person does perceive it unless he desires, as from himself, to see its Internal quality. It cannot be forced upon any man by sectarian or dogmatic assertion. All the Good that a man does, and all the Truth that he acquires, seem to originate from his own exertions, just the same as he feeds his physical body, when the substances which he eats, and the sustaining of life by the nourishment derived from the food, are from the Lord alone.

THE GOLDEN AGE, OR THE CELESTIAL DEGREE.

219. The Celestial principles of the Word will be revealed to all who from affection for righteousness obey the Truth which en-

Heavenly men.	Open communication with Heaven.

lightens their minds. The internal quality of their lives is such that they then have a clear perception of the principles of the Divine Love and Wisdom, the Lord JESUS CHRIST, who has always been the same from eternity, and who is now perceived in the Human Form, or Human Principle of the Word which is inscribed on their hearts, or within their minds. They are Celestial or Heavenly men, and have immediate revelation from the Lord by conjunction with the angels and spirits of the Word, by whom they are taught these Heavenly Principles. They possess an internal perception of the principles of the Word, abstracted from the personifications there recorded, and the Celestial and Spiritual principles of the Word are the Angels and Spirits by means of which they have conjunction with the Lord. Thus they have open communication with Heaven and with Angels and Spirits by means of the Literal Sense of the Word, for this open communication is the revelation to the natural mind of the Heavenly principles within the Word to those whose lives are being regenerated and vivified by its Truths. Conjunction with these Divine principles of the Word constitutes Heaven, for Heaven is in the Internal Sense of the Word, and the natural thought of man is in the Literal Sense, wherefore the conjunction of Heaven with the natural world of thought is by means of the Literal Sense of the Word and its Interior principles.

220. As their whole lives are governed by principles of internal worship, they do not require the representative rites and ceremonies which prevail with those who are in natural thought concerning the Word, because they enjoy open communication with, or perception of its Celestial and Spiritual principles. Although they are vividly sensible of the external objects relating to their physical bodies and the world of nature, they are not absorbed with them, because by means of the science of correspondence, they perceive the spiritual principles represented by all these things.

Perception of spiritual principles.   External style of the Word.

Thus when looking upon a high mountain, the thought of its being a mountain does not impress them, but they perceive the high or interior heavenly principle represented, and thus their minds are led to Heaven and the Lord. From this circumstance it is written in the Word that the Lord "dwells on high," * and that He is called the "HIGHEST,"† and "EXALTED."‡

When they awake in the morning, their minds do not rest in the appearance of the rising sun, but as the dawn of more wisdom from the Lord. Hence the Lord is called the "MORNING,"§ the "EAST,"‖ and the "DAY SPRING from on high."¶ Also when they behold trees, with the fruit and leaves, they do not think of them as physical objects, but perceive the living principle of the mind represented thereby, the "fruit" denoting love and charity, and the "leaves" representing faith. Thus trees are in many places in the Word spoken of as representative of regenerating men, and do not mean trees in the physical world. *"For ye shall go out with joy, and be led forth with peace; the mountains and the hills shall break forth before you into singing, and all the trees of the field shall clap their hands."*

THE STYLE OF THE LITERAL SENSE.

221. The Literal Sense of the Word is written in several different styles. The First Style is illustrative of Celestial and Spiritual principles by representative language, as related in the account of the Creation, the Garden of Eden, the Fall, the Deluge, etc.

The Second Style is that of Spiritual History illustrating the successive steps of regeneration, or making the human nature Divine by means of the Word. This style begins with Abram and continues through the Pentateuch, and afterwards in the Books called Joshua, Judges, Samuel, Kings, and the four Gospels

---

* Ps. cxiii. 5.   † Luke vi. 35.   ‡ Is. xii. 14.
§ Ezek. vii. 7.   ‖ Ezek. xliii. 2.   ¶ Luke i. 78.

| The Prophetical style. | Correspondential writing. |

of the Evangelists, in which the facts of spiritual history actually take place within the regenerating man in the order in which they are related in the Literal Sense, and when the Internal Sense is revealed, the spiritual facts are altogether different from the earthly appearances in which the mind first rests.

222. A Third Style is the Prophetical, which is not connected in the Literal Sense, and is not historical in appearance excepting in the Book called Daniel, but is broken and interrupted, being scarcely ever intelligible excepting in the Internal Sense, in which the heavenly principles succeed each other in a beautiful and orderly connection, and relate to the Internal and External mind in the various states of regeneration, treating of the Interior principles of Heavenly Life, and in their Inmost Principles they relate to the Lord. This Internal Sense of the Word is perceived by angelic men who derive their spiritual food from this Fountain, abstracted from the idea of the worldly things which the Literal Sense conveys to the natural mind, and they do not have an idea of persons, objects or places, but of the spiritual principles which these words convey. In this Style all the prophetical books of the Old Testament, and the Revelation in the New Testament, are written.

Another Style is that of the Psalms, which is intermediate between the Prophetical Style and that of common speech, where the Lord is treated of in the regenerating man in the representation of David as a King.

The Book of Job consists of writings handed down from ancient times, containing apparent history, full of correspondences, according to the mode of writing at that time, and is a book of great excellence and usefulness in the illustration of spiritual correspondence with natural objects. The Book of Proverbs and Ecclesiastes are replete with illustrations of the law of Love to the Neighbor and the opposite principle, while the Canticles, or

Song of Solomon, consists of correspondential language significative of spiritual principles concerning the marriage, or conjunction of Good and Truth in man.

223. The Epistles are filled with quotations from the Word, and everywhere teach the truths of Love to the Neighbor as set forth in the Gospels, and they are " *profitable for doctrine, for reproof, for correction, for instruction in righteousness: that the man of God may be perfect, throughly furnished unto all good works* "* They consist of doctrinal writings which are given to the religious world in order that the Literal Sense may be more clearly and intimately understood and applied to the life, in preparation for the opening of the Internal Sense of the Word when it is revealed. The Doctrine of Life, of Charity and Brotherly Love, is clearly revealed in the Epistles in more minute particulars than elsewhere in the Literal Sense, and they are all correspondential in their interpretation, especially in all the quotations from the preceding Word which constitutes their foundation.

The Style of the Word consists altogether of correspondences, whereby it is effective of Immediate communication with Heaven; but doctrinal writings are teachings explanatory of the Word in a different style, which also have communication with Heaven, but Mediately, because adapted to a more exterior plane of thought, from which the mind is led to perceive the Interior Principles of the Word when the Internal Sense is revealed.

224. The thoughtful reader having been gradually led to perceive the nature of the Literal Sense of the Word, its Sacred Pages will now be opened at the Book of Genesis for a glimpse of some of its Internal Principles as applied to the mind of a regenerating man, and to prove its Spiritual Coherence. After the principles of the First Day of Creation have been illustrated, parallel descriptions of the same principles will also be briefly

---
* 2 Tim. iii. 16, 17.

THE NATURE OF THE WORD OF GOD. 115

The Literal Word exists from its Internal principle.

given from the Gospel History of the Advent, to demonstrate the Divinity of the Word as it is applied to the elevation of the nature of man to higher planes of thought than can be found in the perishing things of this world, bearing continually in mind that the Literal Sense exists from the Internal Sense which gives it life.

The many different verses of Scripture which may be found from the marginal references on the preceding pages, are illustrative of the Spiritual Principles which are referred to within their adjoining paragraphs, and the same principles will be illustrated from the references in the succeeding pages, by the laws of correspondence, and if the reader sincerely desires, from love and obedience to the truths of the Word, his mind will be illuminated to clearly perceive that the Word treats of more important things than transitory earthly affairs, and that the same words throughout the Scriptures convey the same corresponding Spiritual Principles, whether occurring in the Old or New Testament.

Scientific facts.	Spiritual Principles.

THE
FIRST CHAPTER OF GENESIS.

Ex. 18 : 16	225. The Scientist, on reading the First Chapter of Genesis, observes that it does not
Is. 48 : 3	agree with determined scientific discovery, and
Job 34 : 4	from a natural or literal point of view, unhesi-
2 Sam.14 : 20	tatingly declares that it is not true; for he
Job 38 : 19	reads that light is created, and that the earth
Job 38 : 7	was productive of grass, herbs, and trees yield-
Ps. 104 : 14	ing fruit, before the sun was created, when
Job 37 : 15	science proves that all natural life in the vege-
2 Sam. 23 : 4	table kingdom exists by means of the fructify- ing influence of the natural sun. He knows
Jer. 16 : 21	that this Literal statement cannot be reconciled
Zech. 10 : 1	with physical science, for all the truths of
Job 37 : 21	natural science and life, are the revelation of
Job 33 : 24	natural principles which exist from spiritual
Job 33 : 33	causes, but he is not yet aware that the Word
Job 38 : 36	of God reveals spiritual principles only, and
Prov. 9 : 10	that the first verse of the Word refers to the
John 8 : 25	"Beginning" of spiritual life in the man who
Ps. 17 : 2	is to be regenerated. In order to illustrate the
Ezek. 40 : 32	coherence of the Internal Sense of the Word
Ps. 19 : 14	of God, a simple outline will be given of the
Ex. 20 : 11	meaning of the Six Days of Creation as applied

| Heaven and Earth. | Sensual perception. |

to the order of regeneration with men in general, observing the many spiritual principles which the Word will reveal.

<small>Luke 13: 14
Ezek. 40: 4
Ezek. 44: 5</small>

In the beginning God created the Heaven and the Earth.

<small>Gen. 1: 1
Ps. 135: 6</small>

226. Abstracting the mind from the physical frame when thinking of man, by "Heaven" in this verse is signified the Internal mind, and by "Earth" is meant the External mind, or the internal and external principles of the mind of the man who is in a state of reformation from evil, frequently termed repentance. Principles which are Above natural things are called Internal, while those which are natural and sensual, are Below, toward the earth. Thus, a man's head represents high, interior or celestial principles, because therein is located the brain, the organ of affection and thought; while the feet which rest upon the surface of the earth represent the Natural or Sensual principle, which is the most external of the mind, it being in the circumference of the spiritual circle of Affection and Thought. By the Sensual principle is not meant the lust of the bodily appetites, but that perception of the External mind which exists through the external senses, which is lowest in the mind. Spiritual life originates with the Lord by means

<small>Micah 7: 7
Ps. 60: 34
Jer. 23: 24
Num. 14: 21
1 Chron, 29: 11
1 Kings 8: 27
Is. 8: 22
Ex. 25: 22
Ps. 57: 5
§ :8)
Is. 51: 6
Ps. 23: 5
Ps. 3: 3
Z·ch 14: 4
Luke 1: 79
Ps. 122: 2
Ezek. 47: 2
¶ 181
John 20: 25
John 20: 27
John 6: 33</small>

Progressive qualities of mind.   Insanity of Self-intelligence.

of the Truths from Him in the Word which was in the "Beginning" with God. The word "Earth" also signifies the Literal Sense of the Word which is received by the External mind.

John 6 : 63
John 1 : 2

STATES.

Gal. 4 : 10
Ezek. 12 : 22
Ezek. 12 : 23
Ezek 39 : 8
Ps. 39 : 5
Ps. 12 : 45
2 Cor 13 : 11
John 15 : 11
2 Kings 20 : 19
Is. 40 : 8
John 2 : 18
Mark 8 : 12
John 4 : 40
John 11 : 6
Gen. 19 : 1
Gen. 19 : 6
Luke 5 : 22
Rom. 2 : 13
Rom. 2 : 19
Deut. 28 : 34
Rom. 1 : 22
Ezek. 30 : 4
Ezek. 30 : 12
Hos. 9 : 7
Jer. 50 : 38
Ps. 40 : 3
Micah 6 : 9
Ps. 101 : 2
Ps. 101 : 3

227. All hours, days, weeks, months and years, in the Word, have reference to the quality or nature of the Affections and Thoughts in their progressive or successive degrees of regeneration, and the word STATE is used in the Internal Sense to express this mental condition. State is predicated of love, of life, of wisdom, of the affections and the joys thence derived ; in general of Good and Truth. Degrees of time and distance of space are used in the Word to represent State, but the mind in perceiving the spiritual meaning must be abstracted from the Literal Sense.

228. There are Two States of a man's life, the External and the Internal. When he is in the External state, he speaks and acts rationally and wisely, like any intelligent man in the world, and he can teach others many things concerning moral and civil life. When a man's Internal state is awakened to reflection, if he is in the Love of Self, instead of becoming Rational, he becomes Sensual, and instead of becoming wise, he becomes insane in regard to spiritual things : for he thinks then from the evil of his will and its delight, and therefore from self-derived intelligence. But with those who permit themselves to be regenerated, when they are let into an internal state from an external, they increase in the knowledge of spiritual principles and love them.

THE NATURE OF THE WORD OF GOD. 119

The First State.   Reformation.

229. No man can enter the kingdom of God except he is "born again," for unless he is made a spiritual man in opposition to the natural evils into which he was born, and becomes filled with holy principles, the Kingdom of Heaven cannot reign within him, for to be "born again" is to be regenerated, or made spiritual.

230. There are Three States pertaining to regeneration. The FIRST STATE is the absence of spiritual life,—the Natural state,—which is the Death from which Resurrection is to take place. In this state he is born with the Love of Self and the World predominant. The delights of these loves lead him and prevent him from knowing that he is in evils and falses, because every man is delighted with whatever he loves, whether it is good or evil.

231. The SECOND STATE of the man is that of Reformation, and begins to exist when he thinks of Immortal life and Heaven, from the joy which he hopes to experience, and thus he is led to think of God, from whom the joy of Heaven is derived. At first he thinks of the delight of the Love of Self which is commingled with his thoughts of Heaven, and while the delight of this love reigns, together with the evils flowing from it, he cannot understand otherwise but that the Way to Heaven is to make many prayers, listen to sermons, partake of the Holy Supper, giving money to the poor, helping the needy, and giving of his possessions for the building of religious or charitable edifices, all of which acts, although highly commendable, are in themselves external, and may be prompted by no inward spiritual motive.

232. In this State of Reformation, which is generally called Repentance, it is permitted that a man shall

1 Cor. 6 : 9
John 3 : 4
John 3 : 8
Is. 43 : 19
Ezek. 18 : 30
John 3 : 18
Matt. 18 : 3
Matt. 13 : 11
Eph. 2 : 2
Eph. 2 : 3
Eph. 2 : 4-6
Eph. 2 : 12
Rom. 3 : 12
Eph. 4 : 18
Rom. 12 : 2
Rom. 1 : 32
Rom. 6 : 12
Matt. 19 : 16
Rom. 2 : 6
Rom. 2 : 7
Mark 10 : 30
Rom. 14 : 17
Mark 10 : 37
Matt. 19 : 27
1 Thess. 5 : 17
Acts. 2 : 42
Acts 10 : 4
Matt. 19 : 21
Matt. 19 : 28
Matt. 19 : 20
John 4 : 7
Matt. 3 : 8
Jer. 11 : 23

The "schoolmaster."   Deeds of the Law.

<small>
Je.. 11:3
Jer. 11;4
Jer. 11:5
Is. 40:11
Is. 40:27
Is. 41:10
Is. 41:13
Is. 43:1
Is. 43:2
Is. 43:3
Is. 43:4
Is. 43:5
Is. 43:26
Is. 43:25
Is. 41:20
Ps. 60:11
Ps. 6:2
Gal. 4:23
Gal. 4:24
</small>

think that he is able to resist evil in his own strength, so that he will not be forced into a religious life against his own will, although the Lord is gently moving upon his internal nature. At first he does not inwardly believe that the Lord is reforming him, neither does he believe that every Good and True thought is infused into his mind, and the Lord permits this Appearance of Truth to exist in his mind so that he will use effort with the strength given him, to overcome evil, and not passively await some special outpouring of Divine Power. By exerting what seems to be his own strength, he will in due season be led to recognize his utter helplessness, and call upon the Lord for aid, and the law which he is endeavouring to fulfil in his own strength is the "schoolmaster" which will lead him to the Word.

<small>
Gal. 2:16
Phil. 3:9
Rom. 3:28
Rom. 7:18
Rom. 7:23
Rom. 7:24
Jas. 4:10
Rom. 7:7
Rom. 7:8
Rom. 7:10
Rom. 7:11
Rom. 7:12
Rom. 7:13
James 4:7
Luke 13:24
</small>

233. In the Epistles, this state of self-righteousness is indicated by the " works " or " deeds of the law by which no flesh shall be justified." The seventh chapter of Romans treats of this state of reformation, ar d illustrates the mental conflict and despair which results in the exclamation, " *O wretched man that I am! who shall deliver me from the body of this death?*" In due time he is led to think and perceive that there is such a thing as sin, which has its origin in his own nature, and this state becomes progressive when he examines his motives to see if their tendency in all his acts is toward evil, and when he recognizes this inclination, exerts his WILL against the evil so that it shall not be carried into act.

<small>Rev. 3:14</small>

234. The THIRD STATE which is the Beginning of Regeneration, progresses from the previous state, and

| Redemption. | The spiritual marriage. |

begins when, with the acknowledgement of the need of Divine help, a man desists from and strives against the evils which he sees within himself, and which will be overcome if he persists in the combat. In this order, regeneration proceeds until from a Natural state of mind he is made a Spiritual man by means of the Word, and thus he is redeemed from sin. By continually struggling against the evil he naturally loves, it becomes repulsive to him, and when he hates it, it will be overcome, and this will be a continual work during his earthly life, if he attains the limit of the years of mankind. This work must be consummated on the earth, before he can enter the abode, or state of Heaven.

Is. 33 : 13
Is. 1 : 16
Jer. 3 : 13
Rom. 12 : 21
Rom. 6 : 13
Eph. 5 : 19
Eph. 5 : 20
Gal. 6 : 4
Gal. 3 : 13
Gal. 5 : 24
Gal. 6 : 9
Prov. 8 : 13
Luke 1 : 71
Eph. 6 : 13
Eph. 6 : 14
Eph. 6 : 15
Ps. 91 : 14
Luke 23 : 42
Ps. 102 : 24

235. With the consciousness that all the power is derived from the Lord, he grows less self-righteous in his progression as he perceives that he has no inherent good principle within himself. A man is made spiritual only in proportion as he knows Truths from the Word and obeys them in his Will, because every man who attains spiritual life is thus regenerated. By means of the Truths from the Word, he knows the life he ought to lead, and by living according to them, he performs them, or causes them to govern his external life by internally determining to do them. He thus conjoins Goodness in the will, to Truth in the understanding, and this is the Spiritual Marriage which constitutes the Kingdom of Heaven within the regenerating man. Thus, to Know and Will the Truths of the Word, is LOVING THE LORD, and making them manifest in the external life, is LOVING THE NEIGHBOR.

1 Tim 1 : 17
Deut. 8 : 18
Ps. 66 : 7
Ps. 53 : 1
Ps. 59 : 16
Deut. 4 : 40
Ps. 59 : 26.
Ps. 89 : 28
John 13 : 17
Ps. 62 : 12
John 13 : 15
Ps. 34 : 14
Gen. 17 : 2
Gen. 17 : 7
Matt. 25 : 10
Jer. 3 : 14
1 John 5 : 3
John 13 : 34
John 13 : 35

THE FIRST DAY OF CREATION;

OR,

THE FIRST STATE OF REGENERATION.

Zech. 14 : 0 — "*And the LORD shall be King over all the earth; in that day shall there be one Lord, and His Name shall be One.*"

Luke 1 : 33 — "*And He shall reign over the house of Jacob for ever; and of His Kingdom there shall be no end.*"

Gen. 1 : 2 — And the earth was without form, and void; and darkness was upon the face of the deep. And the Spirit of God moved upon the face of the waters.

Dan. 10 : 12
Dan. 10 : 14
Ps. 102 : 25
Prov 8 : 23
1 Kings 3 : 7
Dan. 10 : 18
1 Kings 3 : 9, 11, 12, 13, 14
Gen. 47 : 23
Prov. 1 : 8
Prov. 4 : 1
Prov. 4 : 4
Jer. 4 : 23

236. The First State of regeneration includes the state which has just been described and which is included in the "Beginning" when "God created the heaven and the earth." It includes the state of infancy in spiritual things, during which the mind is instructed in the simple Truths of the Word, and the duties which must be performed in obeying these Truths. Before these seeds of Truth from the Word are sown or implanted in the "earth," or the External mind, by means of instruction from parents or teachers, or from personal reading,—or before a man makes these Truths the rule of his life,—his conception of spiritual principles are "without form," for it has been

No spiritual ground.	Emptiness and darkness.

illustrated that the form of the Human Principle in man is the conjunction of Good and Truth in the will and understanding and thence in the life.

§ 154
Jer. 32 : 39
Jer. 32 : 40
Jer. 32 : 41

237. As there is no conjunction of these two Living Principles in the "earth" of the unregenerated man, no spiritual seed has found root, and consequently this "earth" is "void." This State is meant by the words "*The Son of Man hath not where to lay his head*," by which is signified that the Divine Truth of the Literal Sense is not implanted in the External mind. The "head" signifying what is superior or interior, by which inferior things are governed, as the whole body is ruled by the head, inferior things being external, and thus the "earth" or External mind when "void" has no resting place for the Internal Principles of Heavenly Life.

Is. 24 : 4
Is. 24 : 3
Is. 24 : 5
Matt. 8 : 20
Is. 66 : 1
Jer. 6 : 16
§ 150
Col. 2 : 19
Micah 7 : 13
Ps. 22 : 6
Gen. 47 : 19

238. From this state of emptiness there exists "darkness," or a dulness of perception and ignorance concerning all things which have relation to faith in the Lord, such as the Doctrine of Life from the Commandments, and the true spiritual nature of the Word. This "darkness" is "upon the face of the deep." Throughout the Word, things which are superior or high, signify Interior principles, and things which are low and inferior, signify Exterior

Jer. 51 : 43
Gen. 15 : 12
Jer. 4 : 22
Joel 2 : 10
Joel 2 : 31
Joel 2 : 11

§ 181

principles; thus, upward or Height, and downward or Depth, signify their respective principles in relation to the mind of man.

239. Since Heaven is the antipode of Hell, and the principle of Love to the Lord is opposite to the Love of Self, so the "deep" here mentioned, refers to the evil and false principles which govern the unregenerated mind which the "darkness" covers, for there is no spiritual light or Living Truth in this "deep." The "face" denotes the state of the Affections and Thoughts, because the face of man is a representative external likeness of the qualities of the mind which animate its expression; therefore the "face of the deep" signifies the lusts or evil desires of the unregenerated man, and the false principles thence originating, in which his life and thoughts are entirely immersed, because these evils and falsities obscure all the rays of spiritual light. In many places in the Word such persons or principles are called "depths," the "great deep," or the "pit."

240. When the unregenerate man becomes conscious of his spiritual condition, and has the faintest desire to turn from evil principles, then the Spirit of God "moves upon the face of the waters." This is the Divine Mercy of the Lord which has constantly sought entrance to the mind, and as soon as man in his freedom makes

Margin references:
Ps. 69 : 14
Ps. 69 : 2
Ex. 15 : 5
Ps. 69 : 15

Ps. 6 : 5

Jer. 5 : 3
Ezek 1 : 10
Eccles. 8 : 1
Job 38 : 30
Rev. 7 : 9

Is. 24 : 17
Is. 51 : 10

Is. 42 : 3
Is. 42 : 4
Jer. 46 : 7
Is. 42 : 1
Luke 1 : 50
Ps. 23 : 6

the least effort to open the door, He "moves" or sheds His rays of warmth and light into the coldness and darkness of the natural mind to make known the Love and Wisdom which created him for Heaven. This "moving" is also compared to brooding, as a hen broods over her eggs and causes them to hatch into life.

The waters in motion.

Ps. 81 : 10
Titus 3 : 6
Matt. 24 : 12
Is. 42 : 6
Luke 13 : 34

241. WATER, throughout the Word, signifies Truth. All earthly objects which are used to signify spiritual principles, possess certain qualities which serve for spiritual illustration. Water nourishes the physical life as Truth from the Word sustains the spiritual life. Water cleanses from impurity as Truth, or a life according to the Truth, cleanses from sin. In order to cleanse, water must be put in motion, and so Truths or knowledges from the Word must be moved upon by effort on the part of man who is actuated by the Spirit of God.

Gen. 26 : 3
Num. 21 : 16
Deut. 8 : 7, 8, 9, 10
I Kings 17 : 10
Is. 44 : 3
Eph. 5 : 16
Ps. 72 : 6
Is. 1 : 16
John 9 : 7

242. The "face of the waters" signifies the quality of the Affections and Thoughts in regard to the knowledges of Good and Truth from the Word, which during the past years from childhood have been stored up in the memory by the Lord in readiness to be brought forth into the understanding and life, when the Spirit of God moves upon these Truths or knowledges signified by the "waters."

The face of the waters.

§ 19
1 Tim. 2 : 3
1 Tim. 2 : 4
Is. 1 : 9
Rom. 8 : 11
Rom. 8 : 14

Luke 1:76	243. This fact illustrates the importance of attending to the thorough study of the Literal Sense of the Word in early years, especially in the religious education of children. In teaching and learning the Word, those most general truths with which the Literal Sense abounds should first be considered. Children may be taught the stories of the Literal Sense, and told that they are representative of spiritual principles which they will understand in later years if they obey the simple commandments which are given.
Luke 1:77	
Deut. 6:5	
Deut. 6:7	
Deut. 6:6	
Deut. 6:8	
Deut. 6:9	
Deut. 6:10	
Deut. 6:17	
Deut. 6:18	
Eph. 3:3	
Eph 3:4	
	244. This simple Truth from the Literal Sense of the Word when obeyed is the "Messenger" which prepares the way for the perception of the Internal Sense, of whom it is said, *"Behold I send my messenger before thy face, which shall prepare thy way before thee. The voice of one crying in the wilderness, Prepare ye the way of the Lord, make His paths straight."* This State is also represented by the Virgin Mary to whom the angel said,
Luke 7:27	
Mark 1:2	
Mark 1:3	
Luke 1:30	*"Fear not, Mary; for thou hast found favor with God." "Behold a virgin shall conceive, and bear a son, and shall call his name Immanuel."*
Is. 7:14	
Jer. 31:4	245. In the Word, a Virgin signifies one who loves truths because they elevate the thoughts. A "Woman" also signifies the Affection for Truth, irrespective of sex. This correspondence
Luke 1:28	
Rev. 12:1	
Zech 8:4	

The nature of woman.

may be perceived from the very nature of woman, which is affection, and she is so mentally constituted that the will or affection prevails over the understanding, and in the regeneration of man, "Woman," in the Word, signifies the spiritual principle of Affection, and does not mean a person. In this First State of regeneration, when man begins to desire to know the Truths of the Word, it is said of the Virgin Mary,

"*The Holy Ghost shall come upon thee, and the power of the Highest shall overshadow thee; therefore also that holy thing which shall be born of thee shall be called the Son of God.*"

Gal. 4 : 4
John 4 : 30
Luke 1 : 46
Jer. 44 : 24
Ps. 145 : 19
Luke 1 : 35
Prov. 4 : 7
Luke 22 : 60

And God said, Let there be Light : and there was Light.

Gen. 1 : 3

246. "And God said." Man communicates thought to another person by means of speech, writing, or signs. "Saying," or speech, implies hearing, and hearing implies perception of the thoughts contained within the speech. The communication of Divine Truth to the mind throughout the Word is represented by the Lord "speaking," or by the "Voice of the Lord." The spiritual inflowing of Divine Truth into the mind of man is not perceived by any of the organs of the physical frame, such as the ear, which hears sounds only which emanate

Hab. 3 : 2
Jer. 1 : 17
Ex. 4 : 12
Deut. 5 : 27
Prov. 20 : 12
Deut. 1 : 14
John 7 : 46
Josh. 23 : 14
Deut. 5 : 24
Deut. 5 : 29
2 Sam. 7 : 28
Mark 8 : 17
Mark. 8 : 18

Mark 11:15	from earthly objects, or the eye which sees
2 Kings 6:20	only the forms of physical material things, and
Matt. 20:33 Matt. 20:34	there has not been heard by any earthly ear an
Is. 30:30	audible, physical Voice of God, for the Lord,
Dan. 10:9	in all past history, has only spoken with man
Ps 103:20	by means of the Word in some tangible form,
Is. 66:5	
Luke 22:71	by which Divine Truth has been communicated
John 18:37	to the natural mind.
Acts 11:1	247. By the Word of God is not only meant
Is. 37:26	the Sacred Scriptures in their present form,
Ps. 102:25	but also all Divine Revelation which is derived
Ps. 44:1	from the Interior principles of the Word, and
Is. 25:6	written by the Science of Correspondences.
1 Pet. 1:21	All practical truths of life found in other books
Prov 2:6	are derived from that Word which exists from
Acts 17:25	the Internal Sense in its spiritual meaning.
Luke 8:10	By the Truths of the Word are not meant the
	natural laws of God as they are found revealed
Jer. 14:22	in the objects of the earthly universe, although
	what are termed the Laws of Nature exist from
	a spiritual origin.
Is. 55:10	248. The Word of God is the Mouth by which
Is. 55:11	the Lord Jesus Christ speaks with man. "*And*
Matt. 5:2	*he opened his mouth and taught them.*" He
Is. 45:23	thus speaks with those who are in a state of
Matt. 11:27	life to perceive that He is the Life of the Word;
Deut. 30:11	that the Word is from Him, and is the Body in
Deut. 30:12	which He manifests Himself and dwells among
Deut. 30:13	us; not as a dead material book of paper and

THE NATURE OF THE WORD OF GOD.

Light from the Word.	The entrance of light.

ink containing words which in themselves are dead, but in the Life within us from the Living Truths contained within those dead words. Thus "GOD SAID, "*Let there be light.*"   Deut. 30:14   1 Kings 8:53   Jer. 9:4

249. When a man has entered this First State of Regeneration, he begins to recognize that the principles of Goodness and Truth from the Word are of a superior nature. Men who are immersed in external natural thought, do not know what is meant by Goodness and Truth, for they imagine all things to be Good which relate to the Love of Self, without being aware that what they call Good, is evil, and that what they call Truth is falsity. But when the spiritual life of the regenerating man begins, he then first perceives that what he felt to be his own good, is evil, especially when he becomes enlightened to see that all Life and Light, or Good and Truth, is from the Word, or the Lord alone.   Micah 2:7   Ps. 71:10   Mark 12:24   Prov. 21:2   Mal. 2:17   Is. 5:20   Heb. 5:13   Heb. 5:14   Ps. 19:28   Eph. 1:19   Ps. 86:10

250. Until a man recognizes this Truth, no Light can enter from above, or from the Internal into the External mind. This Light is the perception and acknowledgement that the Lord Jesus Christ is the Lord Jehovah, who "*In the beginning was the Word, and the Word was with God, and the Word was God. All things were made by Him; and without Him was not anything made that was made. In Him*   John 8:24   Is. 13:10   1 Kings 22:25   2 Kings 6:17   Ps. 14:2   Is. 33:17   John 1:1   John 1:3

| The source of Light. | The Light glorified. |

<table>
<tr><td>John 1:5
John 1:9</td><td>was Life, and the Life was the Light of men. And the Light shineth in darkness; and the darkness comprehended it not. That was the true Light which lighteth every man that cometh into the world."</td></tr>
<tr><td>John 3:13
Jer. 4:25
Heb. 7:3
Matt. 1:20
Luke 1:42
1 John 4:15
1 Cor. 12:3
Luke 8:11
Mark 4:14
John 3:35
Gal. 4:23</td><td>251. This Light does not shine from the physical frame of any man who was born in time and space, but from the Seed which is conceived in the womb of the true Virgin Mary, the Interior Affection of the man who now first receives and acknowledges the Lord Jesus as the Word. "*The seed is the Word.*" All conception of true doctrine from the Word is from the Father, or the Divine Love; and all birth or re-generation is from the Divine Wisdom as a Mother.</td></tr>
<tr><td>Jude 21
1 Pet. 1:9
Luke 8:15
Luke 8:8
Ps. 107:35
Rom. 5:21
Rom. 6:22</td><td>252. Only the man who is in the Affection for Truth, or in the desire to know and obey the Truth, can receive this Seed, which must be sown in good "earth" in order to spring up and become fruitful. This good "earth" is the will and understanding of the External mind which desires to be filled with Love and Wisdom, the Seed of the Word from which Eternal Life is born.</td></tr>
<tr><td>John 3:17
Matt. 5:14
Hag. 1:8
John 13:32</td><td>253. This is the "earth" or world into which the "true Light" is to be born and glorified, and in the order of regeneration it becomes a fact of true spiritual history that the Son of</td></tr>
</table>

THE NATURE OF THE WORD OF GOD. 131

True spiritual façts.

God is born of the Virgin Mary, and that He has no earthly father, but in the regeneration of men He is conceived and born from the Lord Jehovah according to the laws of Divine Order.

Gal. 4 : 4
Luke 3: 23
John 5 : 26

254. The will and understanding of man are the voluntary and intellectual principles of his life; the will, or volition, acting through the cerebellum of the physical brain, and the understanding, or intellect, acting through the cerebrum, both principles acting as ONE in the nerves which proceed and radiate from the brain. This Voluntary and Intellectual principle constitutes the Individuality or Self-hood of man. In the following pages, the Latin word Proprium, by which is meant those principles which are proper to a man's individuality, will be used to indicate this characteristic.

Matt. 12: 35
Lev. 19 : 5
Prov. 2: 1
Prov. 2: 2
1 Cor.14 : 20
Prov. 15: 21
§ 155
§ 143
Dan. 11: 16
Prov. 2: 10
Prov. 2 : 11
Prov. 2 : 12

THE PROPRIUM OF MAN.

255. The Proprium of man is his hereditary nature residing in the External mind, which in itself consists only of evil and false principles successively accruing through past generations and condensed in each individual. Evil is the tendency to actual sin. Man is not responsible for his hereditary evil nature, for he was born into this physical world without his own volition, and the evils derived from his ancestors are accumulated in his Proprium. The Lord ever pities this poor, weak, erring nature, and surrounds all men

Eccles. 1 : 4
Ezek. 22 : 30
§ 35
Ex. 20 : 5
Ex. 34 : 7
Prov. 4 : 23
Deut. 4 : 23
Num. 14 : 18
Jer. 3 : 25
Ps. 103 : 13

| Human responsibility. | The evil Proprium. |

Ps. 91: 11 Ps. 91: 15 Ez k. 18 : 20 Deut. 24 : 16 Prov. 4: 2 Rev. 21 : 23 Rev. 21 : 25 Rev. 21 : 27 Rom. 8: 7 Rom. 8: 8 Eph. 4 : 24 Prov. 15 : 24 Gal. 4 : 3 Ps. 52 : 3 Ps. 52: 4 Ps. 50 : 16 Matt. 24 : 2 Matt. 22: 29 Jas. 2 : 26 Ps. 52: 5	with every possible protecting influence without destroying their freedom of volition. 256. A man is responsible for all the actual sin he wills and does, or even he thinks. The Light from the Sun of Heaven shines so clearly to every man who has the Word, that he sees the nature of sin before he yields to the evil which tempts. The Proprium of every person resides in the sensual or natural mind, and not in the spiritual or regenerating mind in which he is elevated above his Proprium. From the Proprium, man believes only in himself, and loves evil instead of good, and falsity and self-intelligence rather than Truth from the Word, believing that nothing is there true excepting what he perceives materially or sensually, not knowing that those things in themselves without the Spiritual Sense are as dead as his physical frame would be without the spirit which resides within it.
Deut. 8 : 3 Ezek. 34 : 15 Mark 5 : 14 Luke 8 : 29 Luke 8 : 30 Luke 8 : 31-34 Luke 8 : 35-36 Gal. 5 : 19 Gal. 5 : 20 Gal. 5 : 21 Rom. 1 : 23 Prov. 16 : 25 Prov. 16 : 2 Prov. 12 : 15	257. As the spiritual mind is nourished by the "flesh and blood" of the Word which creates Heavenly life, so the Proprium is fed with influences from hell, and all the combats between the Divine Truth and the evil and false principles of the Proprium occur in the natural or External mind; for as Heaven exists from the Lord by mutual love, so hell exists from the Proprium of man by the Love of Self and the World. Every man, as to his Proprium, is mere evil, and if left to himself would breathe nothing but hatred, revenge, cruelty and adultery. Those who are in the Love of Self cannot perceive this evil Proprium, because all things within them favor the Proprium.

THE NATURE OF THE WORD OF GOD. 133

A two-fold Proprium. The source of life.

258. But in the process of regeneration, it will be encouraging to learn that there is a two-fold Proprium, —that which belongs to man as his own, from hell, and the Celestial or regenerated Proprium which is from the Lord alone by means of the Word. The Proprium of man is natural love separated from spiritual love, and since it is of such an evil nature, the Lord in His Divine Mercy has provided means by which it may be removed. The means are furnished by the Word, and when man thinks and speaks, or wills and acts according to the precepts of this Divine Word, he is then kept by the Lord in Divine Principles, and is thus withheld from his Proprium. As he perseveres in this course of life, a new voluntary and intellectual Proprium is formed within him by the Lord, which is altogether separated from his own Proprium. Thus man is created anew, and this is what is called his reformation and regeneration by truths from the Word, and by a life according to them.

Is. 40: 31
2 Cor. 4:16
2 Cor. 4:15
2 Cor. 6:17
2 Cor. 6:18
Rom. 13:1
Ps. 17:4
Ps. 25:4
Ps. 25:21
Ezek. 34:11
Ezek. 34:12
Ezek. 34:13
Ezek. 34:16
Ezek. 34:21-24
Ezek. 34:25
Ezek. 34:26
Ezek. 34:27-28
Ezek. 34:30

259. Nothing evil and false can possibly exist which is not from the Proprium of man; so true is this, that if a man should be permitted to see his own Proprium, he would be struck with horror, and desire to flee from himself as though he were a devil.

Ps. 55:11
Jer. 2:19
Lam. 5:10
Ps. 40:2
Ezek. 26:21
Ps. 38:7

260. The Proprium of man in itself is dead, or destitute of spiritual life, for no person has any life from himself, and he does not even think from himself, for all ideas of thought flow into his mind, and he uses these ideas according to the nature of his Proprium as though they were his own. Whoever therefore supposes that he lives and thinks from himself, is in error, for he then appropriates to himself every evil and

Is. 26:14
2 Cor 13:3
2 Cor. 13:4
Ps. 10:4
Deut. 32:5

| Preservation of individuality. | Seeing the light. |

Ps. 17 : 9
Ps. 40 : 12
Ps. 35 : 7

false idea which flows into his mind from such evil spirits who are of a like nature with himself, because they are his own evils and falses which are personified as enemies and evil spirits in the Word.

Is. 13 : 13

261. In the gradual removal of the Proprium, the individuality of the regenerating man is not taken away, but his talents and faculties will be developed and brought into higher exercise, with the motive of being useful to others, rather than seeking the gratification of the Love of Self, and he is thus led by the Word from darkness toward that Light which ever after will brighten his whole existence.

Ps. 87 : 7
Rom. 14 : 7
Rom. 15 : 1
Rom. 7 : 17
Is. 9 : 2

Gen. 1 : 4

And God saw the light, that it was good ; and God divided the light from the darkness.

Ps. 53 : 2
Prov. 1 : 2
Prov. 1 : 3
Prov. 1 : 5
Prov 1 : 6
Ps. 8 : 3
Ps. 8 : 1
Ps. 18 : 22
Ps. 9 : 1
Ezek. 10 : 4
Luke 11 : 36

262. When "seeing" in the Word is spoken of man, it signifies to perceive, or to understand, according to what is said, and that the External mind is illuminated by a more interior perception of the Truth enclosed within the Literal Sense. When a man surveys the starry heavens with his physical eyes, and thinks of the Lord who made them ; or when he reads the apparent truths of the Word, and is thereby led to see and obey the spiritual principles which are thus conveyed, his mind is illuminated so that he has clearer perception.

Matt. 6 : 22

263. The physical eye sees from the sight of the spirit which is within, and external sight

THE NATURE OF THE WORD OF GOD.

The gift of sight.   *Lovely and agreeable objects.*

was given man in order that from beholding objects in the physical world, he might be led continually to reflect on the true principles which govern the "other life," because he is created for that life, or degree of spiritual attainment in which the mind is elevated above earthly thought, and in which all natural objects become means of heavenly instruction.   Ps. 25: 15 / Zech. 9: 1 / Ps. 73: 24 / Is. 43: 7 / Job 14: 1 / Is. 44: 7

264. A man to whom the Spiritual Sense of the Word has been revealed, is so imbued with the reality of the spiritual world which is opened to him by means of the Word, that when he sees the sun, his mind instantly reverts to the Lord as the Sun of Heaven. When he beholds the first dawn of the morning light, he meditates on the rise of all true principles from the Word and their progress in the order of regeneration to the full day of wisdom. Also, when he looks on gardens, orchards, and beds of flowers, his eye is not confined to any particular tree, plant, or blossom and fruit, but he is led to a contemplation of the heavenly things represented by them.   Zech. 13: 1 / Rev. 19: 11 / Is. 30: 26 / Mal. 4: 2 / 2 Pet. 1: 19 / Matt. 28: 1 / Matt. 28: 2 / Matt. 28: 3 / Jer. 20: 5 / Eccles. 2: 5 / Cant. 2: 12 / Hos. 14: 5 / Ps. 143: 5 / Ps. 143: 6

265. When he sees the beautiful color and formation of the flowers, he is led to regard the spiritual principles which they represent in the other life, for there is not a single object existing in the sky or earth which is lovely and agreeable, but which is in some way represen-   Eccles. 3: 11 / Is. 52: 1 / Col. 1: 16 / Ps. 135: 6 / Ps. 36: 5

tative of the Lord's Kingdom. Those persons who perceive the Spiritual Sense of the Word, do not confine their sight to mere external objects, but continually from them behold Interior Principles which are essentially things relating to spiritual life, which is the life of regeneration. They do not regard the Word of God from the Literal Sense alone, but consider those things described in the Letter of the Word as representative and significative of heavenly principles, and thus the Literal Sense is only an instrumental means of leading the thoughts upward or to more Interior Truths.

266. In the verse under consideration it is said that "God saw the light." When "seeing" is predicated of God, in the Internal Sense it denotes faith in the regenerating man which is received from Him by the Truths of the Word. As the Word is God, all its Truths which are implanted in the mind of man are from Him, and enable man to see spiritual principles. To have faith in God is to see Him in the Word and obey its precepts from Affection for these Truths. Since the Lord is Infinite Omniscience in Himself, this expression has relation to the Light in the regenerating man which he perceives is from God; therefore this Light is "good."

THE NATURE OF THE WORD OF GOD.

Intellectual Sight.   **Separation between light and darkness.**

267. As the sight of the physical eye corresponds to the Understanding, therefore "seeing" is attributed to this faculty, and in the Word signifies Intellectual Sight. It is quite common to say that ideas or thoughts are "seen" when they are understood. Light is also predicated of the Understanding as well as darkness and obscurity, and these analogies are of ordinary occurrence in speech or illustration, because they correspond to each other.

Is. 11 : 3
Matt. 11 : 5
Ex. 24 : 17
John 3 : 11
Ps. 98 : 3
Ps. 97 : 11
Ps. 107 : 10
Job 15 : 17
Job 15 : 18

And God divided the light from the darkness.   Gen. 1 : 4

268. "Darkness" signifies all those evil and false principles which before the beginning of regeneration appear like light, because in that state evil seemed like good, and falsity had the appearance of truth, when in reality all was darkness resulting from the Proprium which is to be removed through the progressive states of regeneration.

Ps. 107 : 14
Eph. 5 : 11
Matt. 6 : 23
Is. 5 : 20
1 Kings 18 : 18
Prov. 28 : 5
Job 10 : 22

269. The Divine Truth of the Word now enlightens the regenerating man in regard to the nature of his Proprium, and shows him the separation there is between the True Light which shines from obedience to the Word and the Appearance of Light which has hitherto illuminated his mind, but which, emanating from his own false principles, was "darkness rather than light."

Jer. 10 : 10
Ps. 97 : 4
Phil. 3 : 8
Rom. 8 : 5
John 3 : 21
Ezek. 32 : 6
Ezek. 32 : 7
Ezek. 32 : 8

| The assertion of Divine Truth. | Night. |

Gen. 1:5 — And God called the light Day, and the darkness he called Night.

Ps. 147:4
John 10:3
Is. 45:4

Heb. 4:12

Ps. 33:9

2 Sam. 23:3

270. "Calling," or giving a name to any principle in man, signifies a perception of its quality, whether it is good or evil, or true or false. As God is Omniscient, He knows all the qualities in the nature of man, and this form of expression is used in the Literal Sense to indicate that it is Divine Truth, therefore in this form of words it is stated that "God said," or "God spoke all these words," or "God called."

Prov. 22:1

Zech. 10:12
Eccles. 7:1
Micah 4:5
Ezek. 43:35
Ezek. 24:2
Deut. 33:25

John 11:10
John 13:30
Josh. 1:8
Zech 2:11
Is. 60:11

271. When we speak the name of a person, not only do his features and bodily form present themselves before our minds, but the qualities of his life as we have known him also appear before us. Thus the quality of the true Light which now illumines the regenerating man is recognized and called "Day," because it is from the Lord, and is compared to the light of day; but whatever belongs to man's unregenerated Proprium is in darkness, and is called "Night." The comparisons of "day" and "night" are frequently used in the Word to illustrate these principles, and represent the States of man in his entrance to regenerate life.

| Evening | | Morning. |

And the evening and the morning were the first day.	Gen. 1:5
272. The "Evening" denotes all the preceding states which were preparatory to the "Beginning" of spiritual life, which were in obscurity and falsity and therefore were in the shade signified by the word "evening," when man exists in the life of his Proprium, which is "darkness." In the order of regeneration, "Evening" must always precede the "Morning," because before the light dawns there is always darkness, and in the subsequent states of regeneration, each preceding state is compared to evening in relation to the one which follows, just in the same manner as in the natural world of thought, what is light to us to-day will be as evening compared with our attainments in spiritual knowledge in the future, which will then be Morning, or the dawn of superior intelligence.	John 6:16 Ezek. 33:22 Job 10:22 Is. 17:14 Jer. 5:6 Dan. 8:26 Ps. 55:17 Jer. 6;4 Ps. 112:4 Is. 21:12 Is. 9:2 Zech. 14:7 Is. 50:4 Luke 21:38
273. "Morning" signifies clearer revelation from the Lord by means of the Word, and the consequent increase of spiritual perception as the Proprium is vivified by its Living Truths. Each Advent of the Lord into the world of the mind of the regenerating man by means of clearer perception of the Living Principles of the Word is "Morning." This state is not	Ps. 59:16 Ex. 16:7 Ex. 16:12 Ex. 16:13 Is. 58:8 Hos. 6:3 2 Sam. 23:4 Ps. 5:3

Spiritual glory. Entering the First Day.

<small>2 Pet. 1 : 19
Job 7 : 4

Dan. 7 : 27
2 Sam. 22 : 29
Zech. 2 : 5

Phil. 3 : 10
Phil. 3 : 11
Matt. 28 : 1
Is. 22 : 16
Matt. 28 : 2
Mark 15 : 46
Luke 24 : 1
Mark 16 : 2
Lev. 8 : 33
Ezek. 43 : 26
2 Chron. 29 : 31
Micah 4 : 13
Eph. 3 : 11
Mal. 4 : 2
Eph. 5 : 14
Lam. 3 : 23

Phil. 1 : 6
2 Cor. 3 : 7
Is. 43 : 11
Is. 55 : 11
Ps. 18 : 7
Ezek. 37 : 12</small>

simply compared to the morning, but is called the "Day-dawn" or the dawning of the Day," because when the Lord appears, and His Kingdom in the Word begins to rule over the Proprium of man, there shines an effulgence of spiritual glory resembling the morning twilight or dawn of day.

274. The Resurrection of the Lord from the grave of man's natural thought, by the opening of the sepulchre of the earth of the Literal Sense of the Word,—the Divine Truth descending from Heaven and rolling back the stone of Sensual or Material truth,—takes place in the "early morning," and upon the "First Day of the week." A "Week," or Seven Days, signifies the whole period of a man's life, not the life of the physical frame in this world, but the whole regenerate life through all its states to eternity, and in the minds of all who are being regenerated He not only arises daily at the dawn of the morning, but through every moment of life.

275. Thus the regenerating man has entered upon the First Day of Creation, and the Lord, by means of the Literal Truths from the Word, has given "form" to them in his External mind, so that where they were "void," "empty," and "darkness," they are now "moved upon" by the Giver of Life, so that he freely opens

THE NATURE OF THE WORD OF GOD. 141

The Conception. | The espousal.

the thick shutters of his Proprium to admit the warmth and light of the morning sun to purify the vitiated air which he has been breathing to his own destruction, and the Resurrection Morn is coming to him whose death is taking place.

| Mark 16 : 3
| Ezek. 8: 16
| Prov. 16: 6
| Ezek. 37 : 8
| Bz k. 37 : 9
| Ezek. 37 : 1(

276. It is during this First day of Regeneration that the Conception of the Son of God takes place within the mind of the regenerating man whose Will is warmed with affection for the Literal Truths of the Word, when the Virgin Mary conceives by the Power of the Holy Ghost.

| Num. 28: 8
| Is. 43 : 10
| Col. 1 : 23
| Col. 1 : 27
| Col, 1 : 28
| Luke 1 : 3*
| Luke 1 : 35

277. The espousal of Joseph and Mary signifies the State of Reformation which precedes the "Beginning" of regenerate life, before the Rational Faculty is enlightened to clearly perceive the Internal Sense of the Word, excepting by the obscure perceptions which are indicated by the Angel appearing unto Joseph in a dream, in which a premonition is communicated that the Internal Sense of the Word will appear in coherent order in succeeding states. The formation and birth of the Holy Child will be more fully illustrated under the subjects of the Second and Third Days of Creation.

| Matt. 1: 13
| Matt. 3: 8
| Rom. 2: 4
| Matt. 1: 19
| Zech. 14: 8
| Matt. 1 : 20
| Mark 1: 21
| Acts 4 : 30

THE SECOND DAY OF CREATION;

OR,

THE SECOND STATE OF REGENERATION.

Gen. 1 : 6

And God said, Let there be a Firmament in the midst of the waters, and let it divide the waters from the waters.

Ps. 19 : 1
Ps. 150 : 1

§ 180
Ezek. 34 : 14
Ps. 136 : 23
Is. 12 : 6
Is. 8 : 7

Is. 8 : 8

278. The natural idea of the "Firmament" is of the space or expanse which is above or encircling the earth, and it has been illustrated that things which are above are representative of Interior principles, and things which are below denote Exterior principles. "In the midst" denotes Within, and "waters" signify Knowledges of Truths from the Literal Sense of the Word upon which the Spirit of God has been moving and warming into life.

Ezek. 1 : 22
Ezek. 1 : 25
Ps. 87 : 5
Ps. 84 : 10
Dan. 12 : 3
Ps. 119 : 152
Ps. 25 : 10
Prov. 2 : 15

279. The "Firmament" signifies an Interior Principle which is created in the midst of these knowledges, which the Mercy of the Lord, or Power of the Highest has brought forth into "Day," in which a perception is communicated to the regenerating man that the Word is the only True Spiritual Light, and that the Lord within its expressions is Goodness and Truth alone, while the Proprium of man is evil and false.

THE RATIONAL FACULTY.

280. This "Firmament" or Interior Principle, is the Rational Faculty, which now begins to discern and separate Actual Truths from the Appearances of Truth as they exist in the Literal Sense of the Word, and discriminates between True Doctrines derived therefrom, and those which favor the Love of Self, for any false doctrine may be confirmed from the letter of the Word when the mind does not recognize that the expressions contain an Internal Sense.

281. The Rational Faculty is taught to distinguish or "divide" the Internal mind, or "heaven" from the External mind, or "earth." Before regeneration begins, a man is not aware that an Internal mind exists, and therefore he has no knowledge of its nature and quality, because he is so occupied with corporeal and worldly things that he cannot conceive that there is any difference between the Internal and External nature of his mind, and thus he forms confused and indistinct ideas which emanate from two perfectly distinct principles.

282. All the Wisdom, Intelligence, Reason, and Science which fill the understanding, are from the Lord alone, although these principles appear to emanate from man. The true order of Life flowing into the understanding, is, first, Wisdom from the Lord, from wisdom, Intelligence, from intelligence, Reason, and by reason, the Scientifics of the memory are vivified.

283. When the regenerating man enters the Second State of Regeneration, a division takes place by means of the Rational Faculty perceiving such principles which flow in from the Lord, and those which arise from the Proprium. Those principles which are from the Lord, are all the knowledges and Truths of the Word

The Remnant, or External memory.   *Scientific principles.*

which have hitherto been stored up in the External memory, which are spoken of in the Word as a "Remnant," and they are not made manifest until this Second State is entered upon.

284. The Internal mind forms the Inmost Principle of man, which distinguishes him from animals which do not possess such a principle, and this is the entrance to man for the Lord by the Truths of the Word. Beneath this Inmost Principle of the mind, the Rational Faculty exists, and it appears to a man as though it were derived from himself, because he thinks from this faculty, and before regeneration begins, it belongs to his Proprium; but afterwards, when he is led to believe in the Word as the Lord, it becomes "good ground" into which the Seed of the Word as it falls, "springs up and bears much fruit."

285. The Rational Faculty, or "Firmament," pertains to the External mind, and it acts as a Medium or Intermediate Principle between the Internal and External mind. The External mind consists of Three Principles, the Rational, or inmost principle, the Scientific, or intermediate principle, and the Sensual, or exterior principle. The Rational Principle conjoins the Internal mind with the External, and this conjunction is according to the nature and quality of the Rational Principle. If Divine Love flows into the Rational Faculty by obedience to the Truths of the Word, from Affection for every good principle which constitutes Love to the Lord, it then becomes of a spiritual nature, which is perverted to the opposite quality when the Love of Self flows into it.

286. By Scientific principles are meant all the means employed by external aids to increase in knowledge, which is stored up in the External memory. In a general sense all earthly education is meant by the word Scientific, and in a specific sense when applied to the regenerating man, is meant all knowledges and doctrines pertaining to the Literal Sense of the Word, which are the means by which a person may become wise in spiritual things.

THE NATURE OF THE WORD OF GOD. 145

The Sensual principle.	Appearances.

The Rational Faculty examines all scientifics and doctrines to observe if they are according to the laws of Divine Order before they are believed and confirmed in the life.

287. By the Sensual, or Corporeal principle, is meant the senses of sight, hearing, touch, smelling and taste, which act from the External mind through the organs of the physical frame, and it must be constantly kept in view that these principles are being considered without any reference to the physical frame, which in itself is simply an instrument or machine which is operated by the mind which fills its form.

THE OPENING OF THE RATIONAL FACULTY.

288. Every regenerating man has a natural and a spiritual mind, or a natural and a spiritual will and understanding. The natural mind wills and thinks concerning the things of the physical world and concerning things of natural thought, and the things of the Literal Sense of the Word, while the spiritual mind wills and thinks according to the Interior Truths of the Word, or as an angel of Heaven. If a man acts and speaks from himself alone, and thinks from self concerning the Word, he has only natural thought, but if he acknowledges the Lord within the Word, and perceives that it treats of Internal principles concerning heavenly life, he will be led from natural to spiritual thought if he obeys its precepts. When a man has been led to spiritual thought, it appears as if he had attained this degree of elevated thought by himself alone, yet this is only an Appearance, in order that he may be led in freedom, for the Lord is leading him by the Word.

289. As the natural mind is opened and formed by the things of this world, and by the Appearances which exist in the Literal Sense of the Word, and the spiritual mind is opened and formed by heavenly principles, it is essential that the Rational Faculty

J

Obedience to the Word.	Abstaining from evil.

should be opened and formed by the Internal principles of the Word, because they are divine and constitute Heaven. The Word contains Truths which are to be known and thought, and Goods which are to be willed and performed, by both of which the Rational Faculty is to be enlightened and perfected. If the Precepts of the Word are not obeyed, but an act of mental faith alone is substituted for them, there will be no discernment of the Interior principles of the Word, and the natural mind will possess only a natural or historical faith, which is merely a scientific or natural light from which the natural mind thinks.

290. In order that the Rational Faculty may be opened and formed, it is essential that it should have a storehouse from which it may be supplied with its requisite food. This storehouse of supply consists of the natural or external memory, in which every good thing that it is possible to know shall be stored up for use, and thence called forth as occasion may require. This storehouse must be filled with Truths from the Word, which are to be believed, and Goods which are to be done, and these must be learned from the earliest dawn of religious thought. These simple Goods and Truths must be taught by parents to their children, by precept and example, so that the door of this storehouse may be readily opened to transmit these knowledges. But all these things from the Word stored in the memory, even to the greatest abundance, are only natural, or scientific, until the Rational Faculty is opened to perceive a more Interior meaning.

291. The Rational Faculty has its first dawn by abstaining from doing evils, because they are contrary to the Divine Precepts of the Word. If a man abstains from evil from any other motive, for any selfish end, the Rational Faculty will not be opened. A man must first remove the evils he sees in himself, with the strength given him, acknowledging the Lord, for all evils which are in the External mind keep Heaven closed, and as

THE NATURE OF THE WORD OF GOD. 147

| The entrance of the Word. | Elevated Truths. |

the Lord is the Word, they who abstain from doing evils, because they are contrary to the Divine Precepts in the Word, abstain from them with power from the Lord. In proportion as evil is removed, in the same proportion Goodness enters from the Lord, which constitutes Heaven. If unchaste thoughts are removed, the mind becomes pure; if intemperance is removed, temperance enters; if deceitfulness is removed, sincerity enters; if hatred and revenge are removed, love and friendship enter, and thus it is with all other evils which are to be overcome in the order of regeneration.

THE FORMATION OF THE RATIONAL FACULTY.

292. The Rational Faculty is formed from those things which are stored in the memory from the Word. When a man loves to obey the Truth because he sees that it is true, and that it will elevate his being with higher principles of obedience, an affection for the Truth flows into the mind from the Lord as evils are removed. This affection is given from the Lord alone, for the Lord in Heaven is Divine Truth, and thus this affection is given by the Word. The things of the Literal Sense of the Word which are stored in the memory, are then elevated and purified by the Internal Sense being revealed by the Lord, and Genuine Truths are discriminated and separated from the Appearances of Truth, for the Rational Faculty can only be formed from Genuine Truths, as Heaven, or the Internal Sense, can exist, in no other form.

293. The Genuine Truths of the Word are elevated by the Lord, and the mind perceives them while in a higher degree of thought, which is effected by the inflowing of heavenly principles according to Divine Order. These elevated Truths are not in a natural form, but are in a spiritual form, abstracted from time, space, and objective persons. Truths in a natural form are such as those which are in the Literal Sense of the Word, and when the Rational

"After death."	Natural life.

Faculty is opened, which takes place "after death," or when natural thought has ceased to exist without being actuated by spiritual thought, the regenerating man thinks and speaks spiritually according to the Genuine Truths of the Internal Sense. While he lives in the state of natural thought alone, he is not aware that even natural thought exists from a correspondence with spiritual principles, but when the Rational Faculty is opened, this natural state of thought is changed, and he thinks according to the spiritual principles of the Word.

294. When the Rational Faculty is opened and formed, then the Lord re-forms the natural mind, because there is then an orderly inflowing of principles from the Internal mind, which is in Heaven, and the natural mind, being in the world, cannot be re-created with heavenly principles excepting by receiving the elevating principles of the Internal Sense of the Word, whereby the principles of the natural mind are brought into orderly subjection, so as to correspond with the principles of the spiritual mind, or with the principles of the Internal Sense, which fill the spiritual mind. The Truths which are in the natural mind from the spiritual, are called rational, moral, natural, and in general, Scientific Truths, and the Goods which are in the natural mind from the spiritual are called affections and desires for those Truths, and from them are derived thoughts, speech, and actions, which are called uses. All those principles which exist in the natural mind from the Spiritual Sense of the Word received into the Rational Faculty, enter the intuition and perception of the regenerating man, and thence actuate the natural principles, so that this " earth is the Lord's and the fulness thereof."

295. As the Rational Faculty is formed, the regenerating man is perfected in intelligence and wisdom, and becomes a man, for no man is a man from his natural mind, which in itself alone is simple natural animal life, but he becomes a man by principles of

intelligence and wisdom from the Lord, or the Word, and in proportion as he receives these heavenly principles he is a beautiful man, and is already an angel of Heaven; but when these Divine principles of the Word are rejected and perverted, the natural mind takes the form of a monster and not of a man, because all the principles which form a divine life are suffocated and distorted. Man is not a man from his parents by hereditary descent, but becomes a man from the Lord who creates him anew by the Word, and thus the process of regeneration forms a man. This process must take place within every man, without which there can be no spiritual life, or Heaven, and all men throughout the coming ages of time must be led from evil to good.

THE MATERIAL DEGREE OF THE MIND.

296. The Material Principle of the External mind is the first receptacle of the Literal Sense of the Word, which constitutes the Material Human Principle which the Son of Man first assumes in the order of the regeneration of man. This Material Principle does not consist of physical substances, neither does the Literal Sense of the Word culminate in fixed physical events, but it rests in the ultimate or Material Principle of the External mind, or lowest plane of Natural Thought.

297. This is an important distinction which should be clearly comprehended at this point, in order to avoid confusion of mind in following the order of thought in the succeeding pages, and especially in studying the Interior Truths concerning the assumption and glorification of the Material Human Principle in man by the Lord, or the Word.

298. The Literal Sense of the Word is adapted to the Natural Thought of the Material Principle of the External mind, and

The division.	The waters above and below.

since it originates from the Internal Sense by correspondence between natural and spiritual principles, it does not lead to physical occurrences as the mind recognizes an Internal Principle. From the degree of Natural Thought, the understanding may be elevated to perceive the Internal Sense within, but if the mind is led away from spiritual truths to ideas of earthly physical history, there will result confliction and a tendency toward material rather than spiritual thoughts concerning the Word.

Gen. 1: 7

And God made the Firmament, and divided the waters which were under the Firmament from the waters which were above the Firmament; and it was so.

299. It will be noticed that in the previous verse of the Word, the "Firmament" was first created " in the midst of the waters," but in this verse, "the waters which were under the firmament" are divided "from the waters which were above." In the progress of his regeneration, the man begins to know that there is an Internal mind within him, and that the principles which fill this Internal mind are Heavenly, and are from the Lord alone. Thus the Rational Faculty begins to be vivified with a perception that its life is from the Lord, and that He "made the Firmament," and that "the waters" below and above are divided by the Lord by means of the Rational Faculty.

Ps. 133 : 7
Ps. 77 : 10
Ex. 14 : 21
Ex. 14 : 22
Joel 2 : 27
Deut. 10: 14
Heb. 11 : 16
Heb. 12 : 22
Heb. 12: 23
Deut. 4 : 39
Ps. 33 : 11
Ps. 146: 5
Ps. 146 : 6
Is. 51 : 15

External motives.   Mental affliction.

300. At this stage of the progress of regeneration, the External mind is of such a nature that the man supposes the good which he does to emanate from his own power, and the truths which he speaks to be spoken of himself. By these Appearances he is led by the Lord, as by things of his own individuality, or Proprium, to do good and speak truth, and these external principles are "the waters which were under the firmament." | Ps. 71 : 20
Prov. 8 : 26
Ps. 46 : 10
Is. 29 : 4
Is. 48 : 17
Deut. 32 : 12
Gen. 50 : 20
Ezek. 47 : 1

301. In attaining this era in one's spiritual history, this state of regeneration is generally accompanied by suffering, temptation, loss of property, misfortune, sorrow, or mental affliction, and the combat begins between the unregenerated External mind and the Internal Internal mind, because all things which appertain to the External mind which have reference to the affairs of this world, in which the Proprium resides, are to be brought into a state of quiescence or subjection, the experience of which is akin to death, and which becomes the "valley of the shadow of death" through which the regenerating man must walk, for the things belonging to the External mind must be separated from the Internal mind by means of the vivified Rational Faculty or "Firmament" which the Lord has made. | 1 Cor 3 : 13
1 Cor. 3 : 15
1 Cor. 10 : 13
1 Pet. 4 : 12
Jonah 2 : 2
1 Pet. 4 : 17
1 Pet. 1 : 3
1 Pet. 1 : 4
1 Pet. 1 : 5
1 Pet. 1 : 6
1 Pet. 1 : 7
2 Cor. 7 : 10
Ps. 23 : 4
1 Pet. 1 13
1 Pet. 1 : 14
1 Pet. 1 : 15
1 Pet. 1 : 16
1 Pet. 1 : 23

| Trouble and anguish. | Substitution. |

Jer. 6 : 24
Micah 4 : 9
Micah 4 : 10
Jer. 30 : 6
Ps. 48 : 6
Ps. 18 : 5
Ps. 119 : 143

302. Now the pains of labor and travail begin, which attend the birth of the Lord upon the "earth," or the External mind of the regenerating man. "*Ask ye now, and see whether a man doth travail with child.*" "*Fear took hold upon them there, and pain, as of a woman in travail.*" "*Trouble and anguish have taken hold on me.*"

Eph. 6 : 12
Ps. 18 : 4
2 Pet. 2 : 18
Rom. 8 : 38
Rom. 8 : 39
Deut. 32 : 4
2 Sam. 22 : 2
2 Sam. 22 : 3
Matt. 16 : 18
Is. 48 : 21
Joel 3 : 18
Is. 51 : 8
Micah 4 : 1

303. Now the evil powers of the Proprium exert their utmost influence to obscure the Light from the Word, to destroy his spiritual life, but the Lord has "made" the Rational Faculty into which the Divine Truth is entering with power, and this Truth is a solid Rock upon which the anxious and perplexed mind can surely rest, "*and the gates of hell shall not prevail against it,*" for Heavenly Principles are flowing in from the Lord, which are filled with Life, while the "flesh and blood," or evil and falsity of the Proprium, must die in the regeneration of man, and the resurrection into Life Eternal will soon take place.

Is. 63 : 1
Is. 63 : 2
Is. 63 : 3
Is. 63 : 4
Is. 63 : 5
Is. 63 : 6
Is. 63 : 7

304. The regeneration of the External mind becomes the true Substitution of the Life of the Lord in man in place of the natural Proprium. It is the power of the Lord alone which gives strength to man in fighting against the influences of hell in the External mind, and subdues them, and this is His Merit and

Righteousness, without any self-merit on the part of man. The Lord alone regenerates man, and this regeneration cannot be accomplished without severe combats and temptations, from which comes salvation from sin.

305. The temptations arise from the evils which infest the Proprium. They are personified as evil spirits, and are like men who live in the physical frame in this world, who in freedom shut out the Light of Heaven from themselves, and whose delight is to ruin man, and these evil spirits endeavor to kill his perception of spiritual life, by filling his mind with such temptations which will be most likely to allure him toward natural or material thought, by exciting the Love of Self. Unless these evil spirits, or evil and false principles, are overcome and driven away by the aggression of the Heavenly Principles of the Word, men could not be saved from sin. By the Word alone can the Lord conquer and save, and thus the Word becomes Merit and Righteousness in the regenerating man, instead of self-righteousness.

	Is. 63 : 8
	Is. 63 : 9
	Is. 2 : 12
	Mark. 13: 7
	Mark 13: 8
	2 Thess. 2: 7
	2 Thess. 2 : 8
	Mark 3 : 11
	Ps. 5 : 9
	2 Thess. 2 : 10
	Ps. 62 : 4
	Ps. 27 : 2
	Ezek 8 : 17
	2 Cor.11 : 13
	2 Cor.11 : 14
	James 1 : 14
	1 John 2 : 13
	Ex. 6 : 1
	Ex. 6 : 2
	Acts 4 : 12
	John 4 : 42
	Ps. 48 : 10
	Is. 54 : 17

306. During this Second Day, the Rational Faculty is being formed by the Affection for the Truths of the Word. These Truths must be learned from the Literal Sense of the Word, and received into the natural or material principle of the External mind by means of the

	Ps. 71 : 6
	Is. 25 : 1
	Ps. 77 : 6
	Ex. 3 : 5

The pulpit and the press.   Water above.

Ps. 77:5
Rom. 15:4
Eccles. 12:9
Eccles. 12:10
Ex. 20:24
Eph. 3:4
Job 42:5
Neh. 8:2
Job 19:23
Deut. 17:19
John 6:56
Eccles. 7:25
Luke 24:15
1 Cor. 2:13
1 Cor. 3:15
1 Cor. 3:16
1 Cor. 3:17

sense of sight or hearing. In former centuries, when the education of mankind was in obscurity, the simple Truths of the Word were proclaimed by the mouth of religious teachers from pulpits and in places of public worship, to people who could not read and reflect, and these Truths were received by the sense of hearing; but in the present era, the Lord has provided the printing-press as a Voice or Teacher by which the acute sense of sight may absorb the Divine Truth and the Appearances of Truth in the Word, so that the Rational Faculty may be enabled to perceive, compare, and discriminate, for the Word treats both of the Lord, and the false principles of the Proprium which lead men away from the Living Principles of the Word.

Zech. 8:12
Hag. 2:19
Judges 9:12
Joel 2:22
Micah 4:4
Ps. 119:50
Ps. 119:93
Eph. 1:18
Ps. 56:13
Mark 15:39
Acts 3:26

307. The "Seed" of the Word having been sown in the External memory, the Rational Faculty perceives the Truth which is contained therein, and as the Affection for this Truth flows from the Internal mind into this Rational Faculty, it becomes quickened with life and is made Divine, and in due time there will be illumination given to perceive that this Interior Divine Truth is the Son of God, which has been conceived by the Holy Spirit, or the Divine Proceeding of the Word. These Divine Truths are the "waters which are above the firmament."

THE NATURE OF THE WORD OF GOD.

Heaven.	Combat and conjunction.

And God called the firmament Heaven. — Gen. 1:8

308. The Rational Faculty is now called "Heaven," because the regenerating man now perceives that it is vivified from Heavenly Principles, as the Proprium gradually dies and is removed, for the External mind then begins to be ruled by the Kingdom of Heaven which is within the Internal mind.

Ezek 8:3
Acts 9:3
Rom. 8:13
Ps. 47:2
Ps. 103:19
Luke 17:21

And the Evening and the Morning were the Second Day. — Gen. 1:8

309. Thus each and every moment of regeneration proceeds from the obscurity of the Truths of the Literal Sense of the Word as received by the External mind, to the clearer light of their spiritual meaning as they are perceived by the Rational Faculty which is vivified by the Living Principles from the Lord in the Internal mind.

2 Pet. 3:12
Ps. 19:2
Rom. 13:12
1 Thess. 5:5
Acts 26:13
Ezek. 33:19
Ezek. 74:9

210. The Second Day therefore is the state in which the conjunction of the External mind with the Internal begins to take place through the illumination of the Rational Faculty, and it also signifies the state of labor and combat which exists in subduing the Proprium so that this conjunction may eventually occur.

Heb. 8:13
Is. 59:20
Is. 60:20
Is. 33:2
Ps. 9:9
Ps. 9:10

PARALLEL ILLUSTRATIONS
FROM THE GOSPEL HISTORY,

OF THE PRINCIPLES OF THE SECOND DAY.

THE MATERNITY OF THE VIRGIN MARY.

Luke 2 : 4 — And Joseph also went up from Galilee, out of the city of Nazareth, into Judea, unto the city of David, which is called Bethlehem (because he was of the house and lineage of David).

§ 02

Ps. 81 : 5
Luke 1 : 27
Ps. 80 : 1
Gen. 49 : 22
Gen. 45 : 26
Gen. 39 : 2
Deut. 33 : 13
Deut. 33 : 16

311. The names of all persons, places and things in the Word are representative of Spiritual Principles. The word "Joseph," whether in the Old or New Testament, represents the Rational Faculty, and in this verse it signifies the state of this Interior Principle which has hitherto not been aware of the existence of the Internal mind, and is the same as the "Firmament" which was "in the midst of the waters,"

Is. 9 : 1
Matt. 4 : 25
Mark 3 : 7
Matt. 27 : 55
Mark 1 : 39
John 7 : 52
John 7 : 41
Luke 24 : 6

312. "Galilee" represents the External mind of the regenerating man who is in the external good or natural affection for the Truths of the Literal Sense of the Word, in the life of Love to the Neighbor, without the knowledge that there is an Internal Sense of the Word, by the revelation of which, it is made known that there is an Internal mind.

A city.   The city of David.

313. A "City" signifies Truth, or the Doctrine of Truth from the Word. "Nazareth" is a City of "Galilee," and here signifies external doctrine or the Truth of the Literal Sense of the Word, or the scientific principle of the External mind.

| Prov. 8 : 3 |
| Ps. 48 : 1 |
| Luke 1 : 26 |
| Luke 4 : 16 |
| Matt. 21 : 11 |
| John 1 : 46 |

314. In the Book of Judges it will be found that Samson was a Nazarite, and that his strength was in his hair. As the hair is the most exterior of all things belonging to the physical frame, it corresponds to the merely exterior principles of the External mind, therefore by the strength of the hair of Samson, is represented the power of external truths which must first be attended to in the order of regeneration, and thus in the personification of Samson is manifested the power which is contained in the Literal Sense of the Word when its Truths are applied to the life, for they lead the Rational Faculty to "divide the waters which are beneath," or the exterior Appearances of Truth, from the "waters which are above the firmament," or the Interior Divine Truths of the Word.

| Judges 13 : 5 |
| Judges 13 : 7 |
| Judges 16 : 17 |
| Gen. 27 : 11 |
| Num. 6 : 2 |
| Num. 6 : 5 |
| Num. 6 : 13 |
| Num. 6 : 21 |
| Is. 7 : 20 |
| Matt. 10 : 30 |
| Luke 12 : 7 |
| Judges 16 : 29 |
| Ezek. 8 : 3 |
| Ps. 74 : 12 |
| Ps. 74 : 13 |
| Ezek. 5 : 1 |
| § 321 |
| § 323 |

315. In the order of regeneration, "Joseph," or the Rational Faculty, enters from this state "into Judea, unto the City of David, which is called Bethlehem." Since the country of "Galilee" represents the External mind, the

| Acts 10 : 37 |

Amos 7 : 12	country of "Judea" denotes the Internal mind,
Ps. 105 : 17	to which "Joseph" or the Rational Faculty, is
Ps. 148 : 4	led, bearing the same relation to the Rational Faculty as the "waters which are above" do to the "Firmament."
Is. 55 : 8	316. "David" signifies the Lord as to the
Is. 9 : 7	Divine Truth of the Word, and therefore the
Matt. 22 : 42	Internal Sense of the Word, and the "City of
2 Sam. 5 : 9	David" denotes true doctrine derived from the
1 Kings 8 : 1	Internal Sense.
John 7 : 42	317. "Bethlehem" is the city or doctrine in
2 Sam. 33 : 15	which the Internal Sense of the Word is born,
1 Sam. 20 : 6	and into which the Rational Faculty rests, for
Ps. 1:6 : 7	"Joseph" now perceives that the Interior
Gen. 29 : 31	Truth of the Word originates from the Lord,
Ps. 116 : 8	and the regenerating man is now warmed with
Ps. 116 : 17	affection for the Word, from the Lord who fills
Ps. 118 : 28	the Internal mind, whereas, when he was in the
Ps. 116 : 1	state represented by "Nazareth" in "Galilee,"
Ps. 116 : 2	he thought that his good desires originated in
Is. 29 : 16	himself, and now perceives that such ascription
Job 14 : 4	was suggested by the Proprium of the External
Ps. 138 : 6	mind.
Luke 2 : 4	318. "Because he was of the house and
Gen. 13 : 15	lineage of David," signifies that he has a per-
Ps. 119 : 2	ception that all the Goods and Truths which
Ps. 119 : 27	now enter the Rational Faculty are from the
Ps. 119 : 68	Lord, or ᐯthe Word. "House" denotes the
Amos 7 : 16	origin of a family, and the family relationship

| Lineage. | Internal worship. |

represents the conjunction of Good and Truth which is from the Lord. "Lineage" denotes descent, and here signifies the descent of "David," or the Divine Truth from above into the Internal mind, and thence into the Rational Faculty.

	Jer. 31 : 1
	Eph. 3 : 15
	Heb. 7 : 3
	Ps. 133 : 3
	Rev. 21 : 10

To be taxed with Mary his espoused wife, being great with child. — Luke 2 : 5

319. By "Joseph" going to "Bethlehem" "to be taxed with Mary" is signified that worship is to be rendered from the Affection of Good and Truth which is conjoined in the Rational Faculty. To pay a "tax," signifies to render worship, and "Mary," the espoused wife, signifies the Affection of Good and Truth in the External mind, in which the state of Reformation has been fulfilled. This worship is from internal motives, and consists in profound adoration and humiliation of heart before the Lord, and True Love for the Neighbor, in the constant duties of daily life, independent of specific religious rites and ceremonies. A daily life according to true doctrine from the Word constitutes Internal worship.

	Luke 2 : 1
	Luke 2 : 3
	Ps. 29 : 1
	Ps. 20 : 2
	Ps. 76 : 11
	Jer. 2 : 2
	Hos. 2 : 19
	Hos. 2 : 20
	Is. 27 : 13
	Rev. 7 : 12
	Ps. 145 : 14
	Zech. 8 : 16
	Zech. 8 : 17
	Heb. 9 : 1
	Heb. 9 : 11
	Heb. 9 : 12

320. "Being great with child," also signifies this state of Internal worship which is formed by the Affection for Truths of the Word by obedience to them as they are given in the

	Luke 1 : 15
	Deut. 7 : 9
	Ps. 69 : 30

| Phil. 2 : 10 | Literal Sense. "Great" is predicated of Good,
| Luke 1 : 32 | and "being great with child," signifies the
| Deut. 7 : 13 | formation of principles of Good in the will, by
| Judges 5 : 31 | means of Truth in the understanding, derived
| Lev. 26 : 3,4 | from the Literal Sense of the Word.

| Luke 2 : 6 | And so it was, that, while they were there, the days were accomplished that she should be delivered.

| Is. 11 : 24 | 321. "And so it was," is equivalent to the
| § 273 | expression "And God said," with its Internal
| Jer. 18 : 2 | meaning. "That while they were there," signi-
| Acts 22 : 10 | fies that in this state of regeneration concerning
| Ezek. 12 : 23 | the Rational Faculty, "the days were accom-
| Ezek. 12 : 28 | plished that she should be delivered," in which
| Job 30 : 16 | the time of travail and labor will arrive, when
| Heb. 10 : 32 | from this state of combat between the Internal
| Heb. 10 : 35 | and External principles of the mind, the hour
| Heb. 10 : 36 | of delivery shall come, for the Rational Faculty
| Heb. 10 : 37 | is being formed within the "Mother," or the
| Eccles. 11 : 5 | Affection for the spiritual truths which have
| Ps. 40 : 8 | been received by the External mind from the
| Deut. 12 : 7 | Literal Sense of the Word.
| Joel 2 : 21 |

322. It will be observed that in this place
| Is. 11 : 1 | where the birth and development of the Rational
| Zech. 6 : 12 | Faculty are being treated of in the Internal
| Zech. 6 : 13 | Sense of the Word, that the different words have relation to this same principle. Thus "Joseph," and "Bethlehem," as well as the

Child which is being formed within the mother Mary, each have reference to spiritual principles concerning the Rational Faculty. "Joseph" is not the father of the yet unborn child, and therefore no life emanates from him, and the Rational Faculty has no life in itself, because in the order of regeneration, spiritual life descends from above, or through Inmost Principles.

Matt. 1 : 18

James 1 : 17
Rev. 3 : 12

323. During this Second Day, the Knowledges from the Literal Sense of the Word acquired in the External memory, are taking the form of man in the womb of the Virgin Mary, for the conception, gestation and birth of the Lord in the spiritual principles of the mind, by the law of spiritual correspondence, are in the order of the conception, gestation, and birth of the physical frame into this physical world.

Ps. 22 : 27
Ps. 103 : 13
Jer. 15 : 11
Jer. 1 : 5
Is. 49 : 1
Is. 44 : 2
Is. 44 : 21
Is. 44 : 23
Hos. 9 : 11
Jas. 1 : 15

324. The Rational Faculty is vivified by the Father, but the "Mother" is the Affection for the scientifics and knowledges of the Literal Sense of the Word, which have been acquired by means of the external or material senses of the spiritual body.

John 15 : 26
Ps. 139 : 13
Is. 11 : 9
Is. 7 : 16
Is. 8 : 4

325. Conception is the first life of the Rational Faculty, and it receives this first life from the Lord flowing through the Internal mind into the Affection of knowledges and sciences belonging to the External mind. The

Mark 9 : 1
Hab. 3 : 3
Rom. 1 : 4
Dan. 1 : 4

Rev. 7:17	Life from the Lord within this Affection for knowledge and science from the Word, gives to the Rational Faculty a body which is being formed within this Affection, or "Mother," and this body which is being formed, clothes the Internal principle of the mind which is within, as the body of the unborn infant clothes its spiritual body, which, although quiescent, is already conceived within the mother.
John 10:11	
1 Cor.15:38	
Is. 61:10	
Is. 61:11	
Job 29:14	

Ezek. 19:10	326. The "Mother" is not the sciences and knowledges themselves which are stored in the External memory, but is the Affection for them. No one can become truly rational unless he is actuated by a principle of Affection, and this Affection is the true essential Maternal Life, for "Mother" in the Internal Sense signifies Affection for the Truth, and it is in this Second State of regeneration that *"the days were accomplished that she should be delivered."*
Ezek. 19:11	
1 John 4:16	
Matt. 12:49	
Matt. 12:50	
Luke 8:21	
Luke 2:6	

PRAYER.

Luke 18:1	327. During the Second Day of Creation, the regenerating man continually calls upon the Lord for help to overcome the evil of his Proprium. Prayer is discoursing with the Lord by means of the Truths of the Word, in which there is an internal intuition which flows into the perceptions in such a manner that the Internal mind is opened toward the Lord, if the supplication contains no desire to favor the Love of Self.
Ps. 5:2	
Ps. 4:1	
1 Thess. 5:17	
Luke 18:35, 43	
Ezek. 43:2	
Prov. 23:9	

THE NATURE OF THE WORD OF GOD. 163

Answer to prayer. | A mountain.

328. When the Rational Faculty is illuminated by the perception of the Interior Truths of the Word, the regenerating man is taught not to pray for anything which would be contrary to the laws of Divine Order, and in regard to the affairs of this world, he learns to trust so implicitly in the Divine Providence, that in all his personal relations to others, he endeavors to fulfil the law of Love to the Neighbor, and in the breathing of his spiritual lungs he constantly whispers, "*Teach me to do thy will; for thou art my God. Thy Spirit is good; lead me into the land of uprightness,*" and he has no anxiety for the morrow, and utters no complaint against the Mercy of the Lord.

Ps. 139: 1
Ps. 139: 2
Ps. 139: 3
Ps. 139: 4
Matt. 6: 31
Matt. 6: 32
Rom. 13, 14
2 Cor. 8: 21
James 2: 8
Lam. 3: 56
Ps. 143: 10
Matt. 7: 11
Matt. 6: 34
Phil. 2: 14

329. In his struggles against his evils he acknowledges his need of Divine Help, for he has learned that he is helpless in himself alone, and in the progress of his regeneration it is revealed to him that "all things are possible with God," and that "*Whosoever shall say unto this mountain, Be thou removed, and be cast into the sea; and shall not doubt in his heart, but shall believe that those things which he saith shall come to pass; he shall have whatsover he saith.*"

Ps. 35: 1
Ps. 86: 1
Ps. 12: 1
Ps. 142
Ps. 22: 11
Mark 9: 23
Mark 10: 27
Mark 11: 23
Matt. 21: 21
Matt. 21: 22
John 16: 23
John 16: 24

330. A "mountain," in a good sense, signifies Love to the Lord, or the Celestial Principle, and in an evil sense it signifies the Love of Self. The "sea" in which "waters" terminate and are collected, signifies the most exterior terminations of the Divine Truth of the Literal Sense of the Word in the Material Principle of the External mind, and in the evil sense it signifies hell, and thus the "mountain" of Self Love which rears its head above all the "earth" is to be cast down even to hell, and thus removed, if the prayer is sincere, and if

Ps. 30: 7
Is. 2: 2
Ezek 11: 23
Luke 8: 32
Ps. 72: 8
Is. 42: 10
Zech. 9: 10
Rev. 14: 7
Matt. 8: 32
Amos 6: 1
Is. 54: 10
Ps. 46: 2

Vain repetitions.	The Lord's Prayer.

1 Cor. 13:2 1 Thess. 5:15 Matt. 7:8	faith is made alive by living according to the Truths of the Word, for true Faith implies obedience to the commands of the Decalogue. Thus the prayer will be answered, for "every one that asketh, receiveth."
 Matt. 6:5 Matt. 6:6 Matt. 6:7 Matt. 6:8	331. Such prayer is not made "standing in the synagogues and in the corners of the streets," but within the mind, independent of the observation of other men. Neither are "vain repetitions" made, for the Rational Faculty perceives that "your Father knoweth what things ye have need of, before ye ask Him."
1 John 5:14 Lev. 1:2 Lev. 1:3 Lev. 10:5 Ps. 34:18 Ps. 102:17 Ps. 13:3 Luke 17:5 Is. 40:29 Matt. 5:44 Luke 6:27 Luke 6:28 1 John 5:15 1 Pet. 5:6 1 Pet. 5:7	332. A truly rational man would not pray that the will of another person might be changed, because he knows that the Lord cannot violate the freedom of the will of man through Eternity, for no man can be regenerated without his own desire and co-operation with Divine Principles. The most that a regenerating man can pray for, is Divine Light to illumine his path and the increase of his Affection for the Truth, which is the strength of his spiritual life, and the Lord permits that the man shall be the instrument by which his prayers are answered, through a life of obedience to the Truths of the Word. Prayer denotes humility of heart in acknowledging all Power and Life to emanate from the Lord, which must be a constant recognition on the part of man through Eternity.

THE LORD'S PRAYER.

333. THE LORD'S PRAYER which appears so brief in the Literal Sense of the Word, contains within it all the principles of Heavenly Life which man is to attain, and the quality of the lives of angelic men is formed by their perception of the Internal Principles within these words.

Interior principles.   The heavenly kingdom.

334. Within the contents of this Prayer more Interior Principles will be revealed to the regenerating man in proportion as his thought is open toward Heaven; but with those whose spiritual thoughts are closed by the Love of Self, the Interior principles do not appear within the Literal Sense. Within its words, all the Spiritual Principles follow each other in the Divine Order of Regeneration, each depending on the preceding principle in a series from the highest or inmost, and adding successively until the internal principles become Infinite, because they proceed from the Lord who is the Word. Thus this Prayer contains all the principles of the Word, and is the Lord Himself breathing in the Internal mind of the regenerating man.

335. The "Beginning" of Spiritual Life is created by OUR FATHER WHICH IS IN HEAVEN, from whom the universal Heaven exists, the Divine Love within the Word by whom the Internal mind is to be nourished and sustained. HALLOWED BE THY NAME is a recognition of the Holiness of the Word in the mind and life of the man who obeys its Precepts. "Name" signifies the quality of the Divine Love and Wisdom, or of the Lord Jesus Christ, as expressed in the Word. The name of a person on this earth calls before our mental vision all the qualities which we know concerning his life; and thus all that we know of the character of the Lord is by means of the Word, which is His Name. This Word we are to make holy, or hallow His Name, by the knowledge derived from the study of its Literal and Internal Sense. *"For there is none other name under heaven given among men whereby we must be saved.*"*

336. THY KINGDOM COME, expresses the desire to have the Divine Truths of the Word enter our will and understanding, filling our minds with affection for them so that we shall be willing to give up our Self-love and Self-intelligence; making us willing to take up this cross, and to suffer, in order that our pride

*Acts 4 : 12

may be subdued, and this cannot take place without the External mind experiencing anguish, for all mental pain exists only in the External mind, or spiritual body, just as all physical pain exists only in the physical body. Through Eternity the Lord seeks to enter the life of every immortal creature, but the culmination of this desire can only be answered by the manifestation of the Kingdom of God in our own lives, so that others may be led toward the Light by our silent and unobtrusive example, rather than influenced toward evil. Thus the Heavenly Kingdom will come to all who receive the Divine Love and Wisdom which flows from the Lord by the Word.

337. THY WILL BE DONE ON EARTH AS IT IS IN HEAVEN. The Will of the Lord is Infinite Love and Mercy toward all His creatures. The Word is the expression of His Will to man, and we are to Do, or obey the commandments of the Word. *" Ye are my friends if ye do whatsoever 1 command you." " If ye abide in me, and my words abide in you, ye shall ask what ye will, and it shall be done unto you."*

338. The Internal mind, or "Heaven," is not opened to the perception of any man until he begins to live the life of regeneration. His External mind, or " earth," is then to be regenerated by the Living Truths of the Literal Sense of the Word, so that his external conduct in all his acts, from the Heavenly Principles within his motives, shall fulfil the law of Love to the Neighbor, and thus to him the Literal Sense, or " earth " of the Word, will be seen to contain Living Heavenly Principles.

339. GIVE US THIS DAY OUR DAILY BREAD. The Lord gives freely to every man who receives the Heavenly Principles of the Word in obedience, from which results Affection for its Truths. To receive the Word into the life is to receive the Lord, and "this day" refers to the quality of the life in this State of regeneration, and " daily bread" refers to the perpetual supply of heavenly manna, or spiritual food from the Word.

Heavenly bread.	The forgiveness of sins.

In "this day," the regenerating man will recognize that life and thought are given every moment by the Lord, and this perception will so fill the mind with happiness, that he will have neither care nor anxiety about the future, and especially concerning the affairs of this world, excepting to do his part faithfully, in whatever humble or dignified position in which he may be placed.

340. The "bread which cometh down from Heaven" is the Divine Human Principle of the Word, which is Celestial food, or Love to the Lord and to the Neighbor. Spiritual "bread" or meat is Goodness, or Affection for the Word, or a Living Faith. "*Blessed are they which do hunger and thirst after righteousness : for they shall be filled.*"

341. AND FORGIVE US OUR DEBTS, AS WE FORGIVE OUR DEBTORS. The Lord never withholds His Forgiveness nor Mercy from any person, but the perverse and unregenerated man averts himself from the Lord. By the strong force of the Infinite Love of the Lord, He draws men to Himself by the Word, and enlightens their minds to perceive the gracious invitations, which in the Internal Sense, teach that the Divine Mercy is never removed from any man, but the evils of men are like dense clouds which conceal the Lord, or the Internal Sense of the Word, from their view, because their Internal minds and spiritual perceptions are closed.

342. The Forgiveness of sins or trespasses, implies the giving up of the Love of Self, and thus the giving up of sin. Evils and falses are not washed away by a sovereign decree of the Word, but they are to be fought against and successively removed, and there is no other forgiveness or remission of sins by the Lord. The regenerating man is continually falling of himself, but is constantly raised up by the Lord, in order that he may progress in the attainment of spiritual life, and the Divine Truth, or Blood of the Word is incessantly shed, by the strength of which victory is obtained, for "*without shedding of blood there is no remission.*"

Therefore he who desires the Divine Love and Wisdom to enter his will and understanding, must give up his trespasses, shun all evil, look to the Lord, and do unto others as he would have them do to him.

343. AND LEAD US NOT INTO TEMPTATION, BUT DELIVER US FROM EVIL. The Lord never leads any man into temptation, but in all our struggles and combats against our evils He is closely present with us to strengthen and deliver, although it appears as though we are left entirely to ourselves, and thus this expression "lead us not into temptation" is written according to Appearance, in order that the natural mind may acknowledge a Guiding Hand.

344. Instead of the Lord tempting man, He is continually delivering him from evil, as far as it is possible without violating his freedom. The perception of the presence of Divine Truth in the regenerating man, causes the evil principles in the External mind to give pain until they are removed, just as the living nerve within a decayed tooth causes suffering when it is exposed, and the tooth must either be extracted, or the decayed substance removed, and the cavity cleansed and filled with a material which will resist corruption.

345. When a man is undergoing temptation, prayers alone will not deliver him nor save him from yielding, notwithstanding that they may be ardently poured forth, for in the combats of temptation, all the evils which manifest themselves are to be resisted, fought against, and overcome. The united prayers of the whole world would not save a single man from his sins, without his own volition and action.

346. All temptations in the External mind are infused by evil spirits from hell, or from his own evils and falses, and in all his spiritual battles he should fight as from himself with the power given him, because at the time of conflict he is not conscious of Divine Help, but in order to keep the door open for Divine

THE NATURE OF THE WORD OF GOD.

Overcoming evil. Revelation.

Strength to flow in and aid him, he must inwardly acknowledge and believe that the Lord is his Helper, otherwise he will be filled with pride and self-righteousness, and the powers of evil will gain the victory.

347. As evil is to be overcome, so that the temptation will cease, if a man should give himself up to prayer, and not to the active life of resistance by the determination of his Will, from interior motives, he could not be aided in eradicating his evils, and thus be saved from them, which is the end for which the Word has been given to man. He who thus conquers in temptations knows that it is the Lord within who overcomes.

348. If in the state of temptation, a man should fall upon his knees and spend the night in prayer, awaiting a special inspiration of strength, instead of at once resisting the evil insinuations, —if the temptation should not cease thereby, he would be likely to entertain doubt concerning the Divine assistance, because he does not seem to be heard. Sometimes on such occasions, if he slackens his resistance, he partly yields to the temptation, whereas he should resist evil with the weapon the Lord has placed in his hands, the Power to Resist, if he will use it, for the Lord answers prayer by the means which He clearly indicates. The Answer to Prayer is the revelation to the mind, of the means to be used in overcoming evil, which is only made known by Truths from the Word brought forth into life, and thus He delivers us from evil.

349. Revelation concerning the Divine Truth of the Word is an internal perception of its spiritual nature. By "Revelation" is meant the illumination of the Rational Faculty when the Word is read, by which its Living Truths are perceived. No inspiration of the Word exists until its Truths are appropriated by the life of the man who reads it and stores it in his memory, for they who are actuated by spiritual affection, and desire to know the

Truth, are clearly taught from the Word; but they who have not broken away from the Love of Self, cannot be taught the Divine Principles of the Word, and can only be confirmed in the Appearance of Truth of the Literal Sense, in which they have been instructed from infancy.

350. The Trials and Temptations of the Second Day are principally concerning the things of this world, and are not the spiritual temptations which must be met with in the future progress of the Life of Regeneration.

THE THIRD DAY OF CREATION;

OR,

THE THIRD STATE OF REGENERATION.

Hos. 6 : 2 — "*After two days will He revive us : in the Third Day He will raise us up, and we shall live in His sight.*"

Hos. 6 : 3 — "*Then shall we know, if we follow on to know the Lord.*"

Gen. 1 : 9 — And God said, Let the waters under the heaven be gathered unto one place, and let the dry land appear; and it was so.

Ps. 57 : 1
Ps. 57 : 2
Ps. 57 : 3
Ps. 57 : 10
Ps. 57 : 11
Is. 37 : 30
Is. 37 31
Is. 44 : 19

351. The regenerating man now begins to perceive that there is both an Internal and External principle of the mind, which are receptive of their corresponding principles in the Word of God; and that Love and Wisdom descend from the Lord through the Internal principles into the External, although this order is contrary to appearance, because Truths

The source of the Literal Sense.   Perception.

are first learned from the Literal Sense of the Word which is external, but the affection for these Truths, from the Internal principle, brings them into the life, so that the Internal Sense of the Word is perceived as the source from which the external Literal Sense exists.

Is. 44: 20
Is. 44: 24
Is. 44 : 26
Is. 44 : 28
Is. 45: 1
Is. 45 : 2
Is. 45 : 3

352. All principles from the Word which are learned and received by the mind of the regenerating man are called "Scientifics." These are the "waters under the heaven," and the place where they are gathered together, is the External memory, and these knowledges will be called forth thence by the Lord when they are needful in his spiritual progress. The "dry land" is the External principle of the mind which has been separated from the Internal principle by the Rational Faculty, which is the "Firmament" which divides the "waters" during the Second Day. "And it was so," signifies that the regenerating man perceives that these "waters" are stored in the External memory, and that they have been gathered there by the External mind.

Hab. 2 : 14
Num. 24 : 7
Ex. 15 : 3
Jer. 23 : 3
Jer. 23 : 4
Jer. 23 : 5
Jer. 23 : 6
Ex. 14 : 16
Ps. 95 : 5
Gen. 1 : 6
Is. 51 : 15
Ps. 33 : 7
Deut. 28 : 8

And God called the dry land earth: and the gathering together of the waters called he seas: and God saw that it was good.

Gen. 1 : 10

353. "God called" signifies perception in the mind of the regenerating man, that the "dry

Ps. 50 : 1

Ps. 119: 64	land" or "Earth," is the External mind, which
Ps. 78: 69	is so designated at the "beginning" of regeneration. The "waters" or knowledges of the
Ps. 24: 2	Literal Sense of the Word, are called "Seas,"
Rom. 9: 7	which are gathered together in the External
Ps. 78: 16	memory. "Waters," "Rivers," and "Foun-
Is. 41: 18	tains," throughout the Word, denote know-
Ps. 36:	ledges of Truth, and "Seas," denote Scientifics, which are collective Truths in the complex.

Gen. 24: 13	354. A Well, or Fountain, signifies the Word,
Zech. 13: 1	because it contains "water," or Truth, and
Ps. 84: 6	throughout its pages this meaning will be
Is. 12: 3	apparent to the thoughtful reader, especially in the spiritual narrative of the Woman of
John 4: 7	Samaria at the Well of Jacob. This "Well"
John 4: 6	with its water, signifies the Literal Sense of
John 4: 13	the Word. "*Whosoever drinketh of this water shall thirst again.*" This "Water" must first
Ps. 110: 7	be imbibed by the natural mind, and it will
Ps. 42: 2	cause a "thirst" or desire for more interior
Is. 35: 7	knowledge which will lead to the revealing of
John 7: 37	the Internal Sense, or "Living Water" signi-
John 4: 10	fied in the following verse, "*But whosoever*
Zech. 14: 8	*drinketh of the water that I shall give him shall*
Rev. 7: 16	*never thirst; but the water that I shall give him*
Cant. 4: 15	*shall be in him a well of water springing up*
Rev. 7: 17	*into Everlasting Life.*"

| | 355. "And God saw that it was good," signi- |
| Ps. 129: 5 | fies the perception which is being implanted in |

| Grass. | Green pastures. |

the Rational Faculty that this work of regeneration and the Revelation of the Internal Sense is from the Lord who alone is Good.

Ps. 106 : 1
Ps. 73 : 1
Luke 18 : 19

And God said, Let the earth bring forth grass, the herb yielding seed, and the fruit-tree yielding fruit after his kind: and it was so.

Gen. 1 : 11

356. During the preceding states of regeneration, the "earth," or External mind, has been preparing to receive Heavenly Seeds from the Word, so that Good and True principles may be produced, and now the Lord causes the tender "grass" to spring forth from this "earth." "Grass," in the Word, denotes Scientific Truth by which the Spiritual Truth of the Word is confirmed, and as grass serves for food to animals, so the Scientific Truth of the Word serves for the spiritual nourishment of the mind, or spiritual body. The Scientific Principles of the Word are not physical or material science.

Ex. 15 : 20
Ex. 23 : 20
Ps. 80 : 9
Ps. 126 : 6
Ps. 107 : 37
Ps. 32 : 20
Ps. 85 : 11
Is. 44 : 4
Is. 61 : 11
Ps. 65 : 10
Deut. 11 : 15
1 Kings 18 : 5
Rev. 9 : 4
Zech. 10 : 1
Ps. 119 : 91
Ps. 119 : 144

357. "*He causeth the grass to grow for the cattle.*" "Cattle," signifies the Natural Affections of the External mind, to which "Grass" or Scientific food serves for nourishment. The Literal Sense of the Word is the spiritual pasture for the "cattle" of the External mind to feed in. "Green pastures" signify Living Truth, for grass, when it ceases to be green,

Ps. 104 : 14
Gen. 9 : 9, 10
Ps. 148 : 10
Ps. 147 : 9
Ps. 100 : 3
John 10 : 9
Ps. 23 : 2

Is. 15:6	withers up and is dried. But this "grass" is
Prov. 27:25	not "green," because it is for the natural affec-
Mark 6:30	tions of the External mind, and as yet has not
	much life in it. In the illustration of the Five
John 6:10	Loaves and Two Fishes, it is said, "*Now there was much grass in the place,*" where the scien-
Matt. 14:19	tifics or knowledges of the Literal Sense of the Word are signified.
Gen. 1:11	358. Next in order it is said "the herb yield-
Deut. 11:10	ing seed," by which is signified also the scientific
Is. 26:19	principle which goes forth into use or activity,
Heb. 6:7	by which is meant that the Truth of the Literal Sense is applied to life. This "herb" must be
Job 38:27	rendered productive by being planted in the
Ps. 92:13	"earth," or External mind, which must receive
Is. 18:4	the heat and light of the Spiritual Sun so as to
Is. 61:3	grow to its maturity, and thereby yield its seed,
Ps. 67:6	and thus these scientifics from the Word become
Ps. 107:38	multiplied, and the knowledges perpetuated. "He causeth the grass to grow for the cattle,
Ps. 104:14	*and herb for the service of man; that he may bring*
Ps. 78:25	*forth food out of the earth.*" Thus spiritual
2 Cor. 9:10	nourishment is derived from the Truths of
Deut. 28:4	the Word which have been implanted within
Deut. 28:11	the External mind, or "earth," the "herb" signifying the Truths which are first produced in the life of the regenerating man.
Mark 4:26	359. "Seed," in the Word, denotes its Truth,
Is. 55:10	and the Truth of the Word does not possess

THE NATURE OF THE WORD OF GOD. 175

The seed of the Word. | Sowing seed.

Life for man until it is implanted in the External mind. The Truth, or "seed" of the Word, as it lays in the letters which give it expression, has no more life without the proper soil in which to grow, than the corresponding seeds of the vegetable kingdom would have if lying dry upon a barren rock. These seeds do not sprout and bring forth the tender plant until they are placed within and take root in the earth, where the moisture and salts of the soil permeate the fibres, while the influence of the heat and light of the sun causes the germ to burst its casement, and shoot upwards toward the light, while its root becomes firmly fixed within the ground.

Is. 55 : 11
Num. 20 : 5
John 12 : 24
Ps. 32 : 4
Luke 8 : 6
Mark 4 : 6
Matt. 13 : 23
Ps. 60 : 9
Gen. 8 : 22
Ezek. 36 : 8
Jer. 12 : 2

360. The Truths of the Word first become inrooted when the regenerating man begins to acknowledge and believe them, for previous to this State they have not taken root. The Truths which have been previously received and retained in the memory, have been merely inseminated, or sown like seed scattered upon the ground, and harrowed in, for it does not burst forth and take root until the regenerating man makes the Truths of the Word sprout by living them from inward motives, which is called the Good of Love, because his life is then actuated by a principle of Affection which is derived from the Divine Love, and is there-

Eccles. 11 : 6
John 14 : 1
Luke 8 : 13
Prov. 11 : 18
Jer. 4 : 3
2 Cor. 9 : 6
Hos. 10 : 12
Mark 4 : 20
Hos. 2 : 23
Job. 14 : 7
Prov. 11 : 31
Zech 10 : 9
Jer. 33 : 8
Jer. 30 : 9

fore Good, for Good is from the Divine Love, and Truth is from the Divine Wisdom.

Ex. 33 : 19
Prov. 2 : 9

THE TWO AFFECTIONS.

361. There are Two Affections existing in the regenerating man. The AFFECTION OF (or derived from) GOOD, and the AFFECTION OF TRUTH, the former being as the husband, and the latter as the wife, and these Two Principles, or Affections, are to be conjoined in the will and understanding, as husband and wife, thus constituting the Heavenly Marriage, from which proceeds Spiritual Life.

Eph. 5 : 23
Eph. 5 : 24
Eph. 5 : 28
Eph. 5 : 29
Eph. 5 : 30
Eph. 5 : 31
Eph. 5 : 32

362. The AFFECTION OF TRUTH first exists in the order of regeneration, in which man is actuated by a principle of obedience to the Literal Sense of the Word, and he attends to the external acts of charity, such as doing good to every one whom he imagines to be a neighbor, especially to the poor, because they call themselves poor, in consequence of being destitute of worldly wealth, not being aware that by "poor" in the Word are meant those who are spiritually poor;—they who know and confess in heart that they have nothing of Good and Truth from themselves, but that all things are freely given them. "*Blessed are the poor in spirit: for theirs is the kingdom of heaven.*"

Ex. 24 : 7
Je.. 42 : 6
Acts 20 : 35
Ps. 112 : 5
Matt. 5 : 42
Luke 11 : 41
Ps. 41 : 1
Matt. 19 : 21
Jer. 22 : 16
Luke 6 : 20
Ps. 82 : 4
Zeph. 3 : 12
Ps. 9 : 18
Rev. 21 : 6
Matt. 5 : 3

363. Thus the "poor" are those who desire instruction from the Word, because they know that they have no intelligence in themselves, and the mind is gradually led to perceive the spiritual principle within the natural expression, and thus the idea of Love to the Neighbor, or the Affection of Truth, progresses from the

Ps. 68 : 10
Is. 41 : 17
Ps. 63 : 1
Ps. 65 : 9
Is. 44 : 3
Rom. 13 : 10
Zech. 10 : 12

| The Affection of Good. | Charity. |

external thought of a person, or from the Literal Sense of the Word to the Internal Spiritual Principle, which is the Neighbor to be loved, and the Affection for this principle of the Word, is meant by the Affection of Truth, or Truth warmed into obedience.

Zech. 3 : 10
Zech. 8 : 22
Zech. 8 : 23
Ps. 116 : 1
Ps. 116 : 9
Ps. 116 : 18

364. The Affection of Truth consists in doing good from the Love of the Truth of the Word, first from the Apparent Truth, or Literal Sense, and afterward from the Truth of the Internal or True Sense of the Word, and this Affection properly belongs to the Understanding of the regenerating man.

Ps. 18 : 1
John 5 : 30
Deut. 32 : 4
Is. 5 : 16
Is. 5 : 17
Rev. 16 : 7

365. The AFFECTION OF GOOD consists in doing good from the Love of Good, and properly belongs to the Will, and is grounded in the principle of Celestial love, or Love to the Lord, and in the order of regeneration it succeeds the Affection of Truth. A person who is in the Affection of Good, has an immediate perception of what is Good and True without reasoning if it is so or not, similar to the principle of perception which filled "Adam," in the "generations of old." In all his acts he delights in obedience from his Affection for the Word, or what is the same thing, from his Love to the Lord.

Deut. 5 : 1
Rom. 7 : 22
Lev. 18 : 4
Lev. 18 : 5
Deut. 7 : 11
Deut. 30 : 16
Jer. 31 : 34
Heb. 8 : 10
Heb. 8 : 11
Is. 51 : 9
Mal. 3 : 4
Is. 58 : 8
Is. 58 : 9

366. Those, however, who are in the Affection of Truth for the sake of Truth and Spiritual Life, when they hear or read religious doctrines, search the Word to prove whether they are true or false, and do not remain in false teachings, because they are led to the True Light from the Word. They become so filled with thoughts of charity toward others, that they do not condemn those who differ from them in religious belief, and recognize what is true in the opinions of others.

Is. 58 : 10
2 John 2
Jer. 29 : 12
Jer. 29 : 13
Acts 17 : 11
Jer. 29 : 14
1 Tim. 6 : 20
Is. 2 : 5
1 Cor. 13 : 8
Eph. 4 : 32
Col. 3 : 12
Col. 3 : 13

The herb yielding seed.

Gen. 1 : 11

Gen. 9 : 3

Job 27 : 4
Ps. 145 : 11
Jas. 2 : 22

Ps. 88 : 4
Cor. 8 : 2

2 Kings 19 : 26
2 Kings 19 : 27
2 Kings 19 : 29
2 Kings 19 : 30

Is. 30 : 23
Matt. 13 : 8
Is. 55 : 12

Heb. 6 : 14
Gen. 22 : 17
Ezek. 30 : 30
Ezek. 36 : 35

367. In continuing the subject of the "herb yielding seed" in the man whose regenerating life has been progressing from the Second State, he now begins to talk devoutly and reverently concerning religious things, and to do good actions, which are the external works of charity, but which as yet are inanimate, because they have no inward principle, and therefore he supposes them to originate in himself.

368. These good actions are called the "grass," and the "herb yielding seed," because the scientific principles of the External mind must first be formed from the Literal Sense of the Word, in order that the "seed" may take root. When the "earth," or External mind, is thus prepared to receive Celestial seed from the Word, so that Internal Good and True principles may be produced, the Lord causes the "tender grass" to spring forth : then more productive principles succeed which bear seed in themselves, the "herb yielding seed ;" and next follow principles of Affection which become fruitful. "And the fruit tree yielding fruit after his kind."

CORRESPONDENCES.

369. Every object in Universal Nature represents in some manner the Spiritual Principles of the Lord's Kingdom in Heaven

| Names of physical objects. | A microcosm. |

or in the mind of man, because the Natural Kingdom derives its origin and existence from the Spiritual Kingdom, just as the physical body derives its form and existence from the spiritual body which it clothes, or as the Literal Sense of the Word exists from its Internal Sense.

370. Thus the Spiritual Principles of the Word throughout, are represented by the names of objects in the physical world. All principles of the Spiritual World terminate in the Natural World of thought as the ultimate effect, and yet nothing in this physical world is spiritual in itself, but everything is representative of Spiritual Principles.

371. The Literal Sense of the Word is written entirely by the names and qualities of the representative things of the physical world; and by means of the Science of Correspondence, the spiritual things which at first so obscurely appear in the Literal Sense, are in due order brought plainly before the perception of the regenerating man. The Science of Correspondence is a firmly established Principle which is of universal application, based upon the interior signification of all objective things. It is inherent in the etymology of words, in the qualities of all objects, and in the names of persons when mentioned in the Word, and also in the names of places in which these characteristic persons reside. From these names in the Word, which first exist there, earthly localities are named. Thus the city of Jerusalem is so called, because such a city exists in the Word, and scriptural names are given to men because they first exist in the Word.

372. Throughout the Word, the man within whom spiritual life has begun, is compared to the objects in the Vegetable Kingdom, and especially to Trees, because the whole Vegetable, as well as the Animal and Mineral Kingdom, represent such principles as appertain to the spiritual nature of man, for a regenerated man is a " Heaven," or Spiritual World in the smallest form : hence the mind of man is called a " Microcosm," or little world.

| Leaves, flowers and fruit. | The heart and lungs. |

TREES.

Ezek. 31 : 3
Ezek. 31 : 4
Ezek. 31 : 5
Ezek. 31 : 6
Ezek. 31 : 7
Ezek. 31 : 8
Ezek. 31 : 9

373. In the Word, the regenerating man is either compared to, or is called, a "Tree," and the successive growths of intelligence, of wisdom, and of life, are compared to the production of leaves, flowers, and fruit. His mind is implanted with Divine Good and Truth, the *Seed of the Word from which the Tree begins.

Ex. 24 : 10
John 6 : 33
John 14 : 19
1 Cor 12 : 27
Rev. 22 : 9

374. All things in the physical world have some relation to the Human Form, which is the Form of the universal Heaven, because its Life consists of the Divine Human Principle of the Lord in the lives of angels, or regenerated men.

Eph. 4 : 15
Eph. 4 : 16
Eph. 2 : 21
Matt. 12 : 35
Ezek. 37 : 5

Lev. 17 : 11
Lev. 17 : 14

375. All the minute organs of the physical frame correspond with the spiritual principles of the mind. Nearly every person knows that the Heart corresponds to Love, or Affection, but it is not generally known that the Lungs correspond to Wisdom, or the Understanding. The union of the operation of the heart and lungs causes the blood to circulate and perpetuate the life of the physical frame.

Ezek. 47 : 12

Ezek. 34 : 27
Deut. 20 : 19

376. A Tree has its heart. Its leaves correspond to the lungs in the physical body, and they first appear in spring-time, then the blossoms expand from the buds, and finally the fruit is formed from the inmost principle of the

blossom, and the object of the whole life of the tree is to yield fruit, or in some form be of use to man. | Prov 11: 30

377. The Leaves act as the lungs or respiratory organs, and aid in the circulation of the life-blood of the tree; and a tree spoiled of its leaves will bear no fruit. The Root signifies the extension of intelligence from the spiritual principle of the Internal mind into the External, or "earth," and every Spiritual Tree, or regenerating man must be rooted and grounded in the "earth" or Literal Sense of the Word. | Matt. 24: 32
Rev. 22: 2
Ps. 104: 16
Is. 1: 30
Jer. 12: 2
Job 29: 19
Rom. 11: 16
Jer. 17.: 8
Eph. 3: 17

378. The Branches of the Tree signify sensual and natural Truths in the External mind which are derived from the Literal Sense of the Word. They signify sensual Truths, because the branches of a tree are its most exterior limits, as the material principle of the External mind of man is his ultimate spiritual limit, his corporeal frame being simply a physical machine through which he acts. | Is. 17: 6
Hos. 14: 6
John 15: 2
Jer. 33: 15
Is. 4: 2
John 15: 5
1 Cor. 9: 27

379. By the Leaves of a tree are signified Rational Truths, or the Truths derived from the Word which are received by the Rational Faculty of the Mind after the Appearances of Truth have been separated from the Genuine Truth which is within the Literal Sense. | Mark 13: 28
Zech. 8: 3
John 8: 32
John 16: 7

380. The Blossoms, or Flowers, signify the first Spiritual Truths from the Word which | Ps. 103: 15
Ps. 103: 16

bloom in the Rational Faculty, and the Fruit of the tree signifies these Spiritual Truths made Living, by being brought forth into act, and the fruit yielded is according to the "kind" or quality of the tree. Such is the representative similitude between the fruit-bearing tree, and the man who is being regenerated, which may be discovered from any passage in the Literal Sense of the Word where a tree is being described, either as representative of good or evil principles in man. *"And he shall be like a tree planted by the rivers of water, his leaf shall not wither, and whatsoever he doeth shall prosper."*

381. Trees, in general, signify perceptions and knowledges of Good and Truth from the Word in the regenerating man, according to the quality of his life, and in the Word they are divided into Three Classes: Trees of the Garden, or Fruit Trees, Forest Trees, and Groves. Trees of the Garden, Vineyard, and Orchards, provide fruit for the support of physical life, and afford delight to the sense of taste. Forest trees provide for the building of habitations and furniture for the comfort of man, and they also serve for fuel to give warmth in the cold seasons, and they furnish heat for the preparation of food. Groves afford shelter, and are the places where external worship is held, before the building of temples and tabernacles.

Three principles of the Understanding	Comparisons

382. These Three Divisions of Trees correspond to the Three Principles of the Understanding: the Inmost Principle, or perception of Intellectual things, signified by "gardens"; the Interior Principle, or Perception of Rational things, signified by "forest-trees," such as the cedars of Lebanon; and the Exterior Principle, or perception of Scientific things, or the knowledges of the Literal Sense of the Word, appertaining to the External mind, signified by "groves," and especially by "oak-groves."

Jer. 32: 15
Num. 22: 24
Jer. 29: 23
Is. 41: 8
Ezek. 27: 5
Job 40: 22
Josh. 24: 26
Judges 6: 11
Ezek. 6: 13
Hos. 4: 13

383. All the Comparisons in the Word which have been given for illustration, are also representative of Spiritual Principles by the laws of correspondence. The regenerating man is compared to a Garden in the Word. "*And the Lord shall guide thee continually, and satisfy thy soul in drought, and make fat thy bones; and thou shalt be like a watered garden, and like a spring of water, whose waters fail not.*"

Ps. 80: 6
1 Cor. 2: 13
Is. 58: 11

384. The budding and fructification of a tree represent the re-birth of man: the growing green from the development of the leaves represents the First State of Reformation; the blossoming represents the Second State, or the next before regeneration; and the fructification, or "fruit tree yielding fruit after his kind," represents the Third, which is the State itself of the regenerating man, who is now bearing fruit.

Is. 18: 5
Luke 1: 14
Jer. 17: 8
Hos. 12: 6
Ezek. 36: 9
Ezek. 36: 10
Ezek. 36: 11
Ezek. 36: 12

385. "Whose seed is in itself," signifies the Word of God. All the perceptions of the principles of the understanding represented by the "fruit tree," are from the Word, which is the Human Form the Lord has assumed in the natural world of the mind, and these perceptions flow into the Rational Faculty of the regenerating man from the Lord through the Internal mind. *"The Seed is the Word of God,"* which, with its Interior Divine Truth is the Son of God. *"For as the Father hath life in Himself; so hath He given to the Son to have life in Himself."* Thus the Seed, which is the Word, contains within "Itself" the vital principles of Eternal Life "upon the earth," or Literal Sense, in the External mind of the regenerating man in its outward principle, signified by "upon," which every enlightened person may perceive by thoughtful comparison with the order of growth in the physical world, and looking within his own mental experiences, may comprehend why it is written, "And it was so."

386. *"So is the Kingdom of God, as if a man should cast seed into the ground; and should sleep, and rise night and day, and the seed should spring and grow up, he knoweth not how. For the earth bringeth forth fruit of herself; first the blade, then the ear, after that, the full corn*

Sowing the seed.   The full corn in the ear.

in the ear." He who sows the Seed is the Divine Man of the Word, the Lord Himself; but in this state of regeneration it appears as if the Affections of Good and Truth arose from some innate principle in himself, and thus springs and grows up, "he knoweth not how," for thus the Lord permits a man to be led, rising gradually from obscure perception to clearer light, signified by "night and day."
Mark 4: 13
Matt. 13 : 37
Mark 4: 14
Deut. 8: 13
Deut. 11: 16
Deut. 8: 14
Ex. 15: 13
Prov. 8: 20

387. To the regenerating man it appears as though the Lord was sleeping, because he does not yet perceive that all his intuitions are inflowings from the Divine Wisdom, and therefore it is said according to this State of Appearance, that "the earth bringeth forth fruit of herself," and the order of regeneration is according to natural growth by correspondence with spiritual principles. In due order, the Appearance of Truth in the Literal Sense, which exists in the mind according to the State of the regenerating man, will be substituted by the Truth of the Internal Sense, as soon as the Rational Faculty is developed so that it shall be influenced from the Internal rather than from the External principles of the Word.
Mark 4: 38
Ps. 44: 23
Prov. 2: 7
Is. 37: 30
John 15: 4
Hos. 14: 7
John 20: 3
John 20: 4
Num. 12: 8
John 20: 5
John 20: 6
John 20: 7
John 20: 8

388. This clearer perception of the Internal Sense, or "full corn in the ear," which teaches that the "earth" produces nothing "of herself"; that the Literal Sense of the Word
2 Kings 4: 42
2 Kings 4: 43
2 Kings 4: 44

Bringing forth fruit. Progress in resisting evil.

<table>
<tr><td>John 5:19</td><td>exists only from the Internal Sense ; that even the "Son can do nothing of himself, but what he seeth the Father do," but that the "fruit" is brought forth by the life from the Internal Sense of the Word in the regenerating man, is expressed by the following words : "And the earth brought forth grass, and herb yielding seed after his kind, and the tree yielding fruit, whose seed is in itself, after his kind : And God saw that it was good," signifying that the Rational Faculty is opened to perceive that these spiritual influences are in him from the Lord, and do not originate with himself.</td></tr>
<tr><td>Col. 1:5</td></tr>
<tr><td>Col. 1:6</td></tr>
<tr><td>Col. 1:11</td></tr>
<tr><td>Gen. 1:12</td></tr>
<tr><td>Luke 24:45</td></tr>
<tr><td>John 7:29</td></tr>
<tr><td>John 7:18</td></tr>
</table>

Gen. 1:13   **And the Evening and the Morning were the Third Day.**

389. This Third State of Regeneration is characterized by self-examination, through which the regenerating man is led to see his hereditary evil and sinfulness, with such humiliation of heart that he feels aversion toward each evil as it arises from his Proprium, and he rejects it from his life. In this state of repentance he carefully resists the return of these evils and falses which have been fought against, and he constantly looks to the Lord by the Word for help, and increases in spiritual strength. Thus he progresses from shade to light, or from "evening" to "morning" during the Third Day.

Ps. 26:2
2 Cor. 13:5
Luke 14:11
Is. 57:15
Ps. 139:21
Ps. 139:22
Ps. 139:23
Ps. 139:24
1 Pet. 5:9
Ps. 37:40
Is. 50:7-8
Dan. 8:26
2 Kings 20:5

THE NATURE OF THE WORD OF GOD. 187

The number one.   The number two.

NUMBERS.

390. All Numbers in the Word denote the quality of the State of the regenerating or evil principles in man, according to the subject which is being described. In reference to the First Day of Creation, it treats of the "Beginning" and continuation of the spiritual life of the regenerating man. The number One signifies the conjunction of those principles which form a unity, and One day, week, month or year, denotes a whole period of time or state. | Is. 40 : 26
Ps. 90 : 12
Luke 12 : 7
Dan. 10 : 12
Matt. 23 : 8
John 17 : 23
Ps. 133 : 1
Is. 27 : 4

391. The number Two denotes the Heavenly Marriage of the will and understanding, and also labor and combat as described in the illustration of the Second Day of Creation, between the Proprium and the spiritual principles which are flowing in from the Internal mind. The number Two also denotes the separation between the Internal and External mind by means of the Rational Faculty, but with the man who has attained the Seventh Day, it denotes the Heavenly Marriage of Good and Truth to which all spiritual, natural, and physical things have reference. This Marriage takes place between the will and understanding of the regenerating man on account of the Marriage, or Conjunction which is taking place between his mind and the Word, which is creating him in the Divine Human Form. | Amos 3 : 3
Ezek. 37 : 22
Matt. 6 : 24
Rom. 8 : 6
Rom. 7 : 14
Ex. 32 : 15
Matt. 18 : 19
1 John 3 : 22
Is. 62 : 4
Is. 62 : 5
Ps. 86 : 10
Matt. 19 : 6
Jer. 50 : 5
1 Cor. 6 : 17

392. The number Three is used to denote what is Holy, and what is complete and full from beginning to end, through the successive degrees of End, Cause and Effect, which are necessary for the existence of a One, as the Will, Understanding and Life, in man. | Luke 13 : 32
1 Cor. 15 : 4
Rev. 16 : 10
1 John 5 : 8

| The Coming of the Lord. | The orderly preparation |

Mark 8 : 31
Matt. 15 : 32
Luke 2 : 46
Luke 18 : 32
Jer. 31 : 6
Luke 7 : 14
Luke 15 : 18
Mark 0 : 9
Mark 9 : 10
John 11 : 24
1 John 2 : 24
John 15 : 7

393. The Third Day is used to denote the Coming of the Lord into the spiritual world of man by the Word, and it also indicates every revelation of His Word to the spiritual perceptions. The Coming of the Lord to the mind of the regenerating man, and the Resurrection, are identical, for His Resurrection takes place on the Third Day, when the regenerating man is in a full state of preparation to enter into Spiritual Life, or what is the same thing, for Spiritual Life to enter his mind.

As the studious reader, by means of a Concordance, may refer to any subject in the Word which is being treated of in the succeeding pages, and from the principles explained in the preceding pages may perceive that all the words thus referred to have an interior meaning, the marginal references will now be discontinued. Thus, as under the subject of "Trees," "Seed," "Clothing," or "Garments," "Horses," "Sheep," "Shepherds," "Flocks," "Cattle," "Beasts," "Fishes," "People," "City," "Flesh," "Blood." "Bread," "Water," "Wine," "Light," etc., the illustrations may easily be found, and the correspondences will be firmly stored in the memory by such a comparative study of the Literal Sense of the Word.

394. The Three successive degrees of the Third State of Regeneration, in which the Rational Faculty is imbued with Life from the Lord through the Internal mind, are represented in the preparation for the birth of the Lord, by First, the "Grass," which signifies the Scientific Truth of the Literal Sense of the Word which is confirmed by the Scientific Principles of the External mind. Secondly, by the "Herb yielding seed," which signifies a life according to the Literal Truths of the Word, from which results, Thirdly, perceptions and knowledges of Good and Truth, signified by the "Fruit tree yielding fruit." From this orderly preparation of the life of a regenerating man, the Lord Jesus Christ is born from the Internal mind into the Rational Faculty, where He is first seen as the WORD.

THE BIRTH OF THE HOLY CHILD.

And she brought forth her first born Son, and wrapped him in swaddling clothes, and laid him in a manger; because there was no room for them in the inn. Luke 2 : 7.

395. It was illustrated under the subject of the Second Day of Creation that the Mother of the Infant Jesus in the regenerating man, is the Affection for the Scientifics, or Truths of the Literal Sense of the Word, as they are received by the External mind, and the Rational Faculty is first acted upon by means of these exterior Truths. The Miraculous Conception is the reception of these Truths into the External memory from Affection for them.

396. All Conceptions and Births which are narrated in the Word, are to be understood spiritually and not physically, they having relation to the order of the New Birth or regeneration of man, and the minds of enlightened men are created with the faculty of perceiving higher and more elevating thoughts concerning the Advent of the Lord, according to the laws of Divine Order, if they desire to look above earthly things.

397. When the Rational Faculty, which is intermediate between the Internal and External mind, first perceives the enlightenment that the Word is the Lord, which is caused by the inflowing of the Divine Love from the Internal mind, then the Lord is born within the regen-

erating man, and he ceases to think that either Good or Truth originates in himself, and this Perception is the "First Born Son," for it is in this principle of child-like innocence and in this infantile state that he acknowledges the Internal Sense of the Word and perceives that it is the Lord.

398. Previous to this Perception, his reflections were upon the Literal Truths which were stored within his External memory, and in Appearance it seemed as if he originated his thoughts, which were consequently filled with self-intelligence, but as soon as the Rational Faculty is enlightened from above, or Within, so that the regenerating man sees that the Word is the One Lord, in Heaven and on Earth, then the Affection for the Truth learned from the Word is "brought forth" into the Rational Faculty where it becomes, through the illuminated Perception, the "First Born Son."

399. The Internal Sense of the Word consists of the Essential Divine Truth, but in the Literal Sense there are Truths which are accommodated to the comprehension of those who are principled in external worship. It is essential to their ideas of doctrine and faith, to believe that the Lord Jesus Christ was miraculously conceived and externally born as an infant into this physical world as another and separate finite man, although this idea is contrary to the Laws of Divine Order, and whatever is contrary to these Laws is not the Truth, and a Rational Faith can only accept such principles as the enlightened understanding perceives as true.

400. But with all who are led to obey the Precepts of the Word, the Two Great Commandments of Spiritual Life, even by the Appearance of Truth, as it exists in the Literal Sense, their minds will be so elevated above evil and falsity, that they will be nourished by the Essential Divine Truth, and in their spiritual progress, their perceptions will be enlightened concerning the true Nature of the Word.

401. The Internal Sense of the Word is accommodated to the state of life of those whose Internal mind has been opened, whose lives are principled in the Precepts of the Word, and whose Rational Faculty is so far enlightened, that the illumination is compared to the brightness of the sun and stars. These are they of whom it is said, "*And they that be wise shall shine as the brightness of the firmament.*" "*Then shall the righteous shine forth as the sun in the kingdom of their father.*"

402. Hence it is of great importance that the Literal Truths of the Word should be known and received into the mind and actuate the life, for the Interior Truths are only revealed to those who are principled in love to and faith in the Lord by obedience to the Commandments of the Word. "*But as many as received Him, to them gave He power to become the Sons of God.*" They who are born of God are His sons, because they are principled in the Truths of the Word.

403. "And wrapped him in swaddling clothes, and laid him in a manger." The Truths which now appear to the regenerating man are the truths of innocence, for

he has become an infant in the opening of the perception that all his spiritual life is from the Lord, and he is one of the "little ones" "*That in heaven their angels do always behold the face of my Father which is in Heaven.*" In the Word, "Clothes" signify everything external which enclose spiritual principles. Truth is the "clothing" of Good, because Good is the Life within Truth. "Swaddling clothes" signify the Truths of Innocence with which the Infant Jesus is clothed within the enlightened Rational Faculty of the regenerating man. These Truths of Innocence are the simple Living Truths of the Literal Sense of the Word, by which the spiritual life of the regenerating man is to be nourished, and this Infant is laid "in a manger."

404. A "Manger" signifies the Doctrine of Truth, or spiritual instruction from the Word. A "horse" signifies the understanding of Truth from the Word. All animals mentioned in the Word signify some spiritual principle in the mind of man. "Horses" are many times referred to, especially in the Book of Revelation, in which white, pale, red, and black horses are mentioned. A horse feeds from a "manger," which signifies that the Understanding must receive food, or spiritual instruction from the Word, and thus the Rational Faculty, at this State of regeneration, must be fed by the simple Truths of Innocence from the Word.

405. "Because there was no room for them in the inn. An "Inn" literally denotes a place of rest, or night-abode, and in the Word it signifies a place of

THE NATURE OF THE WORD OF GOD. 193

An Inn.	The representative Face.

instruction, for as in an earthly inn, the physical frame is nourished while journeying, so the mind is fed from the Word, during its progressions from the "night" toward "morning." As an "Inn" is a covering or shelter for the man who rests within, it also signifies the Exterior Natural Principle of the External mind, for the Natural principle also has its interior and exterior principle.

406. The Exterior Natural Principle is that which communicates by means of the senses with the physical world, but it is not the physical frame which is governed by it, but is the principle by which the idea of things in this world flow into the mind.

407. The Interior Natural Principle communicates with the Rational Faculty, through which there is a continual inflowing from the Lord into this Interior degree into the Exterior Natural Principle. With unregenerated men, Good is there turned into evil, and Truth is changed into falsity, but with the regenerating man, Good and Truth from the Lord are presented in the Natural Principle as in a mirror. The Natural Principle is like a face representative of the spiritual principles of the Internal mind, and that face becomes representative of true spiritual principles, when, by a life according to the Truths of the Word, the Exterior principles correspond to the Internal mind. In like manner, the Literal Truths of the Word are the Face of Jesus.

408. When the Rational Faculty is born into the perception of the Divine inflowing through the Internal mind, or that the Life of the Word is the Internal Sense,

it does not take its abode or derive nourishment from the "Inn" of the Exterior Natural Principle, or the Literal Sense of the Word alone, for without a perception of the Internal Sense, there is "no room" or place in the "Inn," and this is why the infantile perception of the Rational Faculty from the Internal mind is laid in the "manger" of spiritual instruction from the Word, and awaits the orderly unfolding of the principles of the Internal Sense.

And there were in the same country shepherds abiding in the field, keeping watch over their flocks by night.
Luke 2 : 8.

409. The "same country" denotes "Bethlehem of Judea," or the State of the Interior perception of the Rational Faculty in which the Lord is born in the regenerating man, for the Lord Jesus is born in this "Bethlehem." As "Shepherds" care for and guide their sheep or flocks, so with the regenerating man, the Truths of the Word lead to Good, which is love and obedience, and they thus become the "Shepherds."

410. "Abiding" signifies living, or the state of the life in which these Truths are received, and "field" signifies the External mind which is being regenerated. "Earth" signifies the External mind, and a "field" is the "earth" in which there is "grass" growing for the nourishment of the "sheep" or "flocks."

411. Throughout the Word, "sheep" or "flocks," signify those who are in the Affection of Good, and who live the innocent life of Love to the Lord and the

Neighbor, and these words also represent the same principles in the regenerating man. "Keeping watch" denotes a course of life according to the Precepts of the Word, or according to a true faith in the Lord. "By night" signifies the obscure state of the External mind concerning spiritual principles, when the Rational Faculty at first begins to open to perceive the Internal Sense of the Word.

And, lo, the angel of the Lord came upon them, and the glory of the Lord shone round about them ; and they were sore afraid. Luke 2 : 9.

412. "And, lo," signifies the perception of the Divine influence, and "the angel of the Lord"* is the Divine Human Principle of the Word, the Lord Himself within the Internal Sense of the Word, which "came upon" the "shepherds," or which is revealed within the Truths of the Word to the regenerating man.

413. "And the glory of the Lord shone round about them." "Glory"† is the intelligence and wisdom derived from the Divine Truth, or the Internal Sense of the Word, which sheds its lustre upon the Literal Truths. This splendor of light which shines from the Word is called "Glory," for it shines round about and within the Truths of the Word, which are the "Shepherds" which lead to the perception of the Internal Sense.

414. When the regenerating man catches the first glimpse of the great Spiritual Truth that the Word is the Lord, and that it is the Son of God who is born into

---
* Ex. 23: 20.   † Matt. 25: 31.

The glory of the Lord.	The guidance of the Lord.

the "earth" of the External mind, an inexpressible "Glory," or elevation, fills his whole being, for Heaven seems opened to his spiritual sight, and the things of time and space for the moment seem to vanish, as he sees the Divine Revelation to be from the Lord, and many mental conflictions concerning the Word, and the Divine Providence, are surmounted, and the paths are made straight for the Rational Faculty to progress in clearer perceptions.

415. He can now look back upon the history of the nations and people of this physical world, until his mind can penetrate no farther into the retrospect, and through the past Eternal ages he perceives One Lord Jesus Christ alone, who has been unchangeable in His Infinite Love and Wisdom, who has been impartial toward all His creatures, although to the obscure judgment of man His apparent dealings with men have seemed unjust, as if one class of men were favored more than others. He has provided His Divine Truth in some form for all, and has led those who have permitted this Truth to enter their lives in the slightest degree, for not all who are surrounded with the most enlightening influences, make the best use of their privileges, and the Lord can only lead those who are guided by the Truths which they know.

416. When this "Glory" within the Divine Truth of the Word is first revealed to the regenerating man, he is "sore afraid." This "fear" is not the fear which evil or unregenerated men have toward their idea of God,

| The fear of the Lord. | Good tidings. |

or which those possess who are in the observance of external worship without the Internal Living principle of spiritual life, but it is a holy state of mind filled with adoration and reverence for Him who is the Word, adjoined to humiliation of heart, and this state is the "*Fear of the Lord,*" which "*is the beginning of wisdom.*"

And the Angel said unto them, Fear not; for, behold I bring you good tidings of great joy, which shall be to all people. Luke 2: 10.

417. By "the Angel said unto them, Fear not," is meant an internal perception from the Lord that this opening of the Rational Faculty to receive the Truths of the Internal Sense of the Word, is by means of a re-creation of spiritual life, by which the Proprium is devastated and put off. At first there is a sense of "fear," arising from the Proprium, which is antagonistic to the "Glory" which has been shining from within, for all who come suddenly from their own proper life, or Proprium, into the "beginning" of spiritual life, are affected with a sense of "fear," which the Lord dissipates as soon as the regenerating man clearly perceives that this illumination is from Him alone, and that it is not a dreamy hallucination of the imagination.

418. "For, behold, I bring you good tidings of great joy," signifies perception that the Word is the Lord, and that the whole Inspired Word is the Gospel, or "Good Tidings," because the whole Word of the Old as well as

the New Testament treats of His Coming into the minds of regenerating men, as has been illustrated thus far concerning the Days of Creation.

419. As all things of the Word in its Internal Sense treat of the Lord alone in His relation to regenerating men, it may clearly be perceived that the Advent of the Lord into the world of time, is not only in the giving of the Literal Sense of the Gospels of the Evangelists, but as often as the Prophecies, Psalms, and the Ancient Spiritual Histories were dictated and recorded, even to the most remote ages, and the Lord Jesus Christ is now as fully present on the earth as at any time in the historical past. The Advent of the Lord into the physical world of time and space is continual, and in general a representative Advent is made in the lowest degree of physical matter as often as each copy of the Word is reproduced from the press, but the True Advent is made only in the life and External mind or "earth" of the regenerating man who with "joy" and gladness receives the Truths of the Word into his will and understanding.

420. "Joy" is predicated of the Affection of Good, and "Gladness" of the Affection of Truth. "Joy" has relation to the heart or Interior representative of the mind, while "Gladness" has relation to the face or Exterior representative of the mind. As there is a marriage of Good and Truth in every part of the Word received into the mind, so the words "joy and gladness" are frequently mentioned together in the same verse of the Scriptures.

Heavenly joy.   Eternal happiness.

421. The "Good Tidings" of the Word, when received into the life of the regenerating man, will, in the "other world" of elevated rational thought, fill his mind with "great joy." This Heavenly joy is from the Lord alone, and in the effort to Love the Neighbor, the constant impulse within his heart is to love others better than himself. This "great joy" does not consist in the gratification of any selfish desire, and his delight arises from the increase of spiritual wisdom, so that through this knowledge from the Word, others may also be led through his intelligence and example, and experience the same holy joy arising from a life and thoughts which are according to Divine Order, by which he is being prepared for that Eternal joy in which his whole future life will be given for the benefit of his fellow men, to which all his energies will be consecrated.

422. Eternal happiness is imparted to those who live in love and faith in the Lord from the Word. The regenerating man enters upon the realization of this joy after the death of natural thought, for then he is within the Kingdom of Heaven which has been forming within him. In the Heavenly State there is a communion of all blessings, in which the peace, intelligence, wisdom and happiness of all are communicated to each other with all the variety of their manifold gifts and talents, and hence it may be conceived how great is the extension of that joy, when the External mind is governed by the Internal, or Heaven.

Unselfish joy. People and nations.

423. They in whom the Love of Self and the World reign, do not know what Heavenly joy is, and it seems incredible to them that there can be any other delight than selfish enjoyment, when yet the joy of Heaven only so far enters the mind as those evil loves are removed. The unselfish happiness which succeeds their removal is so great that it exceeds the comprehension of every man while in merely natural thought.

424. "Which shall be to all people" signifies all whose lives are principled in the Truths of the Word, and specifically by "people" is meant these Truths, or the Affection of Truth in the regenerating man. The reason why Truths are signified by "people," is, because in the Word, those who are governed by a "king" are called "people," and by a "king" is signified Truth. Thus the "King of Kings" signifies the Divine Truth of the Word which governs the lives of regenerating men.

425. "People" and "Nations" are frequently mentioned together in the Word. "Nations," in a general sense, signify all who are receptive of the Celestial principles of Love to the Lord, and specifically is meant this Love, or Affection of Good in the regenerating man, which results from obedience to the Word.

426. In the historical narrative of the Old Testament, the generations of men are distinguished into houses, families, and nations, and throughout the Word these expressions signify the good principles of Love, and of Truth grounded in Love. Thus an accurate distinction is everywhere made between "nations" and "people,"

the former signifying good or evil principles, and the latter true or false principles according to the nature of the subject.

427. As Good is from the Divine Love, the Priesthood of the Old Testament represents the Fatherhood of the Lord, because nations there consist of families and houses, and in the historical narrative, the head of each household is the father who rules in love to his children, and in the patriarchal era, external worship is conducted by the father as a priest of the Lord.

428. The "good tidings of great joy which shall be to all people," fills the man whose Rational Faculty perceives the Interior Truth of the Word; when it is revealed to him that it is not only from the Lord, but constitutes the Lord himself descending through the Internal mind as the Divine Truth, the Son of the Father, or the Divine Love within the Divine Truth of the Word.

429. Thus the Son is not separated from the Father, for the Father is in Him, and He is in the Father, and both these principles of Love and Wisdom are entering the will and understanding of the regenerating man, and yet there is but One Personal Lord who is entering the "earth" of this one man by means of the Word.

For unto you is born this day in the city of David, a Saviour, which is Christ the Lord. Luke 2 : 11.

430. "This day" signifies this state of regeneration. A "City" signifies True Doctrine from the Word accord-

ing to the Truths of the Internal Sense, and its opposite meaning is False Doctrine confirmed from the Appearance of Truth. True Doctrine also implies its reception into the life, for Spiritual Truth has no existence in man until he is nourished by its living within him.

431. "David" in the Word, signifies the Lord as to the Divine Truth, from whom is faith, intelligence, and wisdom, and the name does not mean a physical frame of a man upon this earth in its past history of human events, for throughout the whole Word, names signify Spiritual Principles, and in no case do they mean the apparent persons who represent these principles in the spiritual history of the regeneration of man. Where evil principles are adjoined to the names of representative persons, they signify the evils of the unregenerated Proprium, for no evil can be predicated of the Lord.

432. Concerning "David" it is thus written, "*David my servant shall be king over them; and they shall all have one shepherd:—they, and their children's children, for ever: and my servant David shall be their prince for ever.*"* "*Afterward shall the children of Israel return, and seek the Lord their God, and David their king; and shall fear the Lord and His goodness in the latter days.*"† These prophecies are supposed, from the appearance of literal history, to have been dictated long after the narrative of the history of "David" was given, and yet it is literally declared that he shall be their king and prince: whence it may be evident to every thoughtful

* Ezek. 37: 24, 25.   † Hos. 3: 5.

person that by "David" in the Internal Sense is meant the Divine Truth of the Word, which reigns as a King in the Spiritual World, and this meaning is also the same in all places in the Word where "David" is mentioned.

433. In order to illustrate that the names of kingdoms, of countries, of cities, of men and things, signify Spiritual Principles, without which meaning they are mere dead sounds of words without intelligible coherence, two or three examples may suffice:

"And it shall come to pass in that day, that the Lord shall hiss for the fly that is in the uttermost part of the rivers of Egypt, and for the bee that is in the land of Assyria; and they shall come, and rest all of them in the desolate valleys, and in the holes of the rocks, and upon all thorns, and upon all bushes.

"In the same day will the Lord shave with a razor that is hired, namely, by them beyond the river, by the king of Assyria, the head, and the hair of the feet; and it shall also consume the beard. And it shall come to pass in that day, that a man shall nourish a young cow and two sheep; and it shall come to pass, for the abundance of milk that they shall give, that he shall eat butter; for butter and honey shall every one eat that is left in the land.

"And it shall come to pass in that day, that every place shall be, where there were a thousand vines at a thousand silverlings it shall even be for briers and thorns. With arrows and with bows shall men come thither; because all the land shall become briers and thorns. And on all hills that shall be digged with the mattock, there shall not come thither the fear of briers and thorns; but it shall be for the sending forth of oxen, and for the treading of lesser cattle." [*]

"Therefore, thus saith the Lord God of hosts: O my people that dwellest in Zion, be not afraid of the Assyrian: he shall smite thee with a rod, and shall lift up his staff against thee, after the manner of Egypt. And the Lord of hosts shall stir up a scourge for him according to the slaughter of Midian at the rock of Oreb: and as his rod was upon the

---
[*] Is. 7: 18, 25.

Spiritual correspondences. The Bottomless Pit.

sea, so shall he lift it up after the manner of Egypt.—He is come to Aiath, he is passed to Migron; at Michmash he hath laid up his carriages: They are gone over the passage: they have taken up their lodging at Geba; Ramah is afraid; Gibeah of Saul is fled. Lift up thy voice, O daughter of Gallim; cause it to be heard unto Laish, O poor Anathoth. Madmenah is removed; the inhabitants of Gebim gather themselves to flee. As yet he shall remain at Nob that day: he shall shake his hand against the mount of the daughter of Zion, the hill of Jerusalem. Behold, the Lord, the LORD of hosts, shall lop the bough with terror, and he shall cut down the thickets of the forest with iron, and Lebanon shall fall by a mighty one." *

" And the fifth angel sounded, and I saw a star fall from heaven unto the earth: and to him was given the key to the bottomless pit. And he opened the bottomless pit; and there arose a smoke out of the pit, as the smoke of a great furnace; and the sun and the air were darkened by reason of the smoke of the pit. And there came out of the smoke locusts upon the earth: and unto them was given power, as the scorpions of the earth have power. And it was commanded them that they should not hurt the grass of the earth, neither any green thing, neither any tree; but only those men which have not the seal of God in their foreheads. And to them it was given that they should not kill them, but that they should be tormented five months: and their torment was as the torment of a scorpion when he striketh a man. And the shapes of the locusts were like unto horses prepared unto battle; and on their heads were as it were crowns like gold, and their faces were as the faces of men. And they had hair as the hair of women, and their teeth were as the teeth of lions. And they had breastplates, as it were breastplates of iron: and the sound of their wings was as the sound of chariots of many horses running to battle. And they had tails like unto scorpions, and there were stings in their tails: and their power was to hurt men five months. And they had a king over them, which is the angel of the bottomless pit, whose name in the Hebrew tongue is Abaddon, but in the Greek tongue hath his name Apollyon." †

---

* Is. 10: 24.   † Rev. 9: 1-11.

THE NATURE OF THE WORD OF GOD. 205

An interior signification. The Saviour.

434. Unless these prophetic utterances signified Spiritual Principles, there could result neither sense nor meaning from the words; and if the mind should rest in the mere names, without looking for an inward signification, the Rational Faculty could not acknowledge these passages to be the Word of God. Yet, in the Internal Sense within these strange utterances, the principles are coherent and rational, which the regenerating man will find to be true as he examines, compares and lives the Truth of the Word, for the Internal Sense constitutes Heaven, and the Literal Sense holds the Living Word for man, as he progresses from natural to spiritual life, and enters the " City of David."

435. As "David" signifies the Divine Truth of the Lord, and the Word is the Divine Truth, and therefore is the Lord, so "David" signifies the Word as to the Internal Sense in the mind of the regenerating man, and the "City of David" is the True Doctrine derived from the Internal Sense of the Word, which the Rational Faculty perceives as the Eternal Truth of God, which is born to the perceptions "this day," or in the Third State of Regeneration, and this Divine Truth of the Word is the "Saviour" from sin.

436. This "Saviour" is the " Word made flesh," which, when eaten by the regenerating man, nourishes him with Heavenly Life, and this Divine Humanity can only enter as sin is rejected to make room for the "Saviour," who lifts the regenerating man above his Proprium, and thus redeems him from the power of sin, and this "Saviour" is "Christ the Lord," or the Divine Truth of the Word which "was in the beginning," and which "was God," and who is "the Way, the Truth, and the Life."

437. This Divine Truth of the Word is the Son of God. "*We know that the Son of God is come, and hath given us an understanding, that we may know Him that is True; and we are in Him that is True, even in His Son Jesus Christ. This is the True God, and eternal life.*"* "*Light is come into the world. He that doeth Truth, cometh to the Light.*"† It has been previously stated that no other Principle than the Divine Truth is meant in the Word by the "Messiah," or "Christ"; and they to whom in their regenerating life the Internal Sense of the Word has been revealed, "*have found the Messias, which is, being intrepreted, the Christ.*"‡

438. The Regeneration of man takes place according to the Laws of Divine Order, just as the conception, gestation and birth of every child or creature occurs according to the orderly laws of the physical universe, which are derived from the Laws of Divine Order. Thus the Lord descends to the "earth" of the External mind, from the Internal mind, through the intermediate Rational Faculty, which is prepared for the reception of the Lord, or Interior Divine Truth, by obedience to the Word, which is the Lord Himself received into the life.

439. The Conception and Birth of the Lord Jesus Christ into the Spiritual World, or Rational Faculty of the regenerating man, as narrated in the Gospels, is written purely by the correspondence of the natural order of birth with the Spiritual Birth in the life of a regenerating man. It is according to the Laws of Divine

---
* 1 John 5 : 20.   † John 3 : 19, 21.   ‡ John 1 : 41.

THE NATURE OF THE WORD OF GOD. 207

| The Word is the Saviour. | Confirmation of the Truth. |

Order, that a man should prepare himself for the reception of the Living Truth of the Word; and as he prepares himself with the means given him, so the Truths of the Word enter his mind as into a habitation, for the Word was given that it might be the Saviour, by entering man and thus saving him from sin.

440. This Preparation is made by means of knowledges concerning the Spiritual Principles of the Word, and thus by enlightened wisdom and reason. It is a Law of Divine Order, that as far as man accedes to and approaches the Lord by means of the Word—which he should do altogether as if he had all power from himself in freedom,—so far the Lord accedes to and approaches to man, and by means of the Rational Faculty, conjoins Himself to the regenerating man, by revealing the Spiritual Glory which is within every expression of the Word.

And this shall be a sign unto you: ye shall find the babe wrapped in swaddling clothes, lying in a manger. Luke 2: 12.

441. By a "Sign" or Token, in the Word, is signified a confirmation of Truth in the experience of the regenerating man, united with the study of the Word as a proof that it is so, and therefore it denotes illustration of the Truth from the Word, by which he may examine himself, to perceive if he is in that innocent and childlike state of self-abnegation in which he may "find the babe wrapped in swaddling clothes, lying in a manger."

Signs and Miracles.	A literal miracle.

MIRACLES.

442. The External mind of the regenerating man at first constantly looks into the natural world for "Signs" and Miracles. It looks into the history of nations outside of the Word in the effort to prove the physical occurrences of the facts narrated in the spiritual history of the Word, and in the description of signs and miracles, he first accepts them all as physically true, from a traditional or historical faith which has inculated a reverence for the Word, and from an erroneous opinion concerning the Divine Omnipotence, from which he imagines that "with God all things are possible," until his Rational Faculty is enlightened to see that the Lord never violates His Laws of Divine Order, and that the miracles which are recorded did not have a physical manifestation, but are illustrative of spiritual principles by the laws of correspondence.

443. As soon as the Rational Faculty perceives that the whole Word is a spiritual history of the different States of the Regeneration of men, with infinite variety, adapted to all men on the Eternal Principles of Divine Order, then the whole subject of disorderly physical miracles is at once dissipated, and reverence is implanted for the higher principles which the Word contains.

444. A "Miracle" is a deviation from established natural laws. The External mind of the man who is in natural thought only, is governed by the established laws of his hereditary nature which fill his proprium. The implanting of spiritual life from the Lord through the Internal mind, and enlightening his Rational Faculty by means of the Word, is Super-natural, and is a "Miracle."

445. Such a Miracle deviates from the established or hereditary laws which exist in the unregenerated Proprium, and yet it is according to the Laws of Divine Order. Thus the Rational Faculty of the regenerating man recognizes that within the miracles recorded in the natural language of the Word, there are spiritual principles confirmed which prove its Divine Inspiration.

The Sign of the Son of Man. Physical miracles not true.

All the Miracles have their ultimate culmination in the Literal Sense of the Word, in which they reach the lowest or most exterior degree of natural thought, by the correspondence of physical objects with spiritual principles.

446. "*And then shall appear the sign of the Son of Man in heaven.*" "Heaven" signifies the Rational Faculty enlightened from the Internal mind, which was so called at the close of the Second Day of Creation, which now recognizes that the Divine Truth represented by the Son of Man has appeared in the opening of this Rational Faculty to discern the Living Sense of the Word in which the Lord is Personally present to all who love and obey its Truths, since all the spiritual principles of the Word are from the Lord, and relate to Him alone.

447. Miracles are often recorded in the spiritual history of the Old Testament, concerning the Hebrews, because, in the Word, that nation is representative of the External mind of those who possess the Literal Sense of the Word, and are not aware that it contains an Internal Sense which is Divine Truth, and they represent the principle of external worship which is so exterior, that no true principles of internal worship are discerned, a condition which has always existed in the spiritual history of man, not only in remote ages, but at the present time.

448. When the Literal Sense of the Word only is received, the miracles there recorded are believed in as physical facts, notwithstanding that the laws of the physical world are thereby set aside, and that such interpretation of the Word is not in harmony with the laws of Divine Order from which all natural and physical laws exist. A man in such a state of thought believes in whatever is declared in the Literal Sense of the Word without investigation as to the true meaning, because he has been taught that it is the Word of God.

449. He does not perceive that the Lord in His relation to men has always been the same, and that if it was once possible for miracles to take place in the physical world, such occurrences

Spurious faith.	True faith.

may take place as freely in the present epoch. He marvels at the discoveries which are constantly being developed in the subtle things of the scientific world, which have always existed, but which have not hitherto been manifested, because the world was not ready for their use, and yet all these discoveries are according to the Laws of Order, and for that reason they are not called miracles.

450. If physical miracles, such as appear to be described in the Literal Sense of the Word, were possible, there could be no opening of the Rational Faculty of man, because he would then be compelled to acknowledge certain principles as facts, without freedom to reason whether they were true or not, and what a man is made to believe from appearance, compulsion, or fear, is afterwards dissipated, for it is not true faith.

451. When the Rational Faculty discerns that the Miracles of the Word are spiritually true, the regenerating man freely receives the Internal principles repiesented thereby, and appropriates them into his life, and they remain as Eternal Truth; for into the Internal mind, which is only opened when the Internal Sense of the Word is perceived, nothing enters except by intellectual ideas, which are reasonings concerning what is true, and the ground in which these ideas are received and grow, is the enlightened Rational Faculty, which is illuminated by the Lord alone.

452. If a man to whom the Internal Sense of the Word has been revealed should attempt to believe in the physical reality of the Literal Miracles of the Word, there would be such an opposition and collision between the Internal and External mind, that if the Internal mind should become closed, profanation of the Word would result from the effort to conjoin Truth with falsity; but with the regenerating man whose Rational Faculty is opened to see that all things of the Word have relation to spiritual principles only, this Revelation of the Internal Sense as the Divine Truth becomes to him "none other than the House of God, and this is the Gate of Heaven." * Beyond this Heavenly Portal

---

* Gen. 28 : 17

there is no material barrier for his Rational Faculty to resist, and he can enter and receive all the Light which he is able to bear, because he looks into the Spiritual World which is within the Word, instead of obscurely gazing into the natural world without.

453. But it is not injurious for those men who have no perception of the Internal Sense, to believe in the literal miracles of the Word, for their worship is external, without the internal principle, and no collision or profanation can take place in the mind, because their Rational Faculty is not opened.

454. The belief in the physical miracles of the Word does not contribute anything to an upbuilding of True Faith in the Lord, or the Word, and if such persons should see before their physical sight a multitude of similar miracles, even to bringing the dead physical frame into life, they would not acknowledge them to be done by the Lord, and therefore they would have no effect upon them, for they would not recognize any Divine Internal Principle, any more than they perceive an Internal Sense within the Word. "*If they hear not Moses and the Prophets, neither will they be persuaded though one rose from the dead.*"

And suddenly there was with the Angel a multitude of the heavenly host praising God. Luke 2: 13.

455. In the Internal Sense of the Word, all ideas or expressions which refer to time, signify State, and thence the quality of the state of the regenerating man, or its opposite in the unregenerated principles. "Suddenly," signifies a present state of Affection and Thought which is certain and full on account of the perception that the Word is the Son of God, and that this Word is "Christ the Lord."

The Angel. Divine worship.

456. By the "Angel," is signified the Lord, who is the Divine Truth of the Word, for, in the spiritual sense, Angels represent the Divine Proceeding of the Lord, which is the Word. "Multitude" is predicated of Truth, and "Greatness" or Magnitude is predicated of Good. By the "Heavenly Host" is signified the knowledges of Good and Truth which are from the Word, and "the multitude of the heavenly host" signifies that all these Heavenly Knowledges which have been received into the life of the regenerating man, cause him to confess and worship the Lord, which is denoted by "Praising God-"

DIVINE WORSHIP.

457. The True Worship of God consists in the adoration of His Divine Humanity in humiliation, and in the acknowledgment that in ourselves there is nothing Good nor alive; that in ourselves we are dead, and that we are only receptacles of life and thought from the Lord. The more we possess such inward acknowledgment, the more true will be our humiliation and worship, because our thoughts, words, and actions will be filled with Love to the Lord and the Neighbor, which contain the spiritual principles of Eternal Life. "*O come let us worship and bow down, let us kneel before the Lord our maker.*"

458. This inward humiliation and adoration is represented by "kneeling." In the physical frame of man, the joints of the knees are intermediate between the feet or natural external representative of the External mind, and the thighs, which represent the Affection of Good in the Internal mind. The "knees" correspond to the conjunction of the Internal and External mind, or of Good and Truth in the regenerating man, which takes place by means of the Rational Faculty, from which arises adoration, thanksgiving, and humiliation.

459. "Before" signifies what is Internal, from which all life proceeds to its ultimate effect. "Before the Lord," signifies "Within the Word," for in it alone are revealed those Interior Truths which teach of the Divine Love and Wisdom, and which cannot be imparted from any other source. We therefore "kneel before the Lord" when we receive these revealed Truths into our thoughts and lives.

460. True worship is Internal, for it is grounded in the Interior principle of Love and Faith, and External worship, without this Interior principle, is not true worship. This holy and living principle is the Essential thing of Divine Worship, which should be a constant state of daily life, and true External worship is the manifestation of this Internal principle in the outward life of worldly business and domestic duties, in obedience to the religious, moral and civil laws contained in the Commandments of the Word.

461. All External worship is a formality of Internal worship, for Internal worship is the Essential principle of spiritual life, and to make worship consist of that which is formal, without that which is essential, is but a dead form. They who are ruled by principles of Internal worship, will endeavor to constantly derive spiritual food from the Word, both in the Literal and the Internal Sense. They will do this from Affection for the Truth, and will not try to excuse themselves in their critical self-examination, by affirming that the perishing things of this physical world so engross their thoughts that they have no time or place in which they can open the Word and feed upon the "flesh and blood" within its expressions of love to man.

462. A regenerating man whose Rational Faculty has been opened by the Lord to see Him as the Word, cannot keep its pages closed; for without increasing his wisdom with regular supplies of Heavenly intelligence he cannot live, and his Affections for Good and Truth cannot otherwise be strengthened. A man who attempts to excuse himself from the study of the Word, whereby the Lord is acknowledged, may well doubt

whether the first principles of a regenerating life have entered his mind, because the Divine Truth of the Word enters no farther than a man seeks it in love and freedom, and all spiritual knowledge must be sought from Affection for the Truths of the Word. He who loves the Truth, cannot be kept away from the object of his affection.

463. A regenerating man who worships the Lord from Internal motives is not alone in the world, however isolated he may seem, and he does not murmur nor complain if his fellow-men are not in sympathy with him, although he desires that all may be led to the Light which shines from the Word. He lives consciously in the spiritual world of thought, as well as in the natural world, because everything which he sees, feels or hears, is representative of some Eternal spiritual principle, which becomes more real than the dead objects which surround his external life.

464. In the anticipation of increased spiritual growth, he cheerfully performs every duty which appears at hand, even the most minute, knowing that "*he that is faithful in that which is least, will also be faithful in much*," in all his earthly affairs, and as his work in the Spiritual World is ready for him to take up, the Lord opens his spiritual eyes to perceive his real world.

465. The regenerating man experiences no terror in the thoughts concerning the dissolution of physical life, which so many people dread, for all reference to death in the Word signifies the spiritual death in which the Proprium of man entombs the Rational Faculty. The death of the physical frame of the man who is principled in Internal worship, corresponds to the perishing of merely natural thought, and is thus representative of the entrance into the Spiritual World of thought.

466. He does not assert a superior wisdom to others, nor "occupy the chief seat at the table," for in his humiliation of heart, he knows nothing of himself, and he does not combat to the injury of others, what they hold as true religious doctrine from the Word, but in gentleness and love is ever ready to help all who desire, to that Source of Wisdom to which he has been led by the Lord.

THE NATURE OF THE WORD OF GOD. 215

Internal worship.   Sacrifices and burnt-offerings

They who are in a true state of Internal worship from the celestial principles of the Word, have true wisdom inscribed on their lives, and they immediately perceive whether what they read or hear is Truth or falsity; and when they are asked if it is Truth they simply answer that it is true or that it is not true. Thus it is said concerning them, "*Let your communication be Yea, yea, Nay, nay.*" This constitutes the celestial degree of the mind, or the Third Heaven, which is a state of true wisdom, and is attained in this world by all who immediately apply to life the Divine things they read or hear from the Word, who turn away from their evils, and look to the Lord alone. Such persons, being in innocence, appear to others as though they are infants in comparison with those who possess the pride of self-intelligence. As they do not proclaim their knowledge concerning true wisdom, and do not vaunt themselves in their speech, they appear simple to those who are in worldly thought; yet, when they hear a person speak, they have a perception of the nature of his affections by the sound of his voice, and understand the nature of his intelligence from the words of his speech.

467. The True Worship of the Lord consists in a life of usefulness according to the Precepts of the Word, and is in harmony with the Laws of Divine Order, for it is Essential Life. Public religious worship without this principle is in itself of no avail in salvation from sin, but it becomes Worship to those whose inward motives are principled with Love to the Lord and the Neighbor.

468. In the Old Testament, Divine Worship is represented by sacrifices and burnt-offerings, which signify purification from evils and falsities, which are replaced by the implantation of Good and Truth from the Word, and from the conjunction of these two principles in the External mind, regeneration exists. The man whose life is founded upon the Good and Truth of the Word, which is Love to the Lord and the Neighbor, supplanting the Love of Self and the World, is in genuine worship, for purification from evils and falses consists in desisting from them, and in shunning and holding them in aversion.

Thinking and willing. Rites and ceremonies.

469. The implantation of Good and Truth from the Lord by the Word, consists in thinking and willing what is Good and Truth, and in speaking and doing them ; and the conjunction of both, consists in living from these Precepts ; for when Good and Truth are united in the regenerating man, he then has a new will and a new understanding, and consequently a new life, which is the Lord within him.

470. When a man is thus principled in the life of regeneration in every employment in which he is engaged, there is Divine Worship, for he then has regard to the Divine Principles of the Word in everything which he does. He venerates and loves its Precepts, and consequently he worships the Lord who is thus revealed to him.

471. Notwithstanding the amount of external public worship a man may engage in, no other principle consists of true worship than living according to the Precepts of the Word, for this is true Love and Faith. The man who loves another, and who believes in him, wishes for nothing more than to will and do what the other wills and thinks, for he only desires to know his will and thought, and thus what will be pleasing to him. Thus it is with love to the Lord. "*He that hath my commandments and keepeth them, he it is that loveth me.*" "*If ye keep my commandments, ye shall abide in my love.*" "*This is my commandment, that ye love one another, as I have loved you.*" Thus the life of Love to the Neighbor is the external principle of internal worship, without which principle, all public external worship is meaningless to those who engage in it.

472. Yet it is helpful for those who are in exterior natural thought, to engage in the rites and ceremonies of external worship, even if no interior principle is acknowledged, because all things in this outward worship, are representative of the holy things of the Word, which must be known and obeyed before the Internal Sense can be revealed. Thus the forms of worship of all the various religious organizations are helpful to those who engage

THE NATURE OF THE WORD OF GOD. 217

Danger of formality.	Absence of self-intelligence.

in them, because they become the means of leading their thoughts to the Lord by means of forms derived from the Literal Sense of the Word.

473. Where the Internal principle governs the life of the regenerating man, he may find the External Form of public worship helpful, if he can commingle with those whose minds have been enlightened concerning the Internal Sense of the Word, and in whom the Love of Rule, which is derived from the Love of Self, has been overcome. There is always danger that External public worship will become inoculated with the "traditions of men," by which its Internal principle will become obscured, for External worship is only representative of its Internal principle by correspondence.

474. If each member of a religious society would daily study the Word, and live according to its Precepts, subduing the Love of Self and the Lust of Dominion, looking to the Lord alone, desiring to esteem others better than ourselves, and thus be willing to serve rather than being ministered unto, a heavenly sphere would be formed which would dispel the tendency to become formal and dead. Man has the faculty of knowing more than he lives according to, and when he is permitted to see the glimmering dawn of the Internal Sense of the Word, there is always danger that the pride of self-intelligence will imbue him with a Pharisaical spirit, rather than with that true humility which acknowledges the Lord alone.

475. In order to attain a true state of Internal worship, a man must entirely relinquish the assertion of himself, and take no credit for any good thought or work. His words must be without guile, and inviolable and accurate in the most minute statements concerning every matter, and in all his dealings with men he must be as a living epistle of the Truth of the Word, "known and read of all men." The Truth which seems so clear to him, he must not force upon others who are not yet able to bear it, but he must exercise charity of judgement and adaptation to all for

| A living epistle. | The presence of the Lord. |

the sake of the Truth, and be positive in all righteousness. He must not indulge in combative and useless arguments to gratify his love for superiority over the attainments of others, " knowing that they do gender strife. And the servant of the Lord must not strive; but be gentle unto all men, apt to teach, patient, in meekness instructing those " who desire the Truths which they see manifested in all his words and actions, and which form the corner stone and testimony of his consistent life. *

476. The Proprium of one man in a religious society, often causes such irritation and antagonism, that the sphere of love and unity is destroyed; therefore the Membership of a Society should be formed by a careful and discriminate reception of such persons who in freedom declare that their sincere endeavor is to live according to the principles upon which it is based, and any deviation of members from those principles should be at once remonstrated with in the spirit of love, and if the antagonism is persisted in, such members should be permitted in freedom to withdraw, with the expressions of good will from those who remain.

477. Men who are being regenerated, have their Proprium to contend with, until it is entirely put off, and the opinion of every man must be held in freedom; but before becoming a member of a religious society, he should consider well its statement of principles, and decide for himself whether he wishes to be governed by them, for there must be an orderly government of a religious society.

478. In all religious worship where the Word of God is known, it forms the Source of Divine Instruction, and although from the Literal Sense alone, any doctrine may be confirmed to favor the Proprium of man, yet the Truths of the simple Precepts of Life as contained within the Commandments, are everywhere taught, and these cause the Lord by means of the Word to be present in all forms of worship.

479. With this principle implanted in the life of the worshippers, all peculiar rites and ceremonies belonging to each religious

---
* 2 Tim. 2: 24, 25.

denomination, are representative of the Spiritual Principles or the Word, and they are adapted to the states of those who hold membership in the various societies, for the Lord leads all by the quality and quantity of spiritual light which they are the most able to bear, and the regenerating man whose Rational Faculty has been opened to discern the Interior Truth of the Word, recognizes the Guiding Hand of the Lord, and is only filled with thoughts of charity towards others, even if they condemn him for not affiliating with them in their stated occasions of religious worship.

480. The Truths of the Word are taught by means of parents, religious teachers, religious books, and by reading directly from its pages. All of these means are provided by the Lord, and by them, the Truth simply enters the understanding, but not into the will or heart; but when the regenerating man obeys these Truths, obedience is turned into love, and thus he is filled with Affection for them, and this Good and Truth united internally and externally in the mind or life, constitutes the Lord or the Word immediately in him, and forms the true principle of Internal and External worship.

481. *"For where two or three are gathered together in my name, there am I in the midst of them."* Where "Two or Three" are mentioned in the Word, " Two " is predicated of Good, and " Three " of Truth, and in a general sense, these numbers signify all who are principled in the Goods and Truths of the Word.

482. To be principled in Truths, is to know them and obey them, and to be principled in Goods, is to do them from pure love for them because they are from the Lord, and this is the meaning of being " gathered together in my name," because " Name " signifies the quality of life which results from the conjunction of these Divine Principles from the Word in the " midst," or the Rational Faculty of regenerating men. Thus the Word is the Lord received into the lives of those who love its Truth, and is the Center of all Divine Worship, because it is " in the midst of them."

483. Concerning the nations of this earth, who have not the written Word of God, they are in ignorance concerning the prin-

Gentile worship.	Perverted worship.

ciples of Good and Truth which are from the Internal Sense, but those who obey the Truth according to the light which is infused into their minds, which is natural Love to the Neighbor, are in the Affection of Natural Good without the Internal principle, and they are gifted with a Conscience which is illuminated according to whatever true principles of life exist within their religious doctrines; and although their doctrines are not formed from the prevailing Literal Word, they are formed from traditions derived from this ancient Word.

484. The Mercy of the Lord is universal and everlasting, and is extended to every individual man. The great majority of men who are born in this physical world possess no knowledge of, or instruction from the Word, and it is not their fault that they are ignorant of the Lord who has thus revealed Himself, and not having had the Word in this world, they have not profaned its Divine Truth. All persons are saved from evil, who live in the essential principle of a good natural life from spiritual motives, because this is the "ground" in which the Seed of Truth from the Word will spring up and bear fruit when they are instructed concerning its interior principle. A man is responsible for what he has the privilege of knowing, from which it may be concluded to what a degree of condemnation those persons bring upon themselves in shutting out spiritual light from their minds, who have the Word in their possession, and do not regard its Divine Contents.

IDOLATRY.

485. Idolatry is perverted worship, and contains no inward spiritual principle, but its external form is derived from the Science of Correspondences, which is the science of representation of things in the natural or physical world to illustrate spiritual principles. By this Science, it may be known what spiritual principles are signified by animals of all kinds, and what by mountains, hills, rivers and fountains; what also by the sun, moon and stars; and thus it may be understood why worshippers

have turned their faces toward the East in their Adoration of God, and why they are inclined to make themselves carved images of horses, oxen, calves, lambs, birds, fishes, and serpents, and place them in their houses and other places, in a certain order, according to the spiritual principles of the mind of the regenerating man to which they correspond, or which they represent.

They have placed similar things in their temples, and have worshipped the images themselves as sacred, not knowing that they are only representative of sacred principles, and to worship the representative of a Heavenly Principle is idolatry.

486. From this perversion of worship have originated the idolatries which have filled the whole earth, as well Asia, as Africa, Europe and America. Hence originated the idolatry and mythology of ancient Greece, where the Divine Principles were turned by that people into the mythological gods, over whom they made one supreme, whom they called Jove. The Sacred Writings of the Asiatic nations speak of the Deluge, and refer to other particulars which are treated of by the law of correspondence in the Word, and the mummies of the ancient Egyptian representatives are yet extant, and may be seen in museums.

487. The writings of the Al Koran are received by a large number of the Oriental nations, and they acknowledge the Christ of the Gospels to be the Son of God, the wisest of men, and the greatest of prophets, who came into the world to teach men. These religious doctrines were permitted by the Lord to arise, that they might be instrumental in extirpating the idolatry of Asia, by their accommodation to the genius of the Eastern nations; for they contain principles of Truth to be found in both the Old and New Testaments, and all Truth is derived from the Word.

In the order of spiritual education, the apparent Truth that the Lord came into this world in a physical form, first exists in the mind so that there may be a conception that He is in the Human Form, and thus there is one Being from whom all men derive their life. The believers in the Al Koran do not acknowledge the Son of God as a man to be the God of Heaven and Earth, because the Oriental nations believe in one God as the Creator of the universe, but do not comprehend how He Himself could come into the world and take upon Himself the form of man.

488. There are many also among the more enlightened nations of the world who cannot comprehend how the Lord assumed the Human Principle, neither can they discern how He comes and enters the world, until they resist the evil of Self-love, and look to Him in the Word, do His will, and perceive Him enter their own mental world by the Word assuming control over their lives, in place of the hereditary evil principles which reign before the work of regeneration begins. Then will the Rational Faculty be enlightened to see that the Son of God born into the world, is the Word given to man, and that the Lord Christ is the Divine Truth of the Word from whom all wisdom and intelligence is derived, by which the regenerating man "is renewed in knowledge after the image of Him that created him," and thus Christ, or the Word "*is all and in all*,"* and that Idolatry is Self-Love, or the perverted worship of Self.

MUSIC, AND THE SOUND OF THE VOICE.

489. In the external forms of religious worship, Vocal and Instrumental music have always been employed in "Praising God." Music signifies the harmonious conjunction of the will and understanding with the Lord by the Truth of the Word, and is expressive of joy and gladness for the means of salvation from sin. It denotes exaltation and triumph on account of victory over spiritual enemies.

490. This conquering of evil and falsity is the Glorification of the Lord; the entrance of the Lord of Hosts into the External mind, and is the manifestation of His Divine Humanity, or the Internal Sense of the Word, to the Rational Faculty, which is then in glory or illumination from Heaven. "*All the earth shall worship Thee, and shall sing unto Thee; they shall sing to thy name.*"†

---
* Col. 3 : 10, 11.   † Ps. 66 : 4.

THE NATURE OF THE WORD OF GOD. 223

The voice in singing.   Origin of music.

491. Singing denotes Glorification of the Lord, and to glorify the Lord signifies to live in concord with the Truths of the Word, from which results a glad recognition that the Lord is the Word, for then the heart is in that state of delight which corresponds to the expression of praise which bursts forth into song. The unition of voices in choirs or chorusses signifies agreement between affection and thought, action and speech, or the conjunction of spiritual principles in the regenerating man. Sound corresponds to the Affections, and the words uttered in speech correspond to Thoughts, wherefore Affection utters sound, and Thought speaks, and the voice sings the words of praise.

492. Musical instruments correspond to the delight of the Celestial and Spiritual Affections. Wind instruments, of sustained vibrations, such as the organ, flutes and horns, are expressive of the Affection of Good, while stringed instruments of percussion, such as the harp, or pianoforte, are expressive of the Affection of Truth, on account of the correspondence of sonorous vibrations with the Affections, and all the different qualities of musical tones have a spiritual correspondence. The sound of the trumpet signifies the revelation of Divine Truth from the Word. In the quality of the tone of the human voice in speech, there is an inward indication of the spiritual quality of the person who is speaking, so that the sound of a person's voice reveals his interior nature to those whose spiritual perceptions are acute, similar to the manifestation of character in the expression of the eye, or in the features of the countenance.

493. While the exquisite sense of hearing conveys sounds containing thoughts to the mind, these sounds are actuated by spiritual influences, although in Appearance they seem to originate in the physical world; but as no thought originates in the physical world of nature, and as melody and harmony are instrumental in exciting both the Emotional and Intellectual Affections, it may be clearly evident that Music does not originate in the natural world, but is a euphonious blessing descending from Heaven to assist in leading the material thoughts of men to those

The ear.	Glorification.

Celestial and Spiritual principles from which it is derived, and to which it corresponds. When a man speaks, although the sound of his voice is heard in the natural world, yet the thoughts which lay within the sound, originate in that spiritual world in which his mind lives.

494. The ear receives the sound of the voice, and discerns the thoughts which are thus conveyed. Words uttered by the voice which do not contain thoughts are dead sounds. Thoughts concerning principles or doctrines which do not contain Living Truths are also dead. Hearing signifies perception of the Truth, and obedience to its commands, for the ear receives the sounds which contain words; and words contain thoughts; and thoughts transmit Truths from the Word, which are presented before the Conscience to be incorporated into the life, so that the Lord may be glorified in the regenerated life of man. Thus it is said in the Word, "*If any man have ears to hear, Let him hear.*"

495. Sacred Song, expressed in holy anthems and hymns of praise, when devoutly used in the rites and forms of External Public Worship, becomes truly representative of the Celestial and Spiritual principles of Internal worship, and is like a Triumphal Car which conveys the King of Kings, the Divine Truth of the Word, to the receptive mind through the gateway of the sense of hearing. The acceptance of this Truth, by living in obedience to its teachings, will lead to that State of the delight of the Spiritual Affections which the Melody, Harmony and Quality of musical sounds express.

496. The glorification of the Lord takes place in the elevation of man's spiritual nature to the perception of Heavenly principles within the Word, and the regenerating man gives praise and "glory" to the Lord, when in his heart he acknowledges that there is nothing Good in and of himself, and that he can do nothing from himself, because he perceives that all Good is from the Lord, and that He is Omnipotent.

THE NATURE OF THE WORD OF GOD. 225

Constant humiliation.   Glory.

497. When a man is in this state, the Lord gradually removes his Proprium in which his Self-love resides, and his Internal mind is opened so that the Divine Love and Wisdom can enter with power; hence it is necessary that every man should be in a constant state of humiliation concerning himself, in order that a true acknowledgment of the Lord as the Word, shall enter the mind.

498. In the Order of Regeneration by the Internal Sense of the Word, the Divine Truth enters the Rational Faculty and thence into the External mind, redeeming from evil and falsity, which are thereby removed, so that the Heavenly Principles of the Word are exalted, and "the multitude of the heavenly host," the knowledges of Good and Truth within the regenerating man, cause him to praise the Lord from internal perception, and thus by his life proclaim the ascription, "*Gloria in excelsis Deo!*"

Glory to God in the highest, and on earth peace, good will toward men. Luke 2 : 14

499. This ascription of praise signifies that the enlightened Rational Faculty of the regenerating man perceives the Word in its Interior Divine Light, which shines as "Glory" from the Lord by means of the Revelation to the mind of the Internal Sense, because the Lord is the Word, and the Internal Sense is in the Light of Heaven which proceeds from the Lord as a Sun, which Light is the Divine Truth descending through the highest or inmost principle of the Internal mind.

500. The "earth" refers to the External mind which is filled with tranquillity and delight arising from this interior perception of the Word, when this mind does not rest in the Appearance of Truth, and is not in con-

fliction with the Rational Faculty. While the regenerating man is engaged in temptations and combats with his spiritual enemies, there are intervening states of peace, when the Lord opens his interior perceptions.

501. "Good will toward men," signifies that the will is now made receptive of the Divine Love, which is also perceived by the Rational Faculty, and that it is Infinite toward all "men," or the spiritual principles which constitute men, for the opening of the Internal Sense of the Word to the regenerating man, reveals that the laws of the spiritual world within the Word are Laws of Divine Order, and thus the "pearl of great price" has been found. Thus the "multitude of the heavenly host," the angels and spirits of the Word, or its Goods and Truths actuating the spiritual life of the regenerating man, glorify the Lord and bring peace to the conflictions in the External mind when his thoughts are ruled by love, and all his words and acts are expressions of "goodwill."

THE INFLUENCE OF ANGELS AND SPIRITS.

502. Every regenerating man is taught and governed by the Lord by means of Angels and Spirits, although this fact is not apparent while he is in the material degree of thought concerning the Word, but when the Internal Sense is revealed to him he is in constant and sensible communication with angels, because the sight of his spirit is open to perceive the things or principles of the Spiritual World, for he is a spirit, and his mind is then in the spiritual world of thought. Man, of himself alone, cannot act otherwise than wickedly, and avert himself from the Lord, being incited by the evil spirits of his own nature; for all evil spirits

THE NATURE OF THE WORD OF GOD. 227

The ministry of angels.	The spiritual eye.

thus act from the evil itself which they have done and have incorporated into their lives. Notwithstanding these influences, every man is responsible for the evil he does, and in his own freedom turns himself away from the Lord who never changes in His Love, for He alone gives life to men that He may bless them: and yet man of himself alone, in his own strength, cannot possibly live righteously and turn toward the Lord, excepting by the ministry of Angels. Angelic men cannot live or think excepting from the Lord alone, for they are celestial and spiritual men whose hereditary Proprium has been overcome and supplanted by a Heavenly Proprium. While a man is living merely in the natural world of thought, he does not perceive the influence of Angels and Spirits, because he is in a state of freedom between good and evil, so that he may turn to the Lord as though he had all the power in himself, and if he then felt that he was in any way influenced to will and think, it would tend to destroy that freedom which the Lord sacredly preserves with every man to eternity.

503. It will not be difficult to comprehend the fact of angelic influences, when it is considered that all our knowledge of earthly things has been infused into our minds by other men who have lived, or are yet living in this world, by means of written thoughts in books, or by immediate teaching, for these men have been, or are, spirits within the physical frame. The Lord has permitted regenerating men on earth to see Angels and Spirits, or the Celestial principles of Good and the Spiritual principles of Truth, which they represent as they exist in the Word, by means of the opening of the spiritual sight, or the Rational Faculty, when it is needful for the Interior principles of Divine Revelation to be disclosed, in order that man in his regeneration may perceive the Laws of Divine Order, and his faith in the Word be more fully established.

504. The Eye of the Understanding which looks into the Spiritual World of the Word, and there sees the Angels and Spirits, is the Rational Faculty in intelligent order of thought. The

Spirits looking through the eyes of others.	The "dead."

"spirits of the departed" are sometimes permitted to see the things of the natural world through the spiritual eyes of other men, or through their Rational Faculty, which first feeds upon things of material thought from the Literal Sense of the Word. The "spirits of the departed," here signify the Understanding of those regenerating men who have been elevated above material thought concerning the Word. When a man whose Rational Faculty has been enlightened, writes intelligently, or discourses rationally concerning the material things of the Literal Sense of the Word, the spiritual eyes of other regenerating men who have "risen from the dead," may, through these materially expressed ideas, look into the natural world of thought as represented in the Literal Sense of the Word, and see its coherence and life from Internal Spiritual Principles, which the enlightened reader may perceive in perusing the material words of these pages, if he is in a life of obedience to the Truths of the Word, and if he sees that these thoughts are true in his own experience.

505. If all men were principled in love and faith in the Lord by means of the Word, they could then perceive the reality of the communion of angels and spirits with man, but it is injurious to the spiritual welfare to seek communication with the dead, for then the mind turns to creatures rather than to the Creator, and is not led to the Creator and Source of spiritual life, the Word, for Divine guidance. The Communion of Angels and Spirits with man is Spiritual Instruction by means of the Goods and Truths of the Word.

506. No angel ever manifests himself to the man who seeks intercourse with the "dead," for angels desire to lead men to the Lord, while evil spirits seek to avert them from heavenly life and lead them into evil, and such is their influence over a man who permits himself to be led by them, that they assume angelic wisdom and appear as angels of light, so that he who looks to the "dead," is deceived, and becomes more and more credulous, until he believes in principles which are utterly opposed to the Laws of Order, and is even led to believe in what is termed the

Materialism.	The two angels.

de-materialization of disembodied spirits, or in their assuming at will the physical substances of the corporeal frame and then dissipating them.

507. Thus instead of being led to the Word and to its Interior Principles, he becomes a materialist in thought. Departed spirits do not again assume the conditions or substances of natural existence, because they have entered a spiritual degree of life with which there is no connection with the things of this world excepting by the laws of correspondence.

508. If a man should look to the "dead," or to those who assume that they are in communication with them, for information concerning the future events of his earthly life, he would be in great danger of losing his spiritual freedom, by means of which only he can be regenerated, and he would then become the victim of hallucinations which originate from the evil spirits of the Proprium who desire to communicate with the affections of those who seek them instead of the Lord. They take upon them such form and fraudulent representation, that their emanations often appear to be from good spirits who have entered the succeeding life, but who never seek to communicate with the unregenerated Proprium of man, for they have passed from this natural state of existence, and have no more identity with the events or persons who are in this physical world, than we are aware of their surroundings and circumstances in the world to which they have been removed.

509. The preceding thoughts concerning the influences of angels and spirits have reference to the natural or literal meaning of the words " angels " and " spirits," which in their essence are the principles of Good and Truth from the Word, which re-create the will and understanding of regenerated men. These are the Two Angels who are ever attendant upon the regenerating man to lead him to the Lord.

510. As the recipient vessel signifies the same as that which it contains, so regenerating men who are receptacles of Good and Truth from the Word are also to be understood as Angels or Spirits, according to the quality of their affection of Good or

Evil Spirits. Angels.

Truth; but Evil Spirits are the evil and false principles of the Proprium, which exist from the Love of Self and the World, and which influence the Affections and Thoughts of unregenerated men, therefore men who are governed by their own hereditary natures, are also to be understood by evil and false spirits. The "Dead," signifies those evil and false principles of the Proprium which are destructive to spiritual life, which have been overcome and removed, while "Departed Spirits" signify those who have departed from, or have rejected their evils and falses, and have become recipients of the Truths of the Word, of whom it is said, "*The hour is coming, in the which all that are in the graves shall hear his voice, and shall come forth.*" "*And the graves were opened; and many bodies of the saints which slept, arose, and came out of the graves after the resurrection, and went into the holy city and appeared unto many.*" "*The hour is coming, and now is, when the dead shall hear the voice of the Son of God, and they that hear shall live.*"

511. In the highest sense, by an "Angel" is understood the Lord, who is the Inmost Life within the Word, from whom all Love and Wisdom proceeds, and by "angels" and "spirits" is understood the Good and Truth which is from Him with angelic men, in whose lives Love and Wisdom from the Word have been implanted. Good and Truth are in the knowledges which are derived from the Word, whereby regeneration enters the External mind, and when these knowledges are obeyed from a living spiritual principle within the regenerating man, they become Truths, but if they are not vivified by a spiritual principle of obedience by which they are made alive, they become merely Scientifics, or external knowledges of the Literal Sense of the Word.

512. Thus when "Angels" are mentioned in the Word, the mind is to be abstracted from the natural thought of angelic persons, and the spiritual principle which the name represents, is to be understood, and this same method of interpretation is to be used concerning the Internal Sense in all parts of the Word, in order that the mind may perceive the spiritual truths which are there first personified to the state of natural thought.

Progression.   Confirmation.

And it came to pass, as the angels were gone away from them into heaven, the shepherds said one to another, Let us now go even unto Bethlehem, and see this thing which is come to pass, which the Lord hath made known unto us. Luke 2: 15.

513. "And it came to pass," signifies progression in the life of regeneration. "As the angels were gone away from them into heaven," signifies more interior perception of the Good and Truth of the Word in the Rational Faculty, which is illuminated from the Internal mind, or "Heaven." The "shepherds said one to another," signifies that in the comparison of the Truths of the Word which lead the regenerating man to the life of obedience, the perception of their Divine origin by means of the Internal Sense becomes more evident.

514. "Let us go," signifies the desire for further illumination in the progress of regeneration. "Even unto Bethlehem," signifies the confirmation of these Interior principles within the illuminated Rational Faculty. "And see this thing which has come to pass," signifies that the confirmation of these Interior principles is to be established by a careful study of the Word, in which only "this thing," or these principles may be seen within the Literal Sense which holds the spiritual contents. "Which the Lord hath made known unto us," signifies that the True Divinity of the Word is from the Internal Sense, which can be revealed by the Lord alone to the man whose life is filled with Affection for its Living Precepts; for self-intelligence cannot discover the Life which is within the Internal Sense.

Coming with haste.	The espoused Mary.

And they came with haste, and found Mary and Joseph, and the babe lying in a manger. Luke 2: 16.

515. "And they came with haste," signifies that the confirmation of the Interior principles of the Word is certain, and that they will be fully established in the mind of the regenerating man, for in the Internal Sense "to come with haste" does not denote "quickly," but "surely." Hastening involves time, and in the spiritual world there is no Time, but instead of time there is State. Thus the coming "with haste" relates to a correspondent quality of state of the "Shepherds," or the Truths of the Word in the regenerating man, which lead to Good, or to a perception of the Internal Sense, which is a result from the Affection of Truth, and these "Shepherds" find "Mary and Joseph."

516. "Mary" here signifies the Affection for the Truths of the Literal Sense of the Word in the External mind, within which the conception occurs. "Joseph" here signifies the perception of the Rational Faculty which perceives the Divine Truth of the Internal Sense The Divine Truth of the Internal Sense is the Lord's Divine Humanity, or the Divinity of the Word made Living within the regenerating man.

517. As "Mary" is the espoused wife of "Joseph" at this time, or state, the mentioning of the two words, or principles together, signifies the conjunction of the Literal Sense of the Word, by the Affection for its Truths in the External mind of the regenerating man, with the

THE NATURE OF THE WORD OF GOD.

| Joseph is not the father. | Succession of life. |

perception of the Spiritual Sense within, in the Rational Faculty, which, like Joseph, protects and provides for "the Babe lying in the manger." Although "Joseph" is not the father of the child, the regenerating man recognizes that the Divine Love flowing through the Internal mind into the Rational Faculty, is the Father, and that this Internal Principle which is conceived from the Father and born from the Affection for the Truths of the Word, is the Holy Child which is now "lying in the manger."

THE ORDER OF SPIRITUAL DESCENT.

518. In the succession of human life, man receives through his father, his very soul or life in the order of hereditary descent, and from his mother he derives not only the external covering which constitutes the physical frame, but also the corporeal or material principle of the External mind. The soul itself is implanted through descent from the father, which begins to be clothed with a physical form from within the mother, from whom it thereafter entirely derives its nourishment and growth, until after its birth in the world, and in due time according to the order of natural life, the child lives independently of the mother's nourishment.

519. In the same order of re-creation, according to the laws of spiritual correspondence, the Internal mind of regenerating men is from the Divine Love of the Father by the Internal Sense of the Word. The enlightened Rational Faculty which receives the Divine Truth of the Word is the Son of God; for the receptacle of the Word becomes of the same quality and nature as the Truth which it holds. The child is formed and nourished by the Affection for the Truths of the Literal Sense of the Word which have been received into the External mind, which are the material substances from which the spiritual body of the Divine Infant is developed in the regenerating man. By the expression "material

substances" is not meant physical substances, but the exterior or material principles of the mind which receive the Exterior Truths or Literal Sense of the Word, and which is commonly understood under the expression of "Material Thought." The expressions of the Word when thought of only as physical occurrences, occupy the plane of material thought.

520. At the time or state of the birth of the Divine Truth in the Rational Faculty, the External mind still contains the hereditary principle of the Proprium, which is to be supplanted by the growth of the child Jesus within the regenerating man. The work of regeneration is to be accomplished by putting off the hereditary Proprium, so that the External mind may be united to the Internal by means of the intermediate Rational Faculty, and the progress of this conjunction is signified by the developing life of the Lord Jesus in the world of the regenerating man's spiritual experience, as it is given in the representative history contained in the Literal Sense of the Word.

521. The Internal Principle of this re-created life is the Father, and the Babe is now "lying in the manger," to receive instruction from the principles of the Internal Sense of the Word which are to nourish and strengthen the child Jesus, in entering and overcoming the hereditary Proprium of the External mind, through combats and temptations, by which the evil tendencies are to be subdued. Thus the Righteousness of God will be fulfilled, and the External mind redeemed from iniquity. As this is the work of the Lord in the regenerating man, there can be neither self-righteousness nor self-intelligence implanted where He reigns, for the Lord by acts of redemption in overcoming evil in man makes Himself the Righteousness of man. "*And this is His name whereby He shall be called*: THE LORD OUR RIGHTEOUSNESS."

522. Righteousness is acquired by exercising the works of righteousness, which are, to shun all evil, look to the Lord by the study of, and obedience, to the Precepts of the Word, and in all things fulfilling the law of Love to the Neighbor. Thus a man will show his faith by his works, for "every tree is known by its

fruits," and "except your righteousness shall exceed the righteousness of the Scribes and Pharisees, ye shall in no case enter into the kingdom of heaven."

523. By these acts of righteousness or redemption in the regenerating man, the hereditary evil in the Proprium of the External mind is to be overcome, so that the Lord can descend from the Internal mind into the External, and there assume the place occupied by the Proprium as it is resisted and removed. In this order the Literal Sense of the Word is made Living or Spiritual, and the External mind is gradually united to the Internal, as the Divine Truth of the Internal Sense is revealed and developed in the life. Thus the Lord assumes the Humanity and makes it Divine in every regenerating man.

524. The conjunction of the Lord with the External mind must be mutual and reciprocal on the part of man, and is effected by his acceding to the Lord, and the Lord to him; for it is a fixed and immutable law, that as far as man accedes to the Lord, or voluntarily resists and removes his evils, so far the Lord accedes to him, for He seeks to enter all men with spiritual heat and light, which is Goodness and Truth from the Word. Thus God becomes Man, and man becomes filled with God in one person, and as the Interior life is not his own, he becomes a Divine man, or an angel in Heaven; thus an angelic man is formed by the Word.

525. When the Literal Truths of the Word are filled with life by obedience to them, the regenerating man is actuated by the Affection of Truth from which the Son of Man is born, and when the Internal Sense is revealed in the Word to the Rational Faculty, the Son of God is disclosed, for He is the Internal Divine Truth of the Word manifested in the "flesh" or will of the regenerating man.

526. The perception of the Lord in the Rational Faculty is first born from the primary Truths of the Literal Sense which are written according to the Appearances of Truth, as they seem to the hereditary nature of man. As evil is overcome, the Lord

enters from the Internal mind through the Rational Faculty by the Internal Truth of His Word, and the Appearances of Truth which exist in the External mind concerning the Literal Sense of the Word are gradually dissipated. Thus the Lord in the regenerating man successively puts off all the hereditary material principle of thought of the Word, the human principle derived from the "Mother Mary," as it exists in the External mind which is derived from the natural human mother.

528. The soul which descends through the natural father is the real man, but the covering which is formed from the natural mother, exists only from the soul within it. The external covering of the soul, or the spiritual body which holds it—the External mind—is fed and sustained at first by natural principles of thought, such as exist in the Literal Sense of the Word.

529. When the corporeal principle of the Proprium, which was from the natural mother by hereditary descent, perishes, or when the hereditary material human principle of the External mind is dissipated, as the Literal Sense of the Word is shown to have no life in itself alone, the Soul or Internal principle of man is awakened by the perception of the Internal Sense of the Word, and lives in spiritual life to Eternity. Death must precede resurrection, and with those who attain any advanced degree of the life of regeneration, this death of the merely natural principle of the mind, takes place previous to the opening of the spiritual eyes, or Rational Faculty.

530. During the process of regeneration, the perception of the Divine Principle within the Word is in a state of obscurity and humiliation, which is represented in the Gospel by the sufferings of the Son of Man, and which is described in many places in the Prophecies and the Psalms.

531. The Order of Regeneration of every man must proceed from natural ideas to spiritual perceptions concerning the Word, because he is first born into the natural world of thought, and the External mind is formed from natural and material ideas of things by means of the natural senses.

The Lord is King.	The babe in the manger.

532. When the Interior Principles of the Word have enabled the regenerating man to overcome the hereditary evil of the Proprium, the Lord will reign as King over the External mind from its union with the Internal mind. The conjunction of these two principles of the mind constitute the regenerated man, which is the glorification of the Lord in man, and is represented by the Resurrection.

533. When such a state of conjunction shall be attained by means of the Living Principles revealed in the Internal Sense of the Word, the regenerating man will act from the Lord in freedom with all the power of his individuality, and all the Good which he will then will and do, and all the Truth which he will then think and speak, will be inscribed upon his heart, or in his Will, and thence it will be inwardly in all his actions and speech.

534. Thus the Son of God in the regenerating man will be united to the Father, and the Father to him, and the Human Principle of the Word will be made Divine, because its Internal Sense is not only perceived within the Literal Sense, but these Interior principles have been incorporated into the life. Then the regenerated man will use all things according to order, without being tempted to sin, because his whole life will be the Lord in him, and he will be free from bondage to his Proprium, for *" If the Son therefore shall make you free, ye shall be free indeed."*

And when they had seen it, they made known abroad the saying which was told them concerning this child.
Luke 2 : 17.

535. The " Shepherds," or Truths of the Literal Sense in the External mind of the regenerating man have led the Rational Faculty to perceive the " babe lying in the manger," which is the Infant Jesus, or the innocent state of Affection for the more Interior Truths of the Word, for which the Rational Faculty is awaiting clearer reve-

lation. "Abroad" signifies external principles, because removed from the center. To make "known abroad," signifies the perception of the Rational Faculty, which now from the External or Literal Sense of the Word discerns its Internal principles, which are contained within the Exterior natural expressions, and are now clearly "made known" or disclosed to the External mind.

536. Internal principles are made known to the External mind whenever a regenerating man views any earthly objects with his physical eyes, and is thence led to think of the spiritual principles of the Word. The eye itself is the sight of the spirit making "known abroad," or looking into the natural world, and this principally with the object that from external things he may perceive internal principles, so that from objects in this world he may continnally be led to reflect on the realities of the spiritual world and Eternal Life, because it is for the sake of that life that he was created and lives for a short time in this world.

537. "The saying which was told them concerning this child," signifies that the perception of this Divine Revelation by the Rational Faculty is received into the innocent state of the Interior Affections represented by the "Child." The innocent are those who are in the Interior Affection of Good, and this is the state of innocence of those who are in mature thought concerning the Interior principles of the Word. Innocence consists in acknowledging the Lord, or the Truths of the Word, and

| The Corporeal, or Sensual principle. | Death and life. |

believing by obedience that all Goodness and Truth are from Him by the Word; and thus there exists a state of willingness to be led by the Lord, and not by Self.

THE CORPOREAL PRINCIPLE OF THE MIND.

538. The Corporeal Principle of the External mind is simply a receptacle of sensations communicated by means of the external senses which act through the corporeal-physical frame. When these senses cease to act, the physical body dies and turns to corruption. The physical frame is simply a mechanical instrument through which the corporeal principle acts, this principle being the most exterior of the mind, and they are so intimately connected that they act in unity. When merely natural thought dies, the corporeal principle of the External mind still exists with its senses, so that this death is not destruction, but is the entrance to a more acute perception of life, which actuates the corporeal principle.

539. In the Word, the corporeal things of the physical frame are in no case to be understood when they are mentioned, but the corresponding spiritual principle,—even when the operation of any of the senses is mentioned,—is to be perceived, which belongs to interior thought, to which the senses are but instruments of communication. The external sensual principle, or senses, have relation to the Internal senses or perceptions, and the external senses operate through the nervous system of the physical frame, in order that they may serve the Interior principles of the mind during the life in this world.

540. If these corporeal senses of the natural mind rule over the Internal perceptions, the man is in a state of spiritual death, but regeneration reverses this order and awakens the Internal perceptions into life, and when Internal principles govern the External, the regenerating man lives according to the laws of Divine Order. The Internal principles of the mind can only be perceived by means of the Internal Sense of the Word, by which man alone has spiritual life.

541. All the senses have relation to the Will and Understanding, and therefore to the Internal principles of the mind. The Sense of Sight has especial reference to the Intellectual principle, or Understanding, and this is the first perception that is active in the order of regeneration, for, by the Internal Light, the Conscience is awakened to perceive the Divine Truth of the Word; consequently it belongs to the Intellectual or Rational Faculty to believe, to acknowledge, to know, and to see the Truth, and also what is Good, and this is true Faith.

542. The Sense of Hearing has reference to the Will as well as to the Understanding, and denotes obedience from Affection, because what is heard, passes into the Internal Sight, or Understanding, where it is conjoined to the Will, and is carried forth into act, or life. Hearing, therefore, implies perception and obedience.

543. The Natural principle of the mind is much more easily persuaded and influenced by the spoken and eloquent words of a speaker than in personal reading, because the tones of the voice, being received by the ear, affect the emotional nature which exists from the Will, or Affection; but when the Rational Faculty of the regenerating man is opened, he spiritually hears every Divine Truth of the Word that is presented to his understanding, for he not only perceives the Truth, but he obeys it, and needs no physical voice to either persuade or enlighten him, for he has the Word, which is the Voice and Mouth of the Lord.

And all they that heard it wondered at those things which were told them by the shepherds. Luke 2 : 18 .

544. "All they that heard it," signifies that the Internal principles of the regenerating man, acknowledge, perceive, and obey the Internal principles of the Word. "Wondered" also signifies a state of perception, and these Internal principles have been revealed to the Rational Faculty by the "shepherds," or Truths of the

Keeping the testimonies.   Pondering.

Word, which having been obeyed in Loving the Lord and the Neighbor, have led to the perception of the Internal Sense of the Word.

But Mary kept all these things, and pondered them in her heart. Luke 2 : 19.

545. As previously illustrated, "Mary," or "mother," signifies the Affection for the Truths of the Literal Sense of the Word, which exists in the External mind, and that all "these things" or principles have been "kept" or lived according to by the regenerating man to whom the Internal Sense of the Word has been revealed. "*My mother and my brethren are these which hear the Word of God, and do it.*" "*Blessed are they that keep His testimonies, and that seek Him with the whole heart.*"

546. To "ponder them in the heart," signifies to think interiorly concerning the Truths of the Word of God. The "heart" denotes the life of Affection for the Good and Truth of the Word, and the regenerating man having endeavoured to keep these Literal Precepts, is filled with love for the Divine Truths which now appear, and his meditation is concerning them, for they begin to develop his mind with rational intelligence concerning spiritual principles. "*O how I love Thy law! it is my meditation all the day.*"

And the shepherds returned, glorifying and praising God for all the things that they had heard and seen, as it was told unto them. Luke 2 : 20.

547. By "the shepherds returned," is signified the application of these Interior Truths of the Word to life

P

and thought, in order that all natural ideas derived from the sense of the Letter of the Word, shall be instructive to the Rational Faculty, and from these "things" all external objects of the physical world shall be suggestive of Spiritual Principles.

548. "Glorifying," signifies the union of the Internal mind with the External by means of the enlightened Rational Faculty, which perceives the Internal Sense of the Word, within its External or Literal Sense. This union is not effected at once, but successively through the Six Days of Creation, during which the External mind is in continual progress toward union with the Internal, and becomes Divine when both are absolutely united in the Seventh Day, when the regenerating man has become an angel.

549. "Praising God," signifies true Internal worship of the Lord, which results from the union of the Good and Truth of the Word in the Will and Understanding, by which the regenerating man is saved from all his evils, which salvation he acknowledges to be by means of the Word which is from the Lord alone. Thus he ascribes all glory and praise unto the Lord for all the principles which have been revealed in the Word, and which have been obeyed and manifested in the life, for when the Internal mind is filled with Affection for the Good and Truth of the Word, the External mind must manifest it through the spiritual body, and thence through the physical frame, toward his fellow-men in his speech and actions.

Telling.	Natural thought.

550. "As it was told unto them," signifies the perception of these Interior principles of the Word, for Perception is an internal "telling," wherefore to "perceive," in the historical narrative of the Word is expressed by "telling," and also by "saying," as may frequently be found in both the Old and New Testaments.

THE MATERIAL BODY OF THE LORD.

551. The nature of the External mind of man is such, that he is incapable of forming an idea of thought concerning abstract principles unless he associates them with natural ideas which enter from the tangible things of the physical world, by means of sensual objects, or such things which are perceived by the external senses. Therefore, lest all conception of the Divine Nature of the Lord should perish with men whose thoughts are entirely immersed in corporeal and worldly ideas, the Lord Jesus Christ, or Jehovah, has manifested Himself by the Word. First, according to the thoughts of the natural mind in the Literal Sense of the Word, which is written according to natural ideas of objects in this world, whereby the External mind may gather the primary principles of spiritual life as declared in the Ten Commandments. If nothing more had been given to man than the Literal Ten Commandments, he could be saved from his sins by means of their entrance into his life, but he would have no spiritual history to study, within which there is an Internal Sense which reveals the principles and order of different states of regeneration.

552. All the historical narrations and prophetic utterances of the Word in the Literal Sense, are the earthly or material clothing of the Internal Sense, in which the Lord more fully reveals Himself as He appears in Heaven, as the Word, or Divine Man, for as it has been previously illustrated, the Word in the Internal Sense is in the Divine Human Form, because it is the Lord Himself.

When He enters the natural mind by the Literal Sense, obedience to the Literal Truths prepares the Rational Faculty to perceive its Interior meaning, which reveals that the Lord is the Word, who takes upon Himself the hereditary nature of man, by assuming the corporeal principle of the Literal Sense which is received by the natural External mind.

553. By the correspondence of spiritual principles with natural facts in the order of regeneration, the Lord is born as another man in every respect within the Interior life of the regenerating man, who advances from obscurity to clearer perceptions of the Divine Truth. Jehovah is the Father of this Interior Divine Life, which is the Son of God, or the Interior Truth of the Word, which is made Living by affectionate obedience. The Virgin Mother from whom the Lord is born in man, is the Affection for the Truth of the Literal Sense of the Word. The Literal Sense is the sensual or corporeal principle of spiritual truth which fills its corresponding receptacle in the sensual or corporeal principle of the External mind of the regenerating man, who is elevated from this sensual or material principle of thought, when he perceives that the Internal Sense is from the Lord, and that it is the Lord uniting man to Himself by the Word; and thus the Infinite Nature of the Lord or the Word, differs from finite men, because He is Divine in Himself, and men are only receptacles of this Life.

554. In the first state of regeneration, the External mind thinks from the sensual or corporeal principle concerning the Word, and rests in the Appearances of Truth there recorded. This corporeal principle of thought exists from the hereditary evil derived from the mother, or natural parentage, which closes spiritual perception, and which is only opened through the orderly progress of regeneration. In this corporeal state of thought, the mind only recognizes the corresponding corporeal principle of the Word, which is given to man in this form, so that the Lord may reach every condition of thought whereby the regenerating man may be led from sensual ideas to spiritual thought, and be saved from his sins. Thus the corporeal Appearances of Truth which attribute perverse

Assuming perverse attributes.	Man only is evil.

qualities to the Nature of God on account of the perverse nature of man, by correspondence with the corporeal principles in the unregenerated Proprium, constitutes the hereditary evil which adheres to the personification of the Son of Man in the Word, which is tempted, suffers, and is crucified, for only evil principles can be tempted, or suffer, or be killed.

555. When the Internal Sense of the Word is revealed to the regenerating man who is undergoing the preparatory trials and temptations, the perverse qualities represented in the Appearances of Truth are shown to be falsities, which exist in the Literal Sense on account of the evil nature of man, and these Appearances are dissipated when he understands the nature of and overcomes his Proprium. Thus the Lord, in the Word, assumes the hereditary evil nature of man, and bears the iniquities and evils of mankind, in the Appearances of Truth, so that He might reach men in their lowest ideas of thought and redeem them from sin.

556. When the regenerating man is enlightened as to the True Nature of the Word, and his own fallacies are removed, he perceives the spiritual significance of the Resurrection of the Lord, and discerns in what manner the Corporeal Body of the Lord is dissipated, in which were the Appearances of Truth, but the Actual Truths of the Literal Sense as embodied in the Precepts of Love to the Lord and the Neighbor, constitute the Material Substance of the Word, and form the Material Body which is made Divine in the regenerating man, and which ascends with its Material "flesh and bones" into Heaven.

557. The Divine Nature of the Lord, which is the Internal Life of the Word, is not susceptible of evil, but in order to enable man to overcome evil with the strength which He can impart from the Word, which finite man cannot possess in himself, because he is only evil, the Lord is born in the "earth" as another man, in His Own Word, and thence in the regenerating man by the spiritual correspondence of the conception and birth in the order of physical life; by the Appearance of Truth in the Word, for the sake of man, he has taken upon Himself the sins and infirmities

of men, and bears them, "*That it might be fulfilled which was spoken by Esaias the prophet, saying, Himself took our infirmities and bare our sicknesses.*"

558. Thus the Son of God is conceived, is carried in the womb, and is born in the perception of the Rational Faculty of regenerating men as other men are born into this physical life, by the correspondence of the spiritual principles of the Word received into the life; and by the same laws of correspondence in this spiritual personification of the entrance of the Lord into the regenerating man as the " Holy Child," He is instructed as another man in the growth of the spiritual perception, and continually advances in Heavenly knowledge, to the end that men may attain the highest degree of life for which they were created. Thus, in assuming the Human Principal of the Word, the Lord becomes a Man like a man in the world of natural thought, with this exception, that in entering man and progressing from infancy to manhood in the order of regeneration, He is Infinite and Uncreated, while the man whom He enters is a finite created receptacle of this Divine Life from the Word.

559. The Lord assumes the Humanity of the Word in the External mind of the regenerating man as rapidly as he desists from evil and relinquishes his Proprium, which is accomplished by shunning evil and resisting temptation, and acknowledging the Lord alone to be the Giver of spiritual life and strength by means of the Word. The Lord is not to be thought of as in a corporeal frame like a physical body in the natural world, but the mind when thinking of Him is to be abstracted from time and space, and He will take the Form of the DIVINE MAN when He is discerned as the Inmost Life of the Spiritual Principles of the Word. His Human Body cannot be thought of as either great or small, or of any defined stature or features, because this would limit the idea of Him to a fixed position or wandering through the space and time of the physical universe, neither could a conception of His Omnipresence enter the mind, and instead of thinking of the spiritual principles from Him which constitute

finite men, the thoughts would be dissipated and wander away from the Word, and what is called "Nature" would be substituted for the Living God who forms the Inmost Life of the Word. This Living God is THE MAN in the Human Form, by and from whom all men are created, and sustained in existence. (§ 146.)

560. The Literal Sense of the Word received by the natural mind of the regenerating man is the Material Human Body of the Lord. When these Literal Truths are obeyed from Affection, the Rational Faculty is opened to perceive the Interior Truths of the Word, which, when loved and obeyed, are made Divine, and thus the Humanity of the Lord is glorified; and when the Rational Faculty perceives the Divine Life of the Word to be from its Internal Sense, the Lord rises with His Whole Body, and the Literal Sense of the Word is revered and esteemed Holy, because it is the external manifestation of the Lord's Material Body to the material principle of the External mind, or Natural Thought, and this Body has never appeared to any man excepting in the Literal Sense of the Word. The word "material" here refers to material or natural ideas of thought, and not to physical substances, for the Ultimate Human Principle does not consist of physical flesh and bones, but is the most exterior plane of thought concerning the Literal Sense of the Word, and this is the Human Substance which exists from the Inmost Principles of the Word, and which in the order of regeneration is made Divine Substantial Truth in the man who is being regenerated.

561. Nothing which is Good and True in itself, or which is of the Lord, can ever die. The Body of the Lord which is slain upon the cross, is the Appearance of Truth in the Literal Sense of the Word, which "*bore our sins in His own Body on the tree, that we being dead to sins, should live unto righteousness.*" "*This is my Body which is broken for many.*" The Crucifixion represents the violence done to the Actual Truth of the Literal Sense by those false doctrines which disparage the effort to obey the simple Precepts of the Word. These fallacious teachings are confirmed from the Appearances of Truth, which tend to favor the Love of

The Material Body.	The Spiritual Body.

Self, and which lead to the crucifixion of the Life of the Word in their adherents, thus obscuring all spiritual perceptions, culminating in the death of every receptacle of regenerating principles from the Word, so that to such persons, External worship becomes a dead form, with no Living Jesus within.

562. The MATERIAL BODY of the Lord is the Actual Truth of the Literal Sense of the Word which holds the Internal Sense, and which is "sown a Natural Body," and "is raised a Spiritual Body." "*But he spake of the temple of His Body. When therefore He was risen from the dead, His disciples remembered that He had said this unto them; and they believed the Scripture.*" "*Unto them that look for Him shall He appear the second time without sin unto salvation.*" The SPIRITUAL BODY of the Lord consists of all regenerating men who have received Him by means of the Living Truths of the Word, and have been, and are being re-created in His Form. "*Now ye are the Body of Christ and members in particular.*" Thus the Lord glorifies, or makes the Human Principle of the Word Divine in the regeneration of the man to whom the Internal Sense of the Word is revealed. "*I will praise Thee, O Lord my God, with all my heart, and I will glorify Thy Name forever more.*"

A MIRACLE OF THE THIRD DAY.

And the Third Day there was a marriage in Cana of Galilee; and the mother of Jesus was there. John 2:1.

563. This Spiritual Marriage occurs in the External mind of the regenerating man after a full state of preparation signified by the "Third Day." In illustrating the State represented by the Second Day, it was shown that "Galilee" signifies the man who has externally lived in Love to the Neighbor, without being aware that there is an Internal Principle either within the Word or the mind which is receptive of the Internal Sense. It was also illustrated that a "City" signifies the doctrine of Truth from the Word. "Cana" is a village of Galilee.

564. Where "Cities" and "Villages" are mentioned together in the Word, "Cities" signify the Internal principles of the mind, and "Villages," which are outside of cities, denote the External principles. "Cities" and "Villages" denote these principles, because on the physical earth, men who have minds containing Internal and External principles, live in, and constitute cities and villages.

565. "Cana of Galilee" here signifies the exterior principles of the Natural mind; for the Love of the Neighbor must literally exist in the Natural Affections and be manifested in the external life, before either the Internal principles of the mind, or the Word, can be

revealed, and this state of life has always been found among the Gentile nations of the world who have not had our written Word, and especially with those who have obeyed the Truth which has been given them in any form.

566. It has also been shown that the Proprium, or the hereditary evil self-hood of man, exists only in the External mind, and that this evil is to be overcome in temptation by resistance on the part of the regenerating man, without his freedom being violated, and it has been illustrated that the Work of Regeneration consists in putting off the evil of the hereditary Proprium, so that the Heavenly principles of the Internal mind shall govern the External. This union of the Internal and External mind, by the reception of the Internal and External Truths of the Word, is called a "Marriage," and all Marriages which are alluded to in the Word, signify the union of Good and Truth, or of the Love and Wisdom of the Word in the Will and Understanding of regenerating men.

567. In this Heavenly Marriage which takes place in "Cana of Galilee," the Bride is the vivified Proprium of the External mind of the regenerating man, and the Bridegroom is the Lord, who inseminates principles of innocence, peace, and love, from the Word, as rapidly as evils and falses are resisted and overcome. Hence results that blessedness which is typified by earthly marriages, and which derive their happiness from these Spiritual Principles of the Word, although mankind are not aware of this fact.

The mother of Jesus. The disciples.

568. "And the mother of Jesus was there." It has been shown that the "Mother" is the Affection for the Truths of the Literal Sense of the Word, which has governed the life of the regenerating man previous to the Third Day, and from this Affection, the perception of the Divine Love and Wisdom of the Word illuminates the Rational Faculty, and is born as from a mother "there," or in that State of the perception.

And both Jesus was called, and his disciples, to the marriage. John 2 : 2.

569. "Jesus" signifies the Divine Good, and "Christ" the Divine Truth of the Word, and the words JESUS CHRIST, signify the Divine Marriage of Good and Truth in the Will and Understanding of the regenerating man, making the natural mind Spiritual, or Divine, or God-man in him who is regenerated by the Living Principles of the Word. The reception of these Living Principles of the Word into the mind and life brings salvation from sin, and thus the Lord Jesus Christ is the Saviour.

570. The "Disciples" are all the Goods and Truths of the Word which have entered the memory, and thence have been incorporated into the life of the regenerating man. The first thought which arises in the mind when the word "Disciples" is mentioned, is concerning men who follow the Lord, but when the mind is abstracted from persons and places, it perceives the spiritual principles which govern the life of a disciple, and the Internal meaning appears, so that it may be seen why the Word

treats of spiritual principles, both good and evil, by means of the representations of persons, places and things.

571. By a reference to the Table of the Proper Names in a complete Concordance, the signification of the names of persons and places mentioned in the Word will be found as they appear in their original languages, which when interpreted by the science of correspondence, clearly reveal the spiritual principles represented by these names recorded in the Literal Sense, and which will greatly confirm the reader in the Internal evidence of the Divine Revelation of the Word.

572. By "Called" to the Marriage, is signified the desire of the regenerating man for the conjunction of the Divine Good, or Jesus, with the "Disciples," in order that he may increase in spiritual wisdom, and thence fulfil the object of his creation, which is spiritual usefulness to his fellow-men.

And when they wanted wine, the mother of Jesus saith unto him, They have no wine. John 2: 3.

573. By "Wine," is signified the Interior Divine Truth of the Word which is now desired, or "wanted," by the regenerating man, and which is also expressed by "calling" Jesus and the Disciples to the Marriage. This is the "Wine" which is represented by the Holy Supper, which when received through the Rational Faculty, stimulates the Interior Affections, and opens the understanding to perceive Infinite intelligence within the Word.

574. At the State of regeneration which is represented by these expressions, the "Mother of Jesus" or the

They have no wine.   Desires for clearer revelation.

Affection for the Literal Truth which has been lived thus far, "saith unto him," or perceives that there must be an Interior meaning within the Literal expressions of the Word, and desires a clearer understanding of its Truths, on account of the many conflictions which arise in the Rational Faculty concerning the Literal Sense, which, in itself alone, if no deeper meaning is perceived, has no spiritual life, which is signified by "They have no wine."

Jesus saith unto her, Woman, what have I to do with thee? mine hour is not yet come. John 2: 4.

575. "Jesus saith" signifies instruction from the Word, and "unto her" denotes that this instruction is implanted in the External mind from the Affection for the Truths of the Literal Sense, and that at the proper time, or state, the Divine Providence will reveal clearer perceptions of the Word.

576. As Good and Truth are from the Word alone, and as the principles of the External mind represented by "Woman," originate from the Lord, lest it should appear to the regenerating man that the Affection for the Truth of the Literal Sense originates in himself, because these desires for clearer revelation are manifesting themselves,—and there is danger that the hereditary Proprium will appropriate these desires to itself,—therefore it is written, "Woman, what have I to do with thee!"

577. A careful study of the Literal Sense of the Word will reveal that in the spiritual narrative of the Gospels, the Son of God in no place acknowledges "Mary" to be His mother, because in the regeneration of man, the Lord Jehovah is both the Father and Mother of spiritual life. As in the physical birth of man there must be an instrumental mother, who does not originate the life of the child, so in the spiritual birth of man there must be an instrumental "Mother," which is the Affection for the Literal Sense of the Word. This Affection is also from the Lord, for nothing but evil originates with man. "What have I to do with thee?" is therefore an admonition for careful self-examination in regard to the true Source of spiritual desires or Affections.

578. "Mine hour is not yet come" signifies that until this Source of spiritual life is clearly perceived, the regenerating man has not arrived at the state in which he will be able to bear the revelation of the Internal Sense of the Word, for until his mind is fully prepared by a life in which the Lord alone is recognized in the Word, the Internal Sense would be profaned if it should be prematurely revealed.

579. Words, or natural expressions in themselves, do not constitute the Word of God until the Truths within these expressions are obeyed, for Divine Revelation is the opening of the Rational Faculty to perceive Divine Truth, or the Son of God within the Word, and it becomes a Revelation only to him who from Affection obeys the Divine Truth.

THE NATURE OF THE WORD OF GOD. 255

The perception of ideas.   Servants.

His mother saith unto the servants, Whatsoever he saith unto you, do it. John 2 : 5.

580. "Saith," in the Word, expresses the communication of thought, which in this world is manifested by speech, writing, or gestures. The communication of thought signifies the perception of ideas. By means of the Affection for the Literal Truths of the Word in the External mind, or the "mother," a perception is communicated to the "servants."

581. A "Servant" denotes what is inferior or beneath considered with respect to what is superior. It has been frequently illustrated that things which are beneath, signify external principles, and that superior things represent internal principles. "Servants" therefore denote the exterior natural principles of the External mind, by which the life of the regenerating man is manifested in this physical world of natural thought.

582. When a man is being regenerated, inferior or external principles are made subordinate to superior, or internal principles. The exterior principles become "servants," and the interior principles become "lords" or "rulers," and thus the Lord reigns in the "heaven" and upon the "earth," and all regenerating men become "servants" of the Lord. The Lord speaks to man only by the Word, and to the "servants" or natural principles of the External mind, which receive the Literal Sense of the Word, it is clearly revealed to the perception of the regenerating man as a Divine command, "*Whatsoever he saith unto you, do it.*"

And there were set there six water-pots of stone, after the manner of the purifying of the Jews, containing two or three firkins apiece. John 2 : 6.

583. "And there were set there," signifies in this state of the progress of regeneration. Concerning "Water-pots," it has been shown that "water" signifies Truth from the Word. All vessels in the Word signify receptacles of spiritual principles. "Water" signifies Natural Truth, or the Literal Sense of the Word, and "water-pots" signify the scientific principles of the External mind which receive this Truth.

584. These Scientific principles are the ideas formed from impressions received from terrestrial and physical things by means of the senses, so that when Spiritual Truths are treated of in the Word, they first take a natural form in the mind, from which the Rational Faculty gathers the spiritual meaning when the Laws of Correspondence are understood. Without the natural ideas first appearing as they are given in the Literal Sense of the Word, the External mind could have no tangible objects by which the Truth could be reflected into the Rational Faculty,

585. The "Water-pots" are of "Stone," and a "Stone" also signifies Truth. In the highest sense it signifies the Lord, who is called a "Rock" when the Divine Truth of the Word is represented. It also denotes the lowest form of Truth, which is called Natural Truth, or the fundamental Literal Sense of the Word, and thus the

| Natural ideas. | Cleansing from evil. |

Ten Commandments are represented as being written upon "Tables of Stone," which signify the external plane of the Word, upon which the Literal Sense is inscribed. The "water-pots" being of "stone," signifies the quality of the scientific principles of the External mind, that they are formed from Natural Truths, or the Appearances of Truth in the Literal Sense with which the External mind is first instructed.

586. There are "Six water-pots" set there. "Six" denotes the states of labor and combat which the External mind undergoes in the preparation for the reception of the Internal Sense of the Word, by which the Appearances of Truth are to be dissipated, for all progression in the regenerate life is attained through struggling with the Appearances of Truth until the hereditary Proprium is subdued and overcome, therefore "Six" denotes the full state which precedes the conjunction of the External Truths with the Internal. As the Word of God is in the Human Form, all the spiritual principles which are contained therein have their corresponding receptacles within the minds of regenerating men.

587. "After the manner of the purifying of the Jews," signifies that the cleansing of evil must begin in the regenerating man by means of such Truths as he can apprehend sensually, or by means of the mental senses, and that it is according to the laws of spiritual order that purification, or resisting evil, must be done in the natural mind and in the natural world, because the Internal or spiritual mind thinks and wills in and

through the natural principle of the External mind, while man lives in the corporeal frame in this physical world.

588. The word "Jew" is derived from the word "Judah," and in the highest or Inmost Sense denotes the Lord in His Divine Love, and in the Internal Sense it denotes the Word, therefore the Lord is born as a "Jew," in the Rational Faculty of the regenerating man, when the Internal Sense is revealed. In the narratives of spiritual history, the "Jews" are representative of the principles of the External mind, or Literal Sense of the Word, as indicated by the rites and ceremonies of external worship.

589. When these External principles, or "Jews," have no life from Internal principles, the Love of Self is not subdued, although the external forms of religious worship may be rigidly adhered to, and continually observed. Therefore the Internal Sense cannot appear to such men, for their ideas of the Word are merely natural. The "purifying of the Jews" therefore represents the carrying into the natural principles of the mind, the Truths indicated by the Works of the Law in the Internal Sense of the Word, the way for which is prepared by the effort to obey the Commandments of the Word.

590. "Containing two or three firkins apiece," refers to the capacity or measure of the "water-pots," and therefore signifies the degree of spiritual conjunction, or Truth made Good by obedience, which these receptacles of the mind contain. In the spiritual interpretation of

the Word, the containing receptacle signifies the same principle as the contents which it holds. For example, the world contains men who possess minds containing spiritual principles, wherefore "world" signifies the mind of man, and this is the "world" where the Literal Sense of the Word has its culminating history.

591. "Firkins" are also receptacles, and represent minor Truths as compared with "water-pots," which form the complex. Where "Two or Three" are mentioned together in the Word, "Two" is predicated of Good, and "Three" is predicated of Truth, and the two words signify the conjunction of both principles. In this verse they denote that all the Truths of the Literal Sense of the Word must be received into the External mind and be made Good by the active life of obedience, so that the literal law of Love to the Neighbor shall be fulfilled in the details of daily life before its spiritual meaning can be perceived.

Jesus saith unto them, Fill the waterpots with water. And they filled them up to the brim. John 2 : 7.

592. "Jesus," or the Divine Love which is within the Word, now communicates to the "Servants" the importance of filling the "water-pots with water." The "water-pots" are the scientific or intellectual principles of the External mind, which are to increase in wisdom from the "water," or Literal Sense of the Word, which contains Truth adapted to the natural degree of the mind. The Understanding of the regenerating man is

to be filled or gifted with every knowledge and variety of scientific instruction which can be comprehended and received into the memory, which, when applied to the true meaning of the Word as the Internal Sense is revealed, will aid in opening the inexhaustible mine of spiritual wealth which there lays concealed beneath the surface of the Literal Sense.

593. The more advantage which the regenerating man can secure in every privilege to receive instruction in all branches of science and art, the greater capacity will he possess for usefulness in aiding others to understand the Word, for all knowledge of physical science is from the Lord, although it appears as if it originated with men of rare mental ability.

594. The Internal Sense of the Word is not revealed to the mind of the regenerating man without earnest effort on his part. The External mind must first be filled with the contents and coherence of the Literal historical narratives of the Word throughout. It must be read and re-read until its expressions are fixed in the mind in their order, so that false doctrines and perversions will not act as obstacles to the understanding of the Internal Sense, from isolated interpretations being used to confirm fallacies. The Science of Correspondence should be learned by means of the Word which is written according to those spiritual laws. The Word of God must be studied with all the powers of the mind, in order to see the Lord within. "*And ye shall seek me, and find me, when ye shall search for me with all your heart.*"

595. "And they filled them up to the brim." In the study of the Literal Sense of the Word from the Affection of Truth, the scientific principles of the External mind are filled, beginning with the natural expressions and the Appearances of Truth in which the Word is

Filling up to the brim.   An important decision.

first presented, comparing one portion with another, and obeying the simple Truths of Life as the mind receives them, until the Rational Faculty begins to act, and discovers the antagonisms and conflictions which now begin to appear, and which exist from the Literal Sense alone, before its Spiritual Sense is seen.

596. In this state the External mind is filled "up to the brim" with the Literal Sense, because it has got to the highest boundary to which it alone can lead, and now the understanding begins to look for some rational explanation of the apparent inconsistencies which in many places begin to be manifested, and which were not previously observed.

597. When this confliction is seen, combat and temptation begin in the mind of the regenerating man, and doubt and despair cloud his perceptions. The Literal Sense in itself alone gives no satisfactory answer, for it has not life in itself until it is made living, but when it is made full "to the brim" in the mind and life, the seeker for Divine Truth whose Rational Faculty has been awakened, can only call upon the Lord for enlightenment, with the determination to make it the effort of his life to know from whence the Divinity of the Word proceeds, and in what it consists.

And he saith unto them, Draw out now, and bear unto the governor of the feast. And they bare it. John 2: 5.

598. In answer to this prayer, the Lord leads the regenerating man to perceive that the Word contains an

| The Governor. | Eating and drinking. |

Interior principle, and this perception results from instruction concerning its true nature, that it treats of spiritual science concerning the history or successive states of regeneration, rather than concerning physical science and earthly events. This perception is borne, or disclosed to the "Governor of the feast." The "Governor" is that principle of the Rational Faculty which arranges and disposes into order the receptacles of the External mind which contain the knowledges of the Literal Sense of the Word.

599. The Rational Faculty has also an External and Internal principle. The External principle is formed by the Affection of Truth, and is called the "Governor," and the Internal principle is formed by the Affection of Good, and is called the "Ruler." The "Governor" being formed and developed by Affection for the Truths of the Literal Sense of the Word which bears them forth into life, it discriminates between the Appearances of Truth and the essential Truth of the Word. The "Feast" signifies eating and drinking from the Word. To "Eat" signifies to live according to the Truths of the Word, and to "Drink" signifies to imbibe instruction or doctrine from the Word which teaches how to live.

600. "And they bare it," signifies that the external principles of the mind, or "Servants," are subservient to the "Governor" as the Literal Truth is presented for its disposal, for it is now disclosed from the study of the Word that it has an Interior meaning.

THE NATURE OF THE WORD OF GOD. 263

The Ruler.	Obscure perception.

When the ruler of the feast had tasted the water that was made wine, and knew not whence it was, (but the servants which drew the water knew,) the governor of the feast called the bridegroom. John 2:9.

601. The "Ruler of the feast" is the Internal principle of the Rational Faculty which is formed by the Affection of Good from a life of obedience to the Truths of the Word, and this principle now controls the nourishment which is derived from the Word. "Had tasted the water," signifies the Perception of Truth within the Literal Sense. As physical meat and drink correspond to spiritual food and nourishment from the Word, so "Taste" corresponds to the Perception and the Affection for spiritual food and drink. "That was made wine," signifies that this Literal Truth of the Word has a Living Principle within it, for "Wine" signifies the Divine Truth of the Word, and that the Natural expressions have a spiritual meaning, and to "taste" signifies the Perception of the "Ruler" that the "water was made wine."

602. "And knew not whence it was," signifies that although the Perception has been developed that there is a spiritual meaning to the Word, its origin is not yet clearly perceived, whether it is merely illustrative of the Spiritual Truth of the Word, or is Divine Revelation from the Lord alone.

603. "But the servants which drew the water knew," signifies further progression in the development of this

Drawing water. The Bridegroom.

Perception by "drawing" the "water" by the study of the Word, without which no Spiritual Truth can enter the mind, from which instruction a clearer knowledge of the Literal Sense of the Word serves as the foundation for a more Interior perception of its Internal Sense, for all knowledge of the Word in the spiritual discernment of its Divine Truth can only be imparted by a diligent study of its Literal contents.

604. "The governor of the feast called the bridegroom." The "Bridegroom" is the Lord, or the Inmost Life of the Word, who now enters the External principle of the Rational Faculty through its Internal principle, which from the Affection of Good enlightens the Perception of the Affection of Truth. The "Bride" is the Affection of Truth in the External mind which has received instruction from the Literal Sense of the Word, and the Affection of Good is to be united to the Affection of Truth, as husband and wife. This union constitutes the Heavenly Marriage from which is born the Perception of the Rational Faculty which discerns the Internal Sense of the Word to be from the Lord alone, and that the words which disclose these Interior Truths to the mind which is prepared to receive it, are not the invention of the self-intelligence of a man, but are from Divine Origin, revealing what always has been within, is now, and ever will be in that Word which is "IMMANUEL, GOD WITH US."

THE NATURE OF THE WORD OF GOD. 265

Communication of thought.   Good wine.

And saith unto him, Every man at the beginning doth set forth good wine; and when men have well drunk, then that which is worse: but thou hast kept the good wine until now. John 2 : 10.

605. "Saith unto him," denotes a continuance of Perception, because by "saying" is meant Communication of Thought, and Thought is an influx of Perception. "Every man at the beginning," signifies the state of man in the preparation for a regenerate life, indicated by the "beginning," which is the State of Reformation, when the "earth was without form and void," when all the knowledges in the External memory appear to originate from himself. In this state, the regenerating man is filled with self-intelligence concerning his knowledges and own opinions in the interpretation of the Literal Sense of the Word, and if he possesses and has read the words revealing the principles of the Internal Sense, he feels exalted above others on account of his imaginary spiritual intelligence, which is but an Appearance of "good wine," which emanates from his Proprium, for when the Lord is perceived within the Internal Sense of the Word, the regenerating man humbly acknowledges that he is but a receptacle of life, and that in himself alone he is dead, therefore he neither exalts himself, nor condemns others who as yet do not see Spiritual Truths in the light of his experience.

606. When men from natural principles of thought imbibe the Interior Truths of the Word, without these Internal principles governing their lives, although they

Orderly thought.   Spiritual intemperance.

may delight in searching into Interior doctrines, and learn even the science of correspondences of natural things with spiritual principles, their minds become filled with reasonings to confirm theories which agree with their natural ideas, and thus their thoughts become material and are inverted from the principles of Divine Order, for all true spiritual development proceeds from Interior motives of love and obedience.

607. "And when men have well drunk, then that which is worse," signifies the spiritual drunkenness which results from the self-intelligence of the Proprium. *"But they also have erred through wine; and through strong drink are out of the way, the priest and the people have erred through strong drink, they are swallowed up of wine, they are out of the way through strong drink; they err in vision, they stumble in judgment."* *

608. When men investigate spiritual principles without their lives being guided by obedience to the Truths of the Word, they fall into errors of judgment, because they are led by sensual and philosophical knowledge only. When the thoughts are formed from reasonings concerning terrestrial and earthly objects, if the mind rests in these alone, erroneous opinions will obscure the perceptions, and although such persons "have well drunk" from the fountain of the Word, both in its Literal Sense and Interior interpretations, and think themselves more awake in mental attainments than others, they are in a profound spiritual sleep, for self-

* Is. 28 : 7.

Keeping the good wine. The consummation of the marriage feast.

intelligence is only imaginary wakefulness. "*Woe unto them that are wise in their own eyes, and prudent in their own sight! Woe unto them that are mighty to drink wine, and men of strength to mingle strong drink.*" *

609. "But thou has kept the good wine until now." It is in this Third State of Regeneration that the Rational Faculty perceives the Internal Sense of the Word, from the regenerating man having drunk of the "water" from the well of the Literal Sense, until the Lord has revealed the Living Water, or "good wine," when from the Affection of Good the "Bridegroom" enters the Affection of Truth.

610. This is the consummation of the Marriage Feast of the Third Day, and the Rational Faculty is now awakened into life, and the Light from the Internal Sense of the Word illuminates the Internal principle of the Rational Faculty to perceive that the Lord Jesus Christ is the Inmost Life of the Word, and that He has come in "power and great glory" to the perceptions of the regenerating man, to whom He says, "*From henceforth ye know Him, and have seen Him.*"

This beginning of miracles did Jesus in Cana of Galilee and manifested forth His Glory; and His disciples believed on Him. John 2 : 11.

611. The limits of this work preclude the further illustration of the Third State of Regeneration, and the thoughtful reader will observe the coherence of one part of the Word with another when interpreted by the Spiritual Principles which have always

---
* Ps. 5 : 21.

existed within the Literal Sense, and from which the order of true Spiritual History may be seen. Thus the true meaning of the narration of Miracles may be perceived as orderly spiritual facts in the regeneration of men, but disorderly when accepted literally as physical signs, for no physical water was ever miraculously or supernaturally converted into physical wine.

612. All the incidents and miracles which are narrated in the correspondential language of the Literal Sense of the Word, are representative of different states of regenarating men, or of the evil and false principles of the unregenerated Proprium. It will be simply noted that the Resurrection described in the Gospels, takes place on the Third Day according to prophecy, and this Resurrection is the awakening of the Rational Faculty in its Internal principle to receive the Lord Jesus Christ as the Word, who is the "LORD GOD ALMIGHTY, WHICH WAS, AND IS, AND IS TO COME."

THE FOURTH DAY OF CREATION;

OR,

THE FOURTH STATE OF REGENERATION.

And God said, Let there be Lights in the firmament of the heaven to divide the day from the night; and let them be for signs, and for seasons, and for days, and years. Gen. 1 : 14.

613. Before the "Beginning" of Regeneration, man is in a state of spiritual death, and his life is re-created by the Lord by means of the Good and True principles of the Word. The first dawn of Spiritual Light begins by living according to the Truths of the Literal Sense which have been planted in the External memory, and this is Scientific Faith, or Truth; next by Faith in the Understanding, which is Intellectual Faith; and lastly, by Faith in the Will or heart, which is the Faith of Love, or Saving Faith. By Faith, in the Word, is meant Love to the Lord and the Neighbor, or a life according to those Two Principles which make ONE in the regenerating man, and is the perception or thought of the Rational Faculty concerning the quality of love, or charity, from an Internal Affection for Good and Truth.

614. The very essence of Faith is the Divine Proceeding of the Lord which constitutes the Word, and is a belief in the Son of God who is the Word "made flesh," or the Interior Spiritual Principle of the Word brought

The internal and external Rational Faculty.	Love and Faith.

forth into the Life of the regenerating man. Good and Truth, or Love and Faith from the Lord, are the "Two Great Lights" which rule by "day" and "night." These "Lights" are placed in the "firmament of the heaven," or the Rational Faculty. The Internal principle of the Rational Faculty is a receptacle of Good, and the External principle is a receptacle of Truth from the Word.

615. The perception of the Divine Human Principle of the Word occurs in the Internal principle of the Rational Faculty which is actuated by the Affection of Good, and which is kindled or infused by the Celestial principles of the Word in the Internal mind, for it will be remembered that the Rational Faculty is intermediate between the Internal and External mind, and in the First Day of Creation is called the "Firmament."

616. The External principle of the Rational Faculty is actuated by the Affection of Truth, and manifests itself in the External mind, and thence in the speech and actions. By "Lights in the firmament of the heaven" is signified that the Rational Faculty is now to be actuated by perception from the Internal mind, which is called "Heaven" in the "Beginning."

617. Previous to this State, the Rational Faculty has not been clearly separated into the Internal and External principles alluded to in the "Marriage in Cana of Galilee" (599) and which are now represented by "Day" and "Night," which when taken together signify Love and Faith, because here referring to the "Lights"; for Love is represented by the sun, which rules by day, and as Faith, or Truth, is from Love, as the moon shines by the

reflected light of the sun, so "night," over which the light of the moon governs, here signifies Faith. "Day" also signifies the Internal Sense of the Word, and "Night" the obscurity of the Literal Sense, when used in other places according to the subject which is being illustrated.

618. By "Signs," in the Word, are signified confirmations of the Divine Truth as revealed in the Internal Sense, and that true spiritual knowledge is thus illustrated and communicated to the mind. By "Seasons," are signified the States of the regenerating man as represented by Spring, Summer, Autumn and Winter.

619. Spring signifies the First State of the regenerating man, when spiritual life begins to grow from the "earth" of the Word, in the "earth" of the External mind. Summer signifies a Full State, when the heat and light of the Spiritual Sun, the Word, are vivifying all the principles of the External mind. Autumn, or Harvest-time, signifies the fruition of the Truths of the Word advanced to perfection by Good, or by a life of obedience to them, and it also denotes the decline of love. Winter signifies a state of no love and is the state of coldness which precedes regeneration, which begins in a State of Winter, when there is neither love nor charity.

620. The regenerating man undergoes Changes of State, in which he is in greater or less degrees of love, because in himself he is nothing but evil, for the Lord alone is Good, and during the work of regeneration, he is subject to temptation from the evils of his remaining unregenerated Proprium. These alternations expressed

by "Signs" and "Seasons," are needful, in order that he may be more and more perfected, and brought into conjunction with the Lord.

621. These changes are to be compared to those in the temperate zones, for without Changes of State which correspond to Summer and Winter, as to the Will, and of "Day" and "Night" as to the Understanding, he could not increase in love and wisdom, and thus be perfected. "Days and years" signify all the progressive states of regeneration in general, the qualities of which will be perceived by the Rational Faculty in their order, and by "years" in the Word is not meant periods of earthly time, but full periods of States, and by the Number of years, the quality is indicated by the spiritual correspondence of numbers.

And let them be for Lights in the Firmament of the heaven to give light upon the earth: and it was so. Gen. 1:15.

622. By "Lights in the firmament of heaven," is signified the illumination of the Internal principle of the Rational Faculty, from the Lord within the Internal mind, "to give light upon the earth," or the External mind. "And it was so," signifies confirmation within the mind that this progress is according to Divine Order. It has been illustrated that the "Firmament" is the Rational Faculty which is intermediate between the Internal and External mind, through which conjunction is effected, so that the External mind, or "earth," is caused to act from spiritual principles instead of from selfish and worldly motives.

The Intermediate state.   One point of offence.

INTERIOR MOTIVES.

623. By correspondence, the "Firmament" signifies the Intermediate State into which every person enters at the death of material thought. The order of regeneration takes place similar to the order of physical life in conception, birth, infancy, childhood and manhood, to which its progressive states correspond. Those who attain the years of maturity, form their own ruling loves by their course of life, good or evil, as in freedom they have obeyed whatever form of Truth which has been presented to them, and which they have recognized as Truth according to the capacity of their minds, whether in possession of the written Word or not. When a man's ruling love has been formed, his motives are governed by it, and he inwardly desires to do whatever gives him the greatest delight.

624. Those in whose lives the work of regeneration has begun, love to obey the Precepts of the Word, and love the spiritual welfare of their fellow-beings as they progress in the victory over the Love of Self. Those who are actuated by the Love of Self have no regard for the Interior principles of the Commandments, and though they may externally "keep the whole law, and yet offend in one point," they are "guilty of all." This "one point" is the Love of Self, which being worshipped instead of the Lord, constitutes Idolatry, and in this "one point" all the Commandments are Interiorly broken.

625. By the Commandment, *Thou shalt have no other Gods before me*, in the NATURAL SENSE is meant that no created thing, man or image, is to be worshipped. The SPIRITUAL SENSE is that no other God than the Lord Jesus Christ is to be worshipped, because He is the only Redeemer from sin. The CELESTIAL SENSE is that the Lord Jesus Christ is the One Only Omnipotent, Omniscient, and Omnipresent Jehovah, who Was, Is, and Is to Come.

R

the Almighty, the Inmost Life of the Word, and they who are in the Love of Self do not keep this Commandment because they worship another God.

626. By the Commandment, *Thou shalt not take the name of the Lord thy God in vain,* in the NATURAL SENSE is meant that the Name of the Lord shall not be profanely used in speech or triflingly employed in oaths or perjury. The SPIRITUAL SENSE teaches that the Word is His Name, and that all True Doctrine derived from it shall be reverenced and obeyed, and that the Name of this Word is the Lord Jesus Christ; by the name of Jesus is meant all those principles of salvation from the Word by which man is redeemed from his sins, and by the name of Christ is meant all principles of the doctrine of Divine Truth from the Word. In the CELESTIAL SENSE is meant that there shall be no blasphemy against the Holiness of the Word, which in its Internal Sense is the Divine Humanity of the Lord, which is His Name in the highest sense, and this is the Name which is to be glorified in the regenerating man, and thus by His Name is signified all the Divine Attributes of the Lord which are revealed in the Internal Sense of the Word. They who are in the Love of Self, if they read the Word, and do not obey its Precepts "take His Name in vain."

627. By the Commandment, *Remember the Sabbath Day to keep it holy,* in the NATURAL SENSE is indicated Rest at the end of six days of worldly labor, and that the Sabbath is to be a day of religious instruction and meditation, as also a day in which Love to the Neighbor shall be specially manifested. In the SPIRITUAL SENSE it signifies the Reformation and Regeneration of man by the Lord; by the Six Days of Labor is signified the combats against the evils and falses of the Proprium, and by the Seventh Day is signified his conjunction with the Lord, and thus his Regeneration. In the CELESTIAL SENSE it signifies that state of Heavenly Peace which results from conjunction with the Lord, which evil and falsity can never again invade. They who are in the Love of Self do not keep the Sabbath holy, for this holiness is only attained by a life of Regeneration.

628. By the Commandment, *Honor thy father and thy mother*, in the NATURAL SENSE is indicated that the natural father and mother are to be obeyed, loved and honored, and also all who are in authority for the government of the world. The SPIRITUAL SENSE signifies the Internal Sense of the Word and the Doctrine of Truth therefrom by which man is regenerated, the Internal Sense being the Father and the Spiritual Instruction thence derived being the Mother, for as an earthly mother feeds her children with natural food, so spiritual instruction from the Word provides spiritual food. In the CELESTIAL SENSE it signifies the Lord Jesus Christ as the Father and the Affection of Truth in all regenerating and angelic men, or the Communion of Saints, as the Mother. They who are actuated by the Love of Self do not honor the father and mother, for the Internal Sense of the Word cannot be revealed to them until the work of regeneration has begun.

629. By the Commandment, *Thou shalt not kill*, in the NATURAL Sense is meant literally to inflict no injury upon another person either in his body or reputation, from enmity, hatred, or revenge, either in act or intention. In the SPIRITUAL SENSE is signified any means by which the Divine Truth of the Word is obstructed from regenerating the lives of other men, by perverse example, blasphemous words, or false teaching. In the CELESTIAL SENSE is signified hatred toward the Interior principles of the Word, and thus toward the Lord, and all the Divine Truths proceeding from Him. They who are in the Love of Self care only for themselves, and would not regret even the death of others, provided they would derive benefit themselves thereby.

630. By the Commandment, *Thou shalt not commit adultery*, in the NATURAL SENSE is meant not only that there shall be no adultery in act, but that no thought of lasciviousness or lust shall be cherished, or obscene conversation uttered, for whatever is in the will of man in the intention is the same as if carried into the act, which would be done if there were no external restraint. Abstinence from the act of sin does not constitute chastity, but abstinence from cherishing the thought of sin in the Will, in the

time of temptation, when all external restraints are removed, constitutes chastity, and in this overcoming of lust, a man must seek the Lord's strength; but he is an adulterer who lusts in his heart or speaks obscenely, although he may never indulge in the carnal act. " *Whoever looketh on a woman to lust after her, hath committed adultery with her already in his heart.*" The same principle is true in the woman whose mind is filled with carnal lust, which originates in the Love of Self in its most degrading corporeal principle. " *The adulteress will hunt for the precious life. Whoso committeth adultery with a woman lacketh understanding: he that doeth it destroyeth his own soul.*" " *The adulterer and the adulteress shall surely be put to death,*" for this sin closes every perception of the Truth of the Word, and the result is Spiritual Death. In the SPIRITUAL SENSE it signifies to adulterate the Goods of the Word, and to falsify its Truths by means of false doctrines which obscure the power of the Living Precepts of the Word. In the CELESTIAL SENSE, by committing adultery is meant to deny the Internal Sense of the Word in which its Holiness consists, for when this is denied, the Literal Sense will be profaned to sustain any false doctrine which favors the Love of Self.

631. By the Commandment, *Thou shalt not steal,* in the NATURAL SENSE is meant not to defraud, or take advantage of any person to the least extent, or be unfaithful in any duty, or to receive bribes, or make unjust decisions for the sake of gain. In the SPIRITUAL SENSE is meant that none should be deprived of the Truths of the Word by false doctrines, and that none should teach such doctrines as they may see in the Word for worldly honor or personal gain. In the CELESTIAL SENSE is meant that none should take away the Divine Power of the Lord from the Word by its Internal Sense, or claim to themselves His merit and righteousness instead of putting away their evils in humility and acknowledging the power to be from the Lord by the Word.

632. By the Commandment, *Thou shalt not bear false witness against thy neighbor,* in the NATURAL SENSE is meant that none

shall speak or testify falsely concerning any person or thing, by any stratagem or evil purpose to be subservient to any selfish interest. In the SPIRITUAL SENSE it signifies that there shall be no attempt made to persuade others that false doctrine is the Truth of the Word, and that the evils of life are thereby overlooked and washed away without their being overcome by obedience to the Truths of the Word, and it also signifies to do evil after one knows what Good and Truth are. In the CELESTIAL SENSE by "false witness" is signified to blaspheme and reject the Internal Sense of the Word after recognizing that the Spiritual Principles therein will make a regenerating man "wise unto salvation."

633. In the Commandment, *Thou shalt not covet*, in the NATURAL SENSE is meant that none of the prohibitions mentioned in the previous Commandments shall be lusted for, or inwardly cherished, for a man does not act from internal motives until lusts are overcome and removed, which is accomplished in the work of preparation for regeneration. In the SPIRITUAL SENSE this Commandment prohibits all desires from the Proprium which are contrary to progression in spiritual attainments, or are opposed to obedience to the Truths of the Word; because, unless all coveting or lust is subdued, the Will of the Proprium would gain the ascendancy and lead the man into spiritual death.

634. They who are in the Love of Self, would, if unrestrained by external influences, violate every Commandment to gratify the lust of the Proprium, and if possible lead others into spiritual death. Such is the state of the unregenerated principles of the External mind, and they must undergo the mental suffering incident upon the removal of evil and falsity. Men enter the Intermediate State with the same opinions concerning Divine Principles which they hold at the time of their departure from the natural world of thought, and these opinions, if false, can only be removed when they perceive the Truth, and overcome the evils of the Proprium.

635. The Lord never casts any one away from Him, or remands them to Hell, but seeks to lead every man to the Life of Heaven. Those who are in the life of evil, go their own way to that place or state which gives them the greatest delight in the gratification of their evils, which re-act upon them alone, and in place of desiring that others shall receive blessing, they desire that they may be injured, from which the re-action causes torture and suffering, and all their evil desires culminate in and re-act upon themselves, as anyone may observe, if he will study the operation of his own mind, for the proof of Spiritual Truths is to be found within the mental experience, and not outside in the external world of nature.

636. There are Two Ways which lead to the Rational Faculty; a Superior, or Internal way, by which Good and Truth enter from the Lord by the Internal mind, which is the Kingdom of Heaven within the regenerating man, and an Inferior, or External way, by which evil and falsity enter from Hell, or the Proprium. When the Light is admitted from Heaven, or the Internal mind, a man becomes regenerated and also truly Rational. But if he does not admit this Light from Heaven, he is not Rational, notwithstanding he may appear so to himself.

637. Thus the Rational Faculty corresponds to an Intermediate State. Whatever is above it, corresponds to Heaven, and whatever is below, corresponds to Hell. With the regenerating man, the door above is opened to receive the heat and light from Heaven, and the door below is closed to the influx of evil and falsity from hell; but with the unregenerated principles, the door above is closed, and the door beneath is opened, and they look down to Hell.

638. To look above is to look to the Lord within the Word, who is the Center of all Love and Wisdom, but to look down to Self and the dead things of material thought is to turn away from the Lord, or the Word, to the opposite principle of Spiritual Death, "*I have set the* LORD *always before me: because He is at my right hand I shall not be moved.*" The "hand" signifies the ability, power and confidence which is given to man, because his

work, or usefulness, is performed by his hands, and the "Right Hand" signifies the Intellectual Power, or Rational Faculty, which is vivified by the Truths of the Word. Thus the Lord is at the "right hand" of the regenerating man, and he will not be moved, or led downward by evil and falsity, because the Divine Truth of the Word is firm to uphold in ways of righteousness.

639. It is by correspondence, that in prayer the face or eyes instinctively turn upward, for to look above is to turn the thoughts inwardly, and in whatever direction the Lord is thought of, He is always before the mind. It has been illustrated that "Before," signifies "Within," because the Source of thought is from the Lord, who is "Before all things," and it descends through Interior Principles which precede the ultimate effect. Thus when angelic men think of the Lord, they think of Him as entering within themselves, in the Internal mind. If thought concerning the Lord wanders away from this principle and places Him in vague material space, the idea of God becomes material, and He will then be thought of from natural principles of time and space, and confliction between Spiritual and Natural Principles will take place in the mind.

640. Although the LORD fills all things both within and without by His Omnipresence, Omniscience, and Omnipotence, He is the Inmost Principle of the Life of the Word, and is perceived in the Love and Wisdom which proceeds from Him by the Word into the Affections and Thoughts of regenerating men. He is the Inmost Essential Being of that Spiritual Sun, THE WORD, which sheds its rays of Heat and Light upon the "earth" of regenerating men.

641. The LORD JEHOVAH exists in Himself as the Primary Source of all life, and this erroneous opinion must be carefully guarded against:—that having infused Himself into the lives of angelic and regenerating men, their lives in the complex constitute the Lord. This is not true, for they are only recipients of His Life which He gives from Himself, and unless this fundamental principle of spiritual intelligence is acknowledged in

humility, a man might be led even to think himself to be God, and would thereby close the door above the Rational Faculty, so that the Light could not enter from its Source, the Inmost Essential Life from whom the Literal Sense of the Word exists, and which is made Living when its Truths are received and obeyed by its created receptacle, the regenerating man.

642. When the door above is opened, the Heavenly Lights shine through the firmament of the Rational Faculty, and thence through the lower door, and illuminate the "earth" of the External mind, which is beneath, and with the co-operation of the regenerating man, drive out the evils and falsities of the hereditary Proprium.

And God made Two Great Lights; the greater Light to rule the Day, and the lesser Light to rule the Night: He made the Stars also. Gen. 1: 16.

643. The "Two Great Lights" of the spiritual world of the Rational Faculty are the Sun, or Love, which rules the Will, and the Moon, or Truth, which governs the Understanding; while the "Stars" are the Knowledges of Good and Truth. The rays of the sun warm the receptacle of earth which is planted with seed, for it is according to the order of creation and of regeneration, that seed shall first be planted, and the Spiritual Seed is the Truth of the Word.

644. As Love is the very Essence of Life, and Truth made Living is derived from Love, so the Will, which is the receptacle of Love, is the Life of the Understanding, which is the receptacle of Truth, and the Understanding of the regenerating man becomes the form or clothing of the Will, and is ruled by it. Both of these receptacles of heat and light, or of Love and Wisdom, constitute One mind or man, for what a man then wills and does, he also thinks and intends. But when the Understanding is at

THE NATURE OF THE WORD OF GOD. 281

Stars.	God setting the lights.

variance with the Will, as with those who profess that they have faith, and yet live in contradiction to the simple Truths of the Word, the one mind of such persons is divided into two principles, one of which desires to exalt itself into Heaven, while the other tends toward Hell, or the Proprium; and since the Will rules in every act, the whole mind and life would plunge into evil, unless prevented by the Love and Mercy of the Lord by means of external restraints.

645. As "Stars" signify Knowledges of Good and Truth from the Word, so the "Star in the East," which went before the "wise men," in the historical narrative of the Gospels, "till it came and stood over where the young child was," signifies that these knowledges from the Word, which is the Sun in the East, have led the regenerating man whose mind has been filled with wisdom from obedience, to perceive the Internal Sense of the Word, which reveals the "place" where the "young child" is born, which is in the enlightened Rational Faculty of the man before whom the "Star" appears.

And God set them in the Firmament of the Heaven to give Light upon the Earth. Gen. 1: 17.

646. "And God set them," signifies that the perception is imparted to the regenerating man, that all Love, and consequently all Life, which is from Love alone, is derived solely from the Lord. "In the firmament of the heaven," signifies the Internal principle of the Rational Faculty, which being illuminated from the Internal mind, or "Heaven," gives "light upon the earth," and the External mind is governed by the Internal Truths of the Word.

647. Thus during this Fourth Day, the regenerating man becomes more clearly influenced by the Divine

Love, and is illuminated by the Divine Truth of the Word. In the previous States, his conversation and meditation has been upon religious principles, and he has produced the fruit of good works; but he was then actuated by his unyielding firmness and obedience to the Commandments when laboring under temptation, but not from an Internal principle of Love and Faith, wherefore these principles are now enkindled within his "Firmament," and "give light upon the earth."

648. This Light is from the Internal Sense of the Word which shines through the Rational Faculty and illumines both the Literal Sense and its corresponding receptacles of the External mind, and shows that the origin of the Word is Divine. *"Arise, shine: for thy Light is come, and the glory of the Lord is risen upon thee. Thy sun shall no more go down; neither shall thy moon withdraw itself; for the Lord shall be thine everlasting Light, and the days of thy mourning shall be ended."*

And to rule over the Day and over the Night, and to divide the Light from the Darkness: and God saw that it was good. Gen. 1 : 18.

649. In this verse, by "Day," is meant Good, and by "Night" is signified Evil; wherefore good actions are called Works of the Day, and evil deeds are Works of the Night. By the "Light" is meant Truth, and by "Darkness" is meant Falsity. *"For every one that doeth evil hateth the Light." "He that doeth Truth cometh to*

Light and darkness.   Walking in the day.

the Light, that his deeds may be made manifest, that they are wrought in God." But in the fourteenth verse, "Day" signifies the Will, and "Night" denotes the Understanding, which are receptacles of the Love and Wisdom represented by the Sun and Moon, yet in this verse, "Light" and "Darkness" are mentioned which here qualifies the "Day" and "Night."

650. By the reception of the Love and Wisdom of the Word in obeying its Truths, the "Light in the Rational Faculty discriminates between Truth and Falsity. The "Darkness" is the falsity which envelopes the External mind which is to be filled with Light as evil and falsity are overcome. When the regenerating man is suffering in temptation, the evils and falses which then appear in the Proprium, seem to obscure the Spiritual Heat and Light, but if he resists the evil and looks to the Lord within the Word, the clouds will be dispersed, and he will perceive the Divine Light shining steadily above the clouds.

651. "*If any man walk in the day, he stumbleth not; but if any man walk in the night, he stumbleth because there is no light in him.*" To "walk in the day," signifies to live according to the Truths of the Word, but to "walk in the night," is to be led by the evils and falses of the Proprium, which bring upon the Rational Faculty that state of night and darkness of which it is said, "*Shall the sun be darkened, and the moon shall not give her light, and the stars shall fall from heaven, and the powers of the heavens shall be shaken.*" This prophetic utterance of the Word does not refer to physical events, but to the spiritual state of men whose minds have been become obscured by their own evils and falses, from which false doctrines have been confirmed from the

Appearances of Truth in the Literal Sense, and have obscured the Light which steadily shines from the simple Precepts of the Word. These plain commandments are the " Highway" which lead to the Internal Sense. *"And an Highway shall be there, and a Way, and it shall be called The Way of Holiness; the unclean shall not pass over it; but it shall be for those: the wayfaring men, though fools, shall not err therein." "I am the Way, the Truth, and the Life." "This is the Way, walk ye in it." "Come ye, and let us walk in the light of the Lord."*

And the Evening and the Morning were the Fourth Day. Gen. 1 : 19.

652. Progression into clearer perception of the Divine Truth of the Word, by continued obedience from Affection, effects conjunction between Good and Truth, which union is represented by the number Four, which is the double or multiple of Two, and signifies the fulness of the Fourth State of Regeneration, and it derives its signification from the Four Quarters of the Spiritual World, which are represented by the fixed geographical quarters of the earth in relation to the physical sun, the East, West, North, and South.

SPIRITUAL QUARTERS.

653. These Four Quarters denote states of Good and Truth, and the extension of Good and Truth is described by them in the Word. The "East" denotes the Lord, because He is within the Sun of Heaven, whence comes the Heat and Light of Love and Wisdom, and in particular it denotes Divine Love in a clear perception, by means of the Word, which is the Lord in the East. The West denotes an obscure state of Love, therefore the "Star" is seen "in the East." The South denotes Divine Truth in Light, and the North signifies Truth in obscurity. All principles of spiritual life are derived from the "East," or the Word of God.

The Right Hand of God.	Africans.

654. These States are continually varying with the "earth" of the regenerating man in relation to the Spiritual Sun, as it revolves on its axis and encircles this Sun during each year of regeneration. As the physical sun is the centre of the orbit in which the earth revolves, and is always in the East in respect to the earth as it appears in the order of the revolutions, so the Lord, or the Word, is always in the East in relation to the regenerating man. When a man faces the East, his right hand is towards the South, and the "right hand" of a man signifies Divine Truth received into the life, and the "Right Hand of God" signifies the Internal Sense of the Word, for it is the Divine Power of the Lord in the regeneration of man.

655. The Four Gospels represent the fulness of conjunction of the Internal Sense of the Word with the life of the regenerating man. The name "John" signifies "the Mercy of the Lord," and as this Mercy is from the Inmost Principle of the Divine Love, this Interior Gospel is represented by the East. The word "Matthew" signifies "Reward," by which is denoted a means of conjunction, which in the regenerating man becomes the Affection of Truth, and this being given from the Mercy of the Lord who is in the East, this Gospel is represented by the West. The name "Luke" signifies "Luminous," which is predicated of Divine Truth, and as this Gospel gives light concerning the conception and birth of the Son of God, it is represented by the South. The name "Mark" signifies "Shining," which is also predicated of Divine Truth, but being obscure concerning the Advent, this Gospel is represented by the North.

656. As the world corresponds to the universal mind of man, or one mind with its complex principles, so the names of the geographical quarters signify spiritual principles abstracted from physical locality. The warm country of AFRICA signifies the Affection of Good, the same as the "East," or "John," which is a state of Celestial affection, and thus the "Africans" of the Spiritual World are those who in affection receive the Goods and Truths of the Word into their lives, and whose minds from being black with

the evils and falses of their Proprium, are being made "white in the blood of the Lamb." As the center of Africa is under the influence of the heated climate of the torrid zone, so the spiritual "Africans" have more interior perception and superior judgment concerning the spiritual principles of the Word, and perceive clearly how the Lord descends and presents Himself to the interior sight of men by the Word, which is the Spiritual Sun which sheds greater heat and light at the equator, or within the mind which is constantly open to receive the Divine Love and Wisdom by means of the clear revelation of the interior principles of the Word.

657. ASIA signifies the clear light of intelligence concerning the Word, the same as the "South," or "Luke," and by the inhabitants of Asia in the spiritual world of regeneration, are signified all they who are living in and are illuminated by this clear spiritual light, or in Truths derived from Good. Thus Asia signifies all those principles in the mind of the regenerating man which are enlightened by the Internal Sense of the Word by obedience to its Truths. EUROPE signifies a state of Truth in obscurity concerning the Internal Sense of the Word, the same as the "North," and the spiritual Europeans denote those in the state of regeneration to whom the Internal Sense of the Word is about to be revealed, and in the evil sense they denote those false principles which obscure the mind in regard to the Word, when the doctrine of faith alone predominates over the commandments of Love. AMERICA signifies the Affection of Truth, the same as the "West," or an obscure state of Love, being opposite to the "East" and derived therefrom, and the inhabitants, or principles of this spiritual quarter will be led from the Affection of Truth to the Affection of Good, or to the state signified by Africa, as the regenerating man progresses toward Celestial principles.

Eight days.	Circumcision,

THE CONSECRATION OF THE HOLY CHILD.

And when eight days were accomplished for the circumcising of the child, his name was called Jesus, which was so named of the angel before he was conceived in the womb. Luke 2 : 21.

658. "Eight days," signifies a state of full conjunction of Good and Truth, the same as by "Two" and by "Four," for it is the multiplied product of those numbers. "Eight" also signifies the beginning of a new state of purification from evils which is represented by "Circumcision," which signifies purification from filthy and corporeal evils by means of the Truths of the Word implanted in the life. "Circumcision" is the sign for this purification, which can only exist from an Internal love for that purity and innocence which is represented by the "Child," the quality of which exists from the Divine Love, signified by "his name was called JESUS," which quality was predicated of regeneration, in the Word, concerning the preceding states of Reformation and Repentance which are treated of in the First Day of Creation, "which was so named of the angel before he was conceived in the womb."

659 The "Womb" is the Rational Faculty, and "Conception" is the first life of this Interior receptacle of the mind, which receives its life from the life of the Lord in the Internal mind which flows into the life of

the Affection of the knowledges and sciences belonging to the External mind. The life of this Affection of knowledges and sciences of the Literal Sense of the Word, gives the Rational Faculty a covering or body, which is the "mother" within which the Rational Faculty exists as a receptacle of Seed from the Internal Sense of the Word.

BAPTISM AND CIRCUMCISION.

660. Baptism, in the Literal Sense, is a sign of entrance into regenerating life. The Waters of Baptism denote the Truths of the Word applied to the life, and these Truths are signified by the waters "above" and "below" the "firmament," or the Interior and Literal Truths of the Word. The external application of water to the physical body in any form does not constitute the Baptism of the Word, although it is used as a memorial that men should be purified from their evils; for adulterers and adulteresses may daily wash their bodies with water to the utmost cleanliness, and yet their whole minds be filled with the impurity which results from the Love of Self, although they may have been devoutly baptized in the prescribed external form in which they have been educated. But the Baptism which is described in the Literal Sense of the Word is representative of the entrance upon the work of regeneration, which leads to the internal purification from evil and falsity, and this True Baptism must be daily and constantly performed by obedience to the Truths of the Literal Commandments in the daily external duties of life.

661. Regeneration differs from purification in this respect, which is, that Regeneration precedes, and Purification follows: for no one can be inwardly purified from evils and falses, unless he has entered upon the work of Regeneration. A man who has not entered upon this work may externally withdraw himself from evils, but he is not purified from them, for his will is not changed

| Fulfilment of Baptism. | A week. |

and he remains impure, but the regenerating man is being purified every day. Thus the difference between the signification of Baptism and Circumcision may be perceived; Baptism signifying the entrance upon the work of regeneration, and Circumcision signifying purification from evil and falsity.

662. The external rite of Baptism in itself alone, has no more effect upon the Internal life, than the external rite of Circumcision avails in the Internal purification of evil. The significance of all the external rites and ceremonies recorded in the Literal Sense, refer to spiritual principles which must be fulfilled in the Internal life, of which the external forms narrated in the Letter of the Word are simply representative. "*Neither is that circumcision which is outward in the flesh. Circumcision is that of the heart, in the spirit, and not in the letter.*" * "*Circumcision is nothing, and uncircumcision is nothing, but the keeping of the Commandments of God.*" † "*And the* LORD *thy God will circumcise thine heart, and the heart of thy seed, to love the* LORD *thy God with all thy soul, that thou mayest live.*" ‡

663. A "Week," which is a period of seven days, signifies an entire period of every state of Reformation, Temptation, and Regeneration, and the "Eighth Day" is the beginning of a succeeding state. As "Circumcision" in the representative description of the Word, takes place on the "Eighth Day," this purification from evil must be constantly progressing, and thus be always proceeding as from a new beginning in the removal of Self-love and the Love of the World from the Proprium, for those lusts, while they rule the External mind and the Rational Faculty, so take possession of the thoughts, that they not only reject and suffocate the influx of the Divine Love, but pervert and defile it. This inflowing

* Rom. 2 : 29.   † Cor. 7 : 19.   ‡ Deut. 30 : 6.

S

of Heavenly Love from the Lord is constant with every man, but its reception is opposed and turned to its opposite principle by the evil and falsity of the Proprium of the External mind.

And when the days of her purification according to the law of Moses were accomplished, they brought him to Jerusalem, to present him to the Lord. Luke 2 : 22.

664. The purification of evils and falses takes place in the External mind, which contains the hereditary human principle derived from the mother, and unless this purification is accomplished, the work of regeneration cannot proceed, for otherwise the Divine Love of the Lord cannot enter and assume the place occupied by the hereditary Proprium. The "Law of Moses" denotes the Word of God, and here signifies the Truth of the Literal Commandments of the Word represented by the "Law," by which this purification is accomplished in the External mind. The signification of the word "Moses," is "Taken out of the water," and "water" signifies the Truth of the Literal Sense of the Word, which when obeyed, takes the mind out of natural thought concerning the Word, and lifts it into a spiritual perception of its Interior Truth. Thus instead of a physical man in ancient earthly history, the name "Moses" represents the Lord as to the Commandments of the Word in the various states of the mind of regenerating men.

665. The Purification from the Love of Self and the World is effected by the Two Great Commandments of

the Word, which are signified by the "Law of Moses," and which bring the regenerating man to "Jerusalem." By "Jerusalem," in the Word, is not meant an earthly city, but the Spiritual City, or doctrines formed from the Divine Truth of the Word, which are revealed to the perceptions of the Rational Faculty, and the mind must be abstracted from the appearance of an earthly place in this narration, and the spiritual principle thought of, otherwise the Rational Faculty will be led into the natural world of material thought instead of the Spiritual world which is revealed by the Internal Sense of the Word.

666. "Zion," represents the Celestial Principles of the Word within the regenerating man which are obeyed from the Good of Love, by which is meant life and thought which is actuated by Affection. "Jerusalem," represents the Spiritual Principles of the Word within the regenerating man which exist from the Truth of the Good of Love, by which is meant the thought or understanding which has been opened to perceive the Interior Truths of the Word from obedience to the External Truths of the Commandments, which leads to an Interior principle of Affection, which is higher and warmer than external and cold principles of duty, or obedience. By the "New Jerusalem" is meant the Living Doctrines derived from the Interior Divine Truth of the Word and received into the life of the regenerating man. which are universal in their application.

667. "To present him to the Lord," signifies that by a life according to the simple Literal Truths, the regenerating man has been led to perceive the Divine Truth within the Word, and he is thus "presented," or offered to the Lord, which signifies a life of constant worship from True Doctrines from the Word, because the Internal principle of the Rational Faculty is opened to receive the Divine Love and Wisdom.

> As it is written in the law of the Lord, Every male that openeth the womb shall be called holy to the Lord. Luke 2 : 23.

668. "As it is written" signifies the inscription within, and the impression on the life of the regenerating man. The "Law of the Lord" is the Divine Truth of the Word. Truths are impressed on the life when they are received into the Will, and thence govern the actions and speech. If they are received and remain merely in the Memory, they are only thought of intellectually, but as soon as they are received in the Will, they then become Living, because the very Essence of the Life of man is to Will, and thence to act; and Truths have no power in man until they are made Living. The reason why "it is written" signifies to impress on the life, is because the Art of Writing, or Printing, has been given to mankind, so that Truths and Thoughts may thus be preserved and remembered, and thus be handed down to successive generations.

THE BOOK OF LIFE.

669. The mind of man possesses Two Books, within which are written all his thoughts and actions. These Two Books are his Interior and Exterior memories. Those things which are written on the pages of his Interior Memory, remain to all Eternity, and they will never be blotted out, for they have been from his Will, or ruling love, and here is written the True History of his life as it has progressed in form from Internal motives. Whatever things or principles a man hears and sees, and appropriates into his life, whether they are good or evil, or true or false, are insinuated into his Interior Memory without his being aware of it, just as he may take medicine or poison without being aware how it affects the internal organs of the physical frame.

670. In this Internal Memory not a single impression or inscription which the man has himself written, will ever be lost. The Interior Memory is of such a quality that the inward motives of the most particular things which man has at any time thought, spoken and done, with the most minute circumstances, from his earliest years to extreme old age, are there deeply inscribed. When a man enters the regenerate life he carries with him the memory of all these things, and he is successively brought into recollection of all of them. This is THE BOOK OF HIS LIFE, which is opened in the clearest light whenever the Lord permits, in order that he may not glory in his self-intelligence, but may see and feel that his own Proprium brings nothing but Spiritual Death.

671. In view of this searching fact concerning the opening of the Book of Life, every man who reads the Word should strive to attain Holiness of Life by shunning his evils and looking to the Lord. To look to the Lord is to obey the Precepts of the Word, and thus acknowledge Him. "*And I saw the dead, small and great, stand before God; and the Books were opened; and another Book was opened, which is the Book of Life: and the dead were judged out of those things which were written in the books, according to their works.*"

672. "Every male that openeth the womb shall be called holy to the Lord." In regard to the spiritual principles which constitute the human mind, the Word of God is no respecter of persons in the distinction of physical sex, for an earthly wo-man is a Womb-man who is so created, that in this world there may be a mother to succeeding generations for the perpetuity of life, in order that angels may be created by regeneration. Therefore the Regenerating Man is either male or female in regard to earthly sex, and the Love of Self in its degrading influence, has no degrees of difference between the sexes, and the necessity for regeneration is imperative with both. *"There is neither male nor female: for ye are all one in Christ Jesus."* In the Male or Masculine principle of the mind, Love is the inmost degree, and its feminine covering is Wisdom; whereas in the Female principle of the mind the Wisdom of the male is inmost, and its covering is the Affection thence derived; so that "Male" signifies the Truth from Good, and "Female" is the Affection of that Truth. These two principles represented by "Male" and "Female" exist in the mind of the one regenerating man, the conjunction of which constitutes the Heavenly Marriage, not between two individuals, but between the two principles of the mind, the Will and the Understanding, for two persons cannot become One Person.

673. The "Womb" is the Rational Faculty, and to "Open" is to give power in order that the perception of Truth may be born. The "First-born" is Good, which

Holiness.   Irreverence,

is formed by means of Truths from the Word made Good, or lived according to, and this Good is the power which opens the Rational Faculty, for the "Male" which is first born is Truth from Good, for Good is first conceived from the Lord, and is formed by Truths, and "shall be called holy to the Lord." By "Holy," or "Holiness," is signified Divine Truth and all the principles which proceed therefrom, and the regenerating man is Sanctified or made Holy when his life is governed by Divine Truth, or the Word, for the True Holiness of the Lord in its ultimate degree, exists in the life of the man who obeys its Precepts.

674. The Literal Sense of the Word is Holy, because it contains within its expressions Interior Divine Truth, and it is therefore the Temple of the Lord. It should for this reason always be treated with reverence, both in places of public gatherings and in the home, because therein is the Lord Himself, buried in the sepulchre of the Literal Sense, waiting to arise and re-create the life of the man who opens and reads its sacred pages. "*The Lord is in His Holy Temple, let all the earth keep silence before Him.* "*Holiness becometh Thine House, O Lord, for ever.*"

675. The Literal Sense of the Word should not be used in the language of common conversation, or ever be made the subject of jesting or punning by ludicrous application, and thus abuse made of the receptacles of Interior Divine Truth, because such treatment is trifling with the Source of Spiritual Life, and leads the mind

away from perceiving its true Holiness. Using the Word with irreverence leads to profanity and blasphemy, for it is the Name of the Lord, which "*Thou shalt not take in vain.*" By "called holy to the Lord," is signified a perception that these Divine Truths, which in their Interior meaning have entered the enlightened Rational Faculty, are from the Lord alone, and that He is the Source of their Inspiration, and that they do not originate from the finite instruments which He has employed to record the Literal and its revealed Internal Sense.

And to offer a sacrifice according to that which is said in the law of the Lord, A pair of turtle doves, or two young pigeons. Luke 2 : 24.

676. To "offer a sacrifice" signifies expiation from sin, or the removal of evils and falses. By Expiation, or Propriation, is meant the deliverance from Spiritual Death, by the purification from evils and falses, which is accomplished by resisting and overcoming them. The "Law of the Lord," signifies the Word. A "Turtle dove" is representative of Exterior principles, and a "Young pigeon" signifies Interior principles. By "a "pair" and "two" is signified the conjunction of these two principles, which exist in the Understanding and the Will, which when united by obedience to the Precepts of the Word constitute the Heavenly Marriage. All birds mentioned in the Word signify spiritual principles in the regenerating man which relate to Truth or Faith, and consequently to Intellectual and Rational principles. The gentle, beautiful and clean birds represent principles of Truth, and those which are ravenous and unclean represent false principles.

OFFERING SACRIFICE.

677. An "Offering" signifies Worship, or a life according to the Precepts of the Word, and to "offer" the two spiritual principles of Love and Faith, signified by "young pigeons" and "turtle-doves," implies the sacrifice of the Love of Self, which will suffer until it is removed, and which will occupy the Six Days of Regeneration. Although it appears to the regenerating man as if he removed his own sins by resisting them, this is only an Appearance, which is permitted so that man shall in freedom strive against evil and falsity, for the power to do this is from the Lord alone. Every man must bear the fruit of his own iniquity, for his deeds are recorded by himself in his own Book of Life, and there they will remain, for his works follow him, and the scar of every sin will not be effaced through Eternity.

678. The Lord bears iniquities away and removes them in proportion as men desist from them, and no farther, for He saves a man only through what appears to be his own efforts, for there must be a reciprocal conjunction between the Giver of Life and its receptacle. Yet man of himself alone cannot remove the least evil from his Proprium, although the power is given him to desist from sin if he chooses, and then the Lord removes the evil and enters the Proprium and re-creates it with spiritual principles, bearing the iniquity "without the camp" to the circumference, and saves man from his own evil Proprium, by redeeming or liberating him from the influence of this evil spirit from Hell, or Self Love.

679. The evil that a man has done in the past, cannot be separated from his responsibility, but will remain as his own through Eternity, for the sin which he has committed cannot be imputed to any other person, and therefore it cannot be absolutely detached from his individuality; but so far as the Lord enters by means of love and obedience to the Precepts of the Word, so far the evils and falses of the Proprium are removed to the outer boundary of the individuality of the regenerating man.

680. Heaven does not extinguish Hell, but in the regenerating man, removes those evil and false principles which are from Hell, for the Life of Good and Truth from the Lord by means of the Word, constitutes Heaven, and these are the principles which remove evil and falsity, when man desists from and resists evil. Thus man, who in and of himself alone is a Hell in miniature, by regeneration becomes a Heaven, and as far as Heavenly Life enters his nature, Hell is removed, but the evil he has done in the past will never be separated from his individuality, although the regenerating man will be washed and purified from it in his actual life in the future by means of the Truths of the Word. He can never glory in self-righteousness, but can look back and to the outside, to his past wicked thoughts and actions, which will always be presented before his mental vision, when he is tempted to exalt himself, or look away from the Lord; for whenever he turns away from the Center of his spiritual universe, he looks to the circumference where all his evils and falses are dormant, and he sees his own righteousness as "filthy rags."

And when they had performed all things according to the law of the Lord, they returned into Galilee, to their own city Nazareth. Luke 2: 39.

681. When the Precepts of the Word are obeyed from interior motives of Love conjoined with Truth, which takes place during the Fourth Day of Creation, they enter the Exterior or Natural principles of the External mind and invigorate them with spiritual life, and thus they bring the natural life nearer the Lord and farther away from the hereditary evil of the Proprium, for "Galilee" signifies the Natural principles of the External mind which receive the Natural or Literal Truths of the Word.

THE NATURE OF THE WORD OF GOD. 299

Instruction from the Word. Development of thought.

682. By the "City of Nazareth," is signified the Doctrine or Instruction received from the Literal Sense of the Word, within which the Interior principles of spiritual life reside and are revealed to the mind. As the evil and false principles are removed in the regenerating man, the Appearances of Truth which are upon the surface of the Literal Sense of the Word, are proportionately dispersed, and thus material ideas of the nature of the Word are gradually dissipated, and a true conception of its Divinity is formed within the Rational Faculty, which is born into life, and increases in development.

And the child grew, and waxed strong in spirit, filled with wisdom; and the grace of God was upon him.
Luke 2 : 40.

683. By "the child grew," is signified the further perfection of the Rational Faculty from the entrance of the Lord as a child from the Internal mind, for "growing" signifies advancing in interior knowledges of the Word. "And waxed strong in spirit," signifies increasing perception of the Word, for "strength" is predicated of Truth.

684. The SPIRIT is the whole man himself which is within the physical body, and is the complex of all the faculties of the spiritual body. The SOUL is the Interior life of the spiritual body, or the very Spiritual Essence of man, while the Spirit is the Spiritual Substance of man. The Spirit of man is not a shapeless etherial vapor, but is the real man himself, with all his faculties

as a tangible object of thought. It is not the death of the physical frame which man should fear, but that Death of the Spiritual Perceptions which is caused by disobedience to the Precepts of Life, which turns the Divine Love and Wisdom of the Lord into the Love of Self and the World, and thus into hatred and falsity, so that the Good and Truth of the Word cannot be seen. To save man from this Death, the Lord has entered the world by means of the Word, and made known the Principles of Spiritual Life, by obedience to which, every faculty of the spirit will be kindled into existence, and "wax strong," and be "filled with wisdom."

685. "Filled with wisdom," denotes that the Divine Truth reigns within the whole man, even though all the evils and falses of the Proprium are not yet removed. True Wisdom is derived from Love, and is an Internal perception of the Divine Truth of the Word. Where the Divine Truth reigns, the Proprium of man cannot rule over the Affections, for if a man loves the Truths of the Word by obeying them, they give him such inward delight that Self-love appears to him in a diabolical form, so that he is led to shun those evil and false principles which destroy spiritual life.

686. "And the grace of God was upon him," signifies that humiliation which is derived from the Affection of Truth, denoted by "Grace." This humiliation is the inward acknowledgment that in man alone, there is nothing but evil, and that in his own strength he has not power to look to the Lord, or receive spiritual in-

struction from the Word. "Mercy" signifies humiliation or adoration which is derived from the Affection of Good, and when both words are used together in the Word, Mercy denotes adoration from Love, and Grace represents humiliation. There is no humiliation, or Grace, where the Love of Self reigns, for if a person who is thus ruled, assumes the external appearance of humility, he is filled with Self-righteousness on account of his apparent meekness.

687. Thus the "Grace of God" is upon the External mind of the regenerating man, into which the Lord Jesus is entering as the Holy Child, growing, waxing strong, and being filled with wisdom. This is the "earth" which the Lord is entering by means of the Word, and is the Human Principle He is assuming, which is to be made Divine. The whole work of regeneration is from the Lord alone. The Internal mind is the sinless receptacle of the Lord alone, who has there entered and reigns supremely as Jehovah God.

688. This "Grace of God," or humiliation, exists on account of the hereditary human principle derived from the "mother," or the natural principle of the External mind, which is to be made Divine by being governed by spiritual principles which fill the Internal mind from the Internal Sense of the Word. When the regenerating man is in a true state of humiliation, he divests himself of all ability to think and do anything from himself, and submits himself altogether to the Lord, and thus accedes to the Divine Principles of the Word, or the Lord who fills the Internal mind. This is the conjunction of the Internal mind with the External mind of the regenerating man, and thus of the Internal Sense with the Literal Sense of the Word within him in the order of regeneration, signified by the Fourth Day of Creation.

The waters bringing forth.	Physical science.

THE FIFTH DAY OF CREATION;

OR,

THE FIFTH STATE OF REGENERATION.

And God said, Let the waters bring forth abundantly the moving creature that hath life, and fowl that may fly above the earth in the open firmament of heaven. Gen. 1 : 20.

689. It has been illustrated that "Waters" denote the knowledges and scientific principles which are stored in the External memory concerning the Literal Sense of the Word. To "bring forth" denotes acknowledgment in faith and act, of the Literal Truths of the Word, and "abundantly," which is predicated of Truths from Good, signifies the prolification of the knowledges of these Truths, arising from a life according to them. By "moving," or motion, is denoted a change of state in active progression, and by "creatures that have life," is denoted Scientific Truths in which there is Good, or which have been made alive by obedience.

690. These Scientific Truths are principles connected with the Word of God, and do not refer to the laws and axioms of physical science. All the self-evident truths of physical science exist from the Laws of Divine Order, but they belong to the degree of purely natural thought, and have no relation to the spiritual regeneration of men, excepting by the orderly laws of correspondence, for all natural things correspond to spiritual principles, but are in entirely distinct degrees of life.

| True life. | Moving creatures and fowls. |

691. After the "Great Lights" are kindled and placed in the Internal principle of the Rational Faculty, from which the External principle receives light, the regenerating man then begins to truly live. In the preceding states he was not filled with true spiritual life, because the Good which he did, he supposed originated from himself, and the Truths which he uttered, he imagined he spoke from his own knowledge. Since man in himself alone is spiritually dead, and he originates nothing but what is evil and false, therefore what he produces from himself is not alive, in consequence of his inability to do good from a principle which has no life in itself, for Good can only be derived from the real Fountain of Good, the Inmost Life of the Word.

692. In the development of spiritual life in which the regenerating man is led from the Appearance of Truth to the reality of spiritual principles, the Lord permits him at first to suppose that he does Good and speaks Truth from himself, because in the first states of regeneration he is incapable of conceiving otherwise, nor can he in any other manner be led to perceive and believe that all Goodness and all Truth is from the Lord alone.

693. While in the previous states, the Good and Truths which are in him are compared to the "grass," and also to the "herb yielding seed," and to the "tree yielding fruit," all of which are inanimate ; but when he has arrived at the Fifth State, he is vivified by Love and Faith, and believes that the Lord operates all the Good which he does, and all the Truth which he speaks, and in this State he is compared to the "moving creature that hath life, and fowl that may fly above the earth." "Fowls," or "flying creatures," signify Truths, and in the opposite sense they represent Falsity, and here they signify Spiritual Truths because they fly above the "earth" or External mind. Natural Truths are such as pertain to the Literal Sense of the Word, and which

take their form of expression from the correspondence of things and ideas which exist in the physical world of substance and natural thought, which are exterior to the Interior Principle of the Word, and thus do not originate from any Apparent events or circumstances in this physical world, but which exist from their correspondence with the Spiritual Principles of the Word.

694. The "Open firmament of heaven," is the illuminated Rational Faculty which is open above to receive influx and communication from the Heaven of the Internal mind, which is the Temple of the Lord in the regenerating man, and this "opening" is only by means of the Truths of the Word which are loved and therefore obeyed, and it can only take place by the removal of the Love of Self and the World.

695. The "waters bring forth abundantly the moving creatures," which are called "Fishes" throughout the Word, and they signify the Scientific principles of the External mind, animated by a Living Faith, whether mentioned in the Old or New Testament. A "Fisher" is a spiritual principle which instructs the Natural principle of the mind in the Truths of the Literal Sense of the Word. These "fishes" are the Natural Truths with which the "multitudes" are fed in the Gospel narratives, and which fill the "nets" of the "fishers." By "multitudes" are not signified men, women, and children, but principles of the External mind which are to be fed with the Natural or Literal Truths of the Word. By a "net" is signified the external sensual principle of the mind which is the receptacle of the "moving creatures," or "fishes."

| Birds, beasts and fishes. | The Inmost Life of the Word. |

696. The Literal Sense of the Word abounds in the mention of "birds," "beasts," and "fishes," and any thoughtful person may readily perceive in reading the Word, that Spiritual Principles are indicated by these names, instead of the objects which are mentioned, for without this Interior meaning in the Book called THE WORD OF GOD, the mentioning of such insignificant objects and things would be trifling with the Eternal Principles which save men from sin.

697. All Truths from the Word which are received into the life by obedience, are from the Lord, and contain within them Celestial and Spiritual Principles, which, could they be seen in the world, would appear as a Living Human Principle, because it contains the Life which constitutes man an angel in Heaven when he is regenerated by it. This Living Human Principle is seen in the Gospels of the Evangelists, where it is personified in the Human Form of the Lord Jesus Christ, first in the world of material thought, and to those who love to do His Commandments, He is revealed as the Inmost Life of the Word thus personified to the ultimate degree of natural thought. Every single expression, idea, and least principle of thought received and used by an angelic man has life, because the hereditary Proprium is subdued and removed, and therefore every Thought contains an Affection which proceeds from the Lord who is Life alone, and there is no obstruction from the Love of Self.

And God created great whales, and every living creature that moveth, which the waters brought forth abundantly, after their kind, and every winged fowl after his kind: and God saw that it was good. Gen. 1:21.

698. Every minute principle in the universe of mind and nature is in subordination to some general principle as a means of its existence and subsistence. "Great

"Whales" signify the general principles of the Scientifics of the External mind which are animated by a Living Faith which God creates. By a Living Faith is meant a belief in the Precepts of the Word which govern the life. The "Great Fish" which swallowed the prophet "Jonah," signifies the general knowledges of the Literal Sense of the Word which are applied to confirm false doctrines. A "Prophet" signifies the Divine Truth of the Word which teaches.

699. When the Literal Sense is used to confirm evil and false principles which originate from the Love of Self and the World, the Essential Living Truth of the Word is "swallowed," or obscured by the Appearances of Truth, and the simple Precepts of Love to the Lord and the Neighbor are hidden by the "traditions of men," which tend to place more stress upon matters concerning belief, than a life according to these Two precepts. As Wisdom exists from Love within; as the External proceeds from the Internal; as Truth is from Good, and as the circumference of a circle is projected from its center, so a True Faith results from a life in obedience to the Word from Interior motives, or Affection.

700. The prophet "Jonah" signifies the Lord, or the Internal Sense of the Word, which at the end of "three days and three nights," or a full state of preparation of the regenerating man, is cast out "upon the dry land." The "sea" in which this "great fish" exists, signifies the false principles which are derived from the Love of Self, on which the ship of false doctrine floats, and in which the sensual principles signified by "fishes," confirm all the fallacies of evil and false principles. "Jonah" being cast into the "sea," signifies the temptation which the regenerating man experiences before the "dry land" or External mind perceives the simple Truth of the Word as indicated by the Literal Sense separated from false doctrines; by obedience to which Truth the "ground" is prepared to receive the Life of the Internal Sense.

THE NATURE OF THE WORD OF GOD.

Every living creature.   The blessing of the Lord.

701. "Every living creature that moveth," signifies that all the Scientifics or Natural Truths in the External mind are vivified with a Living Principle derived from Love, which are now brought forth "abundantly" from a principle of Affection, according to their quality, or the requirements of the individuality of the regenerating man, in his preparation for usefulness.

702. "Fowls" signify Thoughts. "Wings" denote Spiritual Truths from the Word, because the Rational Faculty is derived and exists from them, and which sees from the Light of Heaven, which is Spiritual Truth. The wings of fowls, or birds, are like the arms and hands pertaining to man, which signify the power of Divine Truth. "Winged fowls" therefore signify thoughts containing Spiritual Truths which are derived from the Word of God, and the perception is implanted in the regenerating man that these Truths are from the Lord; and that the Word is Divine Truth, which perception is signified as before by the expression "And God saw that it was good."

And God blessed them, saying, Be fruitful and multiply, and fill the waters in the seas, and let fowl multiply on the earth. Gen. 1 : 22.

703. "God blessed them," signifies the presence of the Lord within the spiritual principles which are entering the External mind of the regenerating man, enriching them with Celestial and Spiritual Good. The Lord is present or remote with every man in proportion as he

loves the Neighbor from Internal motives. Every principle or receptacle which contains the Living Presence of the Lord, becomes "fruitful" and "multiplies" itself to a great degree, which does not appear while a man lives in the state of natural thought, but to an incomprehensible degree as the Rational Faculty is illuminated. "Fructification" is predicated of states of Love, and "Multiplication," of states of Truth, or Faith, which now enter and fill the natural scientific receptacles of the External mind, from the Literal Sense of the Word, within which the Spiritual Truths are developed and increased, which is signified by "and fill the seas, and let fowl multiply in the earth."

And the Evening and the Morning were the Fifth Day.
Gen. 1 : 23.

704. Thus the consummation of this State of Regeneration progresses from the obscurity of "evening" toward the light of "morning." The number "Five" signifies "much" and is predicated of Truths, and in this State denotes these Truths which are vivified by animated spiritual principles.

705. During the progress of regeneration, the experience and conflicts which occur in the External mind in the removal of the evils and falsities of the Proprium are represented in the historical narrative of the wise men worshipping the Infant Jesus, and by Herod seeking His life and the consequent flight into Egypt, as given in the second chapter of the Book of Matthew, which will be interpreted by the Spiritual principles illustrated in the preceding pages.

THE INFANCY OF JESUS.

Now when Jesus was born in Bethlehem of Judea, in the days of Herod the King, behold, there came wise men from the East to Jerusalem. Matt. 2: 1.

706. It has been illustrated that "Jesus, born in Bethlehem" is the Rational Faculty which is enlightened to perceive the Internal Sense of the Word, and that this is the Son of God who is born within the mind of the regenerating man, and who is to enter the External mind in proportion as the hereditary evil of the Proprium is removed. The state of the false principles derived from the Love of Self, which govern the unregenerated Proprium is represented by the "Days of Herod the king," but as the Incarnation of the Lord has begun in the External mind, the power of the Proprium must yield, and the influence of its evil and false spirits be gradually overcome and dispersed, for the perception is now implanted that the Word is Divine Truth, which is the Lord Himself.

707. The Truths which teach this knowledge are the "Wise men," who are from the "East," or the Lord, and who come to this "Jerusalem," which here signifies False Doctrine over which "Herod" is the king, because false doctrine is derived from the Appearances of Truth in the Literal Sense of the Word, when a man who is ruled by the Love of Self engages in External worship.

> Saying, Where is he that is born King of the Jews? for we have seen his star in the East, and are come to worship him. Matt. 2: 2.

708. "Saying" signifies communication to the mind, or perception that there should be received further instruction from the Word. The "Jews" here signify the Interior principles of the Word, and the "King" is the Divine Truth, or Internal Sense of the Word, which governs the Truths of the Literal Sense. "For we have seen his Star in the East," signifies that the Truths which have led to this perception were the Heavenly knowledges represented by the "Star in the East," which are from the Divine Wisdom, and are the constant guiding principles of Truth and of Life, which is signified by "and are come to worship him," for to worship the Lord, denotes the faithful performance of every duty in life, by which the Lord is acknowledged and confessed, and the spiritual and temporal welfare is thus regarded.

> When Herod the king had heard these things, he was troubled, and all Jerusalem with him. Matt. 2: 3.

709. When the false principles of the Proprium perceive the entrance of the Divine Truth of the Word illuminating the Rational Faculty, a disturbance occurs in the External mind, for the false doctrines which have been confirmed from the Literal Sense, are brought into confliction with the Light from Heaven. All these facts of Spiritual History occur within the life of the regenerating man, and are not physical events ot a past worldly

history. Concerning these Spiritual events, unless the reader knows something of the operation of his own mind in the word of regeneration, and is attentive to the principles which are operating within his own experience, he cannot know what is meant by the Illumination of the Rational Faculty, and that in this state there is disturbance and trouble at the beginning, and that peace and tranquility do not begin until victory triumphs over each temptation and conflict. The more a man has been absorbed in material and sensual ideas concerning the Word, the more severe will be the conflict between Truth and Falsity. The field of combat is the External mind, which alone is troubled during temptation.

And when he had gathered all the chief priests and scribes of the people together, he demanded of them where Christ should be born. Matt. 2 : 4.

710. The Love of Self which rules the Proprium is represented by "Herod the King," and as he governs the "Jerusalem" which is here treated of, so also the "chief priests and scribes of the people" who are governed by him, represent evil and false principles. In a good sense, the "chief priests" represent the Lord as to his Divine Love, and are the principles of Good in in the Word which lead the regenerating man to obey its Truths. A "Scribe" denotes the Word from which Doctrine, or Spiritual Instruction, is derived, because a scribe records thoughts, and the Word is a record of Divine Thoughts. By "People," is signified Truths.

711. In the opposite sense, "the chief priests and scribes of the people," signify the adulteration of the Goods and the falsification of the Truths of the Literal Sense of the Word. The Internal Sense cannot be falsified, because it is revealed only to the regenerating man whose life is principled in the Good and Truth of the Word, as far as he has comprehended it. By "Demanded" is signified Searching, and the Literal Sense as interpreted by false doctrines, is examined concerning the Humanity of the Lord, which is signified by "where Christ should be born." These are temptations which arise in the External mind of the regenerating man from the yet unregenerated Proprium which is to be overcome.

INTERPRETATION OF SCRIPTURE.

712. The Literal Sense of the Word is for all mankind, however their religious doctrines may differ, and as it reads the same in every language in regard to natural ideas, whether the reader is in the life of true or false doctrines, it is permitted every person to believe freely what seems true to his comprehension, according to his own state of life. If this freedom were not given to each man, there would be no reception of the Word, because there would be no acknowledgement that it is authoritative as a Religious Teacher, and thus even the unregenerated Proprium looks to the Literal Sense, and although it may falsely interpret its meaning to confirm its own state, the words of Spiritual History and Prophetic Utterance remain the same and contain the Interior Principles of Divine Truth.

713. The unregenerated Proprium of the man whose Rational Faculty has been illuminated, is filled with the knowledge of the Literal Sense of the Word, and in the struggle for supremacy, in the Infancy of the Child Jesus, seeks to confirm its own love by

Evil and false confirmations.   Time and place.

doctrines which have been previously implanted in the External memory, and which agree with the evil and false principles of the Proprium. An evil priest and a false scribe may teach the Literal Sense of the Word, for its Truth is the same whether uttered by the voice of a good or evil man, or if written by a true or hypocritical writer.

And they said unto him, In Bethlehem of Judea; for thus it is written by the prophets. Matt. 2 : 5.

714. "And they said unto him," signifies the communication of this knowledge to the understanding of the Proprium, for the unregenerated Proprium is meant by "Herod the King," and as it is ruled by the Love of Self, no Internal principle of the Word can enter the domain of this evil "king" while he reigns, and all perception of its meaning is closed by the natural ideas which occupy the External mind in which the unregenerated Proprium is not yet removed, and which are only thought of when the Word is read; for thoughts of time and place obscure the Spiritual Principles which are held within the Literal form of words. This temptation and obscurity occurs in the experience of every regenerating man until the Appearances of Truth are dissipated by the Love of Self and the World being removed, and the Proprium of the External mind is regenerated and filled with spiritual life.

715. Then it will be discerned that "In Bethlehem of Judea" signifies the Perception of the Rational Faculty illuminated from the Internal mind which is ruled by the Divine Love, and that "thus it is written by the

prophets," signifies that the Divine Truths of the Word are implanted in the life of those who perceive and receive the Internal Sense, for to "write" signifies to implant in the life, and "Prophets" signify the Divine Truths of the Word.

And thou, Bethlehem, in the land of Juda, art not the least among the princes of Juda; for out of thee shall come a Governor, that shall rule my people Israel. Matt. 2:6.

716. The "Land of Juda," signifies the regenerating man who is actuated by the Celestial principle of Love, and "Bethlehem" is the Perception of the Rational Faculty which exists from this principle. "Art not the least among the princes of Juda," signifies that this Perception is the Superior or Interior principle within the Primary Truths of Love to the Lord and the Neighbor, for a "Prince" signifies a primary or leading Truth.

717. Out of this Interior principle of the Rational Faculty the "Governor" will proceed, in the perception of the Divine Truth of the Word in the External principle of the Rational Faculty, which presides over the Literal Truths of the Word which have been obeyed, and illustrates their spiritual meaning. By "Israel" is meant Spiritual Good which has been made alive in the Natural principle of the External mind, by obedience to the Truth which shines through the Literal Sense of the Word to all who love the Lord and the Neighbor. The "Governor" is the Spiritual Sense of the Word received into the External principle of the Rational Faculty.

> Then Herod, when he had privily called the wise men, enquired of them diligently what time the Star appeared. Matt. 2: 7.

718. Self-Love is so insidious in its nature that it seeks in every form to separate the External from the Internal mind, and to this end it assumes the Appearance of Truth as far as it can move the inmost principles of the Natural mind, and communicates with the True Doctrines of Life from the Word, in order to observe the state of the progress of true knowledges from the Word, which will be destructive to the Love of Self. At this state of progress, the regenerating man is not aware of the insinuating nature of Self-Love, and does not perceive its operation, therefore it "privily" calls the "wise men."

> And he sent them to Bethlehem, and said, Go and search diligently for the young child; and when ye have found him, bring me word again, that I may come and worship him also. Matt. 2: 7.

719. The audacity of the Proprium in the time of temptation, when the Light from Heaven seems obscured in the combats of regeneration, is illustrated in this verse. "He sent them to Bethlehem," signifies the directing of the Affections formed by the doctrines from the Word, to the Perception of the Interior principle of the Rational Faculty, to prove if there is a separation between the Rational Faculty and the External mind. The desire of the Proprium to rule over this Affection, is signified by "And when ye have found him, bring me

word again." "That I may come and worship him also," signifies the desire of the Proprium to turn the Perception of the Internal Sense of the Word into self-intelligence, so that profanation will pervert its meaning and thus destroy Internal worship, or Spiritual Life.

720. As the unregenerated Proprium is nothing but evil, all External worship which is performed from it is Idolatry, for there is no inward life in it; but worship which is derived from the Precepts of the Word is alive, because within all the principles of the Word, there is a Spiritual Sense which treats of all things which are from the Lord, and within the Spiritual Sense is the Celestial Sense which treats of the Lord alone. This Inmost Sense is above the comprehension of any man while living in the natural world of thought, but the Sanctity and Life of the Word is from this Source alone, within which is the Divine Being Himself from whom all things exist.

721. The Word is as a Divine Man. The Literal Sense is the Body, and the Internal Sense is the Soul which alone gives life to the Literal Sense, which thus has its Holiness from the Internal Sense within. It appears as if the Literal Sense vanishes or dies when the Internal Sense is revealed, when on the contrary, it does not vanish, but is vivified in the regenerating man by the Internal Sense.

THE LIGHT OF NATURE.

722. It is a common belief among educated men that without the Revealed Word, what is called the "Light of Nature," teaches that there is a God to be worshipped, and that there is an immortal life beyond the death of the physical frame, besides many other facts taught by the natural sciences. Scientific facts are natural truths which exist from Spiritual principles to which they correspond; but man of himself, or in his own self derived intelligence, knows nothing concerning the Divine Principles of Regeneration without the Revelation of the Word of God.

THE NATURE OF THE WORD OF GOD. 317

Natural self-intelligence.   Worship of self.

723. Since man is born into the hereditary evils of the Love of Self, which are such as to preclude the Divine influences entering his mind from the Lord, they open the door for the influx of evil, which causes him to be blind to Spiritual Principles. The "Light of Nature" is the self-intelligence of the Natural mind, which cannot elevate the thoughts above the Proprium into Spiritual Perception, without the Word of God.

724. All the knowledge of Spiritual principles which men have possessed, has not been derived from their self-intelligence, although they may have seemed wise in their own estimation, and have supposed that they were originators of religious teachings, but their wisdom has been derived from doctrines which have in various forms descended through successive generations from those to whom Divine Revelation was given.

725. The entire Word rests upon the two Precepts of Love to the Lord and the Neighbour, which are opposed to the Love of Self and the World, and thus the unregenerated Proprium turns away from the Lord and the Living Truths of the Word, and worships its own loves, using the Literal Sense of the Word to confirm false principles, and it would profane the Interior Truths of the Word if they could be known to that state, but the Love of Self cannot perceive where the "young child" is, and therefore cannot worship him."

When they had heard the king, they departed; and, lo, the star, which they saw in the East, went before them, till it came and stood over where the young child was. Matt. 2:9.

726. "When they had heard the King," signifies that the Truths already implanted within the Rational Faculty perceive the temptations of the Proprium, and "they departed" signifies that they recede from or shun these evil influences. "And, lo, the Star, which they saw in

the East, went before them," signifies clearer perception by means of the knowledge of the Good and Truth of the Word, which leads to more Internal principles. "Till it came and stood over where the young child was," signifies the progression of this perception until the Rational Faculty discerns that this "young child" is the Son of God, and that He is the Word who is being made Divine in the External mind of the regenerating man.

When they saw the Star, they rejoiced with exceeding great joy. Matt. 2: 10.

727. The knowledges which lead to the understanding of the Internal Sense of the Word are obtained by means of the Science of the Correspondence of natural things with Spiritual Principles, and this Science will be made known to all regenerating men who desire to know the true Source of the Divinity of the Word. This knowledge is a cause of "exceeding great joy," because the things of the physical world on every hand become representative of the Spiritual Truths of the Word, not only the tangible objects of sense, but the orderly principles of science and art, and there is not a thing in this world which does not correspond to either Good or Truth, or its opposite evil and falsity.

THE TRUE SOURCE OF INTELLECTUAL CULTURE.

728. The Science of Correspondence is derived from the Internal Sense of the Word, and it is not an earthly science invented by the ingenuity of a finite mind. The Divine Truth

which is made manifest within the Word by the Spiritual Sense, attests its Divinity, and in all time to come, loving hearts will find within the Spiritual Sense of the Word, the most elevating intellectual science which the mind is capable of grasping. With these interior Truths every earthly science and knowledge will co-operate and help illustrate, and regenerating men will rejoice at every discovery in the world of physical science, and refined Art will join hands with the True Source of all enlightenment, for by the Internal Sense of the Word, "*Mercy and Truth are met together; righteousness and peace have kissed each other. Truth shall spring out of the earth; and righteousness shall look down from heaven.*" The adoration of the Word which is expressed in such terms of affection in the One Hundred and Nineteenth Psalm will then be understood by the man who obeys, for in keeping these Divine Precepts "there is great reward," for these are the treasuries which contain the spiritual riches of Heaven.

And when they were come into the house, they saw the young child with Mary his mother, and fell down and worshipped him; and when they had opened their treasures, they presented unto him gifts; gold and frankincense and myrrh. Matt. 2: 11.

729. "House" signifies the Rational Faculty where Good and Truth are conjoined in the regenerating man, because the Marriage of these Two Principles from the Word constitutes one enlightened mind which dwells within, and "to come into the house" signifies the entrance of these Affections for True Doctrine from the Word, or "wise men," which perceive its Internal Sense, which have led to this Affection by obedience, which is signified by "they saw the young child with Mary his mother." The Son of God is the Internal Sense of the

Word which has entered the Affections of the regenerating man who has loved and obeyed its simple Precepts as they are given in the Literal Sense.

730. These Affections which are formed from True Doctrine "fall down," or prostrate themselves in humility and acknowledgment, and worship the Lord from Internal principles. By "when they had opened their treasures," is signified the communication and conjunction of the Divine Truths of the Word within the life of the regenerating man, and the acknowledgment that the Affections and Thoughts which are filled with Good and Truth from the Word, are "gifts" from the Lord alone, is signified by "they presented unto him gifts." These Affections of Good and Truth are "Gold," or Celestial Good; "Frankincense," or Spiritual Good; and "Myrrh," or Natural Good.

731. Celestial Good is Love to the Lord. Spiritual Good is Love to the Neighbour. Natural Good pertains to the natural affections, which give delight to the natural principle of the External mind, from external things in speech and actions with which the natural life communicates. The delight of Natural Good is in the life of usefulness to others. Before Regeneration begins, the Natural Good in man's external life is only an Appearance of Good, because it is not vivified with Spiritual Life from the Living Principles of the Word.

732. All good affections which are within the regenerating man, contain the conjunctive principles of Truth, because in the order of regeneration, in being re-created from natural hereditary evil and falsity to Spiritual Good and Truth, the Affections of Good are formed by means of Truths from the Word, and Good is the Internal principle of Truth, which latter becomes its form or boundary.

THE NATURE OF THE WORD OF GOD. 321

Warning.   The other Life.

And being warned of God in a dream that they should not return to Herod, they departed into their own country another way. Matt. 2: 12.

733. To be "warned of God in a dream," signifies that foresight is implanted within the perception that the Love of Self is fostered by the Appearances of Truth which are in the Literal Sense of the Word, when there is no Internal Sense acknowledged. "They departed into their own country another way," signifies that True Doctrine from the Word recedes from the Appearances of Truth into the Internal Sense from which it is derived, and which is the opposite of false doctrines which favor the Love of Self and thus lead to "Herod," the king of the Proprium.

DREAMS AND VISIONS.

734. During sleep, the exterior thought is quiescent, and in Dreams there is only the appearance of time, because the exterior natural principle of the mind is not operating through the external senses. If men understood the Science of Correspondence with which the Word is written, they could interpret their own spiritual states in every dream which could be retained and brought forth from the external memory. The difference between Dreams and Visions, exists in the fact that in Visions, things or principles are seen in the "other life" by those whose Interior Sight is opened, but which are not seen by the physical eye. This Interior Sight is the Rational Faculty of the regenerating man, and the "Other Life" is the Spiritual World of thought to which his mind has been elevated by the Internal Sense of the Word, which is in this Spiritual World. The "Other Life" should not be thought of as existing in a remote degree of space in distance far away, but as an elevated or spiritual state of Interior Affection and Thought

now existing within the regenerating man. There is no degree of Spiritual Affection and Thought opened to the man who has not begun the work of a regenerate life.

735. There are True and False Visions. Many persons of irrational and credulous minds see Visions in phantasies which are induced by states of their unregenerated Proprium. Such persons are visionaries, and the things which they see are illusions proceeding from memories of external objects fostered into the appearance of reality by the Proprium, which are seen from the obscure light of self-intelligence. Such Visions are dangerous to cherish, because the tendency is to lead them to think that they are specially favored with gifts which others do not possess, and instead of diligently searching the Word by means of which their Interior Sight may be opened in an orderly manner, so that they may have open communication with the Spiritual World, they await a visionary influx of revelation which they vaunt before their neighbors with a parade of mysticism, as though they possessed a key to the mysteries of Heaven, to which others have not the same access. Such is the phantasy induced upon them by their own evils and falses, which are fostered by ignorance of the True Spiritual Principles of the Word.

736. Genuine Visions are the actual sight of the things which exist in the Spiritual World of the Word, which are seen by the eyes of the spirit, or Rational Faculty, and not by the physical eye, and such Visions may be seen by any persons who desire, by leading a regenerate life according to the Truths of the Word. When the Interior Sight of the Rational Faculty is opened, spiritual things are seen in a Light far clearer than the noon-day light of the natural world of self intelligence, and not only the representatives which surround spirits are seen, but the spirits themselves, by a perception of the quality of the life which flows from them. These "Spirits" are the Truths of the Word which form the lives of regenerating men.

737. Such visions are permitted only to the regenerating man when clearer revelation is to be made to the Rational Faculty

concerning the Internal Sense of the Word. All things which appear in the Literal Sense of the Word are for the spiritual knowledge of men who are in the physical world, otherwise they would not have been written in this form of expression, which corresponds in natural thought to their prior existence in the Spiritual World, and the Spiritual Sense may be known to all who desire higher knowledge of Divine things, by means of a life according to the Precepts of the Word. Then will the spiritual state of regenerating men advance upon and within the "earth," in fulfilment of the prophecy in the Book of Joel: "*And it shall come to pass afterward that I will pour out my Spirit upon all flesh; and your sons and your daughters shall prophesy, your old men shall dream dreams, your young men shall see visions; and also upon the servants and upon the handmaids in those days will I pour out my Spirit.*" To "dream dreams" signifies to receive revelation, and to "see visions" signifies to perceive revelation.

738. The Lord reveals the things of the Spiritual World to the "Prophets" not only by Visions, but by Dreams, which are equally representative and significative. There are three kinds of Dreams. The First come immediately through Heaven, or the Internal mind, from the Lord, such as the prophetical dreams recorded in the Word, which are in obscurity until they are coherently interpreted by the laws of correspondence which are derived from the Internal sense of the Word. The second kind occur by means of "angelic spirits," or the Goods and Truths of the Word which teach the spiritual significance of the Literal Sense of the Word to the man who is yet dreaming, and the Third kind result from the influence of spirits who are near man when he is asleep, and which are significative of Divine principles; These "spirits" are the Literal Truths of the Word which are nearest the state of the regenerating man when he is in the sleep of natural thought concerning the Word, before his Rational Faculty is awakened to the perception of the Internal Sense, and that this is the Son of God

739. Evil spirits have the greatest and most burning desire to infest and assault man during the sleep of natural thought; but he is then especially in the care of the Lord, who does not permit the Freedom of the Will to be violated, for Love never sleeps. These "evil spirits" are the lusts of the Proprium which so fiercely assault and infest the regenerating man when he is entering the preparation for spiritual life; but while he is in the state of spiritual sleep concerning the Internal Sense of the Word, the Proprium has no power to overcome him and lead him away from the Lord, or the Word, while he lives in obedience to the Literal Truths of the Word, although he is yet asleep in regard to their Interior meaning.

740. Spiritual Death results from a life of disobedience to the Word, but Spiritual Sleep is a preparatory state of obedience prior to the awakening of the dawn of the Spiritual Sense, to which a Dream is an intermediate state of obscurity; but a Vision is the clear opening or awakening of the Rational Faculty to perceive the things of the Spiritual World of the mind as revealed by the Internal Sense of the Word. Phantastical dreams arise from the Love of Self, and are especially caused by intemperance in drinking and eating, or imbibing and appropriating false doctrines from the Word, which causes incoherence and obscurity concerning the Actual Truths of the Literal Sense.

And when they were departed, behold, the angel of the Lord appeareth to Joseph in a dream, saying, Arise, and take the young child and his mother, and flee into Egypt, and be thou there until I bring thee word; for Herod will seek the young child to destroy him. Matt. 2: 13.

741. When the perceptions of the True Doctrine from the Word have receded from the Appearances of Truth, the Divine Truth of the Word is revealed to the Rational Faculty, signified by "Joseph." "Arise," signifies the

Arising.	Order of Instruction.

elevation of the Rational Faculty from the temptation resulting from the conjunction of the Proprium with the Appearance of Truth, to the Internal Sense of the Word, by the Affection for the Truth which has been fostered by the Literal Sense as a "mother," from which the perception of the Internal Sense is born.

742. The principles of the Internal Sense are now to be confirmed by the Literal Sense, which is signified by "and flee into Egypt," for "Egypt" signifies the scientifics or knowledges of the Literal Sense of the Word in the natural principles of the External mind. Thus the enlightened Rational Faculty, or the "young child," must receive instruction as earthly children gain knowledge, by means of the external objects and thoughts which are communicated by the Literal Sense of the Word. The Interior principle or Internal mind is from the Father, or Inmost Life of the Word, while the External mind which is to be regenerated by the Interior Divine Principles of the Word, is first formed within the Affection for the Truth of the Literal Sense as a "mother," and this External Human Principle of the Word is to be made Divine by the entrance of the Interior Truths into the External mind.

743. The External mind cannot be reduced to correspondence and conjunction with the Internal, excepting by knowledges derived from the Literal Sense of the Word. The External mind is corporeal and sensual, and is not receptive of Celestial and Spiritual principles until these knowledges are previously implanted as

The Life of the Word.	Egypt and magic.

"seeds" in the "ground"; for within these knowledges Celestial principles find their recipient vessels, as "waterpots containing two or three firkins apiece." The Word contains the Life of the Lord in every part, although this fact does not appear in the External form by the Literal Sense alone. In the Internal Sense there is nothing said which has not relation to Him, or does not proceed from Him, for the Literal Sense, or earthly covering of the Word which He assumes for the sake of earthly men, is only an addition to the Internal Sense, or His Divine Essence which exists in the Heavens, and which has existed from Eternity. "Egypt" is the science of knowledges in respect to the Literal Sense of the Word, but when men seek to enter the Divine Principles of the Word from their self-derived intelligence which proceeds from the Love of Self, this science becomes perverted into magic and falsity, for "magic" signifies the perversion of order and the abuse of the Science of Correspondence. The good or evil meaning of "Egypt" in the Word, may be proved throughout the historical and prophetical expressions of the Old Testament. Thus the enlightened Rational Faculty flees into the Literal Sense of the Word with all its knowledges, in order that the Foundation may be laid for true Spiritual Science to be built upon, for the Foundation of all Heavenly Knowledge rests upon the Divinity of the Literal Sense of the Word, just as the spiritual body of man while in this physical world rests within the corporeal frame.

THE NATURE OF THE WORD OF GOD. 327

Further knowledge of the Literal Sense.   Night.

744. "And be thou there until I bring thee word," signifies the state of instruction of the "young child" in the regenerating man, in which the enlightened Rational Faculty must remain until its full state, which will then be made known by the Lord, by clearer revelation concerning the Word, for until the knowledges of the Literal Sense have been fully received into the External memory, there is danger that the Proprium will assert itself in the effort to destroy the spiritual life which has begun to enter the External mind, which is signified by "for Herod will seek the young child to destroy him."

When he arose, he took the young child and his mother by night, and departed into Egypt. Matt. 2: 14.

745. When the Rational Faculty is elevated above the temptations of the Proprium by the enlightenment which is born from the Affection of Truth to discern the obscurity which results from the influence of Self Love, signified by "by night," it resists this temptation and enters the State of Instruction from the Word here signified by "Egypt."

And was there until the death of Herod; that it might be fulfilled which was spoken of the Lord by the prophet, saying, Out of Egypt have I called my son. Matt. 2: 15.

746. This Instruction of the External mind of the regenerating man in the scientifics and knowledges of the Literal Sense of the Word continues until the evils and falses of the Proprium, signified by "Herod," are removed. "That it might be fulfilled which was spoken

of the Lord by the prophet," signifies that the Instruction is according to the Laws of Divine Order in the progress of regeneration according to the Internal Sense, for thus the Prophetic Word reveals to the perception that the Divine Truth, or Son, will be received by those whose lives are governed by the knowledges of the Literal Sense which have been stored in the memory by the study of the Word as it has been given to the natural world of thought, and from which the Science of Correspondence is studied and verified, signified by "Egypt."

> Then Herod, when he saw that he was mocked of the wise men, was exceeding wroth, and sent forth, and slew all the children that were in Bethlehem, and in all the coasts thereof, from two years old and under, according to the time which he had diligently enquired of the wise men. Matt. 2: 16.

747. During this State of Instruction, the evil and false influences of the Proprium are frustrated by the entrance of True Doctrine from the Word which causes separation between Truth and falsity, and this "Herod" is filled with hatred, for the Love of Self turns itself in aversion to the Light which is now entering the External mind of the regenerating man, and this hatred destroys in itself the entrance to that innocent state in which Truth is conjoined to Good in the natural mind, and obscures the perception of the Rational Faculty, so that even the Actual Truths of the Literal Sense, signified by "the "coasts thereof," are not received by the most exterior principles of the External mind, but are hidden by false doctrines.

748. This is the desire and effort of the Proprium, but in the Spiritual World, evil cannot injure or destroy Good, nor can falsity destroy Truth, and all hatred and deceit re-acts upon the evil principle itself and destroys its capacity for receiving Good and Truth from the Word, and thus the unregenerated Proprium destroys itself in the regenerating man, because when it is resisted, the Divine Truth enters with power to overcome its influence. By "two years old and under," is signified during the entire period or state of combat which began when the Proprium endeavored to influence the interior and exterior principles of the External mind by means of the "wise men," by attempting to pervert the Affections concerning True Doctrine from the Word.

Then was fulfilled that which was spoken by Jeremy the prophet, saying, Matt. 2 : 17.

749. Thus it is according to Divine Order that the evils of Self Love should re-act upon themselves according to the prophecy in Jeremiah which treats of the vastation or destruction of the evil Proprium of regenerating men. Where the name of a "Prophet" is mentioned, it does not mean a person, but the Divine Truth of the Prophetic Word which is fulfilled in the regenerating man. The word "Jeremiah" signifies Exaltation, and "exaltation" signifies the power of Divine Truth which exists from the Interior Principle of the Word which devastates and drives out the evils and falses of the Proprium during regeneration, and thus "Jeremy the prophet"

signifies the power of the Divine Truth of the Word which teaches the Rational Faculty in the combat against the Proprium.

> In Rama was there a voice heard, lamentation, and weeping, and great mourning. Rachel weeping for her children, and would not be comforted, because they are not. Matt. 2 : 14.

750. "In Rama," signifies those principles in the regenerating man which are receptive of Spiritual Truth from a Celestial origin, or from the Divine Love. The "Voice" which is heard, is the Divine Truth of the Word which is perceived and obeyed. "Lamentation," signifies the desolation which reigns in the External mind when the Internal Sense is obscured in the state of temptation. "Weeping," signifies the grief of the Understanding, and "Mourning" the grief of the Will. "Weeping" is manifested by tears, which are composed of water mingled with salt. The water of tears signifies grief on account of falsity, and "salt" signifies the spiritual devastation produced by false doctrines, and "tears" therefore signify grief on account of there being no understanding of Truth, while "Mourning" is an inward affection of grief which manifests itself in "Weeping." "Rachel," denotes Affection for the Interior Truth of the Word, and "weeping for her children," signifies the grief of spirit when the understanding of the Interior Goods and Truths of the Word is in darkness, when there is no apparent inflowing of knowledge concerning them, and when there is no perception of their coherent meaning.

Joseph in Egypt. Elevation above temptation.

But when Herod was dead, behold, an angel of the Lord appeareth in a dream to Joseph in Egypt. Matt. 2 : 7.

751. At the end of this state of temptation, the Divine Truth of the Word shines with Interior Light into the Rational Faculty through the External scientifics of the Word, or the knowledges of the Literal Sense, by means of the science of Spiritual Correspondence, signified by "Joseph in Egypt," in which the Rational Faculty is being instructed.

Saying, Arise, and take the young child and his mother, and go into the land of Israel: for they are dead which sought the young child's life. Matt. 2 : 20.

752. The Rational Faculty is now elevated from this state of instruction and temptation, through which the laws of Spiritual Correspondence are perceived, denoted by "Egypt," to the Interior Truth of the Word, for the "Land of Israel" signifies the regenerating man who obeys the Truths of the Word from a principle of Love. "For they are dead which sought the young child's life," signifies the removal of the evil and false principles of the Proprium, over which the Divine Truth from the Lord within the regenerating man has obtained the victory.

And he arose, and took the young child and his mother, and came into the land of Israel. Matt. 2 : 21.

753. This verse signifies the elevation of the Rational Faculty to clearer perception of the Internal Sense, by which this event of spiritual history is confirmed in the experience of the regenerating man, similar to the expression "*And God saw that it was good : and it was so.*"

But when he heard that Archelaus did reign in Judea in the room of his father Herod, he was afraid to go thither ; notwithstanding, being warned of God in a dream, he turned aside into the parts of Galilee. Matt. 2 : 22.

754. " When he heard," signifies further perception of the Rational Faculty. "Archelaus" is the son of " Herod, and in the original language, signifies " a prince of the people." In a good sense the word "prince" signifies a leading Truth, and in the opposite sense it signifies a primary falsity of the Proprium. The word "people," in a good sense, has relation to Truth, and in the opposite sense, to falsity. A " Son," in a good sense, signifies a general Truth, and its opposite meaning denotes falsity. As " Father," in a good sense signifies the Divine Good, in the opposite sense it signifies the evil of the Proprium, " Herod." " Judea," in a good sense, signifies the Celestial principles of the Internal mind, and in the opposite sense it denotes the voluntary principle of the Proprium over which "Archelaus" reigns.

755. The Perception is imparted that the evil and false principles which reign in the will of the unregenerated Proprium are not yet subdued. No evil exists in the Internal mind, and the enlightened Rational Faculty now holds the Proprium in aversion, which is signified by " He was afraid to go thither." " Being warned of God in a dream," signifies instruction derived from the Word, even though the Internal Sense is yet in obscurity, by obedience to which the lusts of the Proprium are

resisted and avoided, and the corporeal and natural principles of the External mind are brought under the subjection of the Rational Faculty, which external principles are signified by "he turned aside into the parts of Galilee."

THE PARTS OF GALILEE.

756. There are Three general principles belonging to the External mind, viz:—The Corporeal, or Sensual principle, the Natural, or Material principle, and the Rational, or Intellectual principle. The Corporeal principle is not the physical frame which contains man, but is the Outermost principle by which the mind communicates through the senses with the corporeal frame, and thus comes in communication with the physical world. The Natural principle is the Middle, in which exists all material thoughts; and the Rational principle is the Interior in which thoughts concerning the Word are Intellectual. So far as one principle prevails in the mind above the other, so far the person is either a Corporeal or Natural, or a Rational man. These Three Parts, or principles, communicate orderly with each other, the Corporeal with the Natural, and the Natural with the Rational.

757. When the life of regeneration first begins, the man is in a Corporeal state of thought, but he possesses a latent faculty which renders him capable of being perfected. Afterwards, he enters a state of Natural thought concerning the Word, and at length he is led to a state of Rational thought. His regeneration takes place according to this progression, and his perception of the Internal sense is educated in this order of the "Parts of Galilee." The Corporeal principle communicates with the Natural by the things of sensuous perception, and the Natural principle communicates with the Rational distinctly by those things which relate to the Understanding, and which pertain to the Will, in order that the regenerating man may be re-created with spiritual life. The sensual principle of the Sight and Hearing, by which the Word

is read and its Truths inwardly heard and obeyed, especially are the external principles which perfect the Rational Faculty, and these have reference to the Understanding, while the correspondence of the sense of Touch, Smell and Taste, have especial respect to the Will.

758. The Corporeal principle of the External mind by means of the senses, communicates with the Natural principle, which is the middle, or intermediate part ; for those ideas of thought which enter by the senses, as in reading or hearing the Word, repose in the Natural principle as in a receptacle, which is the External memory. The delights or enjoyments derived from these Natural Thoughts, pertain to the Will, and are called Natural Goods, whereas the scientifics or knowledges therein relate to the Understanding, and are called Natural Truths, which are the Truths of the Literal Sense of the Word. Every regenerating man is first born into the Corporeal or Sensual degree of existence, in which the five senses which operate through the physical frame are to be opened by use. When he begins to think from the objects which are presented to the mind through these senses, his thoughts become Sensual, and rest in the Appearances of Truth, and in doctrines derived therefrom, from which he becomes Interiorly Sensual. He next advances to the world of Natural thought, and by the study of the Word, and a moral life in harmony with its Precepts, his thoughts become Interiorly Natural, and this is the First or Ultimate degree of Life, which is the receptacle of the Literal Sense of the Word, in which the Foundation is laid for the perception of the Internal Sense, which is discerned only by the Rational Faculty.

759. The Natural principle of the External mind, by means of the thoughts of the things received through the senses, communicates with the Rational Faculty, or the Interior principle of the External mind. The thoughts which are elevated thence toward this Interior principle, repose themselves in the Rational Faculty as in a receptacle, which forms the Interior Memory. All the delights and enjoyments of the things stored within this Interior

THE NATURE OF THE WORD OF GOD. 335

External and internal truths.   Disorderly interpretation.

Memory pertain to the Will, and are called Rational Goods, while Interior views and perceptions of these things are called Rational Truths.

760. The things in the Natural principle which are derived from the exercise of the external senses, which are seen only in the Literal Sense of the Word, are called the External Truths of Good; but those things which are derived from the exercise of the interior senses which receive the Internal principles of the Word, are called Interior Goods and Truths. Those things which are between these, and partake of each principle are Intermediate Goods and Truths. Thus it may be comprehended by the regenerating man whose rational faculty is enlightened, and to him alone, what is signified by "the Parts of Galilee."

761. The mind of the regenerating man receives the Interior Truths of the Word in the order of these Three Principles of the External mind. At first, the thoughts concerning these Divine Truths are Corporeal, in that the ideas of the realities of the spiritual world and spiritual science are pleasing to the corporeal principles of the mind, for at the beginning they take upon themselves a corporeal form somewhat independent of their relation to the Word of God, and are thought of, just as the "angels" and "spirits" of the Word are considered as individualities external to these regenerating principles within the mind, when they are not external persons, but the Goods and Truths of the Word in the regenerating man, for the mind cannot at first conceive of these principles abstractedly, unless they are personified in the human form. Thus these Interior Principles are first seen as an external Face or Frontispiece.

762. Next in order, these Divine Truths become Natural, as the mind perceives their relation to the Word, and endeavors to make a material reality of the spiritual History and Prophecies of the Word, by accepting and attempting to confirm all these spiritual narratives as physical facts, in addition to giving them an internal meaning, notwithstanding this disorderly method of interpreting the Spiritual Sense of the Word, and much conflic-

tion arises in the Rational Faculty concerning Appearances and the spiritual Reality, but the glimmering of light which shines from the Internal sense into the Natural principle constitutes the Gate or Portal which will surely be opened.

763. But when the Rational Faculty becomes the "Ruler" and "Governor" of these subordinate principles of the External mind, the whole Word will be seen in the clear spiritual Light which shines from the Internal Sense, and the names of persons, places, and things will be perceived to be purely significative and representative of Divine principles which culminate in the Literal Sense of the Word, and are thence received into the External mind as the Ultimate of the Word, and thus the Summary of the "Parts of Galilee" will appear in the Rational Faculty of the regenerating man.

764. SIGNIFICATIVES, in the Word, are the words themselves, which denote spiritual principles. REPRESENTATIVES are the descriptions in historical order, or form of narration, which denote successive spiritual principles in the progress of regeneration. CORRESPONDENCES relate to things in the natural world which denote spiritual principles in the Word and man, such as the Eye, denoting the understanding, the Ear, perception and obedience, the Heart, corresponding to love, the Lungs, denoting wisdom, etc., which give an analogy between physical, natural and spiritual things.

And he came and dwelt in a city called Nazareth: that it might be fulfilled which was spoken by the prophets, He shall be called a Nazarene. Matt. 2:23.

765. "And he came and dwelt in a city called Nazareth," signifies that the enlightened Rational Faculty perceives the True Doctrine of Life within the Precepts

A Nazarene.   Elevation of the External mind.

of the Literal Sense of the Word, separated from the Appearances of Truth which the Proprium has hitherto rested in, during the obscure seasons of temptation, and thus the prophetic utterances of the spiritual history of the Word are actually fulfilled in the regeneration of man. "He shall be called a Nazarene," signifies that the exterior principles of the External mind shall be actuated by the Heavenly principles which have been represented in the Fifth Day of Creation, and from these principles the Literal Sense of the Word is perceived as Divine, because it contains the Natural Human Principle of the Lord, which is the Divine Truth in Ultimates, or the Son of Man, which is signified by the word "Nazarene." A "Nazarene" is a regenerating man whose interior and exterior life is actuated by the Affection of Good, or the Celestial Principles of the Word.

766. Thus the Lord alone, by means of the Word, elevates the principles of the External mind above the influences of the Proprium, and fills the Understanding with true intelligence concerning the Word, vivifying both the interior and exterior principles of the External mind with Spiritual Life. "*And I raised up of your sons for prophets, and of your young for Nazarites. Is it not even thus, O ye children of Israel? saith the Lord.*" *

* Amos 2: 11.

THE SIXTH DAY OF CREATION;

OR,

THE SIXTH STATE OF REGENERATION.

Six Days shalt thou labor and do all thy work. Ex. 20 ; 19.

And God said, Let the earth bring forth the living creature after his kind, cattle and creeping thing, and beast of the earth after his kind : and it was so. Gen. 1 : 24.

767. When the regenerating man has arrived at this State, his External mind, or "earth," is influenced by the interior Affections of the Internal mind which have been formed by the Goods and Truths of the Word, instead of the evil and false persuasions of his unregenerated Proprium. The "earth" can produce no fruit unless the "seed" is sown and cultivated, neither can Goodness be produced from the External mind unless the knowledges of Truth from the Word are first implanted whereby he may know what he is to believe and do.

768. It is the office of the Understanding to receive the Truths of the Word, and of the Will, to do them, but before regeneration begins, a man may know the Truth, and have no desire to obey it, because the Truth of the Word is antagonistic to the evil and false principles of the Proprium, so that there is a divided mind which the work of regeneration is to bring into con-

| Winged fowl and living creature. | Animals. |

junction. "*Whosoever heareth these sayings of mine, and doeth them, I will liken him to a wise man who built his house upon a rock: and every one that heareth these sayings of mine, and doeth them not, shall be likened unto a foolish man, who built his house upon the sand.*"

769. In the Fifth State of Regeneration, the principles belonging to the Understanding are signified by "the moving creatures of the waters," and the "winged fowl which fly above the earth in the firmament," but in the Sixth State, the principles of the Will are signified by the "living creature, cattle, creeping thing, and beast of the earth," and hence, the Word being written by pure correspondences, these principles of the Affections are represented by different kinds of animals in the prophecies and historical narratives. Beasts are of two kinds: the good, which are useful and harmless, and the evil, which are injurious. The Good Affections in man are signified by good and gentle beasts, such as cattle, sheep, lambs, etc., and the evil lusts are signified by bears, wolves, dogs, swine, etc. The Internal principles of the Word which actuate the Affections of the regenerating man, enter the External mind as they are revealed to the Rational Faculty, and come in conflict with the lusts of the Proprium, which they supplant with spiritual intelligence concerning the Literal Sense of the Word, and by obedience to its Precepts, the Affection for Goodness and Truth is formed, which is signified by "*Behold, I send you forth as sheep in the midst of wolves: be ye therefore wise as serpents and harmless as doves.*"

770. The inferior things in man, which have more connection with the Corporeal principle of the External mind, and which are lusts and pleasures, are here called the "beasts of the earth." By "Creature," in the Word, is signified the man who possesses faculties capable of being reformed from evil. By "Living Creature," is signified Spiritual Life imparted to these principles according to their quality; thus, "*Go ye into all the world, and preach the Gospel to every creature*," signifies that the regenerating man shall so live from the Spiritual principles of the Word, that the External mind, or "world," shall be regenerated, and thus announce the Coming of the Lord, or the revelation of the Internal Sense of the Word through every faculty of the Will and Understanding.

771. This work must take place within the regenerating man before he can practically announce to his fellow-men the Divine Gospel which proclaims the Advent of the Lord, or the Incarnation of the Human Principle of the Word within the Will and Understanding of men who desire a new-created life according to the Two Great Commandments. Thus within all the receptacles of the mind of the regenerating man, shall "angels," "dragons," "mountains, and all hills"; "fruitful trees, and all cedars;" "beasts, and all cattle;" "creeping things, and all flying fowl, Praise the Lord."

772. By "Cattle," are signified those principles in man which are capable of being sanctified or made holy by regeneration. By "Creeping things" or "Reptiles,"

whose bodies are near the earth, and crawl upon its surface, are signified the corporeal or sensual principles of the External mind, and thus they signify the pleasures and voluptuousness of all the senses, which before regeneration lead men, because they are actuated by the lusts of the Proprium.

And God made the beast of the earth after his kind, and everything that creepeth upon the earth after his kind: and God saw that it was good. Gen. 1 : 25.

773. In the preceding verse, the "earth" brought forth the "Living creature," the "Cattle," and "Creeping thing," by means of the Word, which is signified by "God said," and by the succession of these "creatures," is represented that the order of regeneration is first made manifest in the Corporeal principle of the External mind, because the regenerating man must be led from the corporeal and natural state of thought in which he is first born, to a perception of Spiritual thought from and within the Word.

774. Thus regeneration proceeds from External to Interior principles, which is an Appearance as though the man accomplished it of himself; but the whole work of regeneration is by and from the Lord alone, for all Spiritual Life and power is from Him within the inmost principles of Affection and Thought by means of the Word, and in this Sixth Day, the true order is revealed, for the regenerating man perceives that he is the Work of God, and because he begins to act from Love, as well

as Faith, he becomes a Spiritual Man. Thus the "cattle," the "beasts of the earth," and the "creeping things," are re-created from disorderly lust to order and usefulness. By "lust" is meant all selfish delights and pleasures.

775. The "Creeping things" are the most difficult to subdue, because the whole external life at first derives its pleasures and consciousness of existence from them. These Corporeal and Sensual principles are reduced to submission and order during the work of regeneration, when Internal principles acquire supremacy over the External, but before regeneration the External principles govern the whole man. In the progress of regeneration, the Lord rules over the Affections of the regenerating man by the Goods and Truths of the Word, and the joys which they occasion, sanctify the pleasures with which the external senses are delighted.

PLEASURES.

776. Pleasures are of two kinds, Voluntary, and Intellectual, or of the Will and Understanding. In a general sense the pleasures of the Will arise from the possession of land, houses, money, and religious, political or public honors; they also result from mutual love, and the love toward young children; and from friendship and social fellowship. Intellectual pleasures are excited by reading, writing, and acquiring all knowledges which fill the Understanding with wisdom.

777. The pleasures of the senses are gratified by Sight, from beholding beautiful objects of varied form and color; by Hearing, which is delighted with the sound of good instrumental and vocal music; of Smell, which is regaled by the odors of delicate perfumes; of Taste, which is gratified by the flavors of agreeable

and useful food; and of Touch, which is so exquisitely sensitive with those who are deprived of physical sight. All the senses are designed to give enjoyment when used temperately and orderly. Every recreation is allowable which is in harmony with the Precepts of the Word, but should be so governed by the Rational Faculty as not to be indulged in to excess so as to interfere with the duties of life in the work of regeneration, or to unfit the mind for spiritual meditation. Earthly time is too precious to be wasted in trifling amusements which have no useful end, or which do not tend to the love of the neighbor.

778. Earthly pleasures, being perceived by the senses of the External mind through the physical body are called Corporeal pleasures, although there is no pleasure experienced by the physical senses which does not exist and subsist from its corresponding Interior Affection, and there is no Interior affection which does not exist and subsist from one which is still more Interior, in which is its use and end. While a man lives in a state of merely natural thought, he is insensible to the Interior delights which flow in order from what is Inmost, but it is impossible for any principle to manifest itself externally unless it has an orderly connection with what is Interior, therefore the pleasures of the senses can only consist of ultimate effects from a prior cause.

779. Interior principles are not discovered by any man unless he possesses habits of mature reflection; and they are manifested to the regenerating man in the order in which he is elevated toward Heavenly principles by the Lord. Unless there existed Interior Sight, the External eye could not see, nor could instruction or pleasure be derived from objects of sight. Hence a man may see his spiritual surroundings in clear light, and those who are physically blind, may see the things of the spiritual world within the Word equally as well as those whose external sight has not been dimmed. A man during sleep, sees in his dreams, although his external eye is closed, and this same principle applies equally to the other senses.

Purification from lust.   The Heavenly Universe in Man.

780. When the Lord has entered and rules the Proprium of the regenerating man, all the "creeping things" obey the Laws of Divine Order, and instead of being ruled by the Love of Self, they are purified from lust, and they add to the joy of life, for they are governed by the Spiritual principles of the Word, and and thus by the Lord. *"In thy presence is fulness of joy: at Thy Right Hand there are pleasures for ever more."* *" And in that day will I make a covenant for them with the beasts of the field, and with the fowls of heaven, and with the creeping things of the ground,"* and he looks forward to a life of energetic usefulness by which the spiritual welfare of his fellow-men will be benefited.

781. With the unregenerated man, the filthy pleasures which originate from the lusts of his Proprium, to which all his senses are then subservient, are also signified by " beasts," and " creeping things," according to the context of the words, and they also apply to the yet unregenerated principles of the Proprium of the regenerating man. *"And he said unto me, Go in, and behold the wicked abominations that they do here. So I went in and saw; and, behold, every form of creeping things, and abominable beasts, and all the idols of the house of Israel, portrayed upon the wall round about."*

782. The Lord restores man to order by regeneration, and thus produces an Image of Heaven; wherefore the regenerating man is drawn up and out of his Hell, or Proprium, and is elevated into Heaven, for every regenerated man is a minute Heaven, or an Image of the Universal Heaven, and hence in the Word the Internal mind is called "Heaven." As the Universal Heaven consists of regenerated men who are Images of the Divine Man, or the Lord, who is the Inmost Being or Life of the Word, it is in its Celestial and Spiritual Form as One Man which constitutes the Kingdom of the Lord, for the complex principles of the Word form this One Man. A man who is governed by the Precepts of the Word is a Kingdom of Heaven, for this realm is within him. *"And God saw that it was good."*

783. The contrary is the state of those who make their life consist only in corporeal thoughts of external objects, in lusts and pleasures, and in the sensual gratification of the appetites, for they perceive no delight in anything which is not grounded in the Love of Self and the World, which culminates in hatred to all persons and things which do not favor them. With such men, corporeal and natural principles have dominion over the entire mind, and the Interior faculties are closed. They become Images of Hell, and the Proprium of such persons in the complex, becomes the antipode of Heavenly Order, and has the form of a malignant and infernal spirit, within which no other Lord than Self has the dominion. Such men do not regard the happiness of others, but look forward to a life of ease in which all things will serve them. The complex of the evil and false principles in man is called the Devil and Satan in the Literal Sense of the Word.

And God said, Let us make man in our image, after our likeness, and let them have dominion over the fish of the sea, and over the fowl of the air, and over the cattle, and over all the earth, and over every creeping thing that creepeth upon the earth. Gen. 1 : 26.

784. The regenerating man is now progressing toward a true Manhood, in which his Will and Understanding as receptacles of the Divine Love and Wisdom of the Word, are to be conjoined, so that he will become an Image and Likeness of the Divine Man, the Lord Jesus Christ, from whom all men exist and possess Spiritual Life. The Lord is to be thought of as a Divine Man, not in a physical body, nor in space and time, but according to the qualities of His Divine Love and Wisdom, as made known by the Interior Principles of the Word.

| Thinking of the Lord. | The Unity of the Word. |

785. The first thought concerning the Lord is formed within the External mind from the Literal Sense of the Word, in which He appears to the Corporeal principle of thought as a Man whose Voice is first heard in the fiat of Creation, and who is "walking in the garden in the cool of the day." Then in the form of various "angels" who represent Him, until He appears in the spiritual narrative of the Gospels, personified as the Son of God and the Son of Man, and if the mind cannot discern a more Interior meaning than the Literal Sense, a Father and a Son will exist in the thought as Two Persons, and confliction then arises in the mature mind, and hence originates many and varied doctrines formed from the self-intelligent opinions of learned men, by which the thoughts of others are guided, on account of which the simple Precepts of the Word become obscured.

786. The only tangible way to think of and perceive the Form of the Lord, is to think of Him as the Inmost Life of the Word, and as the regenerating man resists and overcomes his evils, and receives Life from Him by obedience to the Truths of the Word, he will there discern the Divine Human Form as he is re-created into an Image and Likeness of God, who is THE WORD. As his natural life and thoughts at first depend upon the instrumentality of parents, or those who are provided to rear and teach him, so his spiritual thoughts depend upon the "angels" and "spirits," or the Goods and Truths of the Word, which are the only angelic personifications which a regenerating man can perceive, for they re-create and bring salvation from sin, and constitute the presence of the Lord with man. Thus it is said, "*Let us make man*," which cannot be predicated of any finite instrumentality.

787. "In our image," signifies according to the Spiritual principles of the Word, which are within the Commandment of Love to the Neighbor, and "After our likeness," signifies according to the Celestial principles of Love to the Lord. Thus the Two Principles represented by "Image" and "Likeness," form the Unity of the whole Word which regenerates man.

THE NATURE OF THE WORD OF GOD. 347

Scientific discovery.   Mutual love.

788. It will readily be discerned that the apparent history of the Creation, has nothing in common with the supposed time of the physical creation of mankind upon this terrestrial globe, concerning which epoch nothing is known among the traditional records of the past. Every discovery in the scientific world, places the advent of humanity back to a remote and indefinite period of time, concerning which, all speculation or conjecture will be of no avail in solving the mystery, which will always be as obscure as the calculations which have been made concerning the expected "end of the world."

789. The "END OF THE WORLD," to each regenerating man, is the consummation of a full spiritual State before a clearer revelation of the Divine Truth which is within the Word. Thus the "Day of Judgment" comes to every regenerating man in his preparation for Spiritual life, when the things of the natural world, and the Literal Sense of the Word appear to die, in the last conflict which takes place before the Heavenly Light from within the Word dawns upon his Rational Faculty, at the morn of his Resurrection, and thus each morning of spiritual progress becomes a new resurrection.

790. Love toward the Lord makes the regenerating man One with Him, as a "Likeness;" and charity, or Love to the Neighbour, makes him One with the Lord, as an "Image." When one person truly loves another as himself, or more than himself, then he sees the other in himself and himself in the other, which may be perceived by any person if he examines the nature of love, or those who love each other mutually ; for the will of the one is the will of the other, they being interiorly united as to motives, and only distinct in their individuality, which can never be made One Person, as with the Lord. His "Image" and "Likeness" is in the spiritual form of the regenerating man, by the conjunction of the Good and Truth of the Word. This union is signified by the union of the Father and the Son, or the unition of the Divine Love and Wisdom which takes place in the Will and Understand-

ing of the regenerating man. "*At that day ye shall know that I am in my Father, and ye in me, and I in you. He that hath my commandments, and keepeth them, he it is that loveth me.*"

791. When this conjunction is effected in the regenerating man, the Internal mind rules over the "fish of the sea," or Sensual Affections of the External Mind; and over the "fowl of the air," or thoughts of the Understanding; and over the "cattle" or Natural Affections of Good and Truth; and "over all the earth," or all principles of the External mind, even to the "creeping thing that creepeth upon the earth," or the corporeal pleasures which give delight to the senses, and this is the work of the Lord, by the conjunction of the Internal Sense of the Word with its corresponding receptacles in the regenerating man, and no self-righteousness can enter or be appropriated.

THE FORM OF HEAVEN.

792. Instead of thinking of the Lord as another man like men in the physical world, the commandments of the Word, which constitute His Personal Form, are to be loved and obeyed. This Word being in the form of Man, shapes the external mind of the man who receives its spiritual qualities into the mould of Heavenly Order, and he will thus become an angelic "Image" and "Likeness." When the regenerating man looks within the Word, he will see the Lord there personified to his spiritual vision. The Laws of Spiritual Life do not exist in any other place, for there alone is the fixed abode of the Lord, where the Corporeal and Natural principles of the External mind first receive the idea of the Person of the Lord as another man, until the Rational Faculty perceives Him as the Inmost Spiritual Being within the corporeal and natural expressions of the Literal Sense. This Word is "*that which was from the beginning, which we have heard, which we have seen with our eyes, which we have looked upon, and our hands have handled of the Word of Life.*"

793. When the mind, in its abstraction from earthly things and their Appearances in the Word, meditates upon the Divine

| The abode of the Lord. | The Universal Heaven. |

Principles there personified, Spiritual Perception flows in through the Internal mind, which is Heaven, and is the abode of the Lord in the regenerating man. The Universal Heaven which consists of regenerated men, is in the Human Form thus created by the Divine Human Principle of the Word, in which the Lord manifests Himself, and within its Inmost Principle is the Divine Life, from which Heaven is formed and exists. The Universal Heaven is in the Human Form as One Heavenly Body in whom are all regenerated men who have been redeemed from sin by the Word, which is there perceived as the Divine Man. It is this Body of Heavenly Instruction which the Lord takes upon Himself, and makes Divine by entering the life of each regenerating man individually, and unites to Himself by the conjoining Precepts of the Word.

794. During all the ages of Eternity there has been no change in the Oneness or Unity of the Lord, for if His Love and Wisdom were fluctuating and changeable, there could be no Salvation from Sin. In order to accomplish this Salvation, he assumes the Human Principle of the Literal sense of the Word, which He unites to the Divine Human Princlple, or Internal Sense, in the lives of those who by obedience and love are brought into conjunction with its Celestial and Spiritual Principles, which are in the Divine Human Form.

795. The Universal Heaven which is in the Human Form is the Spiritual Body of the Lord Jesus Christ, for it is formed by the qualities of the lives of those who have been redeemed from their sins by the Human Principles of the Word,—of Love to the Lord and the Neighbor. This Heavenly Body has been nourished by the Material Body of the Lord as it has been given in the Literal Sense of the Word. *"And as we have borne the image of the earthy, we shall also bear the image of the heavenly."* They who are governed by the Love of Self and the World do not receive the Body of the Lord when it is broken for them, and do not permit themselves to be re-created into the "Image" and "Likeness" of God.

Natural and Spiritual food.   Male and female.

796. The physical frame of man is sustained by those earthly substances which give it nourishment, and so the spiritual body, the External mind, receives its nourishment from the spiritual substances or doctrines upon which it feeds. If it feeds upon corporeal or natural thoughts alone concerning the Word, as given in the Literal Sense, the External mind becomes Corporeal and Natural in its thought of spiritual principles; but if the Internal Sense of the Word is perceived as the true source of its Divinity, and the whole life is governed by its Two Precepts, the spiritual body of the regenerating man will be a miniature representative of that Heavenly Body which forms the Spiritual Body of the Lord. "*For as the body is one, and hath many members, and all the members of that one body, being many are one body; so also is Christ. For by one Spirit are we all baptized into one Body.*" "*Now ye are the Body of Christ.*" With the individual regenerating man, the Internal mind is the Spiritual Body of the Lord derived from the Internal Truths of the Word, for the Internal mind is "Heaven," and the Universal Heaven is formed by the lives of regenerated men.

So God created man in His image, in the image of God created He him; male and female created He them. Gen. 1 : 27.

797. "Male and female," signifies the two conjoining Principles from the Word in the mind of one regenerating man, either male or female, for the words do not refer to the distinction of physical sex, excepting by the correspondence of spiritual principles with the laws of the physical world. The marriages which are narrated in the Word refer to the reception of its Celestial and Spiritual principles in the Will and Understanding, which constitute the Heavenly Marriage, which is compared to the happiness of the earthly marriage.

Medium of communication.   Man and wife.

798. As the Internal mind of the regenerating man is opened by obedience to the Heavenly Laws of Life, he receives his chief delight from the Internal principles of the Word, viewing the external things of the Literal Sense as a medium to convey to the interior principles of the mind, the Heavenly Principles which they represent. Thus the things of the Literal Sense, as well as the objective things of the physical world, serve as means to lead him to reflect on what is Internal, or Spiritual, and from these to what is Celestial, and thus to the Lord Himself as the Inmost Life of these Principles, in whom his affections and thoughts are centered.

799. In this manner he is led to meditate on the Celestial Marriage of the Will and the Understanding, by the union of the Divine Love and Wisdom within himself as a receptacle, and perceives why marriages are treated of in the Literal Sense of the Word, in order that they may be illustrative of heavenly felicity when the Internal Sense is perceived. For this reason the Word is so written, and the Understanding of the regenerating man is called "Male," and the Will is called "Female," which, when acting in unity, by obeying the Truth that is known, these two principles of the mind are spoken of as "married." A regenerating man who is ruled by the Celestial principles of the Word is called "Daughter," and "Virgin," as the "Daughter of Jerusalem," and also "Wife," from these names representing the Affection of Good.

800. "Male and Female," do not represent the marriage union in the regenerating man which is treated of in the Second chapter of Genesis under the name of "Man and Wife." "Male and Female," denote Truth and Good pertaining to the Intellectual Principle, or the Understanding, while "Man and Wife" denote Truth and Good pertaining to the Voluntary Principle, or Will. Truth cannot spontaneously of itself enter into a marriage with Good, although Good may do so with Truth, because truth is only made Living which is produced from, and thus united with Good; for Truth abstracted from Good, or not incorporated into the life, is but an empty sound, and has no power. *"Though I*

speak with the tongues of men and angels, and have not charity, I am become as sounding brass, or a tinkling cymbal."

801. "Man," when used alone, signifies the perception of Good and the Understanding of Truth derived from the Word, and includes all the spiritual principles represented by "Male and Female," "Man and Woman," "Husband and Wife," "Father and Mother," "Son and Daughter," and "Brother and Sister." By "Man and Woman" is signified Intelligence from the Word united to the Affection of Truth. "Husband and Wife" signifies Truth in conjunction with Good. "Father and Mother" signifies Good in conjunction with the Affection of Truth. "Son and Daughter" denote Truth and Good; for Truth, or the Son, is born from the Father, or Good, and "Daughter" is born from Good and the Affection of Truth, and all conceptions and births in the Word represented by "Sons and Daughters" have reference only to the regenerating principles of the Word. "Brother and Sister" signifies the Affection of Good and the Affection of Truth in conjunction.

802. It will be seen from the Literal sense that "Male and Female" are created before "Eve" is mentioned, for the principle represented by the name "Eve" is not formed until the regenerating man has arrived at the Seventh Day of Creation, described in the Second Chapter of Genesis, after the Six Days of labor and combat are passed, and the work of regeneration is consummated. "Adam" is then first mentioned, and signifies the Celestial principle of spiritual life, or the regenerated Internal principle of the Rational Faculty, and "Eve" signifies the regenerated Proprium of the External mind.

803. The word "Adam" signifies "red earth," and the color "red" is predicated of the Good of Love, because it proceeds from the "fire" of the Spiritual Sun, THE WORD. "Eve" signifies "living," and thus the personification of the "mother of all living" represents the spiritual life which exists in the Proprium in place of the dead hereditary evils. Thus "Adam and Eve," in the "Garden of Eden," represent the holy Celestial and Spiritual state attained by the regenerating man, or the Golden Age.

One Man.	Sons and daughters.

804. The Two Great Precepts which create one regenerated life constitute the Word in the regenerating man, as the Infinite Law of the Eternal Heavens. Thus " Male and Female " exist as one man, for the Lord has created them as two conjoining principles within the mind of him who has chosen His ways of Life and Truth.

And God blessed them; and God said unto them, Be fruitful and multiply, and replenish the earth, and subdue it; and have dominion over the fish of the sea, and over the fowl of the air, and over every living thing that moveth upon the earth. Gen. 1 : 28.

805. "Be fruitful and multiply," signifies filling the "Earth," or External mind, with the Good and Truth of the Word, which constantly develop with more and more interior meaning as they are brought forth into the external life, and rule over all the principles which actuate the thoughts, speech and actions. When the Understanding is united to the Will, or Faith with Love, the External mind of the regenerating man is married. *"For the Lord delighteth in thee, and thy land shall be married."*

806. The fruits thence issuing which are of Truth, are called "Sons," and those which are of Good, are called "Daughters," which may be verified from many portions of the Word. The "Earth" is replenished when there is an abundance of Goodness and Truth; and when the Lord blesses and speaks to man by the Word, and thus causes his spiritual life to bloom, there is a great increase of "fruit." *"The Kingdom of Heaven is like to a grain of mustard-seed, which a man took, and sowed in his field: which indeed is the least of all seeds; but when it is grown, it is the greatest among herbs, and becometh a tree, so that the birds of the air come and lodge in the branches thereof."*

807. A "Grain of mustard-seed" is the goodness which a man thinks he possesses before he becomes spiritual, which is the "least of all seeds," because he then thinks that he does good of himself, and what is of himself is nothing but evil. After regeneration has commenced, there is a beginning of Goodness in him from the Lord, but is the "least of all." At length his faith is joined with Love, or is manifested in Good Works; it grows larger, and becomes an "Herb;" and at last, when the conjunction is perfected, it becomes a "Tree," and then the "birds of the air," which denote Intellectual principles concerning the Word, "come and lodge in the branches," which are the scientific principles of the External mind. When a man is being regenerated, he is in a state of warfare on account of the remaining unregenerated Proprium, and therefore it is said "subdue it," and the Internal mind will "have dominion" over all the creatures of the "Earth," or External mind.

MARRIAGE.

808. The sacredness of the earthly relation of Marriage between husband and wife, is derived from the union of the regenerated Will and Understanding in the man or woman who is thereby filled with Heavenly Life; and all happy marriages contain an inward spiritual conjunction resulting from both the husband and the wife mutually seeking the Life of Regeneration from the Word of God. The true earthly marriage of husband and wife is attained similar to the order of regeneration, and is not a spontaneous outburst of affection which attains the Life of Heaven by an instantaneous conversion into felicitous unity of spirit. It is begun in the Natural Affections, without that Interior principle of Affection which must be formed through the removal of the Love of Self and the World, by means of the Truths of the Word.

809. At the beginning of the State of Marriage, both husband and wife are governed by the External principles of the mind, and their delight in the society of each other is gradually chilled, as the faults of each begin to develop, until often there are states

of aversion to each other. At the beginning, each views the other with that pleasing halo of romance which the ideality of the imagination projects, in which their own love is seen by themselves as in a mirror, for this apparent affection is the Love of Self, although it appears like, and manifests itself as affection for another. But as Spiritual Affection in the regenerating man is only attained through combat and temptation, whereby the Truth enters and illuminates the mind, so true earthly conjugal love is only attained through self-denial, forgivness, charity, and the overcoming of the evil of the Proprium on the part of both husband and wife toward each other, and this work of regeneration must be mutual on the part of each. If one seeks the spiritual life of obedience to the Word while the other gives no heed, the conjugal principle of spiritual conjunction cannot exist, because attainment of the regenerate life must be reciprocal.

810. At first they do not know each other, and in the ideal state which exists before marriage, the delight of one's own Self-Love being reflected back from the image of the other, closes the eye of judgment, until each imagines life to consist of dreamy, transcendental events, intermingled with the variegated hues of the rainbow, which the imagination fondly hopes to grasp and retain. But when Appearances begin to be dissipated, then the trials begin, and there is disjunction instead of conjunction. This disjunction must occur in order that they may learn to know each other through forbearance, and the effort to overcome evil, for the hereditary Proprium of each is to be conquered, and there are many states of coldness and harsh judgment on the part of each in the attainment of a higher love founded upon the Living Truths of the Word. Without the Divine Love and Wisdom warming the Affections, and guiding by the Light of the Word, there can be no true conjugal love, although there may be much tender Natural affection.

811. A husband and wife may live with each other in mutual sympathy many years, without antagonistic elements causing disagreement, but when the work of regeneration begins on the part

of one, without the co-operation of the other, an antagonism often occurs which is hard to bear. This is especially true when one of the pair is led to perceive the Internal Sense of the Word, in which the other has no desire to see its Divine teachings, and the separation of thought, which may for a while exist, must be patiently borne until the Light which so clearly shines to the one, shall so pervade the life with charity and tenderness, and persistent good-will, that the other may also be led to see the Lord within the Word.

812. The one who possesses and carries the Light, must not leave the other to grope in darkness, for the affection which is warm from the Word, will enable the regenerating one to bear all things for the sake of the other without murmuring; for whatever trials any person may experience, are necessary helps in overcoming the Love of Self, and none are permitted to endure more than they are able to bear, for "*all things work together for good to them that love God.*" "*For what knowest thou, O wife, whether thou shalt save thy husband? or how knowest thou, O man, whether thou shalt save thy wife?*"

813. A regenerating man will not take advantage of the earthly law of divorce, which is permitted on account of the "hardness of the heart," or absence of spiritual affection for the Good and Truth of the Word, and take to himself another wife, neither will he put away his wife, nor be an adulterer, for he will regard the spiritual welfare of her whom he has promised to love and cherish, notwithstanding the antagonism which may exist; but if in her freedom she leaves him, not regarding his tenderness and forbearance, he will do all in his power to help her without obtrusion or provoking her aversion.

814. In the case of a regenerating wife whose husband is unfaithful, she must patiently bear what she is called to endure, with the consciousness that all earthly trials exist only in the External mind, and in the faithful performance of her duty, live in the Light which shines from the Word, knowing that the time in the physical frame is short, and the evil which she sees is but

One partner.	Loving the husband or wife spiritually.

a reflection of the Self Love which yet exists in her unregenerated Proprium, which also exists in her children, and in all mankind, until it is overcome by obedience to the Word, and strength will be given her to bear her trials.

815. True conjugal love can be known only to those whose lives are filled with the Good and Truth of the Word, and can only exist between one husband and one wife, for as the marriage relation is an ultimate representative of the conjunction of the regenerated Will and Understanding, it can in no wise exist between more than two persons, and it must be mutual, so that the lives of husband and wife shall be reciprocal in the effort to overcome the evils of the Proprium by obedience to the Word.

816. Marriages formed between two persons from external or corporeal affection alone, without the regenerating principles of Spiritual Life from the Word, are earthly, resembling the natural affection of animals. A marriage which is contracted from beauty of person, wealth, position, or any lower selfish motive, does not exist from conjugal affection, and is therefore not a true marriage, because it is from an external corporeal principle, yet it may become a true marriage when both husband and wife are led to live according to similar principles of Good and Truth from the Word, and when they progress together in the life of regeneration.

817. In order to love another spiritually, instead of loving the personal attractions, such as the form, face, or talents, only those qualities are to be loved which dwell within the person from the Lord, otherwise, if the created receptacle is loved rather than the Regenerating Principles of Life which are from the Word, what is mistaken for love is but an insidious manifestation of the Love of Self, for natural affection is not spiritual love, but is a correspondence of it.

818. As marriages are typical of the Spiritual Marriage in each individual, the creation of Eternal Life depends on the earthly marriage of husband and wife, from whom immortal spirits are first born into the world, before they are fitted for the Life of

Abortion.	An important fact

Heaven, and thus every angelic man has been born of some earthly father and mother, and speculation concerning the time of the origin of mankind becomes as much lost in the retrospect as conjecture concerning their future earthly condition.

819. Hence the sacredness of marriage, which is the entrance of being to every immortal spirit, who, by the care of the father and mother, is to be educated for Heavenly Life, by living example and instruction from the Word. Hence the wicked crime of adultery may appear, which, through its lust, treats with contempt the sacred conception of immortal beings, and hence also may be seen the murderous crime of destroying the life of the unborn infant, whose soul is already forming within the unnatural mother, who, in order to gratify her sensual lust and Love of Self, deliberately kills a life which God has created for immortal existence. The crime of foeticide, or abortion, is secret murder.

820. Earthly marriages between two persons, in themselves are only representative of the Two Spiritual Principles of the Word which re-create the two spiritual receptacles of the one regenerating man, and the differences of physical sex, provided for the descent of earthly generations, do not exist in the Spiritual World, excepting by the laws of Correspondence, for the Spiritual Marriage takes place in each regenerating individual, and the Sons and Daughters which are the fruit of this Heavenly Marriage, are the multiplication of the Truths and Goods of the Word. The beginning of created human life occurs only in the physical world, for no persons are born regenerated, and the regenerated men, called "angels," have their first consciousness from the order of physical birth, no finite angels having been created except by a life according to the Literal Truths of the Word, which are the attendant spirits upon man, while in the world of natural thought.

821. It is very important that the Rational Faculty clearly comprehends this fact, that physical sex and its correspondence with the Spiritual Marriage in the regenerating man, are distinct degrees, otherwise corporeal and sensual thoughts concerning the

THE NATURE OF THE WORD OF GOD. 359

| The lust of "Spiritual Affinity." | The Heavenly Marriage. |

spiritual life will be formed in the mind, and the ultimate result will be spiritual adultery. Many an earthly home has been broken up by fallacious conceptions of the marriage relation, setting aside the legal contract and violating this sacred obligation under the name of "Spiritual Affinity," which covers the most intense lust of Self-Love.

822. The regenerating man is either male or female as regards physical sex, and the Spiritual husband and wife is the Good and Truth of the Word, which are united in the male or female regenerating man. The Goods and Truths of the Word form the "angels of God in Heaven." "*For in the resurrection they neither marry, nor are given in marriage, but are as the angels of God in heaven.*" "*There is neither Jew nor Greek, there is neither bond nor free, there is neither male nor female: for ye are all one in Christ Jesus.*" The name JESUS CHRIST signifies the Divine Marriage of the Love and Wisdom of the Word in the Will and Understanding of the regenerating man, and this is the true Conjugial Marriage to which all marriages refer and represent in the historical and prophetic expressions of the Word. This Heavenly conjunction begets an internal state of happiness from which is born a spirit of usefulness to others, which fills the external life with delight, and life becomes a joy instead of the burden it appears to those who have not entered the Spiritual Marriage.

823. The Heavenly Marriage within the regenerating man takes place in the Proprium, which, when it is regenerated, becomes the "Bride" and "Wife" of the Lord who is within the Internal mind. "*Come hither, and I will show thee the Bride, the Lamb's wife.*" The "Lamb" is the Divine Human Principle of the Word of God which has entered the renewed Proprium of the regenerating man. "*Allelujah, for the Lord God omnipotent reigneth. Let us be glad and rejoice, and give honor to him: for the marriage of the Lamb is come, and his wife hath made herself ready, And to her was granted that she should be arrayed in fine linen, clean and white: for the fine linen is the righteousness of saints.*"

| Impurity. | Carnal temptation. |

ADULTERY.

824. Adultery includes every form of unchastity or filthy lust, and is the hellish opposite of marriage. They whose minds are filled with thoughts of impurity or obscenity cannot enter Heaven, because the corporeal principles of the mind are in the bondage of evil and falsity, which prevent the least entrance of spiritual principles, and they who indulge in impure conversation are adulterers. The fruition of earthly marriage is the creation of immortal spirits who are to be educated for the Life of Heaven, but the crime of Adultery brings into existence helpless infants with no loving parents to teach the Way of Life, and their hereditary natures thus begotten in carnal lust, lead them to sinful lives, and the effort to overcome evil will be attained through great difficulty. Yet the Lord cares for these degraded orphans with the same tender love as for those who enter life under more favorable influences. The adulterer or adulteress closes every avenue to the Kingdom of Heaven, and is a devil incarnate who breaks every Commandment of the Word to gratify the diabolical lust of the Love of Self. *"They commit adultery, and walk in lies; they strengthen also the hands of evil doers, that none return from his wickedness."*

825. The life of an adulter or adulteress is not above that of the unclean beasts, because they have obliterated the suggestions of Conscience, and have destroyed the Human Principle which perceives the Divinity of the Word. Their life is opposed to all order, and after securing the objects of their lust, they conceive aversion toward them, and in the case of seduction, they lead their victims into degrading lives, destroying in them also the desire for spiritual life, and thus they become murderers. Such is the wickedness of this crime, that every thing which tends to unchaste thoughts should be guarded against in every form. The temptations to this sin arise from the Proprium, and the most severe conflicts throughout the work of regeneration occur from this carnal principle of the External mind, because this disorderly passion is the strongest and most seductive in its influence. *"Let him that thinketh he standeth take heed lest he fall."*

THE NATURE OF THE WORD OF GOD. 361

Filthy conversation.	Purification from lust.

826. Those who indulge in obscene thoughts and lascivious jesting, cultivate and inwardly confirm every lust which leads to Adultery. This carnal lust is first to be resisted by obedience to the Literal Command, "*Thou shalt not commit adultery,*" and when it is more clearly revealed to the mind that the thought of Adultery, or unchastity, is sin, as the regenerating man calls upon the Lord, and fills his mind with the Truths of the Word which the Lord gives in answer to his prayer, his thoughts will be purified from lust, and when he is inwardly tempted, he will exclaim in the language of the Word, "*How then can I do this great wickedness, and sin against God?*"

827. As all sin first exists in the intention, so if his mind is purified by the Word from this lustful temptation, he will not commit this great crime; but there is no time during his earthly life but which he must be on his guard against the seductive and deadly influences of this spiritual murder. "*Wherefore lay apart all filthiness and superfluity of naughtiness, and receive with meekness the engrafted Word which is able to save your souls.*" "*Put off filthy communication out of your mouth.*" "*The Commandment of the Lord is pure, enlightening the eyes. Every word of God is pure: He is a shield unto them that put their trust in Him.*" "*In that day there shall be a fountain opened to the house of David, and to the inhabitants of Jerusalem, for sin and for uncleanness.*" "*And I will put my spirit within you, and cause you to walk in my statutes, and ye shall keep my judgments and do them. I will also save you from all your uncleanness.*"

828. In order to obtain this victory in the purification of the sensual principle of the mind from all unchaste and wanton thoughts, the regenerating man will avoid all external temptation, and will ever heed the commandment, "*Watch and pray, lest ye enter into temptation.*" All things which pander to sloth and self-indulgence must be discarded. All books and pictures, or forms of art which feed the carnal imagination, must be shunned. All corrupting dramas which pamper depraved thoughts must be

Intemperance.	Stimulants and narcotics.

proscribed from the sight and hearing. All trifling amusements and recreations which bring the sexes into undue familiarity with each other, should be banished. There should be a kindly reserve in acquaintances between the sexes, so that respect and reverence shall be cultivated and maintained for that sacred union which typifies the marriage of Spiritual Principles from the Word, within the life of the regenerating man. No power but the Truths of the Word, actuating the Will and Understanding, can overcome this deadly evil which is in the hereditary nature of man.

Every avenue which leads to self-indulgence in any form, must be constantly guarded against the entrance of every evil, and every thing which tends to destroy the freedom of orderly thought, speech, and action. "*Denying ungodliness, and worldly lusts, we should live soberly, righteously, and godly in this present world.*" Intemperance in eating and drinking must be eschewed and resisted. The Wine of the Word is not a physical liquor which excites the lower passions, enchaining the freedom of the Will, and which leads to the destruction of spiritual perception, but it is the quickening influence of the Spiritual Truth of the Word, stimulating the interior life with principles which elevate the nature of man above selfish lusts.

A regenerating man cannot conscientiously indulge in the use of intoxicating beverages which inflame the evil spirits of his Proprium, and he will not only abstain from their use, from an internal rational principle, but in true love for the neighbor, he will not present the temptation to others, in any form, from the false custom of mistaken courtesy.

He will not indulge in the use of either stimulants or narcotics. With an inward desire for purity, he will not be under the influence of such habits as the use of tobacco, which is so typical of the Love of Self among earthly-minded men, neither will he, for the sake of gain, assist in dispensing to others, either stimulants or narcotics to pamper their self-indulgence, and thus aid them in fostering habits which will hinder the entrance of pure Spiritual Life from the Word.

Care of the physical frame.	A putrefying corpse.

In order that the regenerating Principles of the Word may have their ultimate culmination in the purification of the corporeal and sensual receptacles of the External mind, and be efficacious in the purification of the physical frame from disease and its adjuncts, the frail tenement of man must be tenderly cared for and preserved in health. It must be cleansed from all impurity, and every precaution observed in guarding it from every obstruction which will prevent the orderly operation of its complicated organs, so that it may be instrumental in fulfiillng the law of Love to the Neighbor, instead of being a hindrance to the spiritual progress of its possessor, and a burden to others. Where its functions are mpaired by disease, he must patiently bear with its infirmities, using every effort for restoration to health, knowing that it is but a temporary habitation, and he must patiently bear the burden until his release.

829. They who commit adultery close the doors of Heaven against themselves, for they are immersed solely in worldly and corporeal things, and the Good and Truth of the Word cannot enter their Rational Faculty. If they speak reverently of the things of the Word and religion, and appear devout in the exercises of public worship, as many adulterers and adulteresses do, their speech is only from the External memory and from the lips, actuated by Self Love or the love of gain; for the Internal mind is closed, and cannot possibly be opened except by earnest repentance and a pure life according to the Precepts of the Word. The lust of unchastity corresponds to the putrefying odor from a dead human body filled with a malignant and infectious disease, blotched and decomposing in the heat of the sun.

If persons abstain from the sin of adultery from any other motive than because it is commanded in the Word, "*Thou shalt not commit adultery*," they are interiorly unchaste, and are adulterers, although they may live, chastely in their external lives. If they abstain from this sin from fear of detection and consequent loss of reputation and honor, from fear of contracting loathsome diseases, or from simple physical and moral reasons, as

Internal purity.   Spiritual food.

not respectable and becoming, or from pride or selfishness, their motives are not pure, for there can be no interior chastity which is not derived from loving obedience to the commandments of the Word, which teach that all sin is contrary to the elevation of the spiritual nature to principles of Heavenly Life, which are Love to the Lord and the Neighbor.

830. Those who take delight in adulteries cannot receive the Good and Truth of the Word, and they deny the Divinity of these Spiritual principles, because the love of Adultery originates from the compact of the evils and falses of the Proprium which exist there on account of the loss of spiritual perception, and which are fostered by the false doctrines favoring the Love of Self which are confirmed by the Appearanses of Truth in the Literal Sense of the Word, when the state of a man's life is evil and false. When these false doctrines are dissipated, and the Commandments of the Word are not obscured, but are the guide of the spiritual life, the minds of the obedient will be purified, and earthly marriage will be reverenced as a Holy Ordinance and as the Seminary of Heaven.

And God said, Behold, I have given you every herb bearing seed, which is upon the face of all the earth, and every tree, in the which is the fruit of a tree yielding seed; to you it shall be for meat. Gen. 1 : 29.

831. The Celestial principles of the regenerating man are treated of in the Second Chapter of Genesis. These principles are delighted with Celestial things alone, which being agreeable to his life, are called Celestial Food. The Spiritual principles are delighted with the Spiritual Food which is signified by the " herb bearing seed," which is every Truth which regards usefulness. "Which is upon the face," signifies the Interior principle of the External mind, which is the Rational Faculty. " Every tree, in the which is the fruit yielding seed," signifies all

the knowledges which the Lord gives from the Word to the regenerating man. "*His delight is in the Law of the Lord: in His Law doth he meditate day and night. And he shall be like a tree planted by the rivers of waters, that bringeth forth his fruit in his season; his leaf shall not wither, and whatsoever he doeth shall prosper.*"

THE HOLY SUPPER.

832. "*Blessed are they which are called unto the Marriage Supper of the Lamb.*" A Supper is representative of reciprocal communion of thought and kindred desire, therefore all feasts which men provide for the delights of their fellow-men, are significative of the joy of mutual fellowship. in a higher or lower degree, as these feasts pertain to the realm of thought or to the bodily appetites. The Marriage Supper is expressive of the joy and peace arising from the conjunction of Good and Truth from the Word within the regenerated Proprium. The food signifies the Divine Love made Good or alive from Affection, and the drink signifies the Divine Wisdom received and made Truth, or Faith, from the Word. The "bread" which is eaten, and the "wine" which is drunken, signify the whole Word of God, which is to be obeyed from principles of love, and its Internal Truths are to be imbibed by rational study, with all the powers of the mind.

833. This is the true Communion Service, of which all external forms are but typical. A man who is being regenerated, partakes daily of the Lord's Supper. Every Truth from the Word which he imbibes and obeys, is wine and bread for the support of his spiritual body. Every meal of which he partakes, is representative of spiritual nourishment from the Word of God. This representative emblem of the Marriage Supper is the WORD, which is within the access of every man who desires spiritual life, and it is of Eternal importance to partake of this Spiritual Food, which contains the Bread and Wine of Heaven, and which is the actual presence of the Lord Jesus Christ with men. "*Lo! I am with you alway.*"

The pleasures of the External mind.	Warfare.

And to every beast of the earth, and to every fowl of the air, and to everything that creepeth upon the earth, wherein there is life, I have given every green herb for meat; and it was so. Gen. 1 : 30.

834. The Natural Affections are signified by the "beast of the earth." The Natural Truths received from the Literal Sense of the Word, are signified by the "fowl of the air," and all the delights and pleasures of the senses which are governed by spiritual principles, are signified by "everything that creepeth upon the earth, wherein there is life." These principles of the External mind are nourished by "every green herb." By "Herb," is signified the Truths of the Literal Sense of the Word, and by "Green," is signified that which is sensitive and living, and thus all the Natural Truths of the Word are made alive, and feed all the hunger and thirst of the External mind, when the Internal Sense is revealed and understood, and thus the Word supplies the Spiritual and Natural Food which supports Eternal Life. "*The Lord is my Shepherd, I shall not want. He maketh me to lie down in green pastures.*"

835. The External mind, in its natural principles, is supported by food consisting of the "green herb," because this is the order in which man is regenerated. While he is being made spiritual, there is continual warfare between the illuminated Rational Faculty and the unregenerated Proprium, on which account he is in a Militant State, for before regeneration begins, the lusts of the Proprium have dominion, with the falsities thence originating. During regeneration, these evils and falses cannot be instantaneously removed, for that would destroy the freedom of man and take away his individuality. Therefore the evil spirits, or

The evil spirits of the Proprium.	The Atoning Sacrifice.

the evils and falsities of his Proprium are permitted to excite his cupidities or selfish affections, which by innumerable modes may be so much weakened by the Truths of the Word, as to be inclined to Goodness, and thus the man be reformed; for in order that evil may be removed, it must be seen as evil, and then be resisted and shunned as something hateful.

836. In the time of combat, the evil spirits of the Proprium exercise the utmost hatred toward the Good and Truth of the Word, or the Divine Love and Wisdom therein, and at such times the Internal Sense is so obscured that the regenerating man has nothing left but Natural Food, which is compared to the "green herb," or the Living Literal Sense. At intervals the Lord gives him glimpses of a more Interior meaning, which becomes the Spiritual Food of the "tree yielding fruit," and the "herb bearing seed," which is the Food of tranquility and peace, with their joys and delights.

837. Unless the Lord defended man every moment, even the smallest part of every moment, he would instantly perish in spiritual death, or relapse into the power of Self Love, in consequence of the indescribably intense and deadly hatred with which the evils and falses of his Proprium are filled toward the Goods and Truths of the Word, and thus the Lord. In order to redeem mankind from this spiritual death, the Lord has entered the Natural world of the External mind, by assuming the Literal Sense of the Word as a covering, or Mediator, whereby the natural mind may approach the Internal Sense, which is "God manifest in the flesh," or the indwelling of the Divine Love and Wisdom in the respective receptacles of the regenerating man, and thus the Literal Sense of the Word becomes the Intercessor between God and man.

838. By resisting the evils and falses of the Proprium according to the simple Truths of the Literal Sense, which plainly declare the duty on the part of man, the Atoning Sacrifice is accomplished by the Lord in the regenerating man, through the sacrifice of his natural hereditary delights of evil and falsity, and

as the Good and Truth of the Word enters, Atonement, or conjunction of the Lord with man is effected, and he is redeemed from sin. "*Seek good, and not evil, that ye may live; and so the* LORD, *the God of Hosts, shall be with you. Hate the evil, and love the good, and establish judgment in the gate.*"

And God saw everything that He had made, and, behold, it was very good. And the Evening and the Morning were the Sixth Day. Gen. 1:31.

839. The culmination of this State of the regenerating man is called "very good," because principles of Truth or Faith make one with Love, and the Heavenly Marriage is consummated between Spiritual and Celestial principles. All things which relate to the Understanding of the regenerating man, such as Knowledges of Truth, or Faith, Intellectual principles, and Thoughts, are called Spiritual, and all things which relate to the Will, such as Love to the Lord and the Neighbor, Goodness, and the Affections, are called Celestial.

840. The times and states of the regeneration of man in general and in particular, are divided into Six, and in the Word are called the Days of Creation, for by degrees he is elevated from a state of spiritual death, in which he possesses none of the qualities which properly constitute a Man, until by successive states he attains to the Sixth Day, when he becomes an "Image" and a "Son of God." "*And it shall come to pass, that in the place where it was said unto them, Ye are not my people, there it shall be said unto them, Ye are the Sons of the Living God.*" "*But as many as received Him, gave He power to become the Sons of God.*"

841. During these states of warfare against his evils, the Lord continually strengthens him and confirms him in the Divine Good and Truth of the Word, which is the power He gives in the time

of combat. The time or state of warfare is the Day of the Lord's operation, and therefore the regenerating man is called the "Work of God," and he advances in spiritual progress until Love becomes his ruling principle, and then the combat will cease. The number Six signifies combat, and also the conjunction indicated by being double the number Three.

842. When the work of regeneration is so far perfected tnat Faith is conjoined to Love, it is then called "very good," because the regenerating man has become made in the "Likeness of God." At the close of the Sixth Day, the "evil spirits" of the Proprium depart, and the Goods of the Word succeed in their place, when he is introduced into the Celestial principle of Heavenly Life.

Thus the heavens and the earth were finished, and all the host of them. Gen. 2 : 1.

843, The regenerating man is now rendered so far Spiritual as to have arrived at the entrance of the Seventh Day. The principles of the Internal and External mind, with the Love, Faith, and the Knowledges thereof, as the "Sun, Moon and Stars," are signified by the "Host of them," and when the Celestial principle of Love begins to rule, the Work of Redemption is finished, and the regenerating man is saved by the Lord, for the "earth" or External mind is redeemed by the Word. "*I have glorified thee on the earth; I have finished the work thou gavest me to do.*" "*I have redeemed thee, I have called thee by thy name; thou art mine, I, even I, am the Lord; and beside me there is no Saviour.*"

x

THE TRANSFIGURATION.

And after Six Days, Jesus taketh Peter, James, and John his brother, and bringeth them up into an high mountain apart, and was transfigured before them; and his face did shine as the sun, and his raiment was white as the light. Matt. 17 : 1, 2.

844. "Peter" signifies a Rock, and a Rock signifies Truth or Faith. "James" signifies Love, or Charity, and "John" signifies the Good Works of charity. The rest of the "disciples" represent Goods and Truths derived from these three principles, in the same manner as the Twelve Tribes of Israel, and the three names, "Peter, James and John" signify the same as the Twelve, or all "His brother" signifies the Affection of Good. It is at the end of a state of combat with the Proprium, that "Jesus," or the Divine Love, "bringeth them up into an high mountain," by which is signified the elevation of the Rational Faculty to perceive the Celestial principles within the Word. No person can see the "Glory of the Lord" within the Word, unless he is principled in a Rational Faith, and in the charity grounded therein, and manifests the living goodness of that Love to the Neighbor. Others are capable of beholding this "glory," but they do not see it, because they do not live the life which leads to the opening of the spiritual sight.

845. The Transfiguration signifies the opening of the perceptions of the Rational Faculty to see that the Son of God is the Interior Truth of the Word received into the life, and that the Word of God is the Divine Humanity, made clearly manifest to the Spiritual Vision of the regenerating man, as a culmination of all his combats with the Proprium. This is a Vision which will never be effaced from his Interior memory, for he has been faithful unto the death of his evils and falses, and this is the crown of

life whose lustre can never be dimmed, and this "glory" will ever more lighten his pathway.

846. By "His face did shine as the sun," is signified the inflowing of the Interior Divine Truth into the Rational Faculty from the Divine Love. By "His raiment was white as the light," is signified the perception of the Divine Truth within the Literal Sense of the Word, which is the clothing of the Internal Sense, and "Raiment," as well as "Light" signify the Divine Truth proceeding from the Lord.

And, behold. there appeared unto them Moses and Elias talking with him. Matt. 17 : 3.

847. By "Moses" is here signified the Historical or Representative Word, and by "Elias," is signified the Prophetical Word. By "talking with him," is signified the communication of perception to the Rational Faculty that the Internal Sense of the Historical and Prophetical forms of expression treats of the same Celestial and Spiritual principles of regeneration.

Then answered Peter, and said unto Jesus, Lord, it is good for us to be here; if thou wilt, let us make here three tabernacles; one for thee, and one for Moses, and one for Elias. Matt. 17 : 4.

848. To "answer" signifies communication, and to "say," signifies perception, thus "Then answered Peter and said unto Jesus," signifies the communication of Divine Truth from the Word, and the perception that it is from the Lord, and "It is good for us to be here," signifies the Heavenly state of the three principles represented by "Peter," "James," and "John," when vivified by the Interior Good and Truth of the Word. "If thou wilt," signifies the inflowing of the Divine Love, and "Let us make here three tabernacles," signifies the conjunction of the Good and Truth of the Word into the Life, by regeneration, which has led to this Celestial state signified by "Three Tabernacles" in which the Divine Humanity of the Lord is seen.

849. The "Tabernacle" in the Word is made of "wood," which signifies Good, while the "Temple" is made of "stone," which signifies Truth. "Three tabernacles" signify the Celestial principles of the Word. "One for Thee" signifies the Divine Love. "One for Moses," signifies the Divine Wisdom, as "Moses" represents the "Law," which is the Divine Truth of the Word, and "One for Elias," signifies the Divine Proceeding, for "Elias" or "Elijah," signifies the Prophetic Word. A "Prophet" signifies True Doctrine from the Word, and the teaching of the Interior Good and Truth of the Word which culminates in a regenerated life, is the Divine Proceeding. Thus the "Three Tabernacles" signify the same principles of the Word as "Father," "Son," and "Holy Spirit."

While he yet spake, behold, a bright cloud overshadowed them: and behold a voice out of the clouds, which said, This is my beloved Son in whom I am well pleased; hear ye him. Matt. 17:5.

850. "While he yet spake," signifies the continuance of this State of Perception. "A bright cloud overshadowed them," signifies the Literal Sense of the Word within which is the Internal Sense, and in which the First Advent of the Lord is made. "*Behold He cometh in clouds, and every eye shall see Him.*" "*Ye men of Galilee, why stand ye gazing up into heaven? This same Jesus, which is taken up from you into heaven, shall so come in like manner as ye have seen him go into heaven.*" "Overshadowed" signifies from within, or above (§180), and these Celestial and Spiritual principles of the Word are clothed by the Literal Sense. "Behold, a voice out of the cloud," signifies annunciation, or communication of Divine Truth from the Word, for a "Voice" is predicted of speech, and the Word is the "Voice" of the Lord, and this Word communicates the expression, "This is my beloved Son," which signifies that this "beloved Son" of the Literal Sense is the Lord's Divine Humanity, or the Interior Divine Truth of the Word thus personified. "In whom I am well pleased," sig-

nifies that this revelation of Divine Truth is from the Lord alone, and the Divine Humanity cannot be manifested in any other form than from the Internal Sense through the Literal Sense. "*They shall see the Son of Man coming in the clouds of heaven with power and great glory.*" This revelation of the Internal Sense of the Word to the regenerating man is the Second Advent of the Lord. "Hear ye him," signifies to obey these Interior Divine Truths of the Word.

And when the disciples heard it, they fell on their face, and were sore afraid. Matt. 17 : 6.

851. "And when the disciples heard it," signifies that when these Interior Truths are taught from the Word, the regenerating man obeys them. "They fell on their face," signifies humility of heart and self abnegation on account of the perception of these Interior Truths. "And they were sore afraid," signifies adoration from the most profound humiliation and holy fear from a consciousness of utter unworthiness.

And Jesus came and touched them, and said, Arise, and be not afraid. Matt. 17 : 7.

852. "And Jesus came," signifies further inflowing of perception from the Divine Love. "And touched them," signifies the reception of this revelation of the Word. "And said, Fear not," signifies the raising up of the Interior life by the Lord while in this state of holy fear. When life enters from the Lord in place of the hereditary Proprium, everything which pertains to the man as a receptacle of life, is dead, and a sacred fear is felt in the interiors of the mind even to their ultimate principles.

And when they had lifted up their eyes, they saw no man, save Jesus only. Matt 17 : 8.

853. "And when they had lifted up their eyes" signifies the elevation of the thoughts toward the Interior Truths of the Word.

The right and left eye.	Descending from the mountain.

or Eternal Life, and this elevation can come only from the Lord by the Word. The "Eye" signifies the understanding, for as the physical eye sees from natural light, the regenerated understanding sees from the Spiritual Light of the Word. The right eye corresponds to the Affection of Good, and the left eye to the Affection of Truth, which two affections are united when the Rational Faculty is elevated by the Lord. The sight of the left eye corresponds to the intellectual principle of Truth, and the sight of the right eye corresponds to the Affection of that principle. No man in his own strength can look above himself, and therefore "no man," or Proprium, is seen in this Transfiguration of the Word in the regenerating man, for this revelation of its Interior Divine Truth is not originated by any man, neither can it be seen from the Natural or corporeal principles of the External mind.

854. "Jesus only," signifies the Divine Love within the Word, for *"No man hath seen God at any time; the only begotten Son, which is in the bosom of the Father, He hath declared Him."* The "Only begotten Son," is the Divine Truth of the Word which the regenerating man obeys and makes living. The "Bosom of the Father," signifies the Spiritual Truth of the Word which proceeds from the Inmost Life of Divine Love, and when this Love and Truth permeates the life of the regenerating man, the Interior Truths flow clearly into his Rational Faculty.

And as they came down from the mountain, Jesus charged them, saying, Tell the vision to no man, until the Son of man be risen again from the dead. Matt 17: 9.

855. This elevation of the Interior Affections and Thoughts is represented as being upon a "high mountain," from which the regenerating mán must descend to attend to the active duties of the natural life, which will be governed by these Celestial and Spiritual principles, and although the warm heart is burning with the desire to communicate this Holy vision to others, so that they

may see this "Glory" within the Word, a perception is communicated to the Rational Faculty to impart this vision to "no man," until the Son of Man be risen again from the dead," which signifies that the regenerating man must yet be on his guard lest the evils and falses of his Proprium obscure this Interior Perception, until these Divine Truths are confirmed from the Literal Sense by being incorporated into the life, while literally is meant that in the desire to communicate these Interior Truths to others, careful discrimmination and judgment should be exercised that they shall not be distorted and profaned by those who cannot receive them, and they can only be communicated and received by such persons who by individual experience have been led to feel that there is an Interior meaning to the Literal Sense of the Word.

856. The Transfiguration signifies the Glory of the whole Word in its Internal and Literal Sense, when its Good and Truth is received by the re-created receptacles in the regenerating man. The Word is then proved to be the Lord himself, for nothing which is created and finite can redeem a man from his sins, and lead him into the Life of Heaven. "*Receive with meekness the ingrafted Word, which is able to save your souls.*"

THE LAST TEMPTATION.

857. As all the incidents narrated in the Spiritual History within the Word have their Heavenly culminations in the lives of regenerated men, it is not essential to salvation from sin to believe that a physical Man was literally crucified upon a cross of wood many centuries ago in the land of Palestine, but it is essential to Salvation, to believe and live according to the Precepts of the Word. The Lord Jesus Christ, the Fountain of Eternal Life within the Word, and the Son of God whom men have created in their systems of religious doctrine, are not identical; but the Divine Truth of the Word, and the Son of God there personified, are one and the same God. Should all records of earthly history be swept out of existence, the spiritual history contained within the Literal

| A mighty fortress. | Sufferings of the External mind. |

Sense of the Word would remain the same for the natural degree of thought to receive first in the order of regeneration. With this perception of the Literal Sense of the Word, the mind will not waver or be shaken in faith when its enemies attack it in any form, for its Divine Precepts become axioms which are seen to be Eternal, the origin of which is anterior to the limitations of time and space.

858. The Lord is crucified in "Sodom and Egypt," in "*the great city, which spiritually is called Sodom and Egypt, where also our Lord was crucified.*" * The " Great City," is the false doctrine originating with the Love of Self, and sanctimoniously confirmed from the Appearances of Truth in the Literal Sense of the Word. "Sodom," signifies the evil of Self Love, and "Egypt," in the evil sense, signifies the self-intelligence and scientifics of the natural principles of the mind which pervert and obscure the plain Living Truths of Love to the Lord and the Neighbor, which are characteristic of false religious doctrines, confirmed from a merely literal interpretation of the Word.

859. The incidents and historical narrations of the Gospels are true in the history of the states of the regenerating man, and are there only to be seen as actual facts. The trials and temptations of the Son of man, ending with the Passion of the Cross, are representative of the sufferings of the External mind during the combats of regeneration by the Truths of the Word. This is the Last Temptation, when the evils and falses of the Proprium have their last struggle with the entrance of the Divine Truth of the Word, and this last struggle is so severe, in whatever form it may be experienced, that all that belongs to the External mind seems to perish, and in this state of death, the Literal Sense of the Word seems also dead, or to have no Divinity within its expressions, and the temptation nearly prevails to reject and cast aside that Word of God which has so sacredly been handed down from one generation to another.

* Rev. 11 : 8.

| Extinction of natural light. | Failure of every earthly help. |

And when the sixth hour was come, there was darkness over the whole land until the ninth hour. And at the ninth hour Jesus cried with a loud voice, saying, Eloi! Eloi! lama sabachthani. Mark. 15 : 33, 34.

860. In this hour of darkness, all light from the natural world is extinguished, and all the material ideas of the regenerating man concerning Heaven are taken from him, and even his previous thoughts concerning Immortality, which have been the ground of his strong hope, and a great resource for his self-intelligence to draw from and discourse about,—all disappear, and nothing finite can give him any help. He has seen his cherished friends and hopes pass out of this earthly existence, and he knows that he himself must soon follow. "*And it was about the sixth hour, and there was darkness over all the land until the ninth hour.*"

861. The number "Six" denotes Combat, while the number "Nine," signifies Conjunction. The "Sixth hour" is the state of devastation and destruction which exists in this last and greatest temptation before the conjunction of the Internal Sense with the Literal is clearly seen, and the desolate spirit of the regenerating man, who has long intellectually accepted these principles, is brought to the experimental proof of his Affection for the Truth, and as he is actuated by the power of the Living Truth of the Word, he now with a "loud voice" in agony cries, "*My God! my God! why hast thou forsaken me?*"

862. As every earthly help fails him in this hour of his struggle, and as the "waters" are about to overwhelm him in oblivion, he finds himself lifted upon a Rock, alone in his individuality, with nothing left of this world's effects but the Word of God, which he firmly clasps in his hands, and which says to him in this "Sixth Hour," "*When thou passest through the waters I will be with thee. For I am the Lord thy God, the Holy One of Israel, thy Saviour.*"

863. Here alone he finds Eternal Truths which in themselves are Immortal, and which clothe him with Immortality. The desire to know the future originates from the love of evil, and it

| Confidence in the Divine Providence. | Implicit trust. |

is taken away from those who believe in the Divine Providence, because they have confidence that the Lord will order all their ways. " *Take no thought for your life, what ye shall eat; neither for the body what ye shall put on, but rather seek ye the Kingdom of God.*" No man can know his own future, or any hidden event before its occurrence, for such fore-knowledge would prevent his becoming regenerated.

The dead do not impart the secrets of the future existence of any man, and none whose physical bodies have been dissolved in the grave, have ever returned to their former life, neither do they who are gone communicate with the mind of man, excepting by their writings or traditions in which their thoughts and lives have been incorporated. The Word itself, which reveals the Spiritual Principles of the Regenerate Life, and exhibits their development and growth in men, as well as illustrating the effects of their rejection both in its Literal and Internal Sense, gives only the manna which must be gathered and eaten To-Day, and does not lift the veil to disclose the mysteries of the actual future of any individual man, for such a disclosure would not only prevent his progress in the attainment of spiritual life, but would destroy his confidence in the Divine Guidance of the Lord, so that instead of becoming regenerated, he would lead and confirm himself in an increasing state of self-love, which would defeat the object of his creation.

The principles of Immortality, or Eternal Life, are contained only in the Living Precepts of the Word, which, when obeyed, continually lead to an increase of Heavenly Love and Intelligence; while the disobedient continually lead themselves away from the Lord, or the Word, to a state of Spiritual Death. " To-day " is always an ETERNAL NOW, and True Faith, according to the Interior Truth of the Word, leads the regenerating man to give up all self-intelligent conjectures, and material ideas concerning the future existence, and the Word teaches him to trust implicitly in the Lord as a little child, and receive the gift of Eternal Life from day to day, and from state to state.

THE NATURE OF THE WORD OF GOD. 379

| Elias. | The superscription on the cross. |

And some of them that stood by, when they heard it, said, Behold, he calleth Elias. Mark 15 : 35.

864. "Elias," signifies the Prophetic Word, and this narrative of the crucifixion is the prophetic utterance of the Last Temptation of the regenerating man when he earnestly seeks the Divine Truth of the Word. In the darkest state of the spiritual obscurity which covers his mental vision, he bows his head in humility as he hears the Voice of Divine Love saying "*It is finished*," which signifies the consummation of this temptation, and in response, with his whole heart he says, "*Father, into thy hands I commend my spirit.*" When this surrender of self occurs, and his life is sincerely consecrated to the Good and Truth of the Word, the "veil of the temple," or the Appearances of Truth which obscure the Literal Truths of the Word, is "rent in the midst," or interiorly opened, by the Divine Truth from within.

865. Now the "Glory of the Lord" shines forth from the Internal Sense of the Word, and the regenerating mind is raised from this Last Temptation, in which all the evil powers of the Proprium have united to crucify the Son of Man. Thus the Lord suffers in each regenerating man, by the Word, for the "sins of the world." When the Proprium is overcome and surrendered, the real Resurrection takes place, at the consummation of the Sixth Day of Labor, and the Seventh Day becomes the beginning of the Holy Week of the External mind, which will be purified from the hereditary evils and falses, "for the Lord has risen indeed," and appears to the "disciples" within the Living Truths of the Word as they are revealed by the Internal Sense. "*And I will raise him up at the Last Day.*"

866. The SUPERSCRIPTION ON THE CROSS is "written in Hebrew, and Greek, and Latin," which is placed at the head, over the crucified Son of Man, and signifies the whole WORD OF GOD, by means of which the regenerating man is enabled to bear the cross, or the temptations from his Proprium, and overcome them. In the Literal Form of the Word the "Hebrew" represents the Natural

Hebrew, Greek and Latin.   The key to the Latin personifications.

principle of the Word as it appears in the external rites of the Old Testament, which in themselves are representative of Celestial and Spiritual principles. The "Greek," represents the Divine principles of the New Testament, which are clearer in their doctrine concerning Celestial and Spiritual principles, but which are also significative, while the "Latin" signifies the Internal Sense of both the Old and New Testament, and therefore of the entire Word, and represents the Intermediate Principle of Conjunction which is received by the Rational Faculty of the regenerating man. While the Revelation of Divine Truth externally written in Hebrew and Greek, consists of the REPRESENTATIVES and SIGNIFICATIVES (763) of the spiritual principles of Regeneration, the principles of the spiritual world revealed within the Internal Sense of the Word, when illustrated in the Latin writings,* are there also personified, and these illustrations are to be interpreted by the SCIENCE OF CORRESPONDENCE, the key to which they also furnish to the Rational Faculty of the Regenerating man.

* *Arcana Cœlestia, Apocalypsis Explicata, Apocalypsis Revelata.*

THE SABBATH.

And on the Seventh Day God ended his work which he had made; and he rested on the Seventh Day from all his works which he had made. Gen. 2: 2.

867. The Regenerating Man is now called the "Seventh Day," for the number "Seven" signifies a Holy State which has been attained by the Work of the Lord during the Six Days of Creation, and the combat between Spiritual principles and the Proprium having ceased, it is here said that the Lord "rested on the Seventh Day." On this account the Seventh Day is sanctified and called the SABBATH, from a Hebrew word signifying "Rest;" and thus man has been created from the "dust of the earth," or earthly principles of thought, and by the Living Truths of the Word, has been formed into the Image and Likeness of God.

868. Among all nations and people who have possessed the Word one day in seven has been set apart for Instruction from the Word, and the cessation from physical labor, and this external observance is derived from its correspondence with the culmination of the Work of Regeneration. This work should occupy the chief thoughts of every man, and he should bend every energy of mind and body in entering the way which leads to Life Eternal, by the study of the Word and obedience to its Precepts. With the regenerating man whose daily life is one of constant worship, all days of labor afford religious instruction, for in every earthly object and event, he sees its spiritual correspondence in the Word, within his own mind, and he acknowledges the Lord in all his ways, and permits Him thus by the Word, to direct his paths.

869. In obedience to the Commandment, and for the sake of others who perceive only the Literal Sense of the Word, he will keep the weekly Sabbath as a day of special religious instruction

and communion with other minds, and refrain from pursuing his daily avocations, enjoying its hours of rest as typical of the cessation of his spiritual warfare. "*The Sabbath was made for man*" and every man possesses the faculty for attaining the Heavenly State for which he was created. In the highest sense, the Lord, or the Word, is the Sabbath, for therein is found rest for the spirit of man, when distracted with the cares and anxieties of the External mind, or "earth."

And God blessed the Seventh Day, and sanctified it; because that in it he had rested from all his work which God created and made. Gen. 2 : 3.

870. The Blessing of God, signifies His presence by the Truths of the Word, which now fill the External mind of the regenerating man of the Seventh Day, whose life is now blessed with tranquillity and joy. The peace which now comforts him is from the Word which sheds Divine Light upon all the ways of Divine Providence, for he has confidence that the Lord governs and provides all things which he needs, and that with those who obey the Word, all things lead to Good. In this State of Peace he fears nothing, and no solicitude concerning the future, gives him any anxiety.

871. All evil, and especially self-confidence, takes away this state of peace. It is commonly believed that an unregenerated man has peace when he is in gladness and tranquillity arising from general success in his worldly affairs; but this is not true peace. It is the delight and tranquillity of selfish love, which counterfeits a state of peace. With the regenerating man, as the exteriors of his mind are successively unfolded to receive the Interior Principles of the Word, even to the Inmost Principles, Peace is the Inmost joy of every delight, and he is affected with Eternal

Successive weeks.	The First and Second Advents.

Happiness, the origin of which is from the Lord Himself by means of His Word. After each Sabbath of Regeneration, a new week of labor is to be begun, for the finite receptacle of life must always receive and advance toward perfection, which can never be fully attained, for the Infinite Lord within the Word alone contains Perfection in Himself.

THE LIFE OF REGENERATION.

872. Regeneration by the Word is a constant and Eternal state of Spiritual progression, and the finite mind will always be a receptacle of increasing Love and Wisdom. *"For since the beginning of the world, men have not heard, nor perceived by the ear, neither hath the eye seen, O God, besides Thee, what He hath prepared for him that waiteth for him.* Is. 64 : 4.

873. In the successive degrees of regenerate life, the first state of a man's life is Natural, from which he becomes Moral, and thence he becomes Spiritual, for he must first obey the Literal Commands of the Word, which constitute the Moral Law, before their Interior Truths can be revealed to him and create the Spiritual and Celestial degrees of his mind.

874. The FIRST ADVENT OF THE LORD, in the order of regeneration, is His entrance to the External mind by obedience to the Truths of the Literal Sense of the Word; and the SECOND ADVENT OF THE LORD is the opening of the Rational Faculty of those to whom He has made the First Advent, to perceive the Internal Sense of the Word, which reveals Jehovah God, or the

| The order of regeneration. | The history of all men. |

Lord Jesus Christ, as THE WORD, within the Divine Truth of which manifestation He can only be found. *" Be ye therefore ready also : for the Son of Man cometh at an hour when ye think not."* Luke 12 : 40.

875. Beginning with the fourth verse of the Second Chapter of Genesis, the formation of the Celestial principles of the Regenerating man are coherently described; concerning which these pages do not treat, they having relation simply to the Spiritual degree of the mind in relation to the Word. The Third Chapter of Genesis treats of the principles of the External mind which cause the Fall of human nature from the innocent and holy state of Celestial and Spiritual Life, from which exists all the sin and suffering which deluges the Spiritual and physical nature of mankind.

876. The twelfth chapter of Genesis begins with the true history of the order of the entrance of the Lord Jesus Christ into the life of the regenerating man, which is depicted by pure correspondences under the form of the historical narrative of " Abram " in the Literal Sense, the Internal Sense of which cannot appear to any man until he has entered upon the State there described, and which cannot be seen if the mental sight is confined to the literal form of history as though these circumstances were fixed physical events, for the Truths contained within these Correspondences must be entirely abstracted from the Literal Sense. " Abram " there does not represent a physical earthly patriarch, but the Lord, who is within the Internal mind of the regenerating man, entering the External mind in the successive order of Infancy, Childhood and Manhood, through the Enlightened Rational Faculty, into the land of the Proprium.

877. The whole Word of God thus becomes representative of the various states of not only one, but of all regenerating men in their griefs, trials, and temptations, as well as in their seasons of delight and peace, and it describes the malignity of the evils of the unregenerated Proprium in order that men may resist the influences of the Love of Self and fear to trust in their own self intelligence.

THE PULPIT AND THE PRESS.

878. In the common order of religious instruction, the teaching of the Truths of the Literal Sense of the Word are enforced upon the mind through the sense of hearing, by means of the influence of the pulpit, or the voice of the clergy. "*So then faith cometh by hearing, and hearing by the Word of God.*" In the order of religious education these ministrations will not cease. The power of speech is given man so that he may communicate to others the thoughts which flow into his mind, and as the object of creation is the regeneration of men, the gift of speech attains its highest use when it is employed in communicating Truths from the Word, rather than in the utterance of self-intelligent speculations.

879. The great power of the pulpit consists in reaching the degree of natural thought in men with living lessons drawn from the fountain of the Literal Sense of the Word, awakening them to obedience, and this method of instruction will always prevail, for in all the successive ages of time, natural thought concerning the Word must first exist, as all men must first be born in the physical world, and first be taught from external objects, and no man has ever been born, or will ever be born with inherent regenerated principles of spiritual life.

880. Therefore the pulpit, which represents oral religious instruction, is to be honored by men for the sake of the Word which it solemnly declares, and which stimulates them to live according to its Truths. Until each hearer who is addressed from the Sacred Desk, makes a personal study of the Word, and in its application endeavors to live according to its Precepts, and thus is prepared to perceive its inner meaning,——until then, the Truths of the Literal Sense must form the burden of all preaching. When the clergy themselves recognize the Internal Sense of the Word, judgment will be given them to adapt their illustrations, so that those who

| The Spiritual Universe of the Word. | A printed memory. |

are in natural thought only, may be led to the perception of spiritual life, and thus to perceive that the Word is Divine from its interior principles of holiness.

881. Since the majority of men do not reflect interiorly, and their minds are fully occupied with the duties and cares of this life, the influence of the pulpit will not retrograde, but will continue to be the great power of lifting them up above worldly life, by presenting in varied forms, the fundamental laws of spiritual life, which inculcate Love to the Lord and the Neighbor, for upon these two things depend all the principles of the Spiritual and Natural Universe of the Word, and all things in the physical universe also have reference to these two principles of Eternal Life, by the laws of correspondence.

882. The inculcation of a holy life according to the Commandments, by looking to the Lord within the Word, and resisting all evils of life, when proclaimed by one whose own life is in harmony with all the teachings of the Word, causes the pulpit to be instrumental in preparing the way for the perception and reception of the Internal Sense by those who are able to bear it. "*I have many things to say unto you, but ye cannot bear them now.*" Thus the Pulpit is representative of the Literal Sense of the Word.

883. The printing of thoughts in religious books is also a Divine means of spiritual instruction for the promulgation of more interior thoughts concerning the Word, for the reason that all the expressions are fixed in their record, so that they may be referred to in their coherent order. An orderly prepared book is a printed memory which may be consulted for confirmation of the subject of which it treats. In listening to the words of speech, the mind is occupied with the meaning expressed within the words in the order of their delivery, and there is no opportunity for reflection and comparison, other than awakening thought which will lead to subsequent investigation. In a book of instruction, its primary declarations may be investigated, stored within the memory, and the succeeding principles may be built

up in regular progression, with the opportunity of reference, for the purpose of establishing the instructions there presented.

884. The Internal Sense of the Word can only be made coherent to the mind of a regenerating man whose Rational Faculty has been enlightened, and which is in active occupation in meditation, comparison, and the rejection of every false principle of thought or doctrine. There can be no growth of this Spiritual faculty, without the employment of the means of nourishment provided through the instrumentality of the Press, which is from the Lord, for He is the Author of every spiritual help, and of every invention which flows into the minds of men for the benefit of mankind. (§306.)

885. The Word itself is held and preserved in its Literal Form by means of the printing-press, as formerly by the slower and more limited method of writing. Text books, such as dictionaries, grammars, concordances and collateral writings, are held in form and are presented to the mind by means of the press, and the records of the principles which teach the laws which reveal the Internal Sense of the Word to the enlightened understanding, are also fixed in printed language. These principles must be studied by the affectionate searcher for the Truth, and also are to be interpreted by the interior thoughts there recorded, to prevent their spiritual instruction being perverted by minds possessing only natural and material ideas concerning Divine principles.

886. From the means thus afforded for study and reflection, and hence giving opportunity in freedom for the acceptance or rejection of recorded thoughts, while the mind is in the intermediate state of receiving instruction, the Press becomes representative of interior thought, or of the Internal Sense of the Word.

When the instruction of the Pulpit is carefully prepared from the Word, and is recorded in printed form so that it may be read and stored within the memory, and by reflection be confirmed and accepted as true, and afterwards be brought forth in the life, then the utterance of the Pulpit from first being external, becomes representative of internal principles when issued from the Press.

The conversion of the world.	Subjective principles

887. The Pulpit and the Press are the external and internal methods of imparting spiritual instruction concerning the Word, and are therefore united as means employed for the conversion of the world to holiness of life. The Voice of the Pulpit declares outwardly, so that the sense of hearing may convey to the mind the truths of life embodied within the sounds, while the Voice of the Press conveys to the mental eye in printed forms, not only the same truths of life, but the means of higher mental development concerning the Word, which would be impossible to attain by oral instruction alone, without the aid of books. Although by means of speech and writing, or printing, the Truths of the Word are first taught objectively to the natural degree of thought, they become subjective principles of Divine Life, when they are inscribed, or printed upon the heart, or Will, for from this interior affection they will then be externally manifested in all the conversation and actions of regenerating men, who are the Angels thus created by the angelic Life of the Word, "*which is Christ in you, the hope of glory : whom we preach, warning every man, and teaching every man in all wisdom ; that we may present every man perfect in Christ Jesus :*" "*To the acknowledgment of the mystery of God, and of the Father, and of Christ ; in whom are hid all the treasures of wisdom and knowledge.*" Col. 1: 2—2: 3.

CONCLUSION.

"*And the book is delivered to him that is not learned, saying, Read this, I pray thee and he saith, I am not learned.*" Is. 29: 12.

"*And in that day shall the deaf hear the words of the book, and the eyes of the blind shall see out of obscurity, and out of darkness.*" Is. 29: 18.

888. At the "Beginning" of Spiritual Life, the regenerating man desired to know the Source of the Inspiration of the Word, and in the progressive order of his re-created life, he is shown its Divinity by its Internal Evidence, and that it is the Fountain of all Spiritual Life and Immortality, and that this Divine Truth in the Ancient Records which have been handed down from generation to generation, is the ROCK OF AGES, which alone is the foundation of the "Earth," and endures when all other things perish. When men wholly surrender themselves to its Divine Teachings, they will see its "Water" and its "Blood," as it flows from the "Wounded Side," or Heart of the Divine Love, and saves from the "Wrath," or evil and falsity of the hereditary nature, and which alone can save men from their sins. Then will they see the Divine Truth of the Word as the "Judgment Throne," on the "Last Day," when all things of Self and the World are closed in their spiritual death, and then in the simple trust of an enlightened Rational Faith will they discern the Spiritual

The use of sacred music.	The spirit of charity.

significance of the Word of God, and also comprehend an interior meaning in such familiar hymns as

> " Rock of Ages, cleft for me,
> Let me hide myself in Thee."

889. When a beautiful piece of sacred music is well sung, there are some who are delighted with the sound of the melody and harmony proceeding from the cultivated voices which vibrate in sympathy with the words which are being clothed with concordant tones. When these external sounds have ceased, there remains in the mind, the thoughts within the words which have been conveyed through the instrumentality of the music, and if the Truths therein are obeyed and incorporated into the life, these harmonious sounds have performed their highest use, in the elevation of the natural thoughts above earthly things. But there are some listeners whose minds are not moved so much by the sound of the music and the voices, as by the Truths which are uttered within the melody and harmony.

890. Every man receives impressions of the Truth according to the obedience and quality of his individuality, and if he understands the operation or form of the human mind, he will not expect the mental features of other persons to be cast in the mould of his own face. He will therefore have charity for others, and be inwardly delighted, if by any means they may be brought to see the Lord within the Word, and led to perceive the Glory of its Internal Sense. If he has more light than his neighbor, he will not arrogantly assert himself as more

highly favored, for the more light that a man receives concerning the nature of the Word of God, the more he recognizes his own weakness, and in humility feels that he is only a receptacle of life from the Lord, and his own hereditary self-hood will be removed to the farthest extreme from the Fountain and Center of Life. He will thus be led solely by the Lord through obedience to the Word.

891. He will seek to aid others through the Truths which shine from the Literal Sense of the Word, and will rejoice when he sees them in the endeavor to live in the loving kindness of the Commandments. His charity will be so warm with affection for the Word that he will not thoughtlessly give offence to others by hastily destroying that form in which the Divine Truth first reaches their minds, and discretion will be given him, if he sinks himself, so that he will be led to communicate the Light from the Internal Sense where it will be received into willing hearts without being profaned or misunderstood.

892. His judgment will be led by knowledges from the Word, as he is filled with good-will toward men, and his own mind will dwell in peace. Instead of being antagonistic toward the religious tenets of others who do not perceive the Interior Principles of the Word which are vital to him, he will recognize Truth in any form which is derived from the Word, and be willing to extend the hand of religious fellowship to all who make the rule of their life according to the Precepts of the Word.

893. Living without offending the "little ones" who are in the innocent life of charity, he will not ruthlessly take away their Lord by the uncharitable presentation of his elevating doctrines, but his "Light will so shine," as he consistently walks through the daily journey of life, that others will intuitively recognize him as a living witness of the Divine Truth which has created him a son of God by means of the Human Form of the Word.

894. There are many devout souls who love to think of the Lord Jesus Christ as a Divine Man on this terrestial globe, going about doing good, healing the sick, casting out devils, restoring sight to the blind, folding the little ones to His Heart, feeding the hungry, and teaching all men to "*Bless them that curse you, do good to them that hate you, and pray for them which despitefully use you.*" If they thus obey the Divine Precepts, He will reveal Himself unto them within the Word, and enable them to live the Life which He teaches by the Word.

895. There are others who see Him personified in the Word which they love and obey, and their thoughts do not go back to earthly events, but they perceive the Lord Jesus Christ present in every part of the Word by the Internal Sense, and recognizing that the External mind of the regenerating man is the "Earth" into which He is born, and perceiving the Humanity which He there assumes in the Literal Sense and makes Divine by the Internal Sense, they see Him in the Human Form of the Word as within the Spiritual Sun which illumines the Heaven of the Internal mind.

| Influence upon others. | Prior existence of the Word. |

897. Upon the Doctrine of Eternal Life embodied in the Two Precepts of the Word, all who recognize the Internal Inspiration of the Holy Scriptures, may strengthen each other in the journey of life, by shunning all evil as sin and death, and looking to the Lord within the Word. Thus will their affections be warmed toward each other, and others be led to the Word, through the effects of its Divine Human Form incarnated in the lives of those who believe and manifest its Humanity. "*He that hath my commandments, and keepeth them, he it is that loveth me: and he that loveth me shall be loved of my Father, and I will love him, and will manifest myself to him.*"

897. There are some natures whose degree of faith requires that they must see the sheathing husk as well as the enclosed kernel of wheat; while there are others who readily discern the nourishing grain, with the knowledge that in its growth it has been clothed with its protecting husk. The wheat itself is the Doctrine of Love to the Lord and the Neighbor brought forth into the life, and this is the Fundamental Truth upon which all religious minds actually unite. From this fruit of the "Earth" of the Literal Sense of the Word, the spiritual life of all devout people is nourished and sustained in their Heavenly voyage. "*He maketh peace in thy borders, and fillest thee with the finest of the wheat.*"

868. The Word of God has existed prior to all the traditions of apparent earthly history which have been derived from its external or Literal contents, (John 1 : 1)

| The Catholic nature of the Word. | Who may see its Divinity |

and the Internal Evidence of this Divine Revelation illustrates that the Principles contained within the Internal Sense are of a Universal or Catholic nature, independent of the many and various forms of religious worship which are prevalent. All Rituals, whether simple or elaborate, which honor the Word of God, will be found to contain a Correspondence with the Heavenly Truths taught from the coherent Interior understanding of this Word.

899. When the Rational Faculty is led to discriminate between the Appearances of Truth which exist in the Literal Sense, and the Actual Truth, by being enlightened through a life according to the Precepts of the Word, the Internal Sense will find welcome reception, and will lead all the powers of the mind to rest firmly on that ROCK OF AGES in which there is Everlasting Strength. The Rational mind of the regenerating man is the "House," in which the Lord enters and dwells by means of the Divine Truth of the Word. "*And the rain descended, and the floods came, and the winds blew, and beat upon that house; and it fell not: for it was founded upon a Rock.*" Matt. 7: 25.

900. From the thoughts presented in the preceding pages, which simply treat of a few principles beheld within the Holy Temple, from its threshold, glimpses of the Divinity of the Letter of the Word may be seen by such readers who love the Truth of Spiritual Life for its own sake, or "*for Christ's sake.*" On the Earth of its Literal Sense may everywhere be seen traversing each

| The Ark of the Covenant. | Beholding the Face of Jesus. |

highway and byway, over mountains veiled in clouds, and down through fertile valleys, a golden chariot of Heavenly Doctrine, drawn by white horses, bearing in radiant glory the Ark of the Covenant, within which are the Two Tables of Stone holding the inscription of those Precepts which form the Foundation of Immortality.

901. During the past ages of earthly history, while the Science of Spiritual Correspondence has been concealed within the Literal Sense of the Word on account of the low degree in which material thought concerning Divine principles has been immersed, its Living Truths have been revered in the hearts and lives of the obedient; tabernacles, temples, houses of worship, and grand cathedrals have been erected to enshrine its sacred pages, and disseminate its Divine Teachings, and thus the Lord has protected THE WORD, which, through the clouds of its Literal Sense, has shed its radiating heat and light, until those who are prepared to receive it have affectionately yearned for more Light concerning its Heavenly Principles, "*to fulfil the Word of God; even the mystery which hath been hid from ages and from generations, but now is made manifest to His saints.*" Col. 1 : 26.

902. The Lord has now permitted the veiled covering to be reverently removed for the Spiritual Sight of these regenerating men, so that they may behold the Living Face of Jesus, which shines as the Sun, for it is the Lord Himself who is manifested by the Internal Sense

of the Word, and who supplies this Sun with warmth and light.

903. "*Behold the Lamb of God which taketh away the Sin of the world!*" By beholding this Lamb of God, the Divine Humanity of the Word, in the innocence of child-like affection, and by partaking of His "flesh," by receiving this Word into the life and thus causing it to shine through the speech and actions, the External mind will become re-created in the Image and Likeness of the Word, and the spiritual countenance, or the form of the affections and thoughts, will correspond to the Face of Jesus. Thus the Lord Jesus Christ will appear in His Second Coming to those who receive Him as the Life of the Word. "*When He shall appear, we shall be like Him, for we shall see Him as He is.*"

SUMMARY.

904. The Summary of this Interwordian Doctrine concerning the Nature of the Sacred Scriptures, as outlined in the preceding pages, teaches that;—

The Word of God in its Literal Sense is written purely by the correspondences of the names of persons, places and things, with its Interior Principles of Divine Love and Wisdom. This Internal Life which is received into the minds of regenerating men, is personified to the natural degree of thought in the names of Jehovah God in the Old Testament, and of Jesus Christ in the New Testament, who are One and the same Lord, and the Interior Truth of this written Word is the Son of God, of whom it treats. Its record of apparent historical narratives, prophecies and miracles, instead of having been physical events of past earthly annals, are facts of true experiences in the order of regeneration from natural to spiritual life, and the Divinity of the Word of God is derived from its Internal Celestial and Spiritual Principles, which culminate in its Natural Principle, or Literal Sense, and not in the apparent occurrences of the external past, nor in the physical coincidences of ancient history.

IF THIS COUNSEL OR THIS WORK BE OF MEN, IT WILL COME TO NOUGHT; BUT IF IT BE OF GOD, YE CANNOT OVERTHROW IT. Acts 5 : 38.

THE TRUTH OF THE LORD ENDURETH FOR EVER. Ps. 117 : 2.

www.ingramcontent.com/pod-product-compliance
Lightning Source LLC
Chambersburg PA
CBHW032147010526
44111CB00035B/1233